Birdfinding in British Columbia

BIRDFINDING

IN

BRITISH COLUMBIA

RUSSELL CANNINGS & RICHARD CANNINGS

GREYSTONE BOOKS

Vancouver/Berkeley

Greystone Books Ltd.
343 Railway Street, Suite 201
Vancouver BC V6A 1A4
www.greystonebooks.com

Cataloguing data available from Library and Archives Canada
ISBN 978-1-77100-003-1 (pbk.)
ISBN 978-1-77100-004-8 (ebook)

Editing by Shirarose Wilensky
Cover design by Setareh Ashrafologhalai and Heather Pringle
Text design by Heather Pringle
Cover photograph by Laure Wilson Neish
(natureniche.zenfolio.com)
Illustrations by Donald Gunn
Maps by James Bradley
Printed and bound in Canada by Friesens
Distributed in the U.S. by Publishers Group West

Every attempt has been made to ensure that the information in this book
is accurate and up to date; however, the authors and publisher assume no
liability for any loss, damage, inconvenience, or injury that may occur to
anyone using this book. All outdoor activities involve an element of the
unknown and thus an element of risk, and you are solely responsible for your
own safety and health at all times. Always check local conditions, know your
own limitations, and consult a map.

We gratefully acknowledge the financial support of the Canada Council for
the Arts, the British Columbia Arts Council, the Province of British Columbia
through the Book Publishing Tax Credit, and the Government of Canada
through the Canada Book Fund for our publishing activities.

Greystone Books is committed to reducing the consumption of old-growth
forests in the books it publishes. This book is one step toward that goal.

CONTENTS

PREFACE

In 2010, I drove the length and breadth of British Columbia in search of its birds. By the end of the year, I had seen 373 species—a new provincial record in the admittedly small world of competitive birding. From the outset, I was planning to write this book afterwards, if only because my father insisted that I accomplish something more tangible from all the kilometres driven. I was able to set this record through the kindness of the birding community, the sharing of birding secrets, the offers of couches for overnight rest stops, and the phone calls reporting rarities throughout the province. When it was all done, I knew the province from the birders' point of view and, in many cases, from the birds' point of view. This book means to get some of that knowledge down on paper.

Whether you've lived here all your life or you're visiting for the first time, we hope that this book can help maximize your enjoyment of the province by showing you fantastic birds and taking you to incredible places you might not have otherwise known about. It would be impossible to include every good birding spot in such a huge place as British Columbia, but we've included the best of the best. Our coverage is almost surely biased by our own experience, and we've placed more emphasis on sites and regions that get more attention from the birding world simply because they're close to where the birders are. So you'll find large sections on the densely populated parts of Vancouver Island and the Lower Mainland, and since we both grew up in the Okanagan Valley, that birding paradise gets a lot of print as well. But we have tried to get the word out about less-travelled routes and rarely visited sites scattered throughout British Columbia. We hope that no matter where you may find yourself in this fine corner of the world, this guide will be able to point you to some of the nearest birding hot spots.

RUSSELL CANNINGS,
January 31, 2012

ACKNOWLEDGEMENTS

We would first like to acknowledge the contribution of both David Mark and Keith Taylor, who pioneered earlier bird guides to the province. Although our book is not affiliated with or based on these past publications, their guides provided a strong base for birding exploration in British Columbia, a base that we have tried to build on to produce a thorough and up-to-date guide.

Without question, this guide could not have come about without the input and guidance of a variety of local experts from around the province. We have had the wonderful opportunity of living and travelling in this beautiful province, but there are many spots that remain unfamiliar to us. And so, it is because of the generosity of others that this book is as thorough, extensive, and (we hope!) accurate as it is. The sharing of birding knowledge is paramount in promoting a greater understanding of our natural environment, as well as forging a stronger community of voices aiming to conserve the ecological splendour of British Columbia. Some local experts who provided lengthy material on their home regions are highlighted within the text itself, but we would like to list here all of our friends and colleagues who helped us along the way:

Art Ahier, Cathy Antoniazzi, Janice Arndt, Avery Bartels, Dave Beeke, Jack Bowling, Gary Breault, Doug Brown, Quentin Brown, Syd Cannings, Chris Charlesworth, George Clulow, Dianne Cooper, Larry Cowan, Christopher Coxson, Ian Cruickshank, Chris Dale, Gary Davidson, Jakob Dulisse, Jamie Fenneman, Gord Gadsden, Jeremy Gatten, Cam Gillies, Tony Greenfield, Larry Halverson, Peter Hamel, Heather Harbord, Alexis Harrington, Margo Hearne, Charles Helm, Nathan Hentze, Jared Hobbs, Rick Howie, Jukka Jantunen, Jeremy Kimm, Sandra Kinsey, Kevin Knight, Nancy Krueger, Laird Law, Adrian Leather, Doug Leighton, Rob Lyske, Derrick Marven, Sandy McCruer, Guy Monty, Mark Phinney, Rosamund Pojar, Ilya Povalyaev, Phil Ranson, Ian Routley, Rick Toochin, John Tschopp, Andrew Tyrrell, Linda Van Damme, Wayne Weber, Diane Weismiller, Ken Wright.

We apologize if this list is missing any names (and it almost surely is), but we give our deepest thanks to you all.

INTRODUCTION

British Columbia is a large and diverse province, and that diversity is especially marked in the bird world. With more than 526 bird species on the provincial list—over 300 of them breeding—there is simply no better place in Canada to look for birds. And some of the hot spots in British Columbia—the Fraser Delta and the Okanagan Valley, for instance, easily rank among the best birding sites on the continent.

The diversity of British Columbia flows from several sources—a variety of ecosystems and habitats, a tremendous range in topography, and the sheer size of the province. It extends from the southern edge of subarctic tundra to the northern limits of the great deserts of the West and is bounded along the sides by the largest ocean on earth and some of the most spectacular mountains on the continent. At almost a million square kilometres, British Columbia is far larger than the mighty state of Texas and almost four times the size of Great Britain. The size of the province can be a daunting prospect to anyone setting out to search for its birds. This is true even for local birders, who mostly live within an hour's drive of the American border and rarely get to the centre of the province during their birding jaunts, let alone explore the Far North.

We have written this book both to overcome this large geography and to take advantage of it. If you're planning an adventurous trip across the Chilcotin Plateau to Bella Coola, for example, or up the Alaska Highway to the Yukon, this book will provide suggestions for where to bird along the way. But if you simply want to find the most birds in the shortest distance from wherever you are, this book should help you plan an efficient birding jaunt.

A QUICK NATURAL HISTORY
OF BRITISH COLUMBIA

To plan any birding trip through British Columbia, it helps to know the basics of its geography and natural history. The mix of topography, climate, and latitude creates a complex mosaic of ecosystems that can change dramatically over the space of a few kilometres—and the bird life changes accordingly. A brief (and admittedly simplistic) geological history of the province may help explain some of this diversity.

If you went back in time to bird British Columbia 200 million years ago, you would encounter two problems. First, you would be stuck in the northeastern corner of the province—everything else was under the waters of the Pacific Ocean. Second, you would have a hard time finding any birds, since they hadn't yet differentiated from their dinosaurian ancestors. Over the next 150 million years, the rest of the province formed through a series of collisions between North America and several large island groups. These collisions added real estate to the west coast of North America, and the force of the impacts thrust up a number of impressive mountain ranges, generally trending from southeast to northwest. The bird list grew accordingly over that period, and by 50 million years ago, you could have seen early ancestors of today's waterfowl, loons, tubenoses, gulls, plovers, and sandpipers. These familiar birds would be mixed in with species unlike anything around today, including large flightless species somewhat like—but not related to—the ostriches, rheas, and emus of the Southern Hemisphere. Things were getting interesting!

In the last 2 million years, a series of cool climate cycles filled the mountains of British Columbia with snow, and huge glaciers flowed out of them to cover essentially the entire province. We can make a much better guess at the bird list of the province at this time of maximal ice coverage—it would be a rather short list, consisting of some high alpine species and an array of seabirds along the coast, and all the species would be familiar to us today. The most recent warming trend began about thirteen thousand years ago, and by ten thousand years ago, British Columbia looked more or less like it does today. The ice had left its mark, turning the coastal plains into deep, beachless fjords that snake into the heart of the Coast Mountains; gouging broad, U-shaped valleys in the Interior; and grinding minor mountain ranges down to rounded hills. The flatland on the coast was more or less restricted to the deltas of the few large rivers, notably the Fraser.

When you look at this modern topography of British Columbia, much of the diversity of climate, habitats, and bird species can be ascribed to two of its salient features. One is that it is a maritime province, bounded on the west by the Pacific Ocean. The other is that it is marked by a series of long, linear mountain ranges that trend from southeast to northwest. Because the prevailing winds at these latitudes are from the west, the Pacific sends weather systems to British Columbia on an almost daily basis. These systems bring rain to the rainforests, snow to the mountaintops, and warm winds to the Interior valleys. The mountain ranges squeeze moisture out of the air as it rises on their western flanks, leaving the valleys in the lee of the mountains warm and dry. In essence, the Pacific provides wind and rain to British Columbia, and the mountains distribute the weather systems in a complex pattern. If you look at a map of Canada showing any detailed environmental variable—be it annual temperature, rainfall, forest type, or bird species diversity—British Columbia looks like a dog's breakfast, whereas the rest of the country is covered by broad swathes of calm patterns. So birding in British Columbia is always interesting—if you want to find something new, just go up the nearest mountain and down the other side.

The Pleistocene glaciations also created one of most interesting aspects of species diversity in British Columbia—contact zones between closely related species or subspecies pairs. As the climate warmed at the end of the Pleistocene, the great ice sheets started to melt away where they were thinnest—in the northeast. It seems counterintuitive, but forests—and thus forest birds—first colonized the part of the province now famous for its cold winters, and the new arrivals came across the boreal forests from the east into the Peace River region and thence across the northern half of British Columbia. Most of these species had survived the period of maximum ice in the forests of southeastern North America, including the diversity of wood-warblers we associate with eastern forests today. The massive river glaciers that filled the southern Interior valleys and coastal inlets melted more slowly, but as they melted away, their forests and birds came from the south. These birds had spent the Pleistocene in the forests of southwestern North America, separated from their eastern cousins by the Great Plains. To complicate matters, there was a third important ice-free area during the Pleistocene—Beringia, the cold, dry tundras of the northern Yukon and Alaska. During the glacial periods, these eastern, western, and northern populations drifted apart from each other genetically, sometimes to the extent of becoming new species or at least recognizable subspecies. So when they met up after the glaciers melted, some didn't mix at all with their cousins and others interbred to varying degrees, creating narrow or broad zones of hybridization and introgression. These patterns of recolonization have created a significant portion of the bird diversity in British Columbia today. Many of you are likely aware of the classic east-west pairs of birds— a partial list would include Red-shafted and Yellow-shafted Flickers, Oregon and Slate-colored Juncos, Audubon and Myrtle Warblers, Bullock's and Baltimore Orioles, Red-naped and Yellow-bellied Sapsuckers, MacGillivray's and Mourning Warblers, Lazuli and Indigo Buntings, Black-headed and Rose-breasted Grosbeaks. The basic pattern is that the "western" forms are found in the southern part of British Columbia, whereas "eastern" forms are found in northern British Columbia—but the situation is different for each pair. For some, the Rockies are the boundary all the way up to the Yukon; others meet up along the Coast Mountain divide. The upshot is that British Columbia has more of these contact zones than anywhere else on the continent, adding spice to birding in the province. Because of this, biologists use British Columbia as a research site to study the processes around the formation of new species. A study of "Traill's Flycatchers" between Lac La Hache and Williams Lake resulted in that species being split into Willow and Alder Flycatchers, and a study of Winter Wrens near Tumbler Ridge resulted in the recognition of the western form as a separate species—the Pacific Wren.

BRITISH COLUMBIA
ECOSYSTEMS

The diverse topography and climate of British Columbia create an equally diverse mix of habitats, each with its own suite of typical bird species. This short list of ecosystems will help you sort out where to look for certain species.

OFFSHORE MARINE WATERS

The open oceans off British Columbia teem with pelagic species that few birders get to see without making a special effort. These birds tend to concentrate at the edge of the continental shelf (west of Vancouver Island, this is about 30 to 40 kilometres offshore), where upwelling currents create a rich mix of plankton, squid, and fish. Typical species include Black-footed Albatross; Northern Fulmar; Pink-footed, Buller's, and Sooty Shearwaters; Fork-tailed Storm-Petrel; Red and Red-necked Phalaropes; South Polar Skua; Pomarine and Long-tailed Jaegers; California and Sabine's Gulls; Black-legged Kittiwake; Arctic Tern; Cassin's Auklet; and Tufted Puffin.

INSHORE MARINE WATERS

The inshore marine waters of British Columbia are a complex mosaic of habitats, the boundaries largely unseen by humans because they are created by patterns of tides, salinity, and nutrients. Deep fjords, hundreds of islands, and the outflow of major and minor rivers add to this mix. Typical species include Harlequin Duck; Surf, White-winged, and Black Scoters; Bufflehead; Common and Barrow's Goldeneyes; Common and Red-breasted Mergansers; Red-throated, Pacific, and Common Loons; Red-necked and Western Grebes; Brandt's, Double-crested, and Pelagic Cormorants; Bonaparte's, Thayer's, and Glaucous-winged Gulls; Common Tern; Pigeon Guillemot; Marbled and Ancient Murrelets; and Rhinoceros Auklet.

ROCKY MARINE SHORES

The rocky shores that make up much of the British Columbia coast are home to a distinct community of birds, including Black Oystercatcher, Surfbird, Wandering Tattler, and Rock Sandpiper.

ESTUARIES AND MUD FLATS

The deltas of large rivers provide most of the flatland on the British Columbia coast and bring tonnes of nutrients to the marine ecosystem. They are often the richest areas for bird diversity on the coast in winter and during spring and fall migration. Typical species include Snow Goose, Brant, Trumpeter Swan, American Wigeon, Northern Pintail, Green-winged Teal, Great Blue Heron, Northern Harrier, Peregrine Falcon, Virginia Rail, Black-bellied Plover, Semipalmated Plover, Whimbrel, Western Sandpiper, Least Sandpiper, Dunlin,

Short-billed Dowitcher, Long-billed Dowitcher, Short-billed Dowitcher, Snowy Owl, Short-eared Owl, Purple Martin, and Marsh Wren.

RIPARIAN WOODLANDS

In a province cloaked in coniferous forests, the deciduous woodlands along creeks, rivers, and lakeshores have a distinct bird community. Occurring at relatively low elevations, they are especially rich during spring migration, when surrounding mountains are still snowbound and offer water and ample food for migrants in the hot days of late summer and early fall. Typical breeding species are Ruffed Grouse, Western Screech-Owl, Long-eared Owl, Vaux's Swift, Black-chinned Hummingbird, Red-naped Sapsucker, Downy Woodpecker, Alder Flycatcher, Willow Flycatcher, Eastern Phoebe, Eastern Kingbird, Warbling Vireo, Red-eyed Vireo, Black-capped Chickadee, Veery, Swainson's Thrush, Cedar Waxwing, Yellow Warbler, Song Sparrow, Black-headed Grosbeak, and Bullock's Oriole.

WET CONIFEROUS FORESTS

The rainforests along the coast and in parts of the Interior are famous for their huge trees, but they are also home to a rich bird fauna, including Sooty Grouse, Band-tailed Pigeon, Spotted Owl (very rare), Barred Owl, Rufous Hummingbird, Hairy Woodpecker, Pileated Woodpecker, Pacific-slope Flycatcher, Hammond's Flycatcher, Hutton's Vireo, Steller's Jay, Chestnut-backed Chickadee, Red-breasted Nuthatch, Brown Creeper, Pacific Wren, Golden-crowned Kinglet, Varied Thrush, Black-throated Gray Warbler, Townsend's Warbler, Purple Finch, and Red Crossbill.

DRY CONIFEROUS FORESTS

The Ponderosa Pine and dry Douglas-fir forests of the southern Interior have an open character that invites exploration. Typical birds include Dusky Grouse, Cooper's Hawk, Mourning Dove, Flammulated Owl, Common Poorwill, Calliope Hummingbird, Lewis's Woodpecker, Williamson's Sapsucker, White-headed Woodpecker, Western Wood-Pewee, Dusky Flycatcher, Gray Flycatcher, Clark's Nutcracker, Mountain Chickadee, Pygmy Nuthatch, White-breasted Nuthatch, House Wren, Western Bluebird, Townsend's Solitaire, Western Tanager, Spotted Towhee, Chipping Sparrow, Cassin's Finch, Red Crossbill, and Evening Grosbeak.

SUBALPINE FORESTS

The high mountain forests of British Columbia are home to a variety of birds, many of them characteristic of higher latitudes, that find suitable habitats farther south at these elevations. Typical species include Sooty Grouse (coastal), Dusky Grouse (Interior), Spruce Grouse, Northern Goshawk, Boreal Owl, Red-breasted Sapsucker (coastal), American Three-toed Woodpecker, Olive-sided Flycatcher, Steller's Jay, Gray Jay, Common Raven, Boreal Chickadee, Pacific Wren, Golden-crowned Kinglet, Ruby-crowned Kinglet, Townsend's Solitaire, Hermit Thrush, Varied Thrush, Townsend's Warbler, MacGillivray's Warbler, Wilson's Warbler, Dark-eyed Junco, and Pine Grosbeak.

BOREAL FORESTS

The mixed forests across the northern half of the province have many similarities with the subalpine forests farther south, but there are also many differences, particularly in the lowlands east of the Rockies. Many "eastern" species are found in these forests of White and Black Spruce, Lodgepole Pine, Trembling Aspen, and White Birch. Typical species include Sharp-shinned Hawk, Northern Goshawk, Northern Hawk Owl, Great Gray Owl, Boreal Owl, Yellow-bellied Sapsucker, American Three-toed Woodpecker, Olive-sided Flycatcher, Yellow-bellied Flycatcher, Least Flycatcher, Blue-headed Vireo, Philadelphia Vireo, Red-eyed Vireo, Gray Jay, Blue Jay, Winter Wren, Golden-crowned Kinglet, Ruby-crowned Kinglet, Hermit Thrush, Bohemian Waxwing, Tennessee Warbler, Connecticut Warbler, Mourning Warbler, Palm Warbler, Magnolia Warbler, Cape May Warbler, Black-throated Green Warbler, Bay-breasted Warbler, Blackpoll Warbler, Black and White Warbler, American Redstart, Ovenbird, Canada Warbler, White-throated Sparrow, Dark-eyed Junco, Rose-breasted Grosbeak, Rusty Blackbird, Pine Grosbeak, White-winged Crossbill, and Evening Grosbeak.

ALPINE TUNDRA AND SUBALPINE MEADOWS

Above the subalpine forests are open parklands with scattered clumps of trees, then the treeless alpine tundra. This ecosystem has a bird fauna with fairly low diversity, but several species are restricted to this harsh environment. Typical species are Spruce Grouse, Willow Ptarmigan, Rock Ptarmigan, Sooty Grouse, Dusky Grouse, Prairie Falcon, American Golden-Plover, Rufous Hummingbird, Clark's Nutcracker, Common Raven, Horned Lark, Mountain Bluebird, Gray-cheeked Thrush, American Pipit, Smith's Longspur, Brewer's (Timberline) Sparrow, Savannah Sparrow, Fox Sparrow, Golden-crowned Sparrow, and White-crowned Sparrow.

GRASSLANDS

Grasslands are largely restricted in British Columbia to a few of the dry valleys and parts of the Cariboo-Chilcotin Plateau. There are remnant patches of coastal savannah on southeastern Vancouver Island and the Gulf Islands, and fragments of prairie grassland remain in the Peace River Lowlands. These endangered ecosystems host a unique bird community, including Gray Partridge, Dusky Grouse, Sharp-tailed Grouse, Northern Harrier, American Kestrel, Upland Sandpiper, Long-billed Curlew, Burrowing Owl, Short-eared Owl, Common Nighthawk, Say's Phoebe, Western Kingbird, Black-billed Magpie, Horned Lark, Tree Swallow, Mountain Bluebird, Sage Thrasher, Clay-colored Sparrow, Brewer's Sparrow, Vesper Sparrow, Lark Sparrow, Savannah Sparrow, Grasshopper Sparrow, Lazuli Bunting, and Bobolink.

INTERIOR CLIFFS AND TALUS SLOPES

This is a very localized habitat with a unique bird fauna, particularly in the valleys of the southern Interior (Thompson-Okanagan, Similkameen, and Kettle Valleys). Typical species are Chukar, Golden Eagle, Prairie Falcon, Peregrine Falcon, Great Horned Owl, White-throated Swift, Say's Phoebe, Violet-green Swallow, Cliff Swallow, Rock Wren, and Canyon Wren.

FRESHWATER WETLANDS

Because of its rugged topography, British Columbia has relatively few extensive marshes and wetlands, but many species rely on these rich habitats for breeding and migration stopovers. Typical breeding species are Canada Goose, Trumpeter Swan, Wood Duck, Gadwall, American Wigeon, Mallard, Blue-winged Teal,

Cinnamon Teal, Northern Shoveler, Northern Pintail, Green-winged Teal, Canvasback, Redhead, Ring-necked Duck, Lesser Scaup, White-winged Scoter, Bufflehead, Common Goldeneye, Barrow's Goldeneye, Hooded Merganser, Common Merganser, Ruddy Duck, Red-throated Loon, Pacific Loon, Common Loon, Pied-billed Grebe, Horned Grebe, Red-necked Grebe, Eared Grebe, Western Grebe, American Bittern, Great Blue Heron, Northern Harrier, Virginia Rail, Sora, American Coot, Sandhill Crane, Killdeer, American Avocet, Spotted Sandpiper, Solitary Sandpiper, Greater Yellowlegs, Lesser Yellowlegs, Wilson's Snipe, Black Tern, Short-eared Owl, Marsh Wren, Common Yellowthroat, Northern Waterthrush, LeConte's Sparrow, Nelson's Sparrow, Song Sparrow, Lincoln's Sparrow, Swamp Sparrow, Red-winged Blackbird, and Yellow-headed Blackbird.

RIVERS AND CREEKS

Rivers and creeks are abundant in the province, but few birds are adapted to feed in their moving waters. Typical species are Trumpeter Swan (winter), Wood Duck, Mallard, Harlequin Duck, Common Goldeneye (winter), Barrow's Goldeneye (winter), Hooded Merganser, Common Merganser, Great Blue Heron, Spotted Sandpiper, Black Swift (waterfalls), Belted Kingfisher, Eastern Phoebe, Bank Swallow, and American Dipper.

LARGE LAKES

Compared to the rest of Canada, British Columbia has few large lakes. Typical birds found along their shores and in their waters include Canada Goose, Mallard, Common Merganser, Horned Grebe (winter), Red-necked Grebe, Western Grebe, American White Pelican, Double-crested Cormorant, Osprey, Bald Eagle, American Coot (winter), Spotted Sandpiper, Bonaparte's Gull,

Mew Gull, Ring-billed Gull, California Gull, Herring Gull, Common Tern, and Belted Kingfisher.

AGRICULTURAL HABITATS

Although many birds have suffered from habitat loss because of agricultural developments, some have flourished in the field crops, feedlots, orchards, and vineyards found primarily in the southern half of the province. These species include Canada Goose, Trumpeter Swan, American Wigeon, Mallard, California Quail, Gray Partridge, Ring-necked Pheasant, Wild Turkey, Northern Harrier, Red-tailed Hawk, Rough-legged Hawk, American Kestrel, Killdeer, Long-billed Curlew, Rock Pigeon, Mourning Dove, Great Horned Owl, Say's Phoebe, Black-billed Magpie, American Crow, Cliff Swallow, Barn Swallow, Mountain Bluebird, American Robin, European Starling, Savannah Sparrow, White-crowned Sparrow, Red-winged Blackbird, Western Meadowlark, Yellow-headed Blackbird, Brewer's Blackbird, Brown-headed Cowbird, House Finch, and House Sparrow.

URBAN AND SUBURBAN HABITATS

A few species have managed to adapt to backyard gardens and even the concrete jungle of downtown landscapes in British Columbia. Typical species include California Quail, Cooper's Hawk, Merlin, Glaucous-winged Gull, Ring-billed Gull, Rock Pigeon, Eurasian Collared-Dove, Anna's Hummingbird, Rufous Hummingbird, Northern Flicker, American Crow, Northwestern Crow, Violet-green Swallow, Black-capped Chickadee, Chestnut-backed Chickadee, House Wren, American Robin, European Starling, Cedar Waxwing, Spotted Towhee, Song Sparrow, Dark-eyed Junco, Bullock's Oriole, Purple Finch, Cassin's Finch, House Finch, Pine Siskin, American Goldfinch, and House Sparrow.

THE BIRDING YEAR

When birding, it always helps to be in the right place at the right time. This book is primarily devoted to putting you in the right place, but this short section may help you to choose the right time to plan your outings. Although you can go birding anywhere and anytime in British Columbia, there are a few wildlife spectacles you shouldn't miss.

JANUARY

Being smack dab in the middle of Canadian winter, January ought to be a time to stay indoors, but for birders, it is one of the most exciting times of the year. While the rest of the world is trying to give up smoking or working out in temporarily crowded gyms, birders are out in the field building their brand new year lists, taking part in the last few Christmas Bird Counts of the year, or just enjoying the Arctic nomads that have been forced south by winter weather. As is the case for the rest of the winter months, the most bird-diverse part of the province in January is the south coast. The Fraser delta in general, and Boundary Bay in particular, is host to huge numbers of waterfowl, shorebirds, and their attendant predators. Upwards of 100,000 Dunlin feed on the tidal flats, with thousands of Northern Pintail, American Wigeon, and other ducks. With all this food around, it's not surprising that the Boundary Bay area hosts one of the largest winter concentrations of hawks, falcons, eagles, and owls in North America! January is also a good time to search rocky shorelines all along the coast for their suite of winter shorebirds— Black Turnstone, Surfbird, and Rock Sandpiper. In the Interior, thousands of Bohemian Waxwings flock into residential areas to feed on Mountain Ash and other berries, while big groups of waterfowl—Redheads, Greater Scaups, and American Coots— concentrate on the unfrozen southern lakes. Much of the world's population of Trumpeter Swans winters in British Columbia, mostly in agricultural habitats along the southern coast, with significant numbers staying in other coastal estuaries as well as ice-free rivers and lakes of the Interior.

FEBRUARY

In direct contrast to January, February is one of the most under-birded months in British Columbia. The excitement of new lists has worn off, and many birders have succumbed to the urge to escape south to see our summer birds in their winter homes in Mexico and Central America. But for those of us who hang in there, February offers excitement of its own. Some years, February is when herring begin to spawn along the south coast—an event always attended by amazing numbers of Bald Eagles, diving ducks, loons, grebes, gulls, and much more. The early signs of spring begin to show in southern British Columbia, including the first returning migrants. Violet-green Swallows and Tree Swallows search for newly hatched insects over streams and rivers. In the grasslands of the southern Interior, Western Meadowlarks begin to sing, and the mournful call of the Say's

Phoebe is heard along the Okanagan River. This is the start of owl nesting season, and Great Horned Owls are hooting all night and much of the day across the province, while Northern Saw-whet Owls fill the night air with their monotonous, whistled toots.

MARCH

Spring is in full swing on the coast—male Rufous Hummingbirds return to set up territories around patches of blooming salmonberry and red flowering currant, and the first migrant Yellow-rumped Warblers show up in city parks and gardens. The herring spawn extravaganza continues on the coast. Williamson's Sapsuckers arrive in late March and are most easily found then, when they drum noisily in larch forests in the southern Interior. Hutton's Vireos can be hard to find at other times of the year but are easily tracked down in March, when they broadcast their monotonous sounds in south coastal forests.

APRIL

Shorebird migration begins in earnest, peaking on the south coast toward the end of the month. Most of the world's population of Western Sandpipers stops to refuel on the mud flats of the Fraser delta, and thousands of Brant stop over on the eelgrass beds around the Strait of Georgia. This is also a good time to visit the southern Interior to enjoy Mountain and Western Bluebirds as they explore nest boxes in the grasslands. While you're there, look up to check for flocks of Sandhill Cranes and Canada Geese on their way north to Alaska. Thousands of these birds migrate up the Okanagan Valley, then over the Douglas Lake plateau and the Kamloops grasslands, and on to the Chilcotin and Bulkley Valley. They are occasionally joined by smaller numbers of American White Pelicans migrating to their breeding colony at Stum Lake in the central Chilcotin. Sparrow migration peaks in late April as large flocks of White-crowned Sparrows flit restlessly through shrub lands of the Interior. April is also a great time for owling, especially for Western Screech-Owl and Boreal Owl, both of which vigorously defend their territories before settling down to nesting duties in May.

MAY

If you polled British Columbia birders about their favourite month, May would likely be the runaway winner. Songbird migration surges north across the province, bringing flycatchers, vireos, and warblers into backyards and favourite birding spots. Birding festivals, such as Wings Over the Rockies in Invermere and the Meadowlark Festival in the south Okanagan, offer visitors an opportunity to enjoy this diverse bounty. This is the best month to do a "Big Day," since the last of the migrant shorebirds and wintering waterfowl mingle with the flood of newly arrived breeding species. By the end of the month, almost every breeding bird has returned.

JUNE

This is the month of birdsong and a time to explore the unbeatable diversity of British Columbia's breeding birds. Visit the Peace River area to add "eastern" warblers to your list, the northwestern mountains for Gray-cheeked Thrush, or the Okanagan Valley for Yellow-breasted Chats and Flammulated Owls. On the coast, this is the one month of the year in which shorebirds and most waterfowl are essentially absent—a good excuse to leave the Fraser delta and head into the forests and hills.

JULY

Birdsong continues into the first week of July, but after that, the forests become quieter as birds concentrate on feeding their nestlings and fledglings. After only a few weeks on their Arctic breeding grounds, adult sandpipers and plovers leave their teenage young behind and pass through British Columbia again, reviving interest in shorebird oases such as Salmon Arm Bay and Iona Island. The snowpack has receded in subalpine habitats, allowing exploration of mountain forests and meadows for high altitude species such as Spruce Grouse, Boreal Chickadee, Horned Lark, and Pine Grosbeak.

AUGUST

The sandpiper flocks swell as adults are replaced by more numerous juveniles on their way to South America, and birders flock to their favourite mud flats and sewage lagoons to scope for rarities in the warm evening sun at places like Witty's Lagoon, Boundary Bay, Duck Lake, Robert Lake, and Salmon Arm Bay. This is the best time to find Wandering Tattlers along the rocky jetties and wave platforms of the south coast. Alpine snowpacks are minimal, making this a good time to do a bit of hiking to find White-tailed Ptarmigan and Gray-crowned Rosy-Finch. As songbirds finish their nesting season, bird observatories around the province gear up with mist nets and banding supplies in anticipation of the great exodus of fall migrants. This is a popular time for pelagic trips off the West Coast, since bird numbers are high and the weather is generally stable.

SEPTEMBER

Shorebird species diversity peaks in the first week of September, providing enthusiasts with their best chance at seeing regular rarities such as Stilt Sandpiper, Buff-breasted Sandpiper, and Hudsonian Godwit. Offshore seabird diversity is also high now, with southern visitors like Buller's Shearwater peaking in numbers. Songbird migration continues in earnest, with many of the warblers starting to be replaced by waves of Savannah and Lincoln's Sparrows. Toward the end of the month, the window opens for Sharp-tailed Sandpiper, giving birders yet another reason to check carefully along the foreshore. The months of September and October are also great for owling. Although they're not nesting, this is when established males start calling again to assert their territorial rights, as juveniles roam around searching out new homes.

OCTOBER

October is the peak of rarity season. From late August to mid-November, lost birds from around the continent (and sometimes Asia) start to pop up in mixed migrant flocks, in the hedges behind the post office or the fields beside the airport. You never know what could turn up, and this makes for some exciting birding. If you want to take this to the extreme, plan a trip to Haida Gwaii at this time of year. Almost anything can show up there, from a Grasshopper Sparrow in 2010 to a Common Crane in 2011. Even if you don't find anything unusual, the rugged beauty of the islands and the non-stop flow of thousands of waterfowl, from geese and dabbling ducks to scoters and grebes, will easily make the trip worthwhile. Have you ever seen fifteen Yellow-billed Loons from a ferry? Enough said.

NOVEMBER

November marks the transition of fall into winter. The last of the warbler flocks trickle south, while some loners hang on for a few more days. Heermann's Gulls, which flew north after breeding to take advantage of the fine British Columbia weather and seafood from August to October, begin a retreat to warmer climes. And the winter birds start to arrive from the north, including Snow Goose, Rock Sandpiper, Northern Shrike, and Snow Bunting. Although they've been rare in recent years, this is often the time when a few Cattle Egrets will stray north, appearing unannounced in fields both on the coast and in the Interior.

DECEMBER

By the beginning of December, birders will have a good idea of the kind of a winter it will be. Will it be a Snowy Owl flight year? Will it be a good Bohemian Waxwing winter or a good redpoll winter? Will it be a white Christmas? Will the lake freeze before the Christmas Bird Count? As the year draws to a close, some birders will be desperately scheming to add those final one or two species to the year list, while others will be thinking of only one bird: turkey. They will reflect on the year that was and wait with giddy anticipation for January 1, when everything is new again . . .

USING THIS GUIDE

This book aims to offer a practical and informative guide to the best birding sites in British Columbia. Some of the locations are relatively well known, whereas others will be completely new to the reader. Included with each site are driving and walking directions, an overview of the area, and a list of bird species that might be found there throughout the year. This is not a field guide; we rarely delve into bird identification but instead provide tips on how best to find a diversity of birds and see some of the most sought-after species. Keep in mind that roadways and site-access issues are constantly changing, so it is likely that some of the birding areas outlined in this book will be subject to subtle or even major changes that may affect your ability to visit a given site, as well as the mix of birds expected for that area.

The province is divided into eleven regions. The Vancouver Island and Lower Mainland regions cover the southern coast of the province, providing the easiest access to rainforest and marine birding opportunities. The drier parts of the southern Interior are divided into the Thompson-Nicola-Lillooet and Okanagan Similkameen regions, and the wetter forests of the southeastern Interior are covered by the Shuswap-Revelstoke and Kootenay regions. The Rocky Mountain Parks region covers the spine of the Rockies in British Columbia, including Mount Robson Provincial Park and Yoho and Kootenay National Parks.

We highly recommend using this guide in conjunction with a road map and a GPS unit. In more remote areas, B.C. Backroad Mapbooks (available at most gas stations and tourist information centres) are extremely useful. The maps included in this book are for the most part extremely basic and designed to give either an overview of certain birding locales in relation to others in the same region or specific trail or driving information about a single site. We recommend that you first read the account of each birding location, and then decide where and when to tackle each spot, depending on what you want to see in conjunction with the season, tide heights, and weather. At the end of the book, we have included an annotated list of birds that many visiting birders might find useful in seeking out some of their most wanted species.

Oh, and don't forget your field guides and binoculars!

VANCOUVER ISLAND

VICTORIA

Because of its location at the southern tip of Vancouver Island, the Greater Victoria region is an ideal area to watch bird migration along the Pacific Flyway. Add this to a variety of habitats, and you have one of the most productive birding areas in the province. Seabirds and the introduced Sky Larks are the two main specialties, but there are plenty of other birds no matter when you visit. Enjoy your time in the capital city!

> Saanich Peninsula

The Swartz Bay ferry terminal is located at the northern tip of the **Saanich Peninsula** and is about a half-hour drive north of downtown Victoria. (To read an account of the Swartz Bay–Tsawwassen ferry route, see page 138.) Between Swartz Bay and Victoria, the rural farmlands and beaches of the Saanich Peninsula offer great opportunities for birding.

Many visiting birders have one target on the Saanich Peninsula: the Sky Lark. Introduced to various locations on the south coast of British Columbia in 1903, the population of this European songbird was established on southern Vancouver Island and increased until the early 1960s. The maximum population

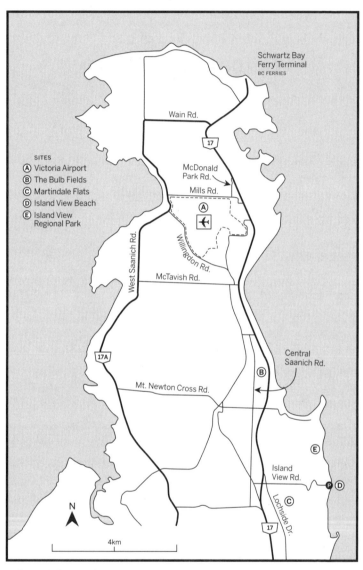

1 Saanich Peninsula

was more than one thousand individuals, but since then, numbers have declined to no more than one hundred birds, largely because of habitat loss. Sky Larks can still be found in open grassy meadows and farmlands all over the Saanich Peninsula, but they are reliable in only three localized areas. The first is the **Victoria International Airport**. From the ferry terminal, drive just over 5 kilometres south toward Victoria, exit right onto McDonald Park Road, then make an immediate left to stay on McDonald; continue south for 850 metres, then turn right at Mills Road. This road skirts the northern perimeter of the airport. Stop at every high point to scan the grassy fields in the area, then continue around the airport complex via West Saanich Road, Willingdon Road, and East Saanich Road (which merges into a variety of other road names along the east side of the airport).

The second and perhaps most reliable location is known simply as the **Bulb Fields** (A K A the Vantreight Bulb Fields). Continue south on the Patricia Bay Highway (Hwy. 17) from the airport and the city of Sidney and watch for the Mount Newton X-Road exit. Turn right (west) here, then turn right again (north) after 200 metres onto Central Saanich Road. From the turn, it's 1.5 kilometres to the Bulb Fields, where Sky Larks can be found on either side of the road. Birders are allowed to walk along the dirt vehicle tracks between the flowers and other crops, but please respect that this is private property and identify yourself as a birder to anyone working in the area. With luck and patience, you will flush a Sky Lark or perhaps even hear one singing (January to July). Savannah Sparrows and American Pipits may also be abundant here, so make sure you get a good look. When it flushes, listen for the lark's rich *cheer up!* call and keep your eye on it, as it can be very difficult to locate again once it lands.

The third location for Sky Lark (and a variety of other species, too) is **Martindale Flats**. Drive 2.5 kilometres south down Hwy. 17 from the Mount Newton X-Road junction and turn

Sky Lark

left (west) on Island View Road—from here, take the first right (Lochside Drive) and stop frequently to scan the fields between here and Martindale Road. Local landowners tolerate birders, but you should try to stay at the edges of the fields, and be wary of thick muck during wet seasons. The best times to find the Sky Larks here are in winter (when the birds are in flocks of ten to twenty) and early spring (when males are singing). The summer breeding season can be very quiet, but the birds are always around somewhere.

Martindale Flats is a fantastic birding area from fall to early spring, when flooded fields and ponds harbour large numbers of waterfowl, raptors, and shorebirds. More than one hundred species can be found in this small area during the winter months, and migration season is even better, with more than thirty-four waterfowl species recorded and a tantalizing rarity list that includes Emperor Goose, Sharp-tailed Sandpiper, Buff-breasted Sandpiper, Ruff, Tropical Kingbird, and Red-throated Pipit (twice). Good fields to check vary depending on water levels, so have fun exploring, particularly the area along Ocean View, Puckle, Lochside, and Martindale Roads. For the most reliable breeding site for Bullock's Oriole in the Victoria area, head south on Welch Road (turn off Martindale east of Lochside) to the cottonwood stand at the corner of Welch Road and Livesay Street. There are usually one or two pairs here each summer. **Island View Beach** is another great spot in this area. Drive to the east end of Island View Road and park in the designated area near the boat ramp. At many times of the year (especially winter), the offshore waters will produce a large number of birds, including cormorants, sea ducks, loons, grebes, gulls, and alcids. Walk north along the trail to **Island View Regional Park**, but remember that the first stretch of the trail passes through private property. In the park, there is a mixture of hedgerows and fields where you might encounter migrant passerines during migration. In winter, look for sparrows, finches, and roving groups of Bushtits. Northern Shrikes are also often around in the winter, and at dusk, you may be lucky enough to run into a Short-eared Owl. Mountain Bluebirds pass through regularly in early spring, and Northern Harriers are present throughout the year. The beach sometimes has a few shorebirds (including Baird's Sandpiper in August and September), but the highlight is offshore, where hundreds of sea ducks such as Surf Scoter, White-winged Scoter, Greater Scaup, Harlequin Duck, and Long-tailed Duck can be seen (particularly in late fall and winter). This is also one of the more reliable sites near Victoria for Black Scoter (outside the breeding season). The northern border of the park ends at the Tsawout First Nation reserve boundary, so do not proceed any farther without permission.

> Sidney Spit Marine Park

Although it's visited infrequently by birders, **Sidney Spit** (on Sidney Island) is perhaps the best shorebird hot spot in the Victoria region. Unless you have a private vessel, the principal way of reaching the site is by taking the daily foot-passenger ferry from

Sidney Wharf on the upper Saanich Peninsula. The ferry typically only runs from spring to fall, so be sure to look up ferry schedules prior to the trip. The twenty-five-minute ride ($19) will take you to the lovely Sidney Island, which the Coast Salish people used as an annual summer camp. Picnicking is most popular during the warm summer months, but most birders visit the spit and the adjacent **Sidney Lagoon** between mid-August and October, when peak shorebird numbers are passing through. Since the site only recently started receiving coverage, the possibility of turning up something mega is exciting!

> Elk/Beaver Lake Regional Park

As you drive between Victoria and Swartz Bay on Hwy. 17, **Elk Lake** is on the west side, just north of Royal Oak Drive. In winter, several waterfowl species occur here that are hard to find elsewhere on southern Vancouver Island, including Canvasback, Redhead (rare), Ruddy Duck, and American Coot. Spring and fall can be interesting times as well, when Townsend's Warblers and other migrants are moving through the many tall conifers in the park.

The main parking area for Elk Lake is reached by turning off Hwy. 17 (west) onto Sayward Road, followed by a left on Hamsterly Road, then a right on Brookleigh Road (which leads to the parking lot). There are several other access points into the park, including the adjacent Beaver Lake to the south.

> Mount Douglas Park

"**Mount Doug**" is accessed via Churchill Drive, which heads up the mountain from the north end of Shelbourne Street (where Shelbourne intersects with Cedar Hill Road). *Note: Churchill Drive is usually gated and locked until noon daily, so you can either walk up (forty-five minutes to the top) or drive up in the early afternoon.*

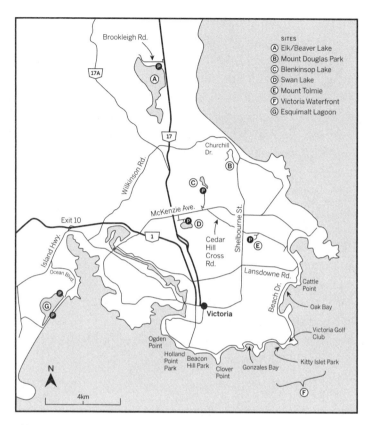

SITES
Ⓐ Elk/Beaver Lake
Ⓑ Mount Douglas Park
Ⓒ Blenkinsop Lake
Ⓓ Swan Lake
Ⓔ Mount Tolmie
Ⓕ Victoria Waterfront
Ⓖ Esquimalt Lagoon

Brookleigh Rd.

17A

Ⓐ

17

Churchill Dr.

Ⓑ

Wilkinson Rd.

Ⓒ
Ⓟ

McKenzie Ave.

Exit 10

Island Hwy.

Ocean Blvd.

1

Ⓟ Ⓓ

Cedar Hill Cross Rd.

Shelbourne St.

Ⓟ Ⓔ

Lansdowne Rd.

Beach Dr.

Cattle Point

Oak Bay

Ⓖ
Ⓟ

Victoria

Victoria Golf Club

Ogden Point

Holland Point Park

Beacon Hill Park

Clover Point

Gonzales Bay

Kitty Islet Park

N

4km

Ⓕ

2 Victoria

At the base of Churchill Drive is mature mixed forest with species typical of this habitat, such as Hutton's Vireo, Varied Thrush, Pacific-slope Flycatcher, Pacific Wren, and Black-throated Gray Warbler. From the summit parking area, walk the trails leading on all sides through the open bluffs and Garry Oak woods. This is a great area for migrant songbirds, especially in spring, and worth checking for "fall-outs" on wet May mornings. Warbler flocks can be spotted, with rarities possible; all the regular flycatchers, vireos, and the like are present in substantial numbers in spring passage. Watch the skies for both Black and Vaux's Swifts. Townsend's Solitaire, Western Kingbird, Mountain Bluebird, and Lazuli Bunting are regular spring visitors, with the bluebird and solitaire seen in fall as well. Breeding species include Western Tanager, Cassin's Vireo, and House Wren. A singing Brewer's Sparrow was present in the broom thickets near the summit in early June 2011, and a Gray-crowned Rosy-Finch was present in late May 2009 at the teacup lookout at the summit, where Horned Larks have also been seen. Another trail access to similar open Garry Oak habitat on Little Mount Douglas is off Blenkinsop Road, just south of Lohbrunner Road East.

In winter, check for Eared Grebe at the beach access down the stairs from the parking lot at the corner of Cedar Hill Road, Cordova Bay Road, and Ash Road (just northeast of Churchill; turnoff along Cedar Hill Road). This site, along with Cordova Bay, is one of the best spots in Victoria for this species. In winter, this is also a good spot to scope for scoter rafts, all three loon species, and an assortment of other water birds.

> Blenkinsop Lake

Situated along the Lochside Trail (crd.bc.ca/parks/lochside), **Blenkinsop Lake** is a pleasant place to visit during spring and summer months, when local breeders such as Warbling Vireo, Yellow Warbler, Black-headed Grosbeak, and Bullock's Oriole (rare) fill the birches with song and colour. The Blenkinsop Trestle—a wooden walking/cycling bridge that crosses the middle section of the small lake—is the best place to watch for birds, both in the surrounding riparian foliage and on the water itself. A number of dabbling ducks visit the lake throughout the year, especially in winter, when Trumpeter Swans may also be present. Green Herons nest in the thick brushy areas around the lake and can sometimes be seen hunting from a perch close to the water's edge.

Whether you're coming from Swartz Bay or downtown Victoria, the simplest way to access the lake is to head east on Mackenzie Avenue off Hwy. 17, then after 1.5 kilometres turn left (north) on Borden Street. Take the first right onto Cedar Hill Cross Road, then the first left onto Lochside Drive—the parking area is near the end (walk north to reach the lake).

> Swan Lake

From the Patricia Bay Highway (Hwy. 17), take the Mackenzie Avenue exit east, then make a right on Rainbow Street, left on Ralph Street, and, finally, a right on Swan Lake Road—the parking area is on the left. **Swan Lake** is a popular sanctuary for photographers and both serious and beginner birders because of the easy access trail boardwalks and quality of habitat. In the nesting season, the lake offers excellent viewing of common residents such as Anna's Hummingbird, Bewick's Wren, Marsh Wren, Bushtit, Cedar Waxwing, Spotted Towhee, Black-headed Grosbeak, Yellow Warbler, and Common Yellowthroat. Freshwater waterfowl are well represented, apart from the breeding season, with Pied-billed Grebe being regular and the occasional Cinnamon or Blue-winged Teal in migration. Up to two American Bitterns have been regular at the lake year-round recently; carefully scan the lakeshore for their cryptic silhouettes in the reeds and watch for them in flight, flying back and forth between the surrounding wet fields and the lake. Green Herons are seen erratically (especially after the young have fledged in late August).

As with most coastal areas, the migration season (particularly late summer and fall) provides the most exciting birding, but Swan Lake can be worth the trip at any time of year. Virginia Rails are generally present year round, often in greater numbers in the fall; they are occasionally seen but more often heard, especially at dawn and dusk. Sora are less common but possible year round. Check the gulls bathing in the lake; Thayer's are regular from September through February, and an occasional rarity has been found, such as Slaty-backed and Franklin's Gulls.

Birding walks, led by local experts, leave the parking area every Wednesday and Sunday at 9 AM. The walks are free, though donations to the sanctuary are much appreciated. For more information, visit swanlake.bc.ca.

➤ Mount Tolmie

Considered one of the premier migrant traps in the Victoria region, **Mount Tolmie Park** is well worth a visit at any time of year but particularly during spring and fall. Like Queen Elizabeth Park and Burnaby Mountain in the Vancouver area, Mount Tolmie is covered in mixed vegetation and surrounded by urban neighbourhoods, making it a magnet for migrants. To reach the park, drive east on Mackenzie Avenue from Hwy. 17. After 1.9 kilometres, turn right on Cedar Hill Cross Road. Follow this road for 2.9 kilometres, then turn right on Glastonbury Road, before making the first left onto Mayfair Drive and proceeding to the top of the hill (the park is well signed).

After parking near the top, you will notice that Mount Tolmie is mostly covered in open Garry Oak woodland. This rare ecosystem used to be widespread across much of southern Vancouver Island, but because of urban development and agriculture, it is now restricted to small fragments like this one. Several rare plant species occur here, and on a clear day, the view of the Greater Victoria region is fabulous. Year-round residents include Anna's Hummingbird (most conspicuous from January to March, when males are singing), Hutton's Vireo, Steller's Jay, Chestnut-backed Chickadee, Bushtit, Bewick's Wren, Spotted Towhee, and Purple Finch. Some of the first migrants, such as Rufous Hummingbird, start arriving in March, but the best time for warblers and flycatchers is from mid-April to early May. Olive-sided, Hammond's, and Pacific-slope are regular migrants, whereas Dusky Fly-catcher is rare but annual. Most of the common warblers pass through, including Black-throated Gray and Townsend's. Nashville Warbler and Lazuli Bunting are locally rare, but this seems to be one of the more reliable sites for one to show up each year. Raptor migration can also be noticeable here, especially for Cooper's and Sharp-shinned Hawks.

> Victoria Waterfront

For most birders, checking the hot spots along the Victoria waterfront is a "must do." Whether you're looking to get a nice view of Pacific seabirds and shorebirds or just hoping to see something rare and exciting, this is a great place to start—and many of the following locations can be checked from the car (perfect for rainy or windy days). There is good birding to be had at any of the waterfront access points, from Gordon Head in northeast Victoria all the way around to Esquimalt, but for the purposes of this book, we will concentrate on the most popular spots in southern Victoria, from the eastern end of Lansdowne Road (just south of Cadboro Bay) down and around to Victoria Harbour.

We start our waterfront sweep at the eastern terminus of Lansdowne Road. Keep right at the Y-intersection on Rutland Road, follow Rutland to the end (crossing Beach Drive), and park. This small access point to the rocky shoreline is not always productive but can sometimes yield shorebirds such as Whimbrel and Rock Sandpiper (rare; November to March). Tides will also be a factor, but at the very least, this site will give you a vantage point for scoping the outer reaches of Cadboro Bay.

Return to Beach Drive and turn left (southwest); only about 500 metres along is **Cattle Point** (on the right). This small park is an excellent place to scope for water birds and check the rocky areas for shorebirds. Winter might be the best time of year to visit, when an impressive variety of waterfowl, loons, grebes, gulls, and cormorants are around, but spring, fall, and even summer can produce some thrilling birds. Black Turnstones (late summer to early spring) and Black Oystercatchers (year round) are often conspicuous near the parking lot and are sometimes joined by Dunlin, Surfbirds, and the odd group of Rock Sandpiper (November to March). In winter, the brushy areas around the park are particularly good for Bushtit, both White-crowned and Golden-crowned Sparrows, and Spotted Towhee, whereas Anna's Hummingbirds are present all year. **Uplands Park** is across the street and can provide more opportunities for "bush birds."

If you continue south on Beach Drive, you'll come to **Oak Bay** and the Oak Bay Marina. This area can be good for wintering diving ducks, and Belted Kingfishers are often seen perching on one of the sailboat masts. As you proceed along Beach Drive, you will pass the **Victoria Golf Club**. In spring and fall, the fairways on the ocean side of the road are worth checking for Whimbrel and other shorebirds, as well as flocks of geese. High tides in the early morning or around dusk (when golfing traffic is minimal) are best. Around the corner, opposite 508 Beach Drive, is **Kitty Islet Park**. This tiny reserve is a great place from which to scan McNeill Bay for seabirds and take in a lovely view. Beach Drive passes Monterey Avenue before cutting inland; instead, turn left onto King George Terrace and follow it as it turns into Crescent Road, which winds around the smaller **Gonzalez Bay** (if you want, you can check this bay by going down one of the small side roads). After Gonzalez Bay, the road names change rapidly, but just try to stay along the shoreline and soon you'll find yourself on Dallas Road. This road will follow the long beach of Ross Bay until it brings you to one of Victoria's most famous birding sites: **Clover Point**.

Consisting only of a parking lot, an open grassy area, and a rocky shoreline, there isn't much to Clover Point—but for whatever reason, the birds seem to like it. With at least sixteen species recorded, gulls are without question the signature bird group here. Winter seems to be the best time for diversity, but each season brings a different mix. Throughout the year, the most abundant species is Glaucous-winged, along with a large number of "mutts," also known as "Olympic Gulls" or "Puget Sound Gulls." These hybrid mixes are mostly crosses between Glaucous-winged and Western Gulls, but sometimes it's hard to tell. Pure Western Gulls are present in small numbers in the winter and to a lesser extent in the fall and spring. Heermann's Gulls are common in late July and early August and remain in the area into fall, before heading back south; California Gulls can be seen through most of the year but especially during spring and fall migration periods; Herring Gulls are less common but are still regularly seen; Ring-billed Gulls are usually more numerous than Herring but are still uncommon; Mew Gulls are common outside of summer; Glaucous Gulls are rare but regular in winter; Thayer's Gulls are common from late fall to early winter, and Iceland (Kumlien's) Gulls are rare, with around one individual reported each winter. Bonaparte's Gulls pass through in significant numbers during spring and fall and are occasionally spotted in winter. The rest of the species list consists of big-time rarities, including Red-legged Kittiwake, Ross's Gull, and Black-tailed Gull.

It's not *all* about the gulls, though; in fact, some days you may see very few. As a prominent point of land, Clover Point is an ideal place to set up a scope and scan the nearby bays and offshore waters. Scoters, Harlequin Ducks, grebes, mergansers, cormorants, and other divers can all be turned up nearby (especially outside of summer), and alcids such as Common Murre, Pigeon Guillemot, Rhinoceros Auklet, and Marbled Murrelet are often visible. Between late November and early March, you might even be lucky enough to see small groups of Ancient Murrelets shuttling back and forth up the Juan de Fuca Strait. In addition to all the gulls and seabirds, open-country passerines such as American Pipit (spring/fall), Snow Bunting (fall/winter), and Lapland Longspurs (fall) are turned up annually in the grassy fringes around the parking area. Shorebirds, too, are often in evidence around the barnacle-encrusted boulders.

West of Clover Point (still on Dallas Road) is **Beacon Hill Park**, Victoria's signature city park. In spring and fall, a few migrant songbirds pass through and can be found mixed in with the resident flocks of Chestnut-backed Chickadees (the only chickadee on Vancouver Island), Bushtits, and Golden-crowned Kinglets. A few feral Indian Peafowl reside in the park as well, but for all intents and purposes, they are not considered "countable" by the checklist committees. Only a couple of hundred metres west of Beacon Hill Park on Dallas Road is **Holland Point Park**. This provides birders with another chance to scope the water and check for shorebirds along the rocky outcrops and beaches. The model-boat pond here attracts a surprising diversity of waterfowl in winter, including Lesser Scaup, Bufflehead, American Wigeon, and the occasional Eurasian Wigeon (Goodacre Lake in Beacon Hill Park is similar in this regard).

Finally, just before Dallas Road turns north and heads toward Victoria Harbour, the conspicuous concrete breakwater of **Ogden Point** comes into view. After finding a safe place to park, walk out along the jetty and check the rocky wave platforms on either side for "rock-pipers." Throughout most of the year, Black Turnstone is the common species in this habitat, but occasionally they are joined by uncommon species such as Ruddy Turnstone and Surfbird. This is also the most reliable and accessible Wandering Tattler site near Victoria, and birds are seen each May, then again in August and September. It's also possible to find other sandpipers, such as Dunlin, Rock Sandpiper (rare), Spotted Sandpiper, and Black-bellied Plover. The long breakwater also allows birders to get closer to birds that are otherwise only visible through a scope, so be sure to bring a scope along for superior views of scoters and other seabirds.

> Ferry to Port Angeles (USA)

The M V *Coho* of Black Ball Ferry Line offers daily vehicle and passenger transport across the Juan de Fuca Strait from Victoria Harbour to Port Angeles, Washington. This gives local or visiting birders an opportunity to get out into the strait and spot some pelagic seabirds that might be straying in from the open ocean. These hard-to-find but annual species include Northern Fulmar, Sooty, Short-tailed and Pink-footed Shearwater, Fork-tailed and Leach's Storm-Petrel, Cassin's Auklet, and Tufted Puffin. You probably won't see any of those species on most trips, but there should be large numbers of more common seabirds, such as scoters, Long-tailed Ducks (mainly winter), all three cormorants, Pacific and Common Loons, Common Murres, Rhinoceros Auklets, Marbled and Ancient Murrelets (in season), and a variety of gulls. The time of year, availability of food, and wind direction will all factor into the diversity of birds you encounter.

This route can be done as a day trip or as an alternate (and less busy) way to travel to Seattle, Washington, and points south. For more information, visit cohoferry.com.

> Esquimalt Lagoon

From downtown Victoria, head north on Douglas Street (which will eventually veer westward and turn into Hwy. 1). Remain on Hwy. 1 for about 1 kilometre, then take the right-hand exit lane (Exit 10) toward Colwood. This road will take you underneath Hwy. 1 before crossing a bridge beside the Six Mile Pub. If you're coming from farther north on the Saanich Peninsula, turn west (right) off the Patricia Bay Highway (Hwy. 17) on Mackenzie Avenue—this will join up with Hwy. 1, where you can follow the same directions given above. Head up the hill and be ready to turn left at the lights immediately past the Juan de Fuca Recreation Centre (onto Ocean Boulevard). After making the left-hand turn onto Ocean Boulevard, proceed for another 300 metres and keep left to continue on Ocean. From here, drive the final 2.2 kilometres to the bottom of the hill, passing through mature conifer forest, where Pacific-slope Flycatcher can be found in spring and summer. At the bottom of the hill, you will come to a one-lane bridge at the mouth of **Esquimalt Lagoon**. There is often room to park on the near side of the bridge; otherwise, there is ample parking beyond the bridge, along the spit that separates the lagoon from the ocean (A K A the Coberg Peninsula).

The birding here is straightforward—walk or drive along the spit (2 kilometres one way) and check out the waterfowl and shorebirds on both sides. Because of the fresh water, the lagoon side tends to have more dabblers, such as Mallard, American Wigeon, Northern Pintail, Green-winged Teal, and Mute Swan, whereas the ocean side can be great for offshore grebes, loons, Bufflehead, Greater Scaup, Harlequin Duck, Long-tailed Duck, Red-breasted Mergansers, cormorants, and several alcid species (October to March typically yields the greatest variety). Flocks of Brant are often present around late winter, and gulls are usually found in substantial numbers on both sides of the spit. In spring and summer, Caspian Terns join the loafing gull flocks and Black Oystercatchers are conspicuous. If there are any exposed gravel bars on the lagoon side during spring or late summer and fall, check them carefully for shorebirds. The protected waters and abutting shrubby area in the narrow section of the lagoon at the far (southwest) end are always worth checking for additional species.

From here, you can either retrace your steps to Victoria and Hwy. 1 or take Lagoon Road north from the southwest end of the spit, then turn left (south) on Metchosin Road to continue to the next birding site.

> Witty's Lagoon

From the junction with Lagoon Road, head south on Metchosin Road for 5.5 kilometres; the parking area for **Witty's Lagoon Regional Park** will be on the left. From here, a trail winds down the hill through a stand of mature coastal forest to the lagoon itself. Common species seen here year round include Steller's Jay, Chestnut-backed Chickadee, Pacific Wren, and Golden-crowned Kinglet. The mud flats of the lagoon attract shorebirds in spring and fall. This is probably the best shorebirding area near Victoria, with such rarities as Curlew Sandpiper, Ruff, and Red-necked Stint being seen over the years. During a rising tide is the best time to visit for maximum numbers, but there are usually a few birds on the sandy spit at the mouth of the lagoon. Look for warblers and other migrants (in season) in the shrubby habitat along the south side of the lagoon, and scan the offshore waters for ducks, grebes, loons, and alcids.

> Pedder Bay

From the Witty's Lagoon parking area, head southwest on Metchosin Road for 1.2 kilometres, then turn right on Happy Valley Road just after passing the Metchosin Country Store. After 550 metres, take the left (southwest) turn onto Rocky Point Road, then follow this road for 5.2 kilometres, with Pedder Bay Road on the left (southeast) side. Follow this road down to the Pedder Bay Marina parking lot.

Pedder Bay is a gorgeous little cove, with overhanging arbutus and spruce trees surrounding a narrow channel that heads out to the Juan de Fuca Strait. The main reason for birders to come here, though, is for the boat rentals. Why? Because you can rent a four-person motorboat for as little as $17.50 an hour! As long as you have a driver's licence, you can rent a boat for a day. For more information, call the marina at 250-478-1771.

If sea conditions are ideal, you can head out of Pedder Bay and get close to **Race Rocks**, a small offshore island that is usually covered in both California and Steller Sea Lions, along with many gulls and shorebirds (in season). On rare occasions, Elephant Seals have hauled up on the rocks, and Harbour Seals and River Otters are common throughout the year. In addition to viewing the spectacle on the rocky islets, you can head out into the open strait (weather permitting) to try for seabirds such as Pacific Loon (outside of summer), Common Murre, Rhinoceros Auklet, and Pigeon Guillemot. These birds can even be seen right in Pedder Bay, along with Marbled and Ancient Murrelets (depending on the season). Shearwaters and fulmars are seen in late summer and early fall, especially after strong westerlies push them into the strait. From late fall through early spring, Black-legged Kittiwakes are a possibility, whereas late summer and early fall are best for gull numbers, including Heermann's and the occasional Western Gull. Overall, the best time is late summer, when the weather is fine and peak numbers of birds are in the area. Be safe and have fun!

> East Sooke

East Sooke is a migration watching hot spot. From the turnoff to Pedder Bay, continue southwest on Rocky Point Road, which will soon turn into East Sooke Road. After 4.8 kilometres, turn left (south) onto Becher Bay Road and follow this for 1.6 kilometres to the end, where there is a parking area at **Aylard Farm**. The fields at Aylard Farm can be productive for songbirds in migration, with the shrubby forest edges concentrating migrants. All regular warblers, vireos, flycatchers, sparrows,

Turkey Vulture

and the like can be seen during spring and fall migration. From the Aylard Farm field, fall raptor watching can be as good as at nearby Beechey Head.

Follow the trail (wide old roadbed) signed for Beechey Head, leading south from the western end of the parking lot opposite the entrance road. After a fifteen-to-twenty-minute walk through the forest, past several trail junctions, watch for signs for Beechey Head where the trail forks into a Y. Take the eastern fork signed for Beechey Head (still a wide old roadbed), and then after roughly 200 metres, look for an unsigned, narrow trail leading to the right, up to a high point of land. This short trail soon emerges at a rock outcrop with wide views: the **Beechey Head hawkwatch site**. In September and early October, especially on sunny days with light northerly winds, the raptor action here is excellent from mid-morning on as the birds congregate over the southern tip of Vancouver Island prior to crossing Juan de Fuca Strait. Among the hundreds of Turkey Vultures, Broad-winged Hawks are regular; and Golden Eagles are regular, especially in the later part of the season. Other species such as Sandhill Cranes and flocks of migrant geese are regular in fall passage, while groups of Band-tailed Pigeons circle the skies and Vaux's Swifts zoom by.

If you continue down the trail signed for Beechey Head, you will reach the bluffs of **Beechey Head** (proper) in ten minutes of rugged, rocky trail past the hawkwatch site. The end of Beechey Head is an excellent sea-watching site, particularly in late summer and fall, and it's best in the first few hours after dawn. Among the feeding frenzies of thousands of California Gulls in late summer and fall, regular species include jaegers; Sooty and, in some years, Pink-footed Shearwaters; Northern Fulmar and Short-tailed Shearwater in later fall; Red-necked Phalaropes; all regular alcids in large numbers; hundreds of Ancient Murrelets in late fall; and gulls, including Thayer's, Bonaparte's and Heermann's, by the hundreds. The occasional Brown Pelican has been seen in all seasons, and it's possible to see rarer species such as Tufted Puffin, Cassin's Auklet, Red Phalarope, and other tubenoses. On the coastal rocks, look for Black Turnstone, Surfbird, Wandering Tattler (May and August), and Black Oystercatcher. This is also a prime spot to watch movements of species such as Brant, ducks, loons, and cormorants during fall, winter, and spring.

> Whiffin Spit Park

To reach this site, you must drive to Sooke. If you are coming from the junction of Becher Bay Road (mentioned in the previous entry), head northwest up East Sooke Road (*not* back toward Pedder Bay) for 2 kilometres, then make a right on Gillespie Road—this will take you out to Sooke Road/Hwy. 14 (5.6 kilometres). Once you're on Sooke Road, turn left (west) and continue into the town of Sooke. About 1.5 kilometres west of downtown, look for Whiffin Spit Road on your left (south) side. Turn down this road and head straight to the bottom, where the parking lot will be obvious, at the base of the spit.

Whiffin Spit Park is a rewarding birding area at any time of year, but not surprisingly, the most birds seem to turn up in spring and fall, when spit-loving species such as shorebirds, gulls, and sparrows are prevalent. Unfortunately (for the birds), this is also a popular dog-walking area. For this reason, it's best to avoid sunny weekends, but there should always be a few birds around regardless. As with most shorebirding areas, a rising tide is usually the ideal time to look. All of the regular shorebird species occur here annually in spring, with Black Turnstones often being the most numerous. Check these flocks for uncommon species such as Ruddy Turnstone, Pacific Golden-Plover, Baird's Sandpiper, and Sharp-tailed Sandpiper (rare in October). In August 2010, a juvenile Ruff stayed for more than a week, and in 1987, a Terek Sandpiper was seen just a bit farther north in Sooke Harbour. Look offshore for a variety of water birds, including Brant, cormorants, sea ducks, loons, grebes, and alcids. It seems that every year brings a new and exciting rarity to the brush and grassy areas along the spit. In 2010, a Lark Sparrow was found, then in the early spring of 2011, Vancouver Island's first ever Lesser Nighthawk was found roosting near the end of the spit. The open grassy area near the east end of the spit usually features migrant sparrows and pipits, along with Western Meadowlarks (fall and some winters) and a sprinkling of Lapland Longspurs and Snow Buntings (both rare but regular on migration).

THE WEST COAST ROAD (Hwy. 14 to Port Renfrew)

For a taste of the real "wet coast," similar to that of Pacific Rim National Park near Tofino, you may want to explore **Juan de Fuca Provincial Park** and other sites along Hwy. 14 west of Sooke. In some years, large numbers of seabirds enter the Juan de Fuca Strait and can be seen from various heads of land as you drive west from Sooke. **Gordon's Beach**, **Otter Point**, **Sheringham Point**, and **French Beach Provincial Park** are all good places to scope the strait before Jordan River (29 kilometres west of Sooke). In summer and fall, look for shearwaters (mainly Sooty and Pink-footed), jaegers, and Heermann's Gulls among the abundant Glaucous-winged, California, and Bonaparte's Gulls. You can see alcids such as Pigeon Guillemot, Common Murre, Marbled Murrelet, and Rhinoceros Auklet all year, and if you're lucky, you might spot a Tufted Puffin. You can find three species of cormorants all year, as well as a variety of shorebirds along the beaches during migration periods. In winter, Black-legged Kittiwakes move into the strait, and Ancient Murrelets become more regular. Gulls congregate at various creek mouths, especially during large fish-spawning events.

There isn't much to the village of **Jordan River**, but Vancouver Island birders know that it can be a hotbed for rarities. As you drive down the hill into town, park by the information kiosk, then explore the area. In spring and fall, the weedy patches of broom and alder can be dynamite spots for migrants. As you poke around behind the houses, you will discover several trails that weave through the adjacent woodland. Just before the highway crosses the Jordan River, there are more trails on the inland side of the highway that are always worth checking. A rule of thumb for coastal rarity seekers: "Always check patches of alder at creek mouths that are surrounded by coniferous forest." This is because the alder is the only suitable habitat in the area for "gleaners" like warblers and vireos; plus, the natural contours of the shoreline force them into a small area—this is called a "rarity trap." Once you find a roving flock, stay with it.

Park at the main pull-off east of the bridge, where there is an information kiosk. There is a slightly overgrown trail that starts across the road and parallels the road, over toward the river. Otherwise, you can park near the main bridge and look for the trails that start on the east side of the Jordan River. The alder and blackberry thickets can host a variety of migrant songbirds, but you should also look through the patches of dry Scotch Broom along the river for sparrows, finches, and California Quail.

Only a few kilometres west of Jordan River you will see signs for the **China Beach** campsite and day-use area, as well as the **Juan de Fuca Marine Trail**. Like the more famous West Coast Trail from Port Renfrew to Bamfield, the Juan de Fuca Marine Trail offers hikers 47 kilometres of scenic beaches, old-growth rainforest, and tidal pools. Visit the B.C. Parks website for more details. For a shorter walk, the 1-kilometre trail from the China Beach parking lot to the beach itself passes through mature forest.

From China Beach, it's another 37 kilometres to **Port Renfrew**, which is located at the western end of the Juan de Fuca Marine Trail and the southern end of the West Coast Trail. When you are near Port Renfrew, continue straight (don't cross the San Juan River) and follow signs for **Botanical Beach** and San Juan Provincial Park. It's an additional 5 kilometres to the parking lot, then only a short walk down to Botanical Beach, which is famous for its tidal pools (so try to arrive during low tide). In May and August, look for migrating Wandering Tattlers on the wave-washed rocks among the more regular Black Turnstones, Surfbirds, and Black Oystercatchers. Sea watching can be productive at certain times of year, as many alcids and shearwaters often pass by the mouth of Port San Juan (the main inlet) to and from foraging grounds in the Juan de Fuca Strait. You will notice that the forests are a lot less diverse in comparison with those around Jordan River and farther east. These thick groves of cedar and hemlock are typical of the wild West Coast, and birds associated with this habitat include Varied Thrush, Hermit Thrush, Pacific Wren, Golden-crowned Kinglet, Townsend's Warbler, Pine Siskin, and Fox Sparrow.

Return to the town of Port Renfrew and check the local gardens carefully, as many strays end up in this area. Eurasian Collared-Doves have become a regular sight along the town's power lines, and as you cross over the San Juan River, check for waterfowl. Soon you will come to a First Nations village beside the **Gordon River Estuary.** This is where hikers ferry across to start or end their journeys on the West Coast Trail. The sand and mud bars in the estuary can provide habitat for shorebirds between spring and fall, and a walk along San Juan Beach (the main beach at the base of Port San Juan) can turn up a few goodies as well. Check the alders along the beach for migrating passerines. From here, you can either retrace your route to Sooke and Victoria, or you can take the **Harris Creek Road** to Cowichan Lake, just west of Duncan. Since this route is nearly 60 kilometres along gravel roads, we advise you to check your fuel, take a back roads map, and only attempt it when weather conditions are ideal. In addition to being a shortcut to the Cowichan Valley, forest birding along this road can be decent—look for Sooty Grouse, Hairy Woodpecker, Varied Thrush, and Red Crossbill, among others.

> Mount Wells Regional Park

To reach Victoria's most reliable site for Sooty Grouse, take Hwy. 1 (Douglas Street) west out of Victoria, following signs for Duncan and Nanaimo. Turn left onto Amy Road/West Shore Parkway 3.2 kilometres west of the exit for Sooke (Hwy. 14), then make a right to stay on Amy Road. Take this road for about 850 metres, then turn left on Sooke Lake Road. Make the third left on Humpback Road, proceed down Humpback, and stay right at the intersection with Irwin Road to continue to the parking lot.

Mount Wells Regional Park is the gateway to Sooke Hills Wilderness Regional Park Reserve, the largest park area in the region at 4,100 hectares. Both parks provide a buffer to the Greater Victoria Water Supply Area and help protect the region's supply of drinking water. The Humpback Reservoir at the base of Mount Wells was once part of the water supply system for Victoria residents. You will cross the old Sooke Lake flow line near the beginning of the **Summit Trail.** From this point on, you are in a Sooty Grouse hot spot! Spring is the best time to visit, when the males are displaying. Listen for their deep hoots, given from up in a tree, on the ground, or along logs in their favourite patches. The trail to the summit is steep and challenging, but you don't need to go all the way to the top for the grouse. Other species found in this Douglas-fir forest habitat include Olive-sided and Pacific-slope Flycatchers, Brown Creepers, and Townsend's Warblers. For spectacular views of the Juan de Fuca Strait, head right to the top.

> Goldstream Provincial Park

To reach Victoria's most popular forest birding destination, take Hwy. 1 (Douglas Street) west out of Victoria (see Map 2), following signs for Duncan and Nanaimo. After passing the turnoff for Mount Wells (see previous entry), the highway turns north and enters the forested **Goldstream Provincial Park**. After approximately 2 kilometres, turn right (east) onto Finlayson Arm Road to access the main parking area.

As you approach the park from Victoria, look for signs for campsites on the west side of the road. The group camping area is often reliable for Northern Pygmy-Owl and soaring Golden Eagle (mainly fall and winter for both species). The trail down to the nature house has American Dipper and Red-breasted Sapsucker at any time of the year, along with the other four regular woodpecker species—Northern Flicker, Pileated, Hairy, and Downy Woodpeckers. During the fall salmon run, gulls mass along the river and estuary, allowing for the possibility of Glaucous Gull and perhaps even rarer species. Fall is an absolutely gorgeous time to visit, as the maple leaves are flush with gold and migrant songbirds are still passing through—and the spawning fish are neat, too! The nature house maintains feeders, which have attracted Rusty Blackbird, and the estuary frequently has one or two Eurasian Wigeon in the fall and winter. A mix of forest

American Dipper

birds attracts both local and visiting birders throughout the year. Although some bird numbers fluctuate (Red Crossbills and Pine Siskins), others remain fairly stable in any season. These include Steller's Jay, Chestnut-backed Chickadee, Red-breasted Nuthatch, and Brown Creeper. Varied Thrush are typically found a little more uphill in breeding season, but outside of fall, they can be regularly seen throughout the park.

COWICHAN VALLEY

> Cherry Point Beach
Turn east off the Trans-Canada Highway (Hwy. 1) at Fisher Road, make a left on Telegraph Road, followed by a right onto Cherry Point Road. After passing Cherry Point Vineyard, turn right onto Garnett Road and follow this to the end. The sandy shoreline of **Cherry Point Nature Park** can sometimes be a magnet for shorebirds, ducks, gulls, and terns. Early morning or on an incoming tide is the most rewarding time. This is one of the better places in the valley to see Red-throated Loons. On a sunny day, the park makes for a fabulous picnicking spot, with a panoramic view of Saltspring Island across the water.

> Cowichan Bay

Without a doubt, **Cowichan Bay** is one of the best birding areas along the east coast of Vancouver Island, so any trip to the Duncan area should include this stop. From the Trans-Canada Highway (Hwy. 1), turn northeast at Bench Road, then continue due north onto Cowichan Bay Road. Once on Cowichan Bay Road, proceed north 950 metres before turning right (east) onto the **Cowichan Bay Dock Road** (AKA CNR Dock Road and Westcan Terminal Road). You can drive down to the main gate (roughly 300 metres) and walk from there. The brushy habitat along the old railway bed is good for migrant sparrows and warblers, and the wet, marshy areas on either side of the road can produce a variety of water birds—especially in spring and fall. Over the years, more than 275 species have been recorded on this road alone, including such rarities as Tufted Duck, Leach's Storm-Petrel, Great Egret, Snowy Egret, Ruff, and Sharp-tailed Sandpiper. When you reach the timber yard near the end of the road, be very careful to stay out of the way of the workers. To the right, look for Purple Martins (April to August) around their boxes mounted on offshore pilings. In summer, nesting ospreys should also be conspicuous. *Do not proceed past the offices on the left, and stay off the main dock!* You can still scope the bay from the timber yard—between fall and spring, when abundance is greatest, is best.

Return to Cowichan Bay Road and turn right (north) on Tzouhalem Road. In 1.5 kilometres, after passing the longhouse and the entrance to a sawmill, the road crosses another large bridge. Be sure to check around the bridge for a secretive Green Heron. From here, you can walk east on the **Blackly Dyke** or west along the river through one of the richest cottonwood riparian areas on Vancouver Island. This latter dyke trail eventually leads back to Duncan (about 5 kilometres). It passes through First Nations land, but it is okay to proceed as long as you stick to the trail. In the cottonwood forest, listen for the persistent song of Red-eyed Vireos in summer, along with other breeders such as Cassin's Vireo, Bewick's Wren, Yellow Warbler, and Black-headed Grosbeak.

With more time, there is another dyke you can access off Lochmanetz Road (just south of Cowichan Bay Dock Road), but you must stay alongside the campground. Parking is available on Cowichan Bay Road opposite the tennis courts. You can walk all the way around the fields on an elevated dyke, looking for many of the same species possible on the Cowichan Bay Dock Road, including waterfowl, American Pipits, shorebirds, and a mix of raptors.

> Mount Tzouhalem Ecological Reserve

From the Trans-Canada Highway (Hwy. 1), turn east onto Trunk Road, then follow this road as it turns into Tzouhalem Road. Stay left at the Y-junction, which will put you on Maple Bay Road, then drive 3 kilometres before turning right on Kingsview Road. Head up Kingsview to Chippewa Road and turn right, then make a left on Kaspa Road—the parking area is at the end of the road near a water tower. If you're coming from Cowichan Bay, proceed north on Cowichan Bay Road, which will turn into Tzouhalem Road. Turn right onto Maple Bay Road, then follow the same directions.

Mount Tzouhalem Ecological Reserve protects one of the finest remaining examples of Garry Oak and wildflower meadows in British Columbia. April is usually the best time for blooming wildflowers and hooting Sooty Grouse. Northern Pygmy Owls are also present throughout most of the year, and a mix of flycatchers, vireos, and warblers can be found here during the nesting season. Scan the skies for circling raptors, including Peregrine Falcons and Turkey Vultures, both of which have nested on the cliff face of the mountain in past years. Townsend's Solitaire and Mountain Bluebirds are occasionally discovered on spring passage, but fall can also be a fantastic time to seek out migrants, from soaring raptors to skulky sparrows. There are several other trailheads that lead up into the Mount Tzouhalem woods. Some of these can be found back along Tzouhalem Road (heading to Cowichan Bay). Look for **Providence Farm** and St. Ann's Catholic Church on the left (mountain) side. You can either bird around Providence Farm itself, where one of the last Cliff Swallow colonies in the area is located, as well as a range of nesting songbirds, or head up the hiking trails to the ridge.

> Quamichan Lake

Quamichan Lake is a perfect spot to eat a picnic lunch and scan for water birds. If you're approaching from Tzouhalem Ecological Reserve, return to Maple Bay Road and turn left, then drive 2.7 kilometres before turning right down Indian Road, which will lead strait to **Art Mann Park** at the south end of Quamichan Lake. From the Trans-Canada Highway or Tzouhalem Road/Cowichan Bay, turn up Maple Bay Road (as if you were heading to the Mount Tzouhalem location in the previous entry), then get in the left turning lane immediately and proceed straight onto Indian Road.

In winter, there can be an assortment (sometimes numbering in the hundreds) of diving ducks on the lake, including Ring-necked Duck, Lesser Scaup, Canvasback, Hooded Merganser, and Ruddy Duck. Waterfowl are present throughout the year, but spring, fall, and winter are best. An Emperor Goose was recorded here in January 1989.

> Somenos Marsh Conservation Area

Another great place for waterfowl and marsh birds, **Somenos Marsh** is located along the east side of Hwy. 1. From Art Mann Park (Quamichan Lake), return to Tzouhalem Road, then turn right (west) and drive for almost 1 kilometre to turn right at Lakes Road. Continue straight to the traffic circle, then head left (west) on Beverly Street, which will take you to the highway. You will pass York Road on the right (north) side, which provides access to the south end of the conservation area—best in fall and winter, when water levels are high. Otherwise, continue to Hwy. 1 and turn right (north). The main parking area for the lake is 2 kilometres north (turn right on Drinkwater Road), where the British Columbia Forest Museum is located, but there are two other parking areas along the way as well. With more than two hundred species on the checklist, there should be enough variety to satisfy birders at any time of year.

Fun fact: Somenos is home to the second-largest wintering flock of Trumpeter Swans on Vancouver Island (after the Comox Valley). For more information, visit somenosmarsh.com.

> ## Mount Prevost

From the Somenos Marsh complex, head north on the Trans-Canada Highway (Hwy. 1), then exit left (west) onto Hwy. 18 (Cowichan Valley Road). Continue for about 1.4 kilometres, then make a right (north) on Somenos Road. Travel north for 2.1 kilometres, then continue straight (keep left) onto Moss Road, where you will make the first left. This road will turn into Mount Prevost Road and will start switchbacking up the hill and turn to gravel after 500 metres. To reach the summit, continue for roughly 8 kilometres along Mount Prevost Road and Prevost Mainline (angling left at the junction about 3.7 kilometres up). The roads are passable in clement weather for two-wheel-drive vehicles, but good clearance is recommended.

Mount Prevost is a likely place to see forest breeders, including Olive-sided Flycatcher, Pacific-slope Flycatcher, Hammond's Flycatcher, Hutton's Vireo, Warbling Vireo, Chestnut-backed Chickadee, Pacific Wren, Swainson's Thrush, MacGillivray's

Warbler, Townsend's Warbler, and Western Tanager. Watch for Sooty Grouse creeping up the roadside, and in winter, look and listen for Gray Jay and Northern Pygmy-Owl. From the summit, there is a fantastic view of the entire Cowichan Valley.

> Crofton Waterfront

From the junction of Hwy. 18 (Cowichan Valley Road), drive north on the Trans-Canada Highway (Hwy. 1) for 6.8 kilometres, then exit right (east) onto Mount Sicker Road (Hwy. 1A). Make the first left onto Westholme Road then turn right onto Crofton Road and follow this into the town of **Crofton**. With a great waterfront boardwalk, this area can at times prove rewarding for diving ducks and loons. It is one of the last remaining reliable spots in the valley for Black Scoter (September to April). Black Oystercatchers are usually seen flying back and forth from the boardwalk, and if you have a small boat, access to the nearby **Shoal Islands** can yield roosting turnstones and other wintering shorebirds. This area is also the only spot in the valley where an eider species has been recorded.

NANAIMO

Known by some as "The Bathtub Racing Capital of the World," Nanaimo is also a prime place for birding, thanks to a plethora of waterfront and inland habitats and a mild climate. Some of the best birding spots are described below; however, there are two species that deserve special consideration because they can be found nowhere else (reliably) on Vancouver Island.

The first is Vesper Sparrow. Formerly widespread throughout the Garry Oak grasslands of Vancouver Island and the Lower Mainland, the Canadian range of this coastal *affinis* subspecies is now restricted to the **Nanaimo Airport** (about twelve individuals circa 2011). As you travel north on the Trans-Canada

Highway (Hwy. 1), the airport will become visible on the right (east) side, about 6.5 kilometres north of Ladysmith. From the Nanaimo direction, look for airport signs nearly 7 kilometres south of the Duke Point Ferry turnoff. The best viewing location for this species is from Simpson Road at the south end of the airport. Take Hwy. 1 to the exit for Cedar Road, which is at the stoplight just south of the airport. Go east on Cedar Road and turn left onto Simpson Road. Follow Simpson until you reach the fence at the south end of the airport. Vesper Sparrows regularly sing from the fence posts on both sides of this road.

For those working on a British Columbia life list, or if you are simply a dabbling duck enthusiast, you better act quickly to catch a glimpse of the province's only population of American Black Duck. This species was first introduced in the 1970s to the **Yellow Point** area, southeast of Nanaimo. Once numbering around one hundred pairs, the population has declined drastically since the late 1990s, principally because of hybridism with Mallards. Check your field guide to see what a "pure" American Black Duck looks like. It is quite possible that by the time you acquire this book, there will be no pure birds left. But just in case, here are directions to an area where you might spy some of the last remaining individuals.

Just south of the Nanaimo Airport, exit the Trans-Canada Highway (Hwy. 1) onto Cedar Road and continue for 2.8 kilometres before turning right on Yellow Point Road. Drive east for 2.3 kilometres, then turn right (south) onto Doole Road. This road is roughly 3 kilometres long and passes by several farm ponds and flooded fields (depending on the season). Michael Lake is also visible from some stretches of the road. Scan all of these habitats because the black ducks can turn up anywhere, though they are most often seen on the small ponds. Between fall and spring, expect large numbers of other dabbling ducks, such as Mallard, American Wigeon, Northern Pintail, Green-winged Teal, and Northern Shoveler.

➤ Nanaimo River Estuary

Just south of Nanaimo, exit east onto Cedar Road. Travel past the landfill (a likely place for eastern birders to pick up Thayer's Gull in fall and winter), then turn left (north) onto Raines Road, just after crossing over the Nanaimo River. Park at the end of the road, then walk through the gate to reach the open expanse of the **Nanaimo River Estuary.** Depending on the season, open-country species are the specialty here, including Rough-legged Hawk, Short-eared Owl, Northern Shrike, Mountain Bluebird, Savannah Sparrow, and Western Meadowlark. Snowy Owls are also regularly seen here in invasion years, and Long-eared Owls have occurred from time to time as well. Ospreys nest nearby in summer, whereas other raptors such as Bald Eagle, Northern Harrier, Cooper's Hawk, and Peregrine Falcon are present all year. Migrant warblers can be found along the river beside Raines Road, whereas Horned Larks, sparrows, and pipits are the more prominent migrants around the estuary itself. This area is a well-known vagrant trap in spring and fall, with May and September producing most of the sightings. Rarities to this area include Buff-breasted Sandpiper, Ruff (up to three birds at once!), American Avocet, Western Kingbird, Eastern Kingbird, Say's Phoebe, Sage Thrasher, Palm Warbler, Vesper Sparrow, and Harris's Sparrow. The river, its side channels, and the tidal flats near the mouth, are all great spots to look for migrating and wintering waterfowl and shorebirds. If you want to get all the way out to the tidal areas near the river mouth, prepare to get muddy!

➤ Duke Point Ferry

In addition to the two main ferry routes to the mainland (Departure Bay–Horseshoe Bay and Swartz Bay–Tsawwassen), B.C.

Ferries offers regular service between Duke Point and Tsawwassen, giving birders more options in planning their route. Because more time is spent out in the middle of the Georgia Strait, this ferry route is usually considered the best one for seeing pelagic species, especially in fall. Fork-tailed Storm-Petrels are regularly seen between August and October, with Leach's Storm-Petrels turning up less frequently. Those who look will often see Parasitic Jaegers, followed by Long-tailed Jaegers, and then Pomarine Jaegers. Rhinoceros Auklets and Common Murres are regular throughout the year. The best time to look for Ancient Murrelets is October to November when the peak of southward migration is happening. If you hit the right day, you might see several hundred on the crossing.

> Colliery Dam Park and Morrell Wildlife Sanctuary

If you're travelling from the south, turn off on the Hwy. 19 bypass for Nanaimo (instead of taking the old highway due north into town, toward Departure Bay). From this junction, drive northwest for close to 6 kilometres, then turn right (east) at the Fifth Street exit. After a few hundred metres on Fifth Street, make your first right (south) on Wakesiah Avenue, then turn right again onto Harewood/Nanaimo Lakes Road. The parking lot for Colliery Dam Park will be on the left, and the turnoff to the Morrell Wildlife Sanctuary is another 550 metres ahead on the right (northwest) side. If you're travelling from the north (along the Hwy. 19 bypass), look for the Fifth Street exit east, then follow the same instructions.

Colliery Dam Park is a small park that is a popular swimming location in summer. Slightly more than 2.5 kilometres of trail loop through dense wooded sections of the twenty-eight-hectare park and around two manmade lakes. The lakes were formed when a dam was created to provide fresh water for a local mine, and they are separated by a concrete dam and spillway. Caves formed during the ice age are accessible from the main park trail, but expect to do a bit of scrambling through brush to access them. Typical breeding species of this young mixed forest include Band-tailed Pigeon, Pacific-slope Flycatcher, Downy Woodpecker, Chestnut-backed Chickadee, Pacific Wren, Cassin's Vireo, Warbling Vireo, Hutton's Vireo, Black-throated Gray Warbler, and Purple Finch (just to name a few).

Morrell Wildlife Sanctuary is generally a less busy and slightly wilder park, popular with local birders. Many of the same species found at Colliery Dam Park will be present here, along with Sooty Grouse, Red-breasted Sapsucker, Hammond's Flycatcher, and Olive-sided Flycatcher. Sometimes there are hundreds of Black Swifts and Common Nighthawks at dusk in late July and August. For more information, visit morrell.bc.ca.

> Buttertubs Marsh

From Nanaimo Lakes Road, return to Wakesiah Road and turn left to proceed north for 1.5 kilometres, where you will turn left onto Jingle Pot Road. In 800 metres, the parking area for **Buttertubs Marsh** will be on the right (north) side. If you're approaching from Hwy. 19, take the Jingle Pot Road exit east for 650 metres— parking will be on the left. From here, you will see that one trail bisects the marsh and another circumnavigates it. In this relatively small area there are usually quite a few birds, from marsh specialists like Pied-billed Grebe, American Bittern, Virginia Rail, Sora (April to August), Wilson's Snipe, Willow Flycatcher, and Marsh Wren to brush birds like California Quail, Anna's Hummingbird, Rufous Hummingbird (spring and summer), Bewick's Wren, Spotted Towhee, Song Sparrow, and Golden-crowned and Fox Sparrows in winter. It's possible but tough to find Green Heron, whereas waterfowl diversity is high all year and five species of swallow are regular in summer.

> Departure Bay to Horseshoe Bay Ferry

The B.C. Ferries terminal at **Departure Bay** is well-signed off the highway passing through Nanaimo. There is regular service across Georgia Strait to Horseshoe Bay and the mainland. Migration periods are usually the best time to make the crossing (April to May, August to November), when large numbers of ducks, loons, grebes, gulls, and alcids are passing through. Expect Rhinoceros Auklet to be fairly common in spring, late summer, and fall, and Common Murre and Pigeon Guillemots are also regular most of the year. This crossing is often fairly quiet bird-wise, but it is still worth it to stay on deck, as you never know when that stray Pink-footed Shearwater or Long-tailed Jaeger is going to cruise by. In February 1997, a Tufted Puffin was sighted from the ferry (quite rare in the strait).

> Piper's Lagoon

After leaving the Departure Bay ferry terminal, turn right (west) on Brechin Road and follow this to a Tim Hortons and a mall complex. Stay straight to proceed on Estevan Road, which turns into Departure Bay Road, where you will drive past the mall on your left side. From the start of Departure Bay Road, drive 2 kilometres, then turn right onto Hammond Bay Road. Follow Hammond Bay Road for 3.2 kilometres, then turn right at Lagoon Road, followed by the first right on Place Road. Park at the end of Place Road. From the Old Island Highway running through Nanaimo, turn north at the Departure Bay Road junction, beside the Tim Hortons and the mall complex mentioned above, then follow the same instructions.

Piper's Lagoon is a beautiful little spot to check out, whether you have only twenty minutes or more than an hour to spare. A variety of shorebirds and a few waterfowl species regularly turn up in the lagoon itself, and the trees and brushy areas on the point provide nesting habitat for Downy Woodpecker, Bewick's

Wren, Spotted Towhee, American Goldfinch, and others. In fall, look for a variety of migrant sparrows, including Fox, Song, Lincoln's, Savannah, Chipping, Golden-crowned, White-crowned, White-throated, and Dark-eyed Junco. The rocky outcrops near the point and the small rocky islets offshore can be good spots for roosting shorebirds at high tide, as well as feeding rock-pipers, such as Black Oystercatcher, Black Turnstone, Surfbird, Wandering Tattler (May, August, September), and Rock Sandpiper (rare; November to March). Out on the waves, look for all three scoter species (especially October to April) and a variety of loons, grebes, cormorants, and alcids. Locally, this is a particularly reliable place to see Barrow's Goldeneye (fall to spring) and Marbled Murrelet.

> Neck Point Park

Continue northwest along Hammond Bay Road from the turn-off to Piper's Lagoon. The turn for **Neck Point Park** will be signed in 1.1 kilometres on the right (ocean) side. This is another spot for sea watching, as well as looking for rock-pipers. The forested area of the park can be a great spot to find migrant warblers in spring and fall; in summer, watch for nesting Black-throated Gray Warblers. Other breeding species to expect from May to August include Pileated Woodpecker, Pacific-slope Flycatcher, Chestnut-backed Chickadee, Bushtit, Red-breasted Nuthatch, Bewick's Wren, Spotted Towhee, and House Finch.

PARKSVILLE AND QUALICUM

> Legacy Marsh

As you pass through the community of Lantzville on Hwy. 19, look for Superior Road (just west of the Ware Road junction), and turn south (inland). Follow Superior Road for 1 kilometre, then turn left onto Normarel Drive. This road dead-ends at **Legacy Marsh**—a great spot for, you guessed it, marsh birds! You can also expect a few forest birds on the opposite side of the road, including the occasional Sooty Grouse that might stroll into view. Virginia Rail and Northern Pygmy-Owl are both regulars here.

> Rathtrevor Beach Provincial Park

Take Exit 46 off Hwy. 19 onto the Old Island Highway into Parksville. About 2.7 kilometres from this turnoff, the entrance to **Rathtrevor Beach Provincial Park** should be signed on the right (northeast) side. A lovely place to visit for birding, picnicking, and camping, Rathtrevor boasts an expansive sandy beach, along with dunes, driftwood, and tall Douglas-firs. A mix of shore- and seabirds can be expected at any time of year, but highest diversity and overall numbers of birds occur in spring and fall (especially March to April, when the herring are spawning). During these times, expect flocks of shorebirds (mainly Black-bellied Plover, Sanderling, Western Sandpiper, and Dunlin), Brant, all three scoters, and large numbers of other divers, such as loons, grebes, Harlequin Ducks, and Greater Scaup. Gulls are prevalent during herring spawn, so carefully scan the regular Glaucous-winged, Herring, Thayer's, Mew, and California for rare but regular species such as Western (uncommon), Glaucous, Iceland, and the occasional Slaty-backed Gull (not seen every year). If lots of Bonaparte's Gulls are around, check these flocks for Little or Black-headed Gulls. Although these latter species are rare in British Columbia, they have been recorded in this area several times over the years. Expect a few forest species in the big firs around the campsite, including Hairy Woodpecker, Hutton's Vireo (February to April is best), Steller's Jay, Red-breasted Nuthatch, Chestnut-backed Chickadee, and Red Crossbill. The central section of the park is an old farm with plenty of overgrown shrubs and fruit trees to attract migrant flycatchers, vireos, warblers,

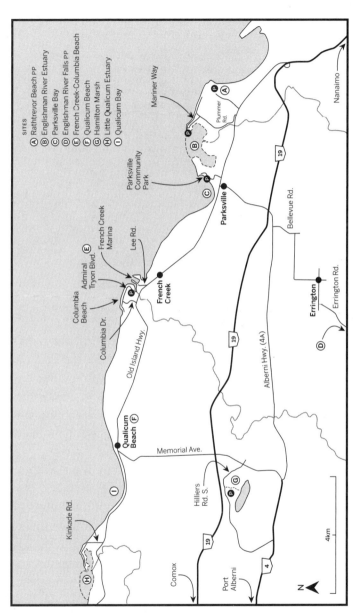

SITES
- (A) Rathtrevor Beach PP
- (B) Englishman River Estuary
- (C) Parksville Bay
- (D) Englishman River Falls PP
- (E) French Creek-Columbia Beach
- (F) Qualicum Beach
- (G) Hamilton Marsh
- (H) Little Qualicum Estuary
- (I) Qualicum Bay

Mariner Way

Plummer Rd.

(P)(A)

(P)(B)

Nanaimo

19

Parksville Community Park

(P)(C)

Parksville

Bellevue Rd.

Errington Rd.

French Creek Marina

Lee Rd.

Admiral Tryon Blvd. (E)

Columbia Beach

(E)

French Creek

Errington

(D)

Columbia Dr.

Old Island Hwy.

19

Alberni Hwy. (4A)

Qualicum Beach (F)

Memorial Ave.

Hilliers Rd. S.

(G)

(P)(G)

Kinkade Rd.

(I)

(H)

Comox

Port Alberni

19

4

N

4km

3 Parksville/Qualicum

Thayer's Gull

and sparrows. Rufous Hummingbird is a common breeder here, as are Bushtit, Bewick's Wren, and Spotted Towhee.

> Englishman River Estuary

From the Rathtrevor park entrance road, return to the Old Island Highway, take a right (west), then take the first right onto Plummer Road. Walk the viewing tower trail from Plummer Road to San Malo Creek. The tidal mud flats of the **Englishman River Estuary** are best outside of summer, when shorebird and waterfowl numbers are highest. The brushy areas along the edges are also good for sparrows and other songbird migrants. For some inspiration, here is a list of some of the rarities that have turned up here over the years: Great Egret, Black-necked Stilt, Hudsonian Godwit, Ruff, Red-necked Stint, Wilson's Phalarope, Long-eared Owl, White-throated Swift, Calliope Hummingbird, Eastern Phoebe, Ash-throated Flycatcher, Bank Swallow, Palm Warbler, American Redstart, Lark Sparrow, and Brambling.

For access to another viewing tower, return to the Old Island Highway, turn right, and then cross over the river, before making your second right onto Shelley Road. The trail to the tower is at the end of this road. This also gives you access to **Parksville Flats**— essentially a mini version of the Nanaimo River Estuary.

> Parksville Bay

Just west of the Englishman River, in downtown Parksville, look for signs for the **Parksville Community Park**, located on **Parksville Bay**. Outside of summer, this is a perfect spot to brush up on your gull identification skills, as there are usually several species present and at close range. Many sit on the grassy areas around the parking lots, and among the Glaucous-wings and strange hybrids, there are usually one or two Glaucous Gulls hanging about (November to April). Thayer's Gulls are usually quite common outside of summer, and Herring and Ring-billed are regular but less numerous. Iceland (Kumlien's) Gulls are annual in March, and it's possible to find almost any gull species here in season, so be vigilant. As the tide rises, groups of shorebirds, gulls, and cormorants will gather on a gravel bar offshore, and a few sea ducks, grebes, and loons should be around during most of the year.

> Englishman River Falls Provincial Park

From the community park at Parksville Bay, turn right (west) onto the Old Island Highway, drive for 170 metres, then turn left (south) onto Alberni Highway. Follow this until it passes the main highway (Hwy. 19), then make the first left on Bellevue Road. Turn right on Ruffels Road, which will turn into Leffler Road after turning south. Next, it's a right on Grafton Road, followed by a left onto Errington Road at the Errington General Store. On Errington, it's almost 7 kilometres to **Englishman River Falls Provincial Park**.

This lovely forested park is usually fairly productive for Island forest specialties such as Red-breasted Sapsucker, Hammond's and Pacific-slope Flycatchers, Chestnut-backed Chickadee, Red-breasted Nuthatch, Brown Creeper, Swainson's Thrush, Townsend's Warbler, Western Tanager, and Dark-eyed Junco. American Dipper is sometimes found near the falls, and watch for Bald Eagle, Turkey Vulture, and Band-tailed Pigeons passing overhead. In previous years, Black Swifts have nested under the waterfall near the upper bridge.

> ### French Creek and Columbia Beach

From the Parksville Community Park, head northwest on the Old Island Highway for 4.6 kilometres, before turning right at Lee Road. At the end of the road, you will arrive at the **French Creek Marina**. Grab a bite at the pub here or pick up some fresh fish, then scan the loafing gull flocks (usually on the marina breakwater and along the beach to the south or at the mouth of French Creek on the north side of the marina). This is also a possible site to find Yellow-billed Loon in winter, so check the diving birds offshore.

To reach the main **French Creek** birding hot spot and access **Columbia Beach**, return to the Old Island Highway, make a right, then take the first right after crossing over French Creek onto Columbia Drive. Take this road down to Admiral Tryon Boulevard, then turn right and park at the cul-de-sac at the end. In recent years, this neighbourhood has produced some impressive rarities, including Tropical Kingbird, Eastern Phoebe, Rock Wren, Northern Wheatear, Orchard Oriole, and Summer Tanager. There are several trails that lead through the thick riparian scrub near the end of the road. One goes along French Creek into the more mature trees and another parallels some houses with regularly stocked bird feeders. Migration season is fantastic here, especially for warblers and sparrows. Gulls and shorebirds can often be seen at the river mouth, along with all three species of mergansers (outside of breeding season), Belted Kingfisher, and Double-crested Cormorants.

To access Columbia Beach, drive back on Admiral Tryon Boulevard and park in the vacant lot just before Columbia Drive. Black Oystercatchers patrol the beach year round and a variety of seabirds can be tallied as they pass by offshore (fall, winter, and spring are best). American Pipits touch down regularly; Lapland Longspurs and Snow Buntings also pass through in fall, though in much smaller numbers. Heermann's Gulls, Caspian Terns, Common Terns, and Parasitic Jaegers are regular in September, and rarer birds such as Leach's Storm Petrel, Long-tailed Jaeger, Franklin's Gull, Black-legged Kittiwakes, and Bar-tailed Godwit have also been seen here.

> Qualicum Beach

From Columbia Beach and French Creek, return to the Old Island Highway and continue west. In almost 5 kilometres, the highway hits **Qualicum Beach** and parallels it for around 2.9 kilometres (last access to the west being the end of Buller Road). Check gull flocks here for unusual species. It's possible to find many of the same shorebirds and seagoing waterfowl mentioned in other locations around Parksville.

> Little Qualicum Estuary

From Qualicum Beach, continue west along the Old Island Highway. Soon after the road turns away from the water, turn right on Kincade Road (600 metres beyond Buller Road). As the road bends to the left, there is a beach access. Continuing to the left, you are now on McFeely Drive. The shrubs and wet meadows on the left are home to migrants in spring and fall and have a large number of sparrows in winter. This road ends at a T-junction (Surfside Drive). To the right, is another beach access; to the left, you can bird part of the **Little Qualicum River Estuary**. At the end of Surfside, there is another beach access from which you can walk along the beach to the west to get to the mouth of the river. This is a great spot to bird between August and May but can be worthwhile in summer as well (the weather's certainly better!). You can expect to find species similar to those found at Rathtrevor Beach and Englishman River Estuary.

> Hamilton Marsh

If you're driving from Qualicum Beach, travel straight out Memorial Drive—near the east end of the beach—toward the new highway (Memorial Drive becomes Hwy. 4 to Port Alberni). Drive under Hwy. 19 and keep going straight. Turn right at the bottom of the first hill onto Hilliers Road South. Drive 1.1 kilometres into the parking lot on the left side of the road. This is the quickest trail in. Otherwise, the first more challenging trail is located at the junction of Hwy. 4 and Hilliers Road South.

Hamilton Marsh is the largest wetland between Nanaimo, Cumberland, and Port Alberni and supports a rich diversity of plant and animal life, including more than 130 species of birds. Waterfowl and other marsh birds are abundant here, but you should also take the time to bird around the second-growth forest, where species such as Ruffed Grouse, Red-breasted Sapsucker, Pacific-slope Flycatcher, MacGillivray's Warbler, and Purple Finch can be found, among many others.

> Qualicum Bay

Not to be confused with Qualicum Beach, **Qualicum Bay** is another fantastic area to scope for seabirds offshore and shorebirds along the shore. From Kincade Road (Little Qualicum Estuary), get back on the Old Island Highway and head west toward Comox. After 12 kilometres, the highway will take you alongside the beach again. This is Qualicum Bay. If you're approaching from the main highway (Hwy. 19), take Exit 75 north (Horne Lake Road), which will take you straight to the Old Island Highway, where you will turn left; Qualicum Bay will come up soon on your right.

This is another great area to look for gulls (especially during the herring spawn and fall and winter). The highway curves north as it follows the contours of the bay; look for Crane Road on the right side, 2.6 kilometres from where the highway first parallels the beach. The end of Crane Road gives you a good place to check the mouth of **Nile Creek** for loafing gulls and the occasional flock of shorebirds.

> ➤ Baynes Sound (Deep Bay to Union Bay)

From the mouth of Nile Creek, proceed northwest on the Old Island Highway. In almost 2 kilometres you will pass through the small community of Bowser. Continue past Bowser for nearly 4 kilometres, then turn right onto Gainsberg Road and stay on this road for 2 kilometres, following signs for **Deep Bay**. Turn right on Burne Road, then left on Deep Bay Drive, and take this to the end. From here, you can scan Deep Bay itself and the southern portion of **Baynes Sound** (the channel between Vancouver Island and Denman Island).

This is one of the best places on Vancouver Island to see a variety of deepwater species during migration and in winter. All three scoters can be seen in season, along with large numbers of Greater Scaup, loons, grebes, cormorants, and gulls. Showy Long-tailed and Harlequin Ducks are a common sight in winter, and several alcid species occur throughout most of the year (particularly Common Murre, Pigeon Guillemot, and Marbled Murrelet). King Eider is a very rare but still realistic possibility among the masses of scoters. In spring, late summer, and fall, look out for jaegers passing through with the more common gull species. Sabine's Gulls are rare but regular in August and September, and

Little Gull has shown up on occasion, mixed in with migrating Bonaparte's Gulls. Scan for Belted Kingfishers near the marina, and in winter, look out for both Greater Yellowlegs and Spotted Sandpipers scouring for invertebrates along the shoreline, docks, or floating logs in the bay.

The shoreline from Deep Bay north to **Buckley Bay** (the main ferry terminal for service to Denman Island) is essentially a continuous stretch of estuarine mud flats and gravelly shores. All of the regular Island shorebirds, such as Black-bellied Plover, Semipalmated Plover, Black Oystercatcher, Black Turnstone, Surfbird, Sanderling, Western Sandpiper, Dunlin, and Short-billed Dowitcher, can be found (in season) in this relatively under-birded area, so who knows what else you can find?

For a taste of forest birding, continue westward on the Old Island Highway for 5.2 kilometres, then turn right (north) onto Berray Road to bird **Rosewell Creek Provincial Park**. The forest along this road can be productive for most typical coastal species, such as Hammond's and Pacific-slope Flycatcher, Chestnut-backed Chickadee, Pacific Wren, Golden-crowned Kinglet, Cassin's Vireo, Townsend's Warbler, and MacGillivray's Warbler.

COMOX VALLEY AND CAMPBELL RIVER

From Cumberland, Royston, and Denman Island up to Campbell River, Quadra Island, and west to the Forbidden Plateau, the Comox Valley–Campbell River region is a fantastic birding area with a diversity of habitats. Lying at the northern end of the dry "East-Island" climate zone, this region is where many species reach their northern coastal breeding limits (Purple Martin, Bushtit, Bewick's Wren, and Bullock's Oriole). Although the region gets less attention than Victoria and Nanaimo-Parksville, it is just as good or better for shorebirds and seabirds alike, and migration watching can be made easier by the bottleneck between Campbell River and Quadra Island. Like the rest of the Island, spring, fall, and winter are considered the best times for bird diversity, but visitors in the summer should still be able to pick up a mix of seabirds and forest specialists.

> ## Sandy Island

Also known as "Tree Island," **Sandy Island** is considered one of the best locations around Vancouver Island for shorebirds and other open-country species, such as Short-eared and Snowy Owls, Horned Lark, American Pipit, Lapland Longspur, and Snow Bunting. The sea birding is also rewarding, especially in spring and fall passage, and the rarity potential is obvious.

Located off the northern tip of Denman Island (just southeast of Comox Harbour), Sandy Island is unfortunately only accessible by boat. Few people have heard about this gem and fewer have had the opportunity to visit. So if you have access to water transportation, we highly recommend making the trip.

> ## Cumberland

Before we get to the well-known beachfront highlights of the Courtenay-Comox area, no birding trip to the Comox Valley is complete without visiting the simple but productive wetlands and second-growth deciduous forests of **Cumberland**. From Hwy. 19, take the exit signed for Cumberland. Follow Cumberland Road into town, then take a right on Dunsmuir Avenue/ Royston Road. Proceed west on Dunsmuir for 500 metres, then turn left (south) on Sutton Road, where you will follow it as it swings right (west), becoming the Comox Lake Road. From this bend, drive for 1 kilometre, then pull into the parking area on the left side at Jumbo's Cabin Historic Site (the last remaining building of the now-dismantled Chinatown). From here, walk back east for 30 to 40 metres and follow the track to the right, which bisects **Cumberland Marsh**.

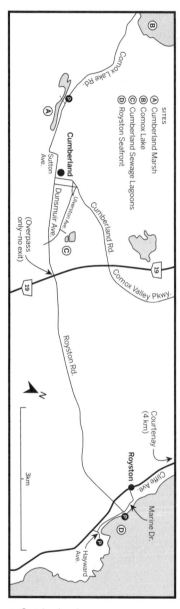

SITES

Ⓐ Cumberland Marsh
Ⓑ Comox Lake
Ⓒ Cumberland Sewage Lagoons
Ⓓ Royston Seafront

4 Cumberland

In spring and summer, this is a fantastic spot for warblers, as Orange-crowned, Townsend's, Black-throated Gray, Yellow-rumped, Wilson's, Yellow, and Common Yellowthroat all nest here. It's possible to spot MacGillivray's on migration, but they no longer nest here now that the vegetation has grown up a bit. Check the marsh on the left side for Virginia Rail, Wood Duck, and other marsh birds and the taller trees farther down the track for Band-tailed Pigeons in the breeding season. Northern Pygmy-Owls are here year round, whereas the resident Western Screech-Owls seem to have disappeared now that Barred Owls have moved in. In addition to the warblers, check the surrounding trees for other colourful breeders, such as Red-breasted Sapsuckers and Black-headed Grosbeaks. In winter, **Comox Lake** itself can be worth checking for waterfowl. Occasionally, huge numbers of gulls come down from the nearby landfill to bathe in the lake. In addition to the abundant Glaucous-winged Gulls, the rare Slaty-backed Gull has been seen here in the past.

One final spot to check in town is the **Cumberland Sewage Lagoons**. Return to Dunsmuir Avenue then turn right and head east on Dunsmuir/Royston Road. Just after leaving the main part of town, look for Ulverston Avenue on the left side. Take this turn then look for the entry road to the lagoons on the right side (350 metres). Unfortunately, the shorebird potential is low, but waterfowl and marsh birds are usually present in significant numbers, and the trees along the entrance road can be rewarding in migration and during the winter.

> Comox Harbour

The birding area known as **Comox Harbour** is essentially an amalgamation of several different sites, from the village of Royston over to the Courtenay River Estuary, then over to Goose Spit at the northeast end of the harbour. It's a fantastic area for waterfowl, especially in winter.

The unincorporated village of **Royston** is located along the Old Island Highway (from Cumberland, take Royston Road east across Hwy. 19 all the way to the end). From the Old Island Highway, turn right on Hayward Avenue, then make a left on Marine Drive to bird the waterfront of Royston (from Hwy. 19, Royston Road ends at Marine). This is a good area for gulls, water birds, and shorebirds (in season).

From the northwest end of Royston, where Marine Drive joins the Old Island Highway, head northwest on the highway (becomes Cliffe Avenue) for 3.7 kilometres, then turn right onto Mansfield Drive, where a parking lot will come up immediately on the right-hand side. From downtown Courtenay, drive south on Cliffe Avenue, then make a left on Mansfield. If you're approaching from Hwy. 19 (from the south), take the Comox Valley Parkway (main exit for Courtenay) all the way to Cliffe, where you will make a left before turning onto Mansfield.

Facing the harbour from the parking area, you can either walk right or left (along the **Courtenay Riverway Heritage Walk**). Walking to the right will take you south along the side of the Courtenay River Estuary/Comox Harbour. Gulls, ducks, shorebird, pipits, and sparrows are all plentiful between fall and spring, and this is where a Black-tailed Gull was found in November 2008. If you head in the other direction, the trail will take you past a few ponds surrounding the **Courtenay Airpark**. This is one of the best sites in the area, boasting prime habitat for migrating and wintering waterfowl, herons, shorebirds, and gulls. The mowed grass around the airpark is a great place to find Horned Lark, American Pipit, Snow Bunting, Lapland Longspur, sparrows, and a few shorebirds, such as Killdeer, Pectoral Sandpiper, and Least Sandpiper. In spring or fall, you just never know what rare shorebird could appear among the usual suspects. Examples from the past include Black-necked Stilt, Willet, Ruff, and Sharp-tailed Sandpiper.

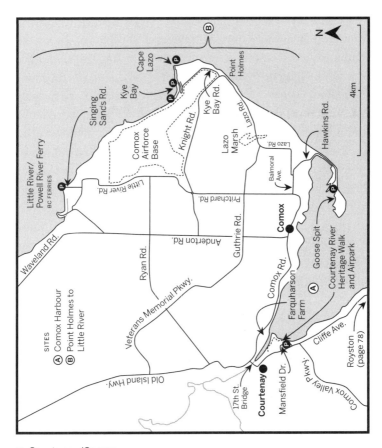

5 Courtenay/Comox

One of the highlights of birding the Comox Valley in winter is the number of Trumpeter Swans. Up to three thousand individuals can be found in the area from late fall into early spring, and many of them hang out close to the estuary. The old **Farquharson Farm** (now known as Comox Bay Farm) is a fairly reliable place to see them. This is just across the Courtenay River from Courtenay Airpark and river trails, along Comox Road (accessed off Cliffe Avenue via the 17th Street Bridge).

To bird the northern half of Comox Harbour, drive east on Comox Road/Avenue, stopping wherever you like. Some of the boathouse roofs around here can sport roosting gulls, and the Comox Marina can be worth checking for diving ducks, loons, and grebes. Eventually, the road will swing to the left and become Pritchard Road. When this happens, look for Balmoral Avenue coming up soon on the right, then drive straight, continuing on Hawkins Road, which will take you down to **Goose Spit**. Like most other spits, this spot can be great for migrating sparrows and the like, along with a few shorebirds. On a calm winter's morning, this can be a fantastic place to watch the sunrise. If the tide is high, it is often easy to get extremely close to wintering flocks of White-winged and Surf Scoters, along with the regular loons, grebes, cormorants, and other ducks, such as Common Goldeneye, Harlequin Duck, Greater Scaup, and Common Merganser.

> Point Holmes to Little River

This is a route recommended for those wanting to see wintering and migrating seabirds, from loons and grebes to ducks, gulls, cormorants, alcids, and even a few tubenoses (rare but possible). From Goose Spit, return to the four-way stop, but instead of heading back to Comox on Balmoral Avenue, turn right on Torrence Road, then make an immediate right on Lazo Road. Continue straight for 800 metres, then turn left to stay on Lazo Road. Two kilometres later, the road passes **Lazo Marsh**, where you may want to stop for some quick forest/marsh birding. There is a path nearby that allows further access to the marsh. After driving 1.4 kilometres past the marsh, the road parallels the water at **Point Holmes**—ideal for gulling and scoping offshore for passing seabirds. When the road curves left, away from the beach, it becomes Knight Road; take the first right onto Kye Bay Road. The first section of this road parallels the **Comox Air Force Base**; scan the mowed grass after periods of rain in spring and fall for shorebirds such as Killdeer, Pacific Golden-Plover, American Golden-Plover, Black-bellied Plover, Pectoral Sandpiper, and Least Sandpiper. Rare possibilities include Buff-breasted Sandpiper (late August to September), Ruff (unrecorded here but possible in May and July to September), and Sharp-tailed Sandpiper (September to October). After passing the airfield, Kye Bay Road winds down the hill; at the second sharp bend, continue straight down the street marked by a yellow No Exit sign. This road dead-ends at **Cape Lazo**, a great spot for sea watching during water bird migration (peak times are March and April and September to December). Like many other similar points of land between here and Nanaimo, migration can be quite the spectacle for those who take the time to look. Thousands of Brant, scoters, and other waterfowl pass by in spring and late fall, along with plenty of alcids, gulls, jaegers, and even a few tubenoses. Although most times of year can be good, the peak time for finding unusual species is fall (September to December), when many scoters, loons, grebes, and alcids are pushing south. Some of the locally rare species that have been seen from Cape Lazo at this time include Leach's Storm-Petrel, Fork-tailed Storm-Petrel, Arctic Loon, Heermann's Gull, Black-legged Kittiwake, Sabine's Gull, and Thick-billed Murre. Birdfinding is all about patience and persistence, as each day can be completely different, depending on the tides, weather, and food.

Return to the main road and pull into the parking area for the Elks and Royal Purple Park—this is **Kye Bay**. This location is well known as a gull watching spot but can be productive for migrant shorebirds in spring and fall, as well as flocks of Dunlin, Sanderling, and Black-bellied Plovers in winter. There is usually no shortage of water birds offshore (especially outside of summer), and in November and December, look for flocks of Ancient Murrelets offshore moving south. Despite a lack of coverage, some fantastic birds have turned up here, including Curlew Sandpiper,

Kamchatka Gull (Siberian form of Mew Gull), Vega Gull (Siberian form of Herring Gull), Slaty-backed Gull, and Black-tailed Gull—most of these records are from fall and winter.

After checking Kye Bay, return to Knight Road then turn right (west) and proceed for 3.9 kilometres before turning right at the traffic circle. Stay on this road, which will turn into Little River Road. Follow this to the end, then turn left on Wilkinson Road before making the first right onto **Singing Sands Road**. The end of this road is another fantastic sea watching spot, with the potential for Yellow-billed Loon in winter (as many as six have been recorded at one time!).

If you want to get closer to the action out in Georgia Strait or are going to the Sunshine Coast, the ferry from Little River to Powell River can be rewarding. Any of the seabirds mentioned in the last entries pages can be found out here, and many will be closer. The only problems are that a scope will be harder to use and the boat doesn't stop for birds! Among the many seabird possibilities, this crossing is most famous for Ancient Murrelets from November to December. If you hit it on the right day, it is possible to see thousands of these beautiful little alcids buzzing by or floating on the surface.

> ### Seal Bay and Bates Beach

For those interested in adding Yellow-billed Loon to a life list, year list, or just-for-fun list, a visit to the Bates Beach area in winter will give you the best shot in southern British Columbia. From the Little River ferry terminal, head south on Eleanor Road (the main access road), then make a right onto Anderson Road, which will turn into Waveland. Continue on this road, staying right at the Y-junction with Larch Road, then make the first left onto Bates Road. Bates Road will take you straight through the middle of **Seal Bay Nature Park**.

On both sides of the road there are pleasant trails that take you through mixed second-growth forest that can be full of birds year round. If you're visiting in winter, expect to encounter Bald Eagle, Hairy Woodpecker, Pileated Woodpecker, Chestnut-backed Chickadee, Brown Creeper, Pacific Wren, Golden-crowned Kinglet, and Varied Thrush, among other species. Trails on the right (east) side lead to the beach, where one can scope offshore (with a slight chance of seeing a Yellow-billed Loon if the viewing conditions are good).

Otherwise, continue northwest along Bates Road past the park, then make the first right turn on Anson Road before turning left on Seacliffe Road and following this to the end, where there is a small turnaround with room for parking near the beach. From the Old Island Highway, turn east onto Coleman Road (to reach the other end of Bates Road), then follow the previous directions in reverse. Walk down the trail a little (10 to 20 metres) to where you get a nice view of Georgia Strait and Seal Bay from an elevated position.

Since **Bates Beach** (also known as Perrey's Beach) first started getting regular winter coverage in 2007, it has consistently produced multiple Yellow-billed Loon sightings, averaging around ten individuals per visit (with a high of fifteen!). This may seem like a guarantee, but be aware that the birds are usually well offshore (1 kilometre out or more). Having a good spotting scope and visiting when conditions are ideal will greatly help your chances. The best viewing is on calm, overcast days or in the afternoon on calm, sunny days. They are usually in groups of one to four, but it is worth remembering that even though most Common Loons stay closer to shore, they usually outnumber the Yellow-bills far out as well. Once one develops an eye for the colour and structure of the Yellow-billed Loons, they are relatively easy to find with a scope (under good conditions). Study photos and your field guide beforehand—in addition to having pale yellow/ white bills, they typically appear brown or pale brown, compared with the dark grey plumage of a Common Loon or Pacific Loon. Furthermore, their faces are usually a lot paler (in winter), and their bill/head posture is more upturned. Nearly all of the Yellow-bills seen here in winter are immatures (or "first-winter"). In addition to these big loons, Bates Beach is also a great place to see a wider variety of seabirds in general, in winter as well as in spring and fall.

> Mount Washington

For an opportunity to get in some upper-elevation birding for species such as American Three-toed Woodpecker, Gray Jay, Sooty Grouse, and White-tailed Ptarmigan (requires a full-day hike to reach true alpine), you may want to make the trip up to the **Mount Washington ski area**. Overall, the birding can be quite slow up there, but it may be worth it if you pick up your target birds, like ptarmigan. This is also a good site to see British Columbia's most famous endemic rodent: the Vancouver Island Marmot.

For more information about reaching Mount Washington, seeing marmots, and accessing the alpine, visit the Courtenay Tourist Information Centre, located along Cliffe Avenue between 21st and 20th Streets.

> Miracle Beach Provincial Park

For those travelling north from the Courtenay area to Campbell River, this may be a place you end up. It's not necessarily a hot spot for birding, but since it's a popular summer picnic locale, it can be a happy compromise on a family road trip. To get there, take Exit 144 from Hwy. 19 for Hamm Road (eastbound). This road will take you to the Old Island Highway, where you will

make a left, then an immediate right onto Miracle Beach Drive—
the park will be signed off this road.

In addition to picnicking opportunities, **Miracle Beach Provincial Park** also has a large campground. Trails lead through
the second-growth forest, around the area, and down to the
sandy beaches. Many typical western forest species can be
encountered here during summer breeding season, including
Band-tailed Pigeon, Hammond's Flycatcher, Pacific-slope Flycatcher, Chestnut-backed Chickadee, Pacific Wren, Cassin's
Vireo, Hutton's Vireo, Black-throated Gray Warbler, Townsend's
Warbler, Spotted Towhee, and Western Tanager. The waterfront here can also be exciting outside of summer, when water
bird diversity is highest.

› Oyster River Estuary

From Miracle Beach, head back along Miracle Beach Drive, but
instead of returning to the highway, make one of the first rights
onto Clarkson Avenue and follow this for 2.2 kilometres to
Eyre Road. There is beach access at the end of Eyre Road, from
which you can walk north to the estuary. Otherwise, you can
continue an additional 550 metres to the Pacific Playgrounds
Marina. Like the other estuaries and sea watching spots along
this coast, the **Oyster River Estuary** can be a wonderful place
during migration and in winter. This is also another spot to see
multiple Yellow-billed Loons in winter.

› Salmon Point and Woodhus Slough

From the side of the Oyster River Estuary, return to the Old
Island Highway by turning west on Eyre Road, then right on Henderson Avenue (which will turn into Saratoga Road), then left at
Regent Road. Make a right onto the highway to proceed north,
then after 2.7 kilometres turn right on Salmon Point Road and

follow this toward the water, staying right to park at the marina/restaurant (note the Nature Trail sign).

For waterfowl and other seabirds, scope offshore from the beach and check the marina itself. Afterwards, walk back up the road to the start of the nature trail. This passes some gravel flats before reaching **Woodhus Slough**. This sand-dune ecosystem is one of the rarest in British Columbia, with many uncommon species of plants and insects. In summer, listen for the *keeks* and *winnies* of both Sora and Virginia Rails, along with the chatter of Marsh Wrens and the *witchities* of Common Yellowthroats. The harsh song of the Red-winged Blackbird is a staple throughout the breeding season, and during the winter months, the birdlife here is dominated by wintering flocks of Canada Geese and Trumpeter Swans. With more than 215 species recorded for the area, many other species are possible throughout the year, so be sure to check carefully around the marsh itself as well as the waves offshore. If you like, you can continue along the trail south of the slough to a stand of tall Douglas-firs. This is **Kuhushan Point**, which offers a stunning view of the north side of the Oyster River Estuary.

> Oyster Bay

For birders travelling to and from Campbell River, we suggest using the Old Island Highway, because it is much better for birding (though not as fast, obviously). For the next hot spot after Salmon Point, return to the highway and continue northwest for 1.2 kilometres, then pull into the rest stop on the right side. This is **Oyster Bay Shoreline Park**—yet another fantastic spot for sea ducks, loons, grebes, cormorants, gulls, jaegers, both Caspian and Common Terns (summer), and alcids during migration. In August and September, huge numbers of Bonaparte's Gulls can be seen between here and Campbell River; check them for rarities such as Little and Franklin's Gull.

Sabine's Gulls are also possible between August and October, and Black-legged Kittiwakes have been seen later on in fall and winter. Flocks of shorebirds can be seen practically any time of year (outside June), with numbers peaking in August and diversity highest in early September. Osprey, Merlin, and Purple Martins are some of the notable nesting species nearby, and in fall and winter, look for Northern Shrike, Horned Lark, American Pipit, Snow Bunting, Lapland Longspur, Western Meadowlark, and various sparrows in the weedy patches of the park and out on the spit.

> Campbell River

From Oyster Bay, it's about 10 kilometres before you reach the main part of **Campbell River**. Along the way, you may want to stop at the various creek mouths and points of land where gulls and shorebirds concentrate. In winter, this area boasts one of the highest concentrations of Pacific Loons and Common Murres in Canada (thousands of both). Continue 1.2 kilometres past the ferry terminal (for Quadra Island), then turn on Spit Road and continue for 1.3 kilometres before parking on the right. This is **Tyee Spit**—a perfect place to watch seabird movements as they pass through the narrow gap between Quadra and Vancouver Islands. Shorebirds and gulls often concentrate out near the tip, but tides will have a big factor in determining this. Murres, loons, and scoters are usually the most numerous birds passing by, but you might also get lucky with some more unusual species, including Storm Petrels and both Red-necked and Red (rare) Phalaropes. Summer is the quietest period to visit, but there is still often a variety of non-breeders that stick around the area.

On the west side of the spit is the **Campbell River Estuary.** Part of it can be birded from the Spit Road area, but another way to access the main river is to return to the Old Island Highway and turn right (west), then make a right in 2.1 kilometres onto Maple Street. At the end of this short street, you can access the Myrt Thompson Trail, which follows the river downstream into the middle of the estuary. Purple Marins, Bushtits, and Bullock's Orioles are all at the northern limits of their breeding ranges on the Island here. There is usually an appealing mix at any time of year, with colourful breeding species such as Rufous Hummingbird, Cedar Waxwing, Yellow Warbler, and Common Yellowthroat being replaced by Fox Sparrow, Golden-crowned Sparrow, and Pacific Wren in the winter. Rarer species found here over the years have included Garganey, Cattle Egret, and Northern Mockingbird.

NORTH ISLAND

Contributed in part by Guy Monty

Although many people make the trip to Port Hardy each year, few if any bird reports come out of the North Island region. So for those looking for something to do along the way, or even planning a dedicated trip just for birding, we hope that the following entries will be useful. After all, there are some fantastic birding locales in this area, highlighted by the Salmon River Estuary in Sayward, seabird watching from Malcolm Island, and backcountry hiking on the outer coast.

> Sayward (Salmon River Estuary)

The **Salmon River Estuary** is one of the more pristine estuaries on the east coast of Vancouver Island and offers excellent birding in a spectacular setting. To reach this area, take the Sayward exit 60 kilometres north of Campbell River. In 7.4 kilometres (after crossing the second bridge over the Salmon River), take a right onto Salmon River Road. After exactly 1 kilometre, you will see a sign for the first **Nature Trust trail** on the right (east) side. This trail is a 1.5-kilometre loop through mature Sitka Spruce forest and estuarine back-channel habitats, bordering on brackish marshland. Red-breasted Sapsucker, Hammond's Flycatcher, and both species of kinglets nest in the forest, and Northern Harrier, five species of swallows, and Savannah Sparrows can be found in the open wetlands. Overhead, Black and Vaux's Swifts are common in summer. Return to your car and drive another 1.1 kilometres (northwest) along Salmon River Road, where a second Nature Trust sign indicates the **Viewing Tower Trail**. Similar species, plus Fox Sparrows and Ruffed Grouse, can be found along this trail. Both of these areas can be very good for migrant waterfowl, raptors, Sandhill Cranes, and shorebirds in migration. Roosevelt Elk and Black Bear can often be seen on the far side of the estuary.

Another 800 metres down Salmon River Road will bring you to the **Sayward Sewage Ponds**, which are located between the road and the estuary. These ponds often hold interesting waterfowl, such as Blue-winged Teal, Canvasback, Lesser Scaup, Ring-necked Duck, and Tufted Duck (once), as well as shorebirds and gulls in migration. Wilson's Snipe, Lesser and Greater Yellowlegs, both dowitcher species, and Baird's and Pectoral Sandpipers are some of the regulars in spring, late summer, and fall; while overhead, nighthawks, swifts, and swallows hawk insects on summer evenings. Across the road is a small lake that can also be a prime spot for waterfowl in migration, and the adjacent playing field attracts migrating geese.

Continuing along the road, you will pass through a log sort, which may be active. Stopping at any of the pullouts along this road allows for views of the estuary, where shorebirds, gulls, terns, and waterfowl are the attraction. Beyond the log-sorting area is a boat launch where one can scope offshore areas for alcids, sea ducks, and gulls. This site frequently hosts

Black-legged Kittiwakes from August to December, as well as interesting marine mammals.

> ## Nimpkish River Estuary

From Sayward, return to Hwy. 19 and drive northwest toward Port McNeill. After 121 kilometres, turn right onto Beaver Cove Road (if you cross the Nimpkish River you have gone too far) and make an immediate left onto a gravel track. On the right side of this old road, you will see a track leading through the woods to the beach. It may be possible to drive all the way to the water, but if not, park in the open area opposite. The massive sand flats of the **Nimpkish River Estuary** feature shorebirds in spring and fall migration, as well as gulls and alcids passing by offshore. Walk down the track through the woods and turn left at the beach to get to the Nimpkish River and **Flagstaff Islet**. Tide height will make a big difference in what birds will be present. During migration and in winter there can be impressive numbers of waterfowl, cormorants, gulls, and alcids offshore between the estuary and Cormorant Island.

> ## Port McNeill and Malcolm Island

From the Beaver Cove turnoff continue along Hwy. 19 for 7 kilometres to where the main road to **Port McNeill** turns off to the right. The waterfront in town can be worth a look, but for the best seabird watching in the area, we recommend taking a trip to Sointula (**Malcolm Island**), either for a day trip or a longer stay. The ferry crossing can be great for spotting birds, then once you're on the island, pick up a local map and head for **Bere Point**. Because of its position in the middle of Queen Charlotte Strait (along with Malcolm Point to the west—accessed by foot from Bere Point), this point of land can be a fantastic place for sea watching. Few birders have made it out to this spot, so with limited effort, the results have been impressive. Both Leach's and Fork-tailed Storm-Petrels are seen regularly outside of winter, and this is possibly the most reliable site from which these two species can be scoped from shore. Black-legged Kittiwake, Sabine's Gull, all three jaeger species, and Sooty Shearwater are all notable regulars that occur in season. Thick-billed Murre and Tufted Puffin (rare on this side of the Island) have also been sighted. The lighthouse at **Putleney Point** (the southwest end of the island) can also be a good place to scope from.

> Cluxewe River Estuary

Fewer than 10 kilometres out of Port McNeill (travelling toward Port Hardy), watch for a sign for the Cluxewe Resort. The resort (which offers campsites) is located on the **Cluxewe River Estuary**— another beautiful place to bird, particularly in spring and late summer and fall, for waterfowl, shorebirds, gulls, and offshore seabirds.

> Port Hardy Airport and Fort Rupert

Continuing north on Hwy. 19, drive 22 kilometres beyond the Cluxewe, then look for signs indicating the **Port Hardy Airport** on the right (northeast) side. Because the airport offers the only significant patch of open grassland in the vicinity, you can see open-country species on migration, such as Short-eared and Snowy Owls, Northern Harrier, Sandhill Cranes, shorebirds, large staging flocks of swallows, and sparrows. The best times for these birds are April to May and August to November.

From the airport, backtrack westward for a short stretch, then turn right after the Budget outlet on Beaver Harbour Road. This will take you into the heart of **Fort Rupert**. During migration season, periods of rain can bring migrants into the area, and similar to the airport, there are few grassy patches available to geese, shorebirds, pipits, larks, and sparrows, so be sure to scan the local ball fields if you are present during these conditions.

The rocky shoreline is favoured by rock-pipers—primarily Black Turnstones—along with large numbers of Surfbird in migration, as well as the odd Ruddy Turnstone and Rock Sandpiper.

> Port Hardy

From Fort Rupert or the airport, head west on Byng Road (the road leading west from the airport) to Hwy. 19, then turn right (toward Port Hardy). After 2.4 kilometres, turn right onto Hardy Bay Road, which will take you along the lower portion of **Hardy Bay**. Park at Babe's Pub then walk back (south) along the footpath. This path will take you down to the **Quatse River Estuary**, which can be a good place for shorebirds and a few forest birds. Otherwise, the entire waterfront of Port Hardy can be productive, especially for large flocks of turnstones and surfbirds in close (late July to April) and sea ducks, loons, grebes, and alcids floating farther out in the bay. Because Port Hardy is remote and surrounded by forest, you never know what lost migrant could turn up around town, so be vigilant!

> Inside Passage (Ferry to Prince Rupert)

For those travelling to and from Prince Rupert (or points north or south), you will be taking the Inside Passage ferry route from Port Hardy. The best part of the trip for birdfinding is the crossing from Port Hardy across **Queen Charlotte Sound** to the protected waters of the Inside Passage. If possible, we recommend booking on a day when you leave or arrive at Port Hardy during daylight so that you have the chance to see Marbled Murrelets, Pigeon Guillemots, a variety of sea ducks, Northern Fulmar, Sooty and Pink-footed Shearwaters, Fork-tailed and Leach's Storm-Petrels, Red-necked Phalarope, jaegers, gulls, alcids, and perhaps a few others depending on the time of year.

Tufted Puffin

> Cape Scott Provincial Park (Access to the West Coast)

If you are up for a bit of an adventure, inquire at the Port Hardy Information Centre about accessing the outer coast near Cape Scott (the northwest tip of Vancouver Island). It is possible to drive via logging roads all the way to the coast to places such as **San Josef Bay** and **Cape Palmerston**. You can also try the multiday hike to **Cape Scott** and back. A back roads map is a must, and be sure to stock up on food and camping supplies as well as a full tank of gas. Birding and camping in this part of the Island can be brutal, but they can also be tremendously rewarding. Storms occur regularly, but they can also bring in some beautiful birds. Sea watching on this side of the Island will give you a shot at a variety of seabirds, including regular rarities such as Manx Shearwater or Horned Puffin. Plus, there is something magical about being "out there," far away from the reach of civilization. Bird diversity in the forest is moderate, but visitors to the area will probably be more than happy waking up to the mystical choruses of Hermit, Swainson's, and Varied Thrushes; Pacific Wrens; Pacific-slope Flycatchers; and Fox Sparrows.

HWY. 4 WEST TO PORT ALBERNI

> Little Qualicum Falls Provincial Park

The first site of interest as you drive along Hwy. 4 toward Port Alberni from the coast is **Little Qualicum Falls Provincial Park**. This 440-hectare park is a family favourite, boasting impressive mountain views, rich forests, and gushing waterfalls. Camping, hiking, and picnicking infrastructure abound, and you can expect to find the usual mix of Vancouver Island forest birds.

> Mount Arrowsmith Regional Park

Continuing west from Little Qualicum Falls, pull into the parking lot on the right (north) side for the **Cameron Lake Picnic Area**. From here you can scan the lake for waterfowl; this is also the starting point for the Arrowsmith Trail, which leads up to the alpine of Mount Cokely and **Mount Arrowsmith Regional Park** for a chance to see high-mountain specialists such as White-tailed Ptarmigan and American Three-toed Woodpecker. The trail begins along an old logging road opposite the Cameron Lake Picnic Area; then, after fifteen to twenty minutes of hiking, starts a steeper climb toward a bridge over McBey Creek. After about 1.5 hours, you will reach a trail junction. The East Loop (left) leads to a lookout with dramatic views of the Strait of Georgia and the Coast Mountains (on the mainland) and continues uphill to Mount Arrowsmith Regional Park and the old ski hill. The West Loop (right) follows the route of the original CPR trail alongside McBey Creek and climbs to the eastern side of the old ski hill. A connector trail just below the ski hill road allows hikers to make a return loop. Expect a variety of forests birds along this hike, and listen for hooting Sooty Grouse in spring. We recommend this hiking route only for those in good physical condition, as there are many steep and uneven sections. Estimated hike times are two hours (one way) to the lookout, four hours (one way) to the ski hill, and six to seven hours round trip to complete the loop.

For those specifically seeking ptarmigan (and other upper-elevation species), the quickest route is to continue 9 kilometres (west) past Cathedral Grove (the next birding hot spot) and turn left onto the main forestry road (formerly the main driving route to the now defunct Mount Arrowsmith ski area). Keep left at kilometres 5.5, 8.2, 9.5, 5.8, 10.4, and 13.5. After travelling southeast for a while, the turn at kilometre 10.4 will take you northwest, where the road will soon begin to switchback up the steep western slopes of **Mount Arrowsmith**. At kilometre 17.5 (just before a wide left turn), an old spur road heads east into a narrow valley before climbing up into a saddle that leads to the summit of **Mount Cokely**. To see White-tailed Ptarmigan you will have to hike to the upper ridges of lichen-clad boulders and alpine meadows. This area is usually covered in snow until mid-July, so unless you have sufficient snow gear, August to September is the best time to visit. Your chances of finding ptarmigan are always low, as there are only a few here and they don't exactly stick out. If you make it up before July, playing a recording can be quite effective in drawing the territorial males in. Otherwise, just hope you bump into a family group somewhere near the top.

To find American Three-toed Woodpecker and Townsend's Solitaire, continue past the spur road turnoff at kilometre 17.5 for 1 kilometre, then bear right to continue to the old ski hill. There is a yellow gate near the start of the road that is sometimes locked. If this is the case, you can walk from here. American Three-toed Woodpeckers are fairly reliable along this road, especially in the mature trees on the steep slope. When you reach the old ski hill (about 2.5 kilometres from the turnoff), listen for the piping calls of Townsend's Solitaires that nest on the ground in the open subalpine meadows. As you drive or hike along the road to the ski hill, keep an eye out for Sooty Grouse, Gray Jay, and other mountain birds. Just before the ski hill, you may notice another trail that heads south up the mountain ridge—this is an alternate hiking route up into the ptarmigan habitat. Depending on road conditions, it takes between thirty and forty-five minutes to drive to the old ski area from Hwy. 4. Expect some challenging steep sections on these hikes. If you want, it is possible to continue south from Mount Cokely summit to the stony peaks of Mount Arrowsmith, but this is only recommended under ideal conditions and with ample return time.

> ## MacMillan Provincial Park and Cathedral Grove
For one of the most beautiful rest stops in Canada, and to witness a lasting example of what British Columbia's towering rainforests once looked like, a stop at **Cathedral Grove** in **MacMillan Provincial Park** is an absolute must. This pull-off area should be obvious about 5.5 kilometres west of the Cameron Lake Picnic Area. The moss-clad buttresses of these giant Douglas-firs and golden light streaming down through the high canopy give this site its name. Several interpretive trails wind through the grove, which was altered drastically in a massive windstorm on New Year's Day 1997. The fallen behemoths are still essential to the forest's ecosystem, as they have opened up the sky for the next generation of giants to grow, and their rotting trunks will supply nutrients to countless plants, fungi, and animals. Visiting birders should keep their eyes and ears peeled for misty mountain denizens such as Sooty Grouse, Northern Goshawk, Hammond's Flycatcher, Brown Creeper, Pacific Wren, Golden-crowned Kinglet, Hermit Thrush, Varied Thrush, Townsend's Warbler, and Dark-eyed Junco.

> Port Alberni

Contributed in part by Sandy McRuer

Located at the end of Alberni Inlet (Vancouver Island's longest inlet), Port Alberni is special in that it's an interior town with ocean access. After an Alaskan earthquake in 1964, the town was hit by two ten-foot-tall tsunamis that washed away fifty-five homes and damaged many others, but luckily there were no injuries. In the years since, dykes have been erected and life has returned to normal. Port Alberni isn't known as a top birding destination, so most visitors are just passing through on their way to Tofino or other locations on the west coast. In fact, the birding can be quite good around town, so if you have some time, why not have a look around? The best time to visit is fall and winter.

Start at the **Harbour Quay.** As you approach the first signs of civilization east of town, angle left/straight (the first paved road on the left) at the visitor's centre onto the old Port Alberni Highway and follow it down the hill as it turns into Redford Street. At the end of Redford turn left (south) on 3rd Avenue and follow this for 1.2 kilometres until you turn right (west) on Argyle Street and follow this to the end. From here, you can scan the upper end of Alberni Inlet for Double-crested Cormorant, Great Blue Heron, Belted Kingfisher, and a variety of waterfowl, grebes, and loons.

> Somass River Estuary and Kitsuksis Dyke

From Harbour Quay, return to 3rd Avenue and head north for 2.3 kilometres, then turn left on Rogers Street, which will swing to the right along the **Somass River.** Pull off in the main parking area on the left, just past the first bridge, and scan the river from there. If you're coming from Hwy. 4, turn left (southeast) onto Victoria Quay at the T-junction in downtown Alberni, then pull into the riverside parking lot.

Kitsuksis Dyke is one of the best birding areas around Port Alberni, and it is easier to access than the main Somass Estuary. From the riverside parking area, drive north on Victoria Quay/ Hwy. 4, past the marina, then make a right onto Beaver Creek Road, before pulling into the parking lot on the right side, just past the restaurant. From here, you can walk a short distance northeast to reach the creek, then up the creek for about 1 kilometre. In spring, the entire walkway is perfect for warblers, such as Orange-crowned, Black-throated Grey, and Wilson's. In the summer, this is a great area to find Green Herons. A resident Merlin is often seen making passes at small birds, such as Song Sparrows or Spotted Towhees. In winter, it's a good idea to walk up to the little pond behind the Co-op gas station, where you often find Ring-necked Ducks, among others.

To get to the **Somass Estuary** itself (from the parking lot by the river), head north to the T-junction and continue straight to River Road/Hwy. 4 (westbound). Continue along the river until you cross a bridge, then make an immediate left onto Mission Road. Drive through the Tseshaht First Nation reserve on this road for about 650 metres until you reach a junction where the paved road bends away from the river and a dirt road continues along the river. Follow the dirt road to a gate and park in the small parking area. Walk under or around the gate and follow the dirt road past a farm building until you reach another gate. *Note: There is a herd of about fourteen horses that runs loose in the area between the gates. They can be dangerous if you have a dog that is off leash or not under control. Do not bring dogs into this area without a leash and do not disturb the horses.*

Near the second gate is a rock with a plaque—this is the **Somass Ducks Unlimited property**. The old air strip and adjacent farm once produced fresh vegetables for the first sawmill in the valley. In operation since 1861, the farm shut down four years later, and it was another twenty years before settlers returned to the valley permanently. In this open country, American Pipits and Savannah Sparrows are common in migration, and Northern Harriers are infrequent visitors. Swamp Sparrows show up periodically, and Short-eared Owls used to be found somewhat regularly but have become decidedly rare in recent years. Another way to bird this area and access the **Port Alberni Sewage Lagoons** is to drive through the Tseshaht First Nation reserve (continuing south on the paved Mission Road) until you come to a big yellow gate. This gate is closed sometimes, so you may have to walk from here. *Do not block the gate or the driveway beside it with your vehicle.* From the gate, drive or walk to where the big white pipeline goes under the road on the left; you can park at the turnout here. Walk across the road to where the pipeline comes out of the ground, then walk onto the elevated wooden walkway beside the pipeline. This is a great way to see the estuary. Follow the walkway until you come to a dirt access road that services both the city sewage lagoon and the mill effluent lagoon. There is a "step-over" the pipeline and a ramp to the road. You can either follow the road back around the hill on the right, which will lead you to the paved road where you left your vehicle, or you can continue on the pipeline until you come to another step-over and a ramp just past the city sewage lagoon. It is best to get off the pipeline here. The road leads out to the mill effluent lagoon. You can walk around both lagoons and then all the way back. This second loop takes about three hours of easygoing birding. Like many other estuarine locations along the British Columbia coast, winter is the best time for high numbers of waterfowl and gulls. Look for Northern Shoveler, Gadwall, Ring-necked Duck, and Lesser Scaup in the effluent and sewage lagoons, along with the occasional Canvasback. Wilson's Snipe and American Coots are seen in small numbers, and Virginia Rail regularly overwinter here; however, they are usually heard but not seen. This is about as far west as

Bewick's Wrens go in central Vancouver Island, and Northern Shrikes are often spotted eyeing up potential prey from a prominent perch (late fall through early spring).

> ## McCoy Lake

This area is interesting in any season. **McCoy Lake** is one of the few places on Vancouver Island where you can find Ruddy Ducks in winter. The winter rains create flooding around the perimeter of the lake and attract a variety of ducks and raptors, as well as Wilson's Snipe and Killdeer. The open fields attract thousands of migrating Savannah Sparrows, American Pipits, Sandhill Cranes, and, sometimes, interesting shorebirds such as Whimbrel and Pectoral Sandpipers in spring and fall. The summer sees substantial populations of four species of swallows: Violet-green, Tree, Cliff, and Barn.

To get here, head west on Hwy. 4 from Port Alberni along the Somass River to the grey iron bridge. After crossing the bridge, look for the second left turn onto McCoy Lake Road, about 500 metres farther on around the bend. The road will take you to the local landfill, and then the view opens up when you get to the agricultural area. The road will bend to the right. Continue straight past the turn onto Stirling Arm Drive. You will go past an old farm, across a small creek, and up onto a knoll with a house on it. This is the most productive area. There are a couple of turnout spots in the area for turning your car around, but the whole road is a good area to walk along. You can continue along this road to meet up with Hwy. 4 again.

> ## Sproat Lake and the Taylor River Estuary

As you head westward from Port Alberni (bound for the outer coast), you will soon come upon a large lake. Although not noted for high waterfowl numbers, **Sproat Lake** can still be a worthwhile place to check out. There are numerous side roads at the east end, but for birders, the west end is most intriguing. Here, the **Taylor River Estuary** promotes a mixture of marshy sloughs and riparian thickets of salmonberry and alder. Look for unmarked trails on both sides of Hwy. 4. The dense shrubbery contains Wilson's, Yellow, Black-throated Grey, Orange-crowned, and MacGillivray's Warblers, as well as Common Yellowthroats, Warbling Vireos, and even a Red-eyed Vireo, if you're lucky. Waterfowl such as Wood Duck, Hooded Mergansers, and Common Loons are often seen at the river mouth, and American Dippers can be found along the river itself.

There is so much more to do and see in the Alberni Valley and surrounding area that we just could not fit in. For those wishing to learn more about the rainforests, rivers, and birds of the region, we highly recommend getting in touch with local expert Sandy McRuer (rainbirdexcursions.com). Sandy has an intimate knowledge of the rich natural and human history of the area, which will no doubt enhance your Island experience.

PACIFIC RIM

In contrast to the American coastal states of Washington, Oregon, and California to the south, the outer coast of British Columbia is not on the continental mainland. From the Olympic Peninsula in Washington right up to Alaska, the coast is cluttered by mazes of rock islets, large islands covered by impenetrable evergreen forests, and long fjords stretching deep into the coastal mountains. Because of this difficult terrain, there are only a few places in British Columbia where birders can easily access the true "West Coast"—the most popular being the area around Pacific Rim National Park. In general, the bird diversity is low, but most birders who visit are not after numbers; they are after seabird species that occur nowhere else in Canada other than the outer coast of British Columbia. These include Black-footed Albatross,

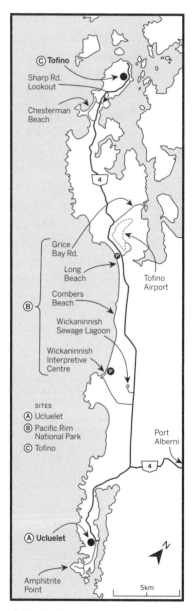

© **Tofino**

Sharp Rd.
Lookout

Chesterman
Beach

4

Grice
Bay Rd.

Long
Beach

Tofino
Airport

Combers
Beach

Ⓑ

Wickaninnish
Sewage Lagoon

Wickaninnish
Interpretive
Centre

P

SITES
Ⓐ Ucluelet
Ⓑ Pacific Rim
National Park
© Tofino

Port
Alberni

4

Ⓐ **Ucluelet**

Amphitrite
Point

N

5km

6 Pacific Rim

Pink-footed Shearwater, Buller's Shearwater, Flesh-footed Shearwater, Short-tailed Shearwater, Fork-tailed Storm-Petrel, Tufted Puffin, and Cassin's Auklet. To see most of these pelagic species, you will have to get out on a dedicated offshore birding or whale-watching trip, though in times of strong westerlies, it is sometimes possible to see albatross and other species from land. Bird variety is slim in these thick temperate rainforests, but many of the residents are specialties to the Pacific Northwest, including Sooty Grouse, Red-breasted Sapsucker, Steller's Jay, Northwestern Crow, Hammond's Flycatcher, Pacific-slope Flycatcher, Hutton's Vireo, Pacific Wren, Varied Thrush, and Townsend's Warbler.

From Port Alberni, it's another 90 kilometres along Hwy. 4 (drive carefully, especially during wet weather) to the Ucluelet-Tofino junction. From here, you can turn right (northwest) for the Long Beach section of Pacific Rim National Park and Tofino or left (southeast) for Ucluelet.

> Ucluelet

The smaller and less touristy village of **Ucluelet** is a delightful place to visit at any time of year. Although it lacks the beaches found farther up the coast, birding can still be rewarding. The best place for sea watching is at **Amphitrite Point**. Follow the main road through town and continue on Peninsula Road. After passing a couple of small inlets, turn right on Coast Guard Drive, following signs for Amphitrite Point Lighthouse. There are several short walking trails that provide an introduction to the native plants in the area—mainly salal, hemlock, and cedar. From the lookout near the lighthouse, take some time to scan the ocean for seabirds. The mix of birds changes with the seasons. Several species of loons, grebes, sea ducks, and alcids are common throughout most of the year, and tubenoses like shearwaters and fulmars are more prevalent between May and

October. Hundreds of Black-legged Kittiwakes can sometimes be seen offshore during the winter months. Look out for a variety of marine mammals as well, including Gray Whale and Orca. Like other remote west coast towns, Ucluelet can turn up rarities, particularly in fall. If you have some extra time, take an hour to walk around the back streets and check the migrant flocks using the feeders and ornamental plantings in peoples' backyards.

> ## Pacific Rim National Park

Return to the Ucluelet-Tofino junction and proceed northwest toward **Tofino**. There is a well-signed turnoff to the **Wickaninnish Interpretive Centre** 4.7 kilometres from the junction. This information centre (open mid-March to mid-October), interpretive facility, and gift shop focusses on the natural and cultural heritage of **Pacific Rim National Park**. There is wheelchair access to the beach, where visitors can walk for miles to the north, swim in the ocean, and go surfing. Sanderling and other shorebirds can be found near the water's edge, and flocks of gulls often loaf around near creek mouths. Both Song and Savannah Sparrows can be seen hopping around the driftwood and are joined by American Pipits in spring and fall. Also, remember to check the alders around the parking lot for migrant flocks.

Return to the highway and continue toward Tofino. Only 1 kilometre along the road, look for a yellow gate on the left side (ocean side) of the road. Park beside the gate, leaving enough room for service vehicles to enter and exit. This is the entrance to the **Wickaninnish Sewage Ponds** (AKA Tofino Sewage Lagoons). Birders used to be able to drive the 300 metres in, but in recent years, things have tightened up a bit. Proceed on foot and, once close to the ponds, proceed quietly because the birds here spook easily. The main pond will be straight ahead of you, but there is often a wet area in the depression on the left. Since there is not a lot of muddy freshwater habitat for migrating waterfowl and shorebirds, this location can attract some real goodies, including Garganey, Ruff, and Sharp-tailed Sandpiper. Return to your vehicle and continue northwest.

There are many beach accesses and walking trails in Pacific Rim National Park, and they are all well-signed off the highway as you drive toward Tofino. Visitors are, of course, encouraged to explore the area as much as possible, but if time is limited, here are a few highlights for birders:

Comber's Beach: Located between the Wickaninnish Interpretive Centre and Green Point, the beach is a short walk downhill from the parking lot. The trail passes through an impressive stand of West Coast rainforest before emerging onto the beach. The large creek that empties out here usually attracts large numbers of loading gulls and occasionally groups of shorebirds. Look for Western and Heermann's Gulls among the more common Glaucous-winged and California Gulls. Outside of summer, Herring and Thayer's Gulls can also be seen regularly.

Long Beach (south parking lot): The south parking lot for Long Beach (opposite Tofino Airport Road) is 3.4 kilometres northwest of Green Point. This is, of course, an opportunity to check out the beach, but another reason to visit is the parking lot itself—lined with alders, it is one of the best spots on the West Coast for migrant passerines. Suitable habitat is relatively scarce out here along the wild coast, so the birds concentrate in these patches of broadleaf trees before continuing south (or north in spring). In late summer, large flocks of warblers—sometimes numbering in the hundreds—can be seen in the area, and this parking lot is one of the best spots for them. Yellow-rumped Warbler, Orange-crowned Warbler, Yellow Warbler, Townsend's Warbler, Warbling Vireo, and Ruby-crowned Kinglet are some of the more common migrants encountered, but almost anything is possible in fall, when many young birds stray off course.

Grice Bay: Drive three kilometres past Airport Road and turn right (north) onto Grice Bay Road. You can turn right immediately, drive to the end of the short road, and park beside the golf course buildings and RV park. From here, you can scan the mowed fields around the airport, which can occasionally attract geese, shorebirds, pipits, and longspurs. Return to Grice Bay Road and drive due north to the bay. The road dead-ends after 3.5 kilometres, but as you will see, there are several places to stop and look at the tidal inlet of Grice Bay. A variety of waterfowl and shorebirds are present throughout the year, including groups of Whimbrel that can sometimes be seen feeding on the flats during spring and late summer.

> ## Tofino

As you draw closer to Tofino, more and more signs for lodges, hotels, and B&Bs will start popping up. Watch for signs pointing to **Chesterman Beach** on the left-hand side. This is one of the more popular beaches in the area, but it can produce some decent beach birding throughout most of the year. Keep your ears open for migrant flocks along Chesterman Beach Road and near the Wickaninnish Inn.

Just a bit farther north, turn right (east) onto Sharp Road at the Dolphin Motel. At the end of this road, there is a short trail ending in a wooden lookout platform where birders can scan the mud flats of Jensen's Bay for shorebirds and waterfowl (a rising tide is best). This spot is known locally as the **Sharp Road Lookout**.

Pelagic Birding

For the best chance at seeing pelagic species such as alcids and tubenoses up close, you need to get out on a pelagic boat trip. In recent years, Tofino has emerged as the place to go for these

Black-footed Albatross

trips, thanks to the efforts and expertise of the staff at the **Tofino Whale Centre** (tofinowhalecentre.com). Pelagic boat trips mainly operate between July and September, when the weather is optimal and seabird numbers are high. You can also contact local nature tour guide George Bradd (justbirding.com) for upcoming scheduled trips or check in at the whale centre, where it is possible to book private trips. At the very least, you can get out on one of the popular whale-watching trips where, in addition to seeing whales, you'll probably nab a few pelagic bird species while you're at it! Near shore, expect to see Sooty Shearwater, Common Murre, Pigeon Guillemot, Rhinoceros Auklet, Marbled Murrelet, Brandt's Cormorant, Pelagic Cormorant, several gulls, and scoters. If you can get out on a trip that goes 20 kilometres or more out to the edge of the continental shelf or Clayoquot Canyon, you have a good chance of seeing Black-footed Albatross, Northern Fulmar, Pink-footed Shearwater, Buller's Shearwater (September to October), Fork-tailed Storm-Petrel, any of the three jaeger species, South Polar Skua (August to October), Tufted Puffin, Cassin's Auklet, and both Red-necked and Red Phalaropes.

Remember: Nothing is Guaranteed! Rarities are always possible birding "Big Blue," so keep your eyes peeled—recent rarities seen in the ocean off Tofino include Short-tailed and Laysan Albatross, Great Shearwater, Solander's Petrel (first photo-documented record for North America), and Parakeet Auklet.

Note: Tofino pelagic trips tend to last around six hours and bathroom facilities are limited in most cases. It is possible to get seasick, sunburnt, and soaking wet all on one trip, so be sure to plan accordingly. Prices for these trips fluctuate but are typically between $160 and $250 per person.

SOUTHERN GULF ISLANDS

The main islands of the southern portion of Georgia Strait (Gabriola, Galiano, Mayne, North and South Pender, Saturna, and Saltspring), known collectively as the Southern Gulf Islands (and accessible by regular ferry service), are a popular destination for tourists and British Columbia residents alike. The relatively dry hillsides of these picturesque islands are cloaked in Douglas-fir and Arbutus, providing habitat for a small but interesting mix of breeding species, including Bald Eagle, Cooper's Hawk, Sooty Grouse, Band-tailed Pigeon, Hutton's Vireo, Pacific-slope Flycatcher, Bewick's Wren, Townsend's Warbler, Spotted Towhee, White-crowned Sparrow, and Purple Finch. Black Oystercatchers nest along the rocky shorelines; in the late summer they are joined by flocks of Black Turnstones and Surfbirds. Scan offshore for migrating and wintering sea ducks, loons, grebes, and alcids such as Rhinoceros Auklet, Pigeon Guillemot, Common Murre, and Marbled Murrelet. For more information about visiting the South, Central, and North Gulf Islands, check out gulfislandseh. com. Click on "Activities" to find out more about the outdoor and birdwatching opportunities for each island.

LOWER MAINLAND
AND
SUNSHINE COAST

VANCOUVER

If this is your first trip to the Pacific Northwest, welcome. The city of Vancouver is truly one of the most beautiful cities in the world (when it's not pouring rain, that is!). The birding is fantastic year round, thanks to a mild climate and a diversity of habitats, from the high peaks of the North Shore Mountains to the rich estuarine habitats of Boundary Bay and the Fraser Delta.

One of the first birds you will notice upon arriving is the Northwestern Crow. If you're thinking, "This looks just like an American Crow," you're not alone. These ones are slightly smaller than their American brethren and have a few different vocalizations, but the difference isn't always apparent. Like other corvids, they are very intelligent and can be a pleasure to watch as they drop clams from great heights to smash them open on the rocks or when they gather each night to roost. If you've ever wanted to see about ten thousand crows in a short time frame,

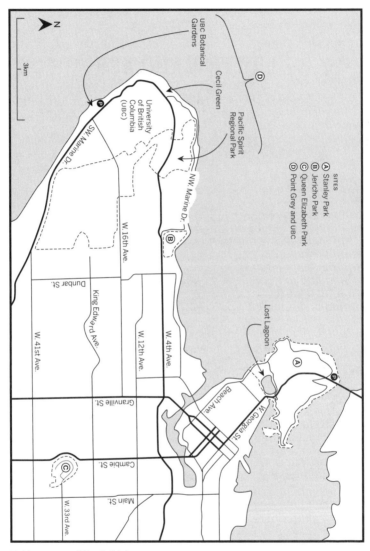

7 Vancouver (West side)

park somewhere by the corner of Boundary Road and Grandview Highway (12th Avenue) around dusk and watch as they stream by to their roost.

The other conspicuous bird in Vancouver is the Glaucous-winged Gull, or rather the variety of hybrids and mutts known as Olympic Gulls. It's best not to get too worried about identifying their parentage, as it can often be a mixture of three species at once (Herring + Glaucous-winged + Western). We suggest that you don't ask questions—just check off the gull and crow on your list and move on to the other birds. Only kidding—enjoy your birding in Van City and hope that the sun shines for you.

> Stanley Park

Probably the most popular park in Vancouver because of its proximity to downtown, **Stanley Park** can be a great spot for newcomers to the area to get a look at some specialties of the Pacific Northwest. Although the park lost more than one thousand of its towering Red Cedar and Douglas-fir trees in a big windstorm in 2006, visitors will still be impressed with the ambiance of this urban park. Stanley Park is bisected by Hwy. 99 and signage will be obvious from either the main entrance off Georgia Street at the south end or across the Lions Gate Bridge to the north (see Map 7).

There are many trails throughout the park that will take you through open coniferous forest, where Pileated, Hairy, and Downy Woodpeckers all nest, along with the common Northern (Red-shafted) Flicker and a few Red-breasted Sapsuckers. Other expected breeders include Pacific-slope Flycatcher, Red-breasted Nuthatch, Brown Creeper, Chestnut-backed and Black-capped Chickadees, Golden-crowned Kinglet, Pacific Wren, Swainson's Thrush, Townsend's Warbler, and Dark-eyed Junco. Varied Thrush occasionally breed here but are more common during the winter months, along with Hermit Thrush, Golden-crowned Sparrow, and Fox Sparrow. The two main freshwater bodies in the park are **Lost Lagoon** and **Beaver Lake**. At any time of year, a variety of waterfowl can be present, but spring through fall is the best time for diversity, with winter usually producing the greatest abundance of birds. Until the early 2000s, thousands of scaup used to come in each winter's day at dusk to roost, and these flocks occasionally held Tufted Ducks. Unfortunately, diving duck numbers have decreased drastically since then, and now only a few scaup are seen at any one time. In winter, other divers such as Ring-necked Duck, Bufflehead, both goldeneye species, and Canvasback are often seen, and both Common and Hooded Mergansers are regular winter residents. Marsh Wrens and Virginia Rails are sometimes heard along the reedy fringes, and Song Sparrows and Mallards are usually the most conspicuous birds here. The flocks of wintering American Wigeon might harbour the odd Eurasian, and practically all the other regular dabblers pass through at various times of the year.

If you're passing by the Vancouver Aquarium, you may want to peer across the fence at the Beluga tank, where an American Dipper sometimes spends the winter, nabbing small invertebrates from the edges of the tank—much to the amusement of the curious Belugas! If you don't want to look like a stereotypical "cheap birder," you can pay the fee to enter the aquarium and have a look from inside. There are plenty of fantastic displays here, showing off the sea life of the Canadian Pacific and Arctic. The dippers are also sometimes seen along the creeks near the aquarium or along the seawall of Stanley Park.

Speaking of the seawall, it is possible to walk, cycle, or drive nearly the entire stretch of coastline around Stanley Park, from English Bay in the southwest up to Prospect Point in the north, then down to Coal Harbour in the southeast corner. Offshore, look for Double-crested and Pelagic Cormorants, along with a mix of scoters, loons, and grebes (the latter species occurring largely outside of the summer breeding season). Barrow's Goldeneyes and Harlequin Ducks favour the rocky shorelines. Be sure to look through these sea duck groups (especially the scoters) for rarities such as Common and King Eider.

> Jericho Park

Like Stanley Park, the smaller **Jericho Park** is a great place to start your birding adventure in Vancouver, offering swimming beaches, duck ponds, brushy habitat, and mature forest. The main parking area is at the western terminus of Cornwall Avenue/Point Grey Road. If you're approaching from the east along 4th Avenue or West Broadway, turn north on Alma Street, then turn left (west) on West 2nd Avenue, and follow it to the very end.

From this parking lot, the main beach will be evident to the north. In summer, the swimming is great, so people traffic is high and bird numbers are low. In the winter, however, the calm waters of Burrard Inlet can showcase water birds—mainly Surf Scoters, Common Goldeneye, Horned and Western Grebe, and all three species of cormorant: Double-crested, Brandt's, and Pelagic. Small flocks of Sanderlings can sometimes be seen working the beach, and Ring-billed, Glaucous-winged, and Mew Gulls are all common out on the water and in the grassy fields of the park. California Gulls pass through in numbers in spring, late summer, and early fall, and Thayer's Gulls can sometimes be seen in late fall and winter.

Large numbers of Mallards and Rock Pigeons are present all year, taking advantage of the bounty of grain thrown out by park visitors. Each fall, a large flock of American Wigeon joins in and can be seen throughout winter and early spring before departing for northern breeding grounds. This flock often contains one or two Eurasian Wigeon as well—the males are obvious with their silvery flanks and maroon faces, but also keep an eye out for the females, which show uniform chocolaty-brown flanks and cheeks (unlike the female Americans, which usually have pinkish sides and grey faces). Other dabblers such as Northern Pintail, Gadwall, and Green-winged Teals are seen regularly in the reed-fringed ponds, whereas Cinnamon and Blue-winged Teal are annual but less frequent (April is best for these two). Sora and Virginia Rail breed in the cattail thickets, and Virginias stick around all winter. For a mix of sparrows, bird the black-berry thickets at the west end of the park in fall, winter, and early spring. Fox, Song, and Golden-crowned Sparrows are the three most common species in winter, and Lincoln's and White-crowned Sparrows are abundant in spring/fall passage, with fewer numbers overwintering. Spotted Towhees are present year round, along with Anna's Hummingbird, Black-capped Chicka-dee, Bushtit, Golden-crowned Kinglet, and Bewick's Wren. In spring and fall, mixed flocks of warblers pass through. Yellow, Orange-crowned, Wilson's, Yellow-rumped, and Townsend's are the most common species, whereas MacGillivray's and Black-throated Gray are regular but uncommon. The trails through the mature forest of Jericho Park are usually fairly low on birds but can turn up a few Pacific northwest specialties, such as Pacific Wren (common all year) and Varied Thrush (common in win-ter and regular but somewhat scarce in spring and fall). Keep your head up though, as Barred, Great Horned, and Northern Saw-whet Owl (winter) can all be discovered while roosting. On September 30, 2003, a Spotted Owl was found here.

> ## Point Grey and the University of British Columbia

Point Grey is a prominent headland separating the Fraser River delta from Burrard Inlet to the north. It is dominated by Pacific Spirit Regional Park and the sprawling campus of the University of British Columbia. The park provides easy access to good forest birding, and the shrubbier parts of the campus can be very productive during spring and fall migration. To visit one of Vancouver's best rarity traps, turn off from northwest Marine Drive onto Cecil Green Park Road (near the northwest tip of Point Grey). Park in the pay-parking area (usually free on weekends and holidays) and walk west along the fence line that skirts the bluff. The alder trees and scrub along this fence line, as well as the mixed woods and grassy patches around the Museum of Anthropology, showcase resident species such as Hutton's Vireo, Bewick's Wren and Spotted Towhee, but many local birders go here in spring and fall to look for surprises. Like many other rarity traps, the birding can be hit or miss. Some days you may only find two or three species, whereas another day could be dynamite. May to June and September to October are the best times to visit **Cecil Green**, when rare migrants are most likely to turn up. Because Cecil Green offers a mixture of habitat on a prominent headland surrounded by water, migrants are often drawn to the area after periods of foul weather. Here is a short list of some of the local rarities that have been found over the years: Ash-throated Flycatcher (several), Tropical Kingbird, Sedge Wren, Hooded Warbler, Chestnut-sided Warbler, Black-and-White Warbler (five), Ovenbird, Lark Bunting, and Gray-crowned Rosy-Finch. In addition to searching for migrant songbirds, the sea birders in the crowd may want to set up a scope atop the grassy hill. From here, you have a good vantage point of the mouth of Burrard Inlet, where you can see flocks of loons, grebes, sea ducks, gulls, and alcids in spring and fall passage.

Pacific Spirit Regional Park buffers the university campus from the city of Vancouver with 763 hectares of mixed forest. There are many trails that wind through the park (most accessed off North West Marine Drive, Chancellor Boulevard, and 16th Avenue), all of which can produce birds typical of the wet coastal forests—such as Barred Owl, Common Raven, Chestnut-backed Chickadee, Brown Creeper, Pacific Wren, and Purple Finch. Imperial Trail, accessed off the west end of 29th Avenue, is a more open trail that offers wider views. The salmonberry patches along this trail are buzzing with Rufous Hummingbirds in spring (mid-March through May). Top Trail, which branches north off Imperial Trail near 29th Avenue, travels by a Great Blue Heron colony.

> Queen Elizabeth Park

Surrounded by urban East Vancouver, this high point of land covered in a variety of trees, shrubs, and ornamental gardens is a natural magnet for migrants and wintering birds. From Main Street, head west on 33rd Avenue and continue up the hill to the main parking lot. "**Queen E.**" is a pleasant place for visitors and locals alike to bird at any time of year, but it is particularly productive in April and May, when fall-outs of migrant passerines can occur during periods of rain or strong north winds that push the birds out of the sky. Common visitors in spring and fall include Olive-sided Flycatcher, Western Wood-Pewee, Hammond's Flycatcher, Pacific-slope Flycatcher, Cassin's Vireo, Orange-crowned Warbler, Wilson's Warbler, Yellow-rumped (both Audubon's and Myrtle types) Warbler, Townsend's Warbler, and Western Tanager. Anna's Hummingbirds are present year round and start displaying and singing their scratchy songs as early as January, whereas Rufous Hummingbirds show up in March and are present throughout summer. A few rarities have shown up in the park—none more mouth-watering for Canadian listers than Hermit Warbler (there have been several records). West Coast specialties such as Hutton's Vireo, Chestnut-backed Chickadee, Bushtit, and Bewick's Wren are possible year round, and a decent mix of waterfowl can be seen on the small ponds in the park, including the occasional Eurasian Wigeon. In winter,

Queen E. is known for sometimes attracting a few species that are rare elsewhere in Vancouver, namely Northern Pygmy-Owl, Townsend's Solitaire, and Pine Grosbeak.

> Trout Lake (John Hendry Park)

A nice little park in the heart of East Vancouver, **John Hendry Park** often has a surprising number of birds, despite being surrounded by the urban hustle-bustle. Winter is the best time to visit, when waterfowl diversity is highest. A pair of Bald Eagles are often perched high in the trees, watching the water birds on **Trout Lake**, much to the displeasure of the resident Merlins. In winter, Trout Lake attracts substantial numbers of gulls and often several species. In addition to the abundant Glaucous-winged Gulls and hybrids, this is one of the most reliable sites in the city for California Gull in winter. A few Thayer's, Ring-billed, and Mew Gulls occasionally join the mix, and in recent years, an apparently pure Western Gull (fairly rare around Vancouver) has been seen frequently. Spring and fall can also be a great time to visit, when mixed flocks of warblers pass through the willows that line the lake. The park is probably not worth a visit for birding in summer.

NORTH SHORE

Contributed in part by Rob Lyske and Quentin Brown

> Maplewood Flats

This site is swiftly becoming one of the more popular birding locations around Vancouver, thanks to the efforts of the Wild Bird Trust of B.C. to protect and restore the area and to the dedicated locals who turn up so many wonderful birds. With more than 240 species now recorded on its checklist (which can be downloaded for free at wildbirdtrust.org), the **Maplewood Flats**

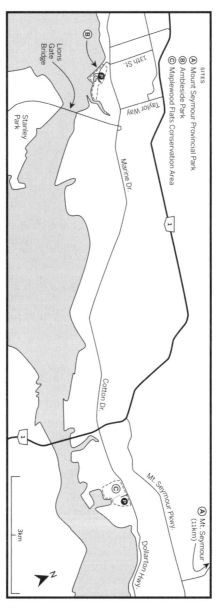

SITES

Ⓐ Mount Seymour Provincial Park
Ⓑ Ambleside Park
Ⓒ Maplewood Flats Conservation Area

Lions
Gate
Bridge

Stanley
Park

13th St.

Taylor Way

Marine Dr.

1

Cotton Dr.

1

Ⓒ

Mt. Seymour Pkwy.

Dollarton Hwy.

Ⓐ Mt. Seymour
(11km)

3km

N

8 North Shore (East)

Conservation Area boasts a variety of habitats in a relatively small area. Among the rarities recorded here are Ash-throated Flycatcher, Sage Thrasher, Black-and-White Warbler, and Chestnut-collared Longspur.

To reach this location, take the Dollarton Highway exit (Exit 23) east off the Trans-Canada Highway (see Map 8). Once on Dollarton, proceed 1.5 kilometres east, and then look for access signs on the right (south) side of the road, where you will find the Wild Bird Trust office and sufficient parking. (There is also parking on the north side of Dollarton on the gravel that surrounds an ironworker's shop). The park is accessible twenty-four hours a day from a walk-in gate just west of the driving entrance. The parking lot is open from 6 AM to 6 PM, Monday to Friday, and 9:30 AM to 4 PM on weekends. It is usually closed on holidays. At the park headquarters there is a white board detailing recent sightings, and this is where people meet for the free birding walks (second Saturday of each month).

From the office, take the trail that heads east toward the mud flats, where large numbers of waterfowl and shorebirds can be found in season (tides will also have an effect on what birds are encountered). From April to midsummer, scope the nest boxes on the old piling for Purple Martins. Although they finish nesting in midsummer, many of the birds hang around into late August and early September, so keep your eyes open. After checking the flats, head south toward the bridge, where you can scan up the barge canal to the north. Continue across and take the right-hand trail, which leads westward toward the cattail ponds. The first pond is usually quiet, but the second pond is great for waterfowl and Virginia Rail in spring. From there, head northward through the woodlot, which starts a loop trail; as you round through the woods, you will end up on the west side of the west pond at a raised viewing area—another good place for Virginia Rail. South of here are a meadow to your left (east) and a salt marsh to the right (west). A little farther along, the trail branches again; the right branch takes you to what locals call **Otter Point**—at low tide a gravel bar is exposed that attracts Black Oystercatcher, among other things. Continuing back to the main trail there is a pocket marsh on the left that has produced Swamp Sparrow, Northern Waterthrush, Rusty Blackbird, and, most recently—Palm Warbler. The trail heads eastward from there and follows the shore more or less back to the bridge. The last or first stop depending on your route is the nursery, which has several feeders. A walk along the Dollarton Highway to the east will bring you to a short trail at the mouth of McCartney Creek—the eastern boundary of the sanctuary. There is a small viewing deck there where American Dipper can sometimes be seen.

> ## Mount Seymour Provincial Park

Located only thirty minutes from downtown Vancouver, **Mount Seymour Provincial Park** provides birders with easy access to the subalpine and alpine habitats of the Coast Mountains. (The best time to visit the high country is June to September, but the lower sections of the park are birdy from April onward). From the Trans-Canada Highway (just north of the Second Narrows Bridge), take Exit 22 onto Mount Seymour Parkway and proceed east for slightly more than 4 kilometres to where Mount Seymour Road is signed on the left. From this junction, it's another 12 kilometres up the mountain to the ski area and most of the hiking trails. As you wind your way up, it may prove worthwhile to stop occasionally and see what's around. The lower reaches of the mountain feature Red-breasted Sapsucker and other woodpeckers, Pacific-slope Flycatcher, Hutton's Vireo, Cassin's Vireo, Chestnut-backed Chickadee, Pacific Wren, Black-throated Gray Warbler (found in mixed maple and conifer stands), and Western Tanager. Other forest birds such as Varied Thrush,

Golden-crowned Kinglet, and Red-breasted Nuthatch are common throughout the park for most of the year. Just past the Baden-Powell Trail access, the road passes an obvious powerline cut. MacGillivray's Warbler can be reliably found here in the breeding season, along with Orange-crowned and Wilson's Warblers. The **Deep Cove Lookout** is a great place to marvel at the view (if the weather co-operates); be sure to look out for both Vaux's and Black Swifts flying past in spring and summer. Continue up to the main parking area for the ski area. From here there are several trails that lead up through the subalpine forest. There are short trails to small nearby lakes and longer trails to the peak of **Mount Seymour** and beyond. White-tailed and Rock Ptarmigan have been recorded above treeline, but both are considered rare and are not always present. Although summer usually provides the best weather and most bird varieties, winter can also be a great time to visit. In years of plentiful cone crops, hundreds of Red Crossbills are sometimes encountered, along with the odd flock of White-winged Crossbills, Pine Grosbeaks, and Common Redpolls (winter only; not present every year). Gray Jays are present year round, but Clark's Nutcrackers are exceedingly rare. Northern Pygmy-Owls can be seen at any time but are most frequently encountered in winter.

> ➤ Ambleside Park

This small but pleasant park is a nice spot to visit, especially in winter, when waterfowl numbers are highest. Take Marine Drive west from Hwy. 99 (use Map 8 for reference). After about 1 kilometre, turn left (south) on 13th Street, which will immediately cross the railroad tracks and become Argyle Avenue. Drive to the end and park where convenient. In the duck department, a variety of both dabblers and divers can be found here—both on the pond and out in Burrard Inlet. Occasionally, a Eurasian Wigeon can be found among their more common American cousins, and elegant Mute Swans (introduced) can be seen year round. Although somewhat unreliable, Green Herons have been known to nest on the island in the middle of the pond, so be sure to scrutinize any likely blobs if you're visiting during the breeding season. For the dreamers in the crowd, British Columbia's only Painted Redstart was found here in November 1978!

> ‣ Lighthouse Park

Continue west along Marine Drive from the Ambleside Park turnoff. After driving nearly 9 kilometres, look for the large wooden sign for **Lighthouse Park** on the left (ocean) side—turn here on Beacon Lane and follow it to the parking area. Lighthouse Park is another fantastic site to visit, as it combines good West Coast birding with beautiful views of Howe Sound and English Bay. Most of the park is covered in old-growth fir and cedar forest, and many West Coast forest species can be reliably found here, including year-round residents such as Sooty Grouse, Band-tailed Pigeon, Red-breasted Sapsucker, Anna's Hummingbird, Hutton's Vireo, Pacific Wren, Varied Thrush, and Chestnut-backed Chickadee. Spring and summer breeders include Pacific-slope Flycatcher, Hammond's Flycatcher, Cassin's Vireo, and both Townsend's and Black-throated Gray Warblers (make sure you familiarize yourself with the different songs, and remember that Townsend's favour tall conifers, whereas Black-throated Grays are more often found in mixed maple and fir). The Hutton's Vireo is a very secretive species and is most easily detected between February and April, when the males are singing. Typically, Sooty Grouse are also difficult to find—the best times are spring and early summer, when the males are hooting and displaying.

In addition to the forest, Lighthouse Park is also regarded as one of the better Vancouver locales for watching seabirds, such as scoters, gulls, and alcids. Late fall and early winter are

Townsend's Warblers

the best times to visit, when large rafts of scoters can be seen around West Vancouver, along with groups of Harlequin Ducks, a sprinkling of Long-tailed Ducks, Marbled Murrelets, Pigeon Guillemots, and the occasional Rhinoceros Auklet or Ancient Murrelet flock. Both Double-crested and Pelagic Cormorants are common year round, whereas Brandt's are only regular in the winter—we recommend using a scope if you want to do some serious sea watching.

The rocky shoreline of Lighthouse Park can be good for rock-pipers (particularly Black Oystercatcher), but for the best chance at seeing species such as Black Turnstone and Surfbird (as well as seabirds), you'll need to visit the nearby **Klootchman Park**. Return to Marine Drive and turn left (west). After only 130 metres, turn left (toward the ocean) on Howe Sound Lane. Watch for a sign on the right once you pass The Byway, also on the right; the sign is set back from the road, so it may be difficult to spot in the shade. There is street parking for about three cars close to this spot. The trail down to the viewpoint at Indian Bluff might be difficult for people with limited mobility, because the terrain is steep and covered in large roots. Many of the same forest species found at

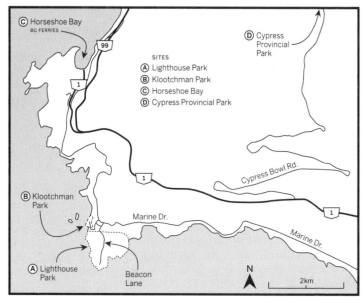

9 North Shore (West)

Lighthouse Park can be seen here, and some of the old Douglas-firs along the trail are majestic; however, the main attraction of this site comes at the viewpoint, where birders will have spectacular views of Georgia Strait and the mouth of Howe Sound. Just offshore, the **Grebe Islets** provide a spot for Black Turnstone in fall, winter, and spring, along with a few Surfbirds during migration. Occasionally (not every year), Rock Sandpipers and Wandering Tattlers are spotted among the regulars. Some winters, large concentrations of Surf Scoters can be seen from this headland, and if you're really lucky, you might be able to pick out a King Eider. Marbled Murrelets are possible at any time of year but are most regular in fall and winter, whereas Common Murre, Pigeon Guillemot, and Rhinoceros Auklets are all less frequent but can be quite numerous on some days, depending on the season and food availability.

> Cypress Provincial Park

Cypress Provincial Park provides the mountain backdrop for most scenic photos of Vancouver, as well as one of the most convenient mountain birding experiences close to the city. From the Trans-Canada Highway (this section is known locally as the Upper Levels Highway), take Exit 8 onto Cypress Bowl Road. The road winds up the mountainside in a series of long traverses punctuated by 180-degree switchback turns. At the second of these turns, about 5.5 kilometres up the road, is the **Highview Lookout**. This is worth a stop not only for the views of the city but for watching forest birds, since you're looking down on the treetops. It is one of the more reliable places in Vancouver to see Band-tailed Pigeon (April to September), and Rufous Hummingbirds forage among the flowering shrubs below (April to July).

Continue up the road and park at the Cypress Mountain ski area—this was the site of the freestyle skiing events at the 2010 Winter Olympics. Walk to the north end of the parking area and look for signs for **Yew Lake Trail**. If you're here on a spring or summer morning (April to early July), you may hear the sweet songs of Fox Sparrows coming from the mountain west of the parking lot—this is one of the only places in the Vancouver area to find this species during the breeding season. This short loop trail goes through beautiful coastal subalpine forest and can be very good for birdfinding. Sooty Grouse are often seen along the trail, and in summer, watch and listen for Vaux's Swifts (May to September) flying overhead—they nest in the large, hollow cedar snags. Typical forest birds at any time of year include Red-breasted Sapsucker, Gray Jay, Steller's Jay, Chestnut-backed Chickadee, Golden-crowned Kinglet, Hermit Thrush, Varied Thrush, and Townsend's Warbler. The toots of a Northern Pygmy-Owl (if you are a skillful whistler or have a recording) will often bring in a flock of forest birds and occasionally the little owl itself. If you want to hike farther into the mountains, the Howe Sound Crest

Trail goes to the north; it is particularly good for watching raptor migration in fall (September to October).

> ## Horseshoe Bay and B.C. Ferries

Horseshoe Bay is the western mainland terminus of the Trans-Canada Highway. From here, B.C. Ferries provides services to Langdale (see page 174 for the Sunshine Coast), Bowen Island, and Nanaimo on Vancouver Island (see page 55). There usually aren't many birds around the ferry terminal other than Glaucous-winged Gulls and Northwestern Crows. In winter, Surf Scoters and Barrow's Goldeneyes can be seen from the terminal, and in spring and summer, scan the skies for Vaux's Swift and Black Swift (uncommon). Band-tailed Pigeon can be seen throughout most of the year, and you may run into a roving flock of Chestnut-backed Chickadees and Bushtits as you walk around town. The ferry trips from here, bound for either Vancouver Island or the Sunshine Coast, are typically uneventful in terms of birdlife. Spring and fall are the best times, as that is when many seabirds and gulls are passing through Georgia Strait. California and Mew Gulls are usually numerous, and it's possible to see several species of alcids, including Rhinoceros Auklet. In late summer and early fall, the odd Fork-tailed or Leach's Storm-Petrel might appear, but otherwise, tubenoses are very rare in the strait. Instead, expect sea ducks, loons, and gulls to be the most abundant groups.

FRASER DELTA

A sprawling expanse of tidal mud flats, marshes, bogs, and farmlands, the delta of the Fraser River is one of the top birding locations on the continent. From October through April, hundreds of thousands of waterfowl (predominantly Green-winged Teal, Mallard, American Wigeon, Northern Pintail, and

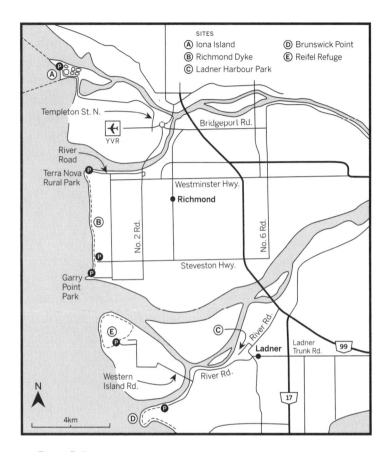

SITES
(A) Iona Island   (D) Brunswick Point
(B) Richmond Dyke   (E) Reifel Refuge
(C) Ladner Harbour Park

10 Fraser Delta

Greater Scaup) and Dunlin feed along the shores of the delta, and in spring (April to May) and fall (July to October), similar numbers of shorebirds (dominated by Western Sandpipers) stop over to refuel on their migration between South America and the Arctic tundra. The eelgrass beds of the delta are an important spring feeding ground (and increasingly important in winter) for Brant, and the surrounding agricultural fields have some of the highest concentrations of wintering raptors in Canada—particularly Bald Eagles, Northern Harriers, and Rough-legged Hawks, with a smattering of Peregrine Falcons. Needless to say, Vancouver birders spend a lot of their time at the many hot spots around the delta.

An important thing to keep in mind when birding the delta is the tide cycle. If you're looking for shorebirds, it is usually best to go out just before high tide so that the birds feeding on the mud flats are forced into shore toward you—otherwise they will be just distant specks when viewed from the dykes. A few sites where you can get close to the water's edge at lower tides are Blackie Spit, Tsawwassen ferry jetty, and Roberts Bank jetty, if the tide charts don't match up with your schedule (see Map 11).

> Iona Island

Located to the northwest of the Vancouver International Airport, **Iona Island** is one of the most popular birding sites in the Vancouver area; despite its relatively small size, close to three hundred species have been recorded, including an astounding total of forty-seven shorebird species. To get there, follow signs to the airport off Hwy. 99 (the main highway from Vancouver to Seattle); once you're on Sea Island (where the airport is), turn right (north) onto Templeton Street North; this will become Grauer Road, then Ferguson Road as you skirt the northern boundary of the airport. After a series of speed bumps, the road turns north and crosses the Iona Island Causeway. Immediately after passing through a yellow road gate, pull over on the right side of the road near the gate in the fence. This is the entrance to the **Iona Sewage Lagoons**. Public access is restricted to these inner ponds, but birders are allowed—you will need a four-digit password to enter. You can get the password either by contacting B.C. Bird Alert (bcbirdalert.blogspot.ca) or by making an inquiry to the Vancouver birding chat group (Yahoo group: birdrepbc) or the Vancouver Natural History Society.

As in most sewage lagoons, the water levels in each cell go up and down throughout the year. If conditions are right during spring and fall, the ponds can fill up with "peeps." Western Sandpipers are usually most numerous in April and August to September, whereas Dunlin take over in late fall and winter. Other regular species (in season) include Semipalmated Plover, Greater and Lesser Yellowlegs, Spotted Sandpiper, Least Sandpiper, Pectoral Sandpiper, and Long-billed Dowitcher. Unfortunately, overall numbers have greatly decreased at this location in recent years—partly because of different sewage treatment practices but also because of the constantly changing ecology of the Fraser Delta. Still, these ponds are always worth a look, as they continue to turn up exciting birds, both in the ponds and in the brushy patches around them. Shorebird highlights include the only photographed Spoon-billed Sandpiper for North America outside Alaska (1978), Curlew Sandpiper, and multiple records of both Little and Red-necked Stints. If that wasn't enough, British Columbia's only record of Common Moorhen is from here, along with records of Garganey, Tropical Kingbird, and Northern Wheatear (August 2011). Shorebird numbers and diversity are highest in August to September, and a visit at high tide (when birds get pushed off the foreshore) will give you the best chance at seeing a lot of birds.

After checking the inner sewage ponds, continue along the road and park in the main lot near the washrooms. From here, you can bird the foreshore and trails through the brambles that lead around the **Outer Ponds**. Many of the typical marsh species nest around these larger ponds, such as Pied-billed Grebe, American Bittern, Virginia Rail, Sora, Marsh Wren, Common Yellowthroat, and Red-winged Blackbird. This is also one of the few local breeding locations of Yellow-headed Blackbird. The trails behind the marshes that lead into the cottonwoods are particularly productive during migration season, and you may run into some biologists who run the local banding station (for more information, visit ionaislandbirdobservatory.blogspot.com). Visit **Iona Beach** and the adjacent foreshore to find shorebirds and gulls, especially on a rising tide. Walking through the mixed grassland and shrubs that border the area can be very rewarding during spring and fall, as you never know what you might discover among the regular pipits, sparrows, and meadowlarks.

Another option is to walk out along the **South Iona jetty**. This 4-kilometre-long jetty is accessible by foot or bicycle only and is attractive to local birders for several reasons. Firstly, it is one of the most reliable spots in Vancouver to see Horned Lark (fall), Snow Bunting (fall and winter), Lapland Longspur (fall), and Gray-crowned Rosy-Finch (winter)—these birds forage on the ground along the edges of the jetty, typically out toward the tip. In the winter of 2004–05, many birders saw a McKay's Bunting hanging out with the Snow Buntings. None of the previously mentioned species are common, but all are seen in some numbers each year. Secondly, the Iona jetty can be a good place to look for rock-loving shorebirds (such as turnstones and surfbirds) in the right season, particularly the locally rare Wandering Tattler (May and August). Flocks of Sanderling, Western Sandpipers, and Dunlin often roost along the rocks near the tip during high tide. Large flocks of gulls (and the occasional jaeger in late summer and fall) sometimes congregate near the tip, where a long pipe pumps out treated sewage water. Since the jetty juts straight out into Georgia Strait, it gives birders a way to get closer to the rafts of scoters, mergansers, loons, grebes, and alcids that are only dots when viewed from the mainland. Sometimes something unusual, such as a King Eider, is picked out of these seabird flocks, so check carefully.

> Richmond Dyke

A string of rarities in recent years, including Emperor Goose, Black Phoebe, and Western Scrub-Jay, has alerted many birders to the potential of this area, though locals have always known its value. The **Richmond Dyke** provides 5.5 kilometres of trail for birders, joggers, dog walkers, and cyclists to explore the outer rim of Lulu Island. From **Terra Nova Rural Park** in the north to **Garry Point** in the south, the natural vegetation and adjacent habitat along the dyke act as a natural north-south corridor for birds on migration, right beside the urban sprawl of Richmond. Starting from the north, the first access point is at the western terminus of River Road (not to be confused with River Road in Ladner). There is ample room for parking here, and birders can either walk along the main dyke path or explore the unique Terra Nova Rural Park—formerly a series of private residences, the homes have been removed and the area has been allowed to grow wild. A small pond has been successfully implanted and is used by a variety of water birds throughout the year. The mix of old trees, weedy patches, and natural shrubs has produced an impressive variety of birds for such a small area—so take your time by checking carefully through the mixed flocks that use the park. The marshes along the outer dyke are similar to Reifel Refuge and Brunswick Point in many respects, though the fall Snow Goose flocks can sometimes be much closer, as they feed along the shoreline here. The western terminus of the Westminster Highway is another place to access the dyke, as is the south end of Terra Nova Rural Park and community garden.

Farther south, if you drive to the west end of the Steveston Highway, there is a small parking area with access to the dyke. There is a farm paddock here that is often partially flooded and attracts large numbers of Wilson's Snipe, as well as other shorebirds such as Pectoral Sandpiper and the occasional Sharp-tailed Sandpiper (mid-September to mid-October). Scan

Sharp-tailed Sandpiper

the wooden structures out at the water's edge for hawks, eagles, cormorants, and herons.

Garry Point is at the south end of the Richmond Dyke Trail (follow Chatham Street west from No. 1 Road). Grab a bite to eat at the famous Pajo's Fish and Chips, then explore the park itself or continue north up the dyke. You may also want to check out the rocky breakwater around the fishing marina, as this is the only regular spot in Richmond for Black Turnstone (August to April).

➤ Ladner Harbour Park

This small park doesn't get a lot of attention from the greater birding community, and perhaps this adds to its value. A mixture of tall cottonwood trees, shrubs, and Fraser Delta cattail sloughs, **Ladner Harbour Park** is a great place to bird in spring, fall, and winter, in particular, and has ample facilities for a group picnic. To access the park, take the River Road exit just south of the George Massey Tunnel, then turn right (north) on McNeely's Way. Or from downtown Ladner, proceed northwest on Elliott Street from the S-bend, then right on River Road, and finally left on McNeely's Way.

For more riparian habitat and access to another part of the same slough, drive northeast up River Road (from the turnoff to Ladner Harbour Park), and make the first left onto **Ferry Road**. There are several sloughs on both sides of the road that can house ducks and marsh birds, and the cottonwood stands along the road are always worth a look during spring and fall migration.

> Brunswick Point

From the junction of Hwy. 17 and Hwy. 10 (Ladner Trunk Road), drive west on Ladner Trunk Road/48 Avenue through downtown Ladner. After passing the main shopping complex, pass through an S-curve and continue west on 47A Avenue, which will turn into River Road in about 1 kilometre. From the S-curve, it's around 6 kilometres to **Brunswick Point** along River Road—note the turnoff to Reifel Refuge/Westham Island (our next location) on the right side as you drive west. At the end of the road, there is ample room to park on the shoulder. From here, walk up onto the dyke and start birding!

The bramble patches and cottonwoods near the parking area can be good spots for migrants in spring and fall. Bewick's Wren and Spotted Towhee are present all year, whereas Golden-crowned, White-crowned, and Fox Sparrows haunt the area mainly in winter. Brunswick Point's geography (at the end of a peninsula) makes it host to impressive bird congregations—mainly shorebirds and waterfowl between fall and spring. As you walk along the outer dyke, check the cattail marshes for Great Blue Heron, American Bittern, Marsh Wren, and Virginia Rails. Huge numbers of dabbling ducks and Snow Geese can be seen close to shore in the right season, and farther out you may be able to see rafts of White-winged and Surf Scoters. Shorebird numbers can also be high in this area, as they feed in the mud flats of **Roberts Bank**. In past years, birders used to be able to drive out along the large super-port jetty, but recently, this has been discouraged. Like Boundary Bay, if you're hoping to see shorebirds, we advise you to show up an hour or more before high tide or afterwards, when the tide is falling. Station yourself on the south side of Brunswick Point and watch the flocks get pushed in as the tide rises. It's possible to see both Short-eared Owls and Snowy Owls in winter, and in the evenings, you may catch a glimpse of a Barn Owl as it leaves its roost to hunt.

> Reifel Refuge

Perhaps the most heavily visited birding site in Western Canada, the George C. Reifel Migratory Bird Sanctuary (AKA Reifel Refuge) is a year-round mecca for birders and bird photographers. More than 280 species have been reported from this small sanctuary. It is also a great place for children and beginner birders, since many of the resident and visiting bird species can be seen at close range. To get to Reifel, turn north off River Road, west of Ladner, following signs for Westham Island and Reifel Refuge. The one-lane bridge over Canoe Pass (an arm of the Fraser separating Westham Island from the mainland) is a reliable place to see "countable" Mute Swans. During migration and in winter, check the muddy banks to the east of the bridge for Long-billed Dowitchers, yellowlegs, and many species of dabbling ducks, including the rare Eurasian race of Green-winged Teal also known as Common Teal. Moving along onto Westham Island, you may encounter swarms of Snow Geese in spring and fall during high tide. In winter, scan the farmlands of Westham Island for flocks of Trumpeter Swans (with the odd Tundra mixed in), along with the regular Great Blue Herons, Red-tailed Hawks, Northern Harriers, and other open-country birds.

Turn left 3.8 kilometres from the bridge, down the Reifel entrance road. Birding can be quite good along this road, so you might want to pull over and check the flocks of Black-capped Chickadees, Golden-crowned Kinglets, and Bushtits for the odd

Hutton's Vireo—or perhaps something extraordinary. After parking, you will have to pay $5 per adult to walk the trails for a day. Recent sightings are posted at the entrance and a binder around the side of the building allows birders to record the highlights of their walk. If this is your first visit to Reifel, the friendly staff will be able to suggest the best areas to check, depending on what you want to see. The birding is rewarding here at any time of year, but many birders prefer the late summer and early fall, when waterfowl and shorebirds are moving through in large numbers.

Large flocks of Snow Geese start arriving at Westham Island by early October and are often referred to as the Fraser-Skagit flock or subpopulation, because they move back and forth between the estuaries of the Fraser and Skagit Rivers. The Lesser Snow Geese visiting this area are part of the Wrangel Island (Pacific Flyway) nesting population. This Russian island lies in the Arctic Ocean, north of Siberia, providing British Columbia birders with around seventy thousand Snow Geese to gawk at each winter. If you are visiting during this time, look for them in the fields around Westham Island, and scan the foreshore from up on the tower in the northwest corner of the sanctuary. The noise and sight of ten thousand or more Snow Geese taking flight is something to behold!

For peak numbers of shorebirds, it's a good idea to arrive around high tide, when the birds are pushed into the shallow ponds around the outer dyke or West Field of Reifel (near the observation tower). In early August, small groups of Short-tailed Dowitchers pass through, but by the end of the month, they are usually replaced by hundreds of juvenile Long-billed Dowitchers, which may stick around as late as November (with smaller numbers carrying on into the winter). Be sure to check carefully through these shorebird flocks for rarer species, as "mega" waders have turned up here, including Spotted Redshank (three!),

Wood Sandpiper, and Temminck's Stint. Thanks to the shallow pools that fill West Field, Reifel is probably the most reliable spot in the Vancouver region for Hudsonian Godwit, Silt Sandpiper, and Sharp-tailed Sandpiper (mid-September to mid-October), all of which prefer the relatively fresh water to the saltwater mud flats of the Fraser Delta's foreshore.

While walking along the outer dyke trail, keep your eyes open for American Bitterns, which sometimes hunt along the trail (especially first thing in the morning), and scan over the marshes for hunting and perched raptors. A pair of Sandhill Cranes lives here year round, and in fall and winter, they are joined by other migrant family groups. Black-crowned Night-Herons are usually present outside of the breeding season near the refuge entrance (ask staff for current locations). A variety of forest and brush birds are present at different times of year, including many western specialties, such as Bewick's Wren, Bushtit, Golden-crowned Sparrow (fall, winter, and spring), and Hutton's Vireo. Like Brunswick Point and Iona Island, Reifel can act as a bit of a trap for migrating songbirds, including the odd rarity, such as Tropical Kingbird, Prothonotary Warbler, and Green-tailed Towhee.

> Tsawwassen Parks

Abutting the American border, Tsawwassen has a nice mix of birding spots in a small area. Turning south onto 56th Street (signed off Hwy. 17) will take you into Tsawwassen proper and the Point Roberts border crossing.

Beach Grove Park is the first hot spot to check out at any time of year but especially during migration. Turn left (east) on 16th Avenue (off 56th Street), then after a few blocks turn left (north) on Duncan Drive. Turn left at the T-junction (17A Avenue), and the park will be obvious on your right-hand side. The mix of trees, thick shrubs, and fields makes this an ideal spot to look

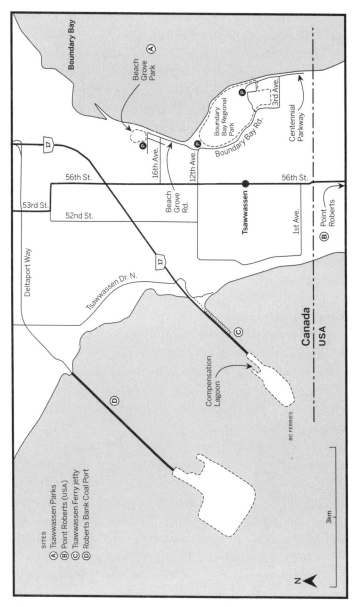

SITES
Ⓐ Tsawwassen Parks
Ⓑ Point Roberts (USA)
Ⓒ Tsawwassen Ferry Jetty
Ⓓ Roberts Bank Coal Port

Boundary Bay

Beach Grove Park Ⓐ

Boundary Bay Regional Park

3rd Ave.

Centennial Parkway

Ⓟ

16th Ave.

12th Ave.

Boundary Bay Rd.

56th St.

53rd St.

52nd St.

Beach Grove Rd.

Tsawwassen

1st Ave.

56th St.

Ⓑ Point Roberts

Deltaport Way

Tsawwassen Dr. N.

17

Ⓒ

Compensation Lagoon

Canada
USA

Ⓓ

BC FERRIES

N

3km

for migrating flycatchers, warblers, and sparrows, as well as local residents such as Great Horned Owl, Vaux's Swift (spring and summer), Bewick's Wren, Bushtit, Black-headed Grosbeak (spring and summer), and Spotted Towhee. For access to the Boundary Bay dyke, walk east on 17A Avenue (only 200 metres from the parking area of Beach Grove).

The best place to find shorebirds in the Tsawwassen section of Boundary Bay is at **Boundary Bay Regional Park**. From Beach Grove, drive to the east end of 17A Avenue, then turn right on Beach Grove Road and follow this for 1.2 kilometres to its intersection with 12th Avenue. There is a small parking area at the eastern end of 12th Avenue. From the main drag in Tsawwassen (56th Street), turn east onto 12th Avenue and follow it to the end. From the parking area, walk east along the main trail—this will take you out to the most westerly corner of Boundary Bay. Along the first stretch of trail, there is a small tidal lagoon on your left (north) side. If there is some exposed mud, look for foraging shorebirds (particularly April to May and July to October). Gulls and Great Blue Herons are usually present in large numbers, and outside of summer, there will be hundreds of birds floating offshore. In winter, these will be mainly Northern Pintail and American Wigeon, but some loons, grebes, and other water birds can be seen in season.

About 800 metres from the start of the trail is a sandy spit and tidal lagoon. In recent years, this has been the best area for foraging and roosting shorebirds—mainly Black-bellied Plovers, Killdeer, Western Sandpipers (spring and fall), and Dunlin (late fall and spring). Occasionally, Marbled Godwits are found here, along with a variety of other shorebirds—you just need to be here at the right moment. The open grassy areas on the inner side of the dyke trail are good for Common Yellowthroat and Red-winged Blackbird during the breeding season, with Song Sparrows, Spotted Towhees, and American Goldfinch present year round. In winter, look for Northern Shrikes perched on top of one of the nearby birches, and sometimes large groups of Great Blue Herons will congregate in the fields. If you happen to be in Tsawwassen when the forecast is calling for a clear day in the morning, you should make a point of watching the sunrise from this trail. If there are a few clouds on the horizon, it can be breathtaking to see the distant Mount Baker (an active volcano to the east) silhouetted in vibrant oranges, reds, and purples.

> Point Roberts (Washington State, USA)

Believe it or not, **Point Roberts**, Washington, is in the Vancouver bird checklist area—it makes sense geographically, but politically it's a little strange. Essentially, it's an easy way for Vancouver birders to get some extra seabirds on their local lists. The end of the peninsula is far enough removed from the muddy outflow of the Fraser River that a number of oceangoing birds (mostly winter residents, migrants, and staging birds) can be seen, with some effort, from a few key spots.

Continue straight south along the main road in downtown Tsawwassen (56th Street) and proceed through the usual border routine (you must have your passport or NEXUS card with you). Once through to the USA, continue driving straight south (Tyee Drive), until you hit the marina, where you will angle right (southwest), following the main road (which turns into Marine Drive, then Edwards Drive). Along the way, you will notice that Point Roberts is relatively undeveloped compared to the rest of the Lower Mainland. This is because their water supply comes from the municipality of Delta, and any development scheme would require some serious cross-border haggling. This makes for a marvellous birding area!

In spring and fall, the hedgerows and old orchards can be teeming with migrants. After passing the marina, scan the man-made pond on the right-hand (north) side for waterfowl—particularly in winter and peak migration periods. Not too far past the pond, the parking lot for **Lighthouse Marine Park** should be obvious on the left side (southwest tip of Point Roberts). This is the most popular spot for birding on Point Roberts, as it gets you closest to birds passing by in the Strait of Georgia. Brant are commonly seen in the area until around mid-May, before returning again in late October. During spring and fall passage, expect substantial numbers of waterfowl, loons, grebes, cormorants and alcids moving past offshore. Tides, weather, and food availability will all contribute to how much you can see at any one time. Large workups of gulls offshore may point you in the direction of feeding frenzies; otherwise, you will just have to be patient and scan back and forth across the strait. Scan the beach and nearby pilings for shorebird flocks, mainly Black-bellied Plovers, Western Sandpipers, Dunlin, Sanderling, and Black Turnstones outside of the breeding season. Surfbirds, Ruddy Turnstones, and the occasional Rock Sandpiper (October to April) or Wandering Tattler (May and August) may also be mixed in.

> Tsawwassen Ferry Jetty

The **Tsawwassen ferry jetty** juts out into the Georgia Strait, which can allow for closer looks at a large number of the migrant water birds that pass through in spring and fall, as well as those that stay here through the winter. The main B.C. Ferries terminal with service to the Gulf Islands and Vancouver Island (via Swartz Bay or Duke Point) is located at the end of the jetty (this is the mainland terminus of Hwy. 17), so most birders travelling from the Vancouver area to Victoria will be passing through here. If you are not catching a ferry or have lots of time to spare, there are two main ways to bird the jetty.

First, drive southwest on Hwy. 17 for 2.5 kilometres past the 56th Street junction and then turn left (south) onto Tsawwassen Drive South at the last set of lights before the long jetty.

The road swings right toward the shore and after 600 metres continues straight onto a wide but pothole-ridden gravel road that parallels the jetty. For around fourteen years, a lone Willet overwintered in this area (August to early April), but it seems that this faithful bird made its last spring flight in 2012 and may never be seen again. One of the largest Great Blue Heron nesting colonies in North America is located in the tall conifers that cloak the nearby hillside, and many of these birds will be seen foraging out on the mud flats at low tide. You can also drive southwest along the gravel track that parallels the jetty. Look along the rocks for Black Oystercatchers (year round) and Black Turnstones (spring, winter, and fall), as well as a variety of other shorebirds, depending on the time of year. Surfbirds are regularly found among the turnstones, whereas Wandering Tattler are rare but seen most years during their southward passage in August.

Out on the water, expect Surf and White-winged Scoters in migration and during winter, as well as both Common and Barrow's Goldeneye; Bufflehead; Red-breasted Merganser; Western, Red-necked, and Horned Grebes; and Common, Pacific, and Red-throated Loons when viewing conditions are good. The breakwater and pilings just south of the ferry terminal are usually covered in cormorants—mostly Double-crested and Pelagic, but there are usually a few Brandt's in the area, with the highest numbers arriving in winter. Because of heightened security around the ferry terminal in recent years, it is nearly impossible to get satisfactory views of the barnacle-encrusted mooring beams where the turnstone flocks are most often seen. The best way to see this is now either from the walk-on passenger lounge or on the ferry itself—particularly from the open vehicle decks. Otherwise, you can park in the short-term parking area (there is a small fee) and walk over to the fence near the southwest end of the terminal and have a look from there.

Finally, the second way for non-ferry traffic to bird the jetty is to drive 1.5 kilometres along the main jetty road (to the ferries), then pull off into the little parking area on the northwest side. This gives birders a place to scope the water between the ferry terminal and the Roberts Bank Coal Port. You will also notice a gravel spit and small lagoon on the ferry jetty side. This is known as **Compensation Lagoon**, which was created when they expanded the ferry terminal. In migration and during winter, flocks of dabbling ducks are often seen here, including a few Eurasian Wigeon. The resident Black Oystercatchers are found on the spit fairly regularly, along with resting cormorants and gulls and a variety of shorebirds, depending on the time of year.

Note: At the time of publication, the causeway out to the ferry terminal was undergoing some significant construction, so some of these directions may be out of date.

> ## Tsawwassen to Swartz Bay

The 1.5-hour sailing from Tsawwassen to Swartz Bay is the most popular route to Vancouver Island. After walking or driving onto the ferry, scan the pilings around the ferry docks for turnstone flocks. Black Turnstone will be most numerous (July to April), Surfbirds are also present during migration and occasionally in winter, and Ruddy Turnstones and Wandering Tattlers are rare but regular in May to August. All three species of cormorants can be seen roosting on the nearby breakwaters throughout most of the year (with Brandt's only being numerous in winter), and Brown Pelican is sometimes sighted in summer. The first leg of the voyage (essentially the entire open part of Georgia Strait before you reach the first of the Gulf Islands) passes through American waters, so anything seen out here can go straight onto your Washington State list! The murky waters here are usually fairly low on birdlife, but occasionally significant numbers of gulls, alcids, grebes, and loons can be seen, especially in spring and fall. Look out for Harbour Porpoise and Killer Whale (Orca) out here, especially as you get closer to the islands.

After crossing the strait, the ferry passes through a tight channel between Galiano Island to the north and Mayne Island to the south. This spot is known as **Active Pass**, which is often the best part of the journey for birds, because of the upwelling of nutrients created by tidal surges between the islands. Pigeon Guillemots are common throughout summer, and Rhinoceros Auklets and Common Murres are also seen regularly. In spring and fall, large numbers of Bonaparte's Gulls concentrate here, and a lucky birder might be able to pick out a rare Little Gull among them. From October to December, look between Active Pass and Swartz Bay for flocks of Ancient Murrelets, along with the more common Marbled Murrelet. Pacific Loons can also be abundant during migration, along with Common and Red-throated Loons and Western, Horned, and Red-necked Grebes. Tubenoses such as shearwaters or fulmars are extremely rare on this side of Vancouver Island, but the occasional Fork-tailed or Leach's Storm-Petrel is observed in fall.

> Boundary Bay

Internationally recognized as one of the most important shorebird and waterfowl stopover points in North America, **Boundary Bay** is worth a visit at any time of year. In winter, the bay is filled with tens of thousands of Northern Pintail, American Wigeon, Green-winged Teal, and other waterfowl, and the exposed mud flats harbour more than fifty thousand Dunlin, as well as many Sanderlings and Black-bellied Plovers. The expansive fields and marshland in the area attract densities of raptors that could rival any location in North America, including hundreds of Bald Eagles, followed by high numbers of Northern Harrier, Red-tailed Hawk, Rough-legged Hawk, Peregrine Falcon, Short-eared Owl in winter, along with the odd

Snowy Owl and Gyrfalcon. Spring and fall are also fantastic times to bird "The Bay," when an impressive variety of shorebirds and other species pass through. The northwest shore of Boundary Bay, which is the most commonly birded stretch, is accessed via six different roads that head due south from Hwy. 10/Ladner Trunk Road (see Map 12). Starting from the west, the first access road is **64th Street** (800 metres east of Hwy. 17 along the Ladner Trunk Road). Head south on 64th Street, following signs for Boundary Bay Dyke Access. From the Ladner Trunk Road, it's 4.5 kilometres to a small parking area; from here, you can walk or cycle along the gravel-surfaced dyke/levee (which follows nearly the entire bay in both directions) and scan for birds. At this access point, the water is usually far out, so shorebirds and waterfowl will be difficult to see. If you walk a few hundred metres to the east, there is a large house with a couple of ponds in front that can be prime spots for waterfowl in season—including locally uncommon or rare species such as Redhead and Canvasback. The main attraction of this particular location, however, is the raptors. Throughout the year, Red-tailed Hawks, Bald Eagles, and Northern Harriers are a common sight, but if you're visiting in fall or winter, scan the logs and grasslands for perched Short-eared Owls. Peregrine Falcons are also a regular sight along the entire bay as they hunt shorebirds. Although they are somewhat rare elsewhere in the Lower Mainland in winter, substantial numbers of Western Meadowlarks and Savannah Sparrows can be found here from November to March.

The next access road over is **72nd Street**. To reach it from 64th Street, you can take a shortcut by driving east on 36th Avenue, which runs perpendicular between the two streets. At high tide, look for shorebird flocks that often roost in the fields in this area. Once you hit 72nd Street, continue another 2.7 kilometres south to the parking area near the dyke. Like 64th Street,

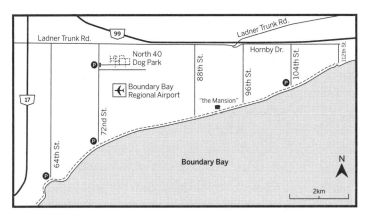

12 Boundary Bay

this is a great area for owls and hawks, and if the tide is high, you should be able to see a few water birds as well. The entire dyke pathway is paralleled by a number of ditches and bramble patches. These thickets can feature migrants in season, as well as sparrows and the odd warbler in winter, so be sure to look in both directions when walking along the dyke. Between November and March, you are almost guaranteed to see Short-eared Owl if you visit near dusk, and in irruption years, Snowy Owls will be conspicuous. The winter of 2011–12 was particularly good for this rare visitor from the north, when more than thirty were present! For the sake of the birds and the habitat, we advise that visitors stay on the dyke paths and refrain from walking down into the grass. With a little patience, there should be plenty of close-up opportunities along the dyke itself.

If you're visiting in spring or fall, you may want to turn east into the small parking area just north of the railway tracks along 72nd Street. This is the entrance to the **North 40 dog park**—an abandoned subdivision that has now gone wild and is fantastic for birding at any time of year but is particularly productive in spring and fall. Yes, there will be dogs, but the area is large enough that you should easily find a quiet corner to look for birds. Today, the "park" is a mixture of weedy meadows dotted with hawthorns and crabapples, along with some mature stands of mixed deciduous trees, making it a natural magnet for migrant passerines.

From the parking area, walk along the old roads that crisscross the area. A Western Scrub-Jay was once found in the line of oak trees in the park, and locally uncommon species like Bullock's Oriole and Lazuli Bunting are suspected to breed here each summer. Despite its position as an ideal migrant trap, the site gets very little coverage, so who knows what you might pick up?

In recent years, **96th and 104th Streets** have been the most rewarding spots for shorebirds on a rising tide (spring, late summer, and fall are the best times). To get to 96th Street, continue east along Ladner Trunk Road and turn right (south) on Hornby Drive at the first set of lights. Hornby continues east and parallels Hwy. 99, giving access to 96th, 104th, and 112th Streets. Along 96th Street, scan the telephone wires for Eurasian Collared-Doves. Like 112th Street, there is no "legal" place to park at the foot of 96th Street, but some birders get away with stashing their car on the south side of the dyke, where 96th meets the gravel jogging/bike path, then walking east or west. Instead, we recommend that you park at the foot of 104th Street, where there is ample space, then walk back toward 96th Street and beyond. From the end of 96th Street, walking west toward "**The Mansion**" (the only large house in the area) can be productive because there is a farm-ditch outflow into the bay. As the tide rises, this can be a fantastic spot for waterfowl, shorebirds, and gulls. Freshwater-loving species such as Greater and Lesser Yellowlegs, Long-billed Dowitcher, and Stilt Sandpiper (August) are more readily found here than elsewhere on the bay. The fields in this area can be full of geese and pipits in spring and fall, and occasionally golden-plovers (either species) and Buff-breasted Sandpipers (August to September) are spotted among the more common wet-field shorebirds such as Killdeer and Pectoral Sandpiper. Halfway between the foot of 96th and 104th Streets, there is a set of pilings where a similar outflow of fresh water attracts groups of yellowlegs and Pectoral Sandpipers in late summer and fall. Look through these shorebird groups for regular rarities such as Buff-breasted Sandpiper (late August to early September) and Sharp-tailed Sandpiper (mid-September to late October).

Working with the tides is critical when looking for shorebirds around 96th and 104th Streets. It's best to arrive at least 1.5 hours before high tide; if the tide is out, you'll see nothing but mud, and if it's all the way in, there is no shoreline for the birds to feed on. Remember that shorebird numbers and species diversity fluctuate throughout the year, with late July to early October being the best time. As the tide comes up, scan the water's edge to determine where the biggest flocks are concentrating. Try positioning yourself so that the tide slowly pushes them toward you. A scope is highly useful. Among the regular species, "megas" like Lesser Sand-Plover, Bristle-thighed Curlew, Far Eastern Curlew, Red-necked Stint, and Little Stint have all been found in the past—one can always dream, right?

The last access road to this section of Boundary Bay is **112th Street**. In the past, it was one of the best spots to be at high tide, but it seems that now the birds are usually farther west. Even so, it's always good to check. Like 96th Street, parking at the end of 112th Street is somewhat awkward, so it's best not to leave your vehicle for too long, and be sure not to block any driveways or tractor throughways. After birding 112th Street, return to the junction of Hornby Drive and Ladner Trunk Road; depending on where you want to go, you can either head back east on Ladner Trunk or merge onto Hwy. 99 (west to Vancouver, east to White Rock and the U.S. border).

Note: The fields behind the Esso gas station often hold large numbers of loafing gulls in winter. About 99 percent of these will be Glaucous-winged, but you may get lucky and pick out something different, such as a Glaucous or Slaty-backed.

SURREY, WHITE ROCK, AND LANGLEY

> Serpentine Fen

This network of freshwater sloughs is a great place to look for marsh birds year round. American Bittern, Virginia Rail, and Marsh Wren are present at any time of year, whereas waterfowl numbers are highest in winter but still impressive at other times. From Hwy. 99, take Exit 10 north for the King George Boulevard (99A). After 600 metres, turn left onto 44th Avenue; the gravel parking area for **Serpentine Fen** will come up on the left. A series of walking trails circles and bisects the wetlands, and there are several viewing towers from which to scope the surrounding area. The northern end of the fen borders on the dyked Serpentine River, where you can usually find a few additional water birds in winter, such as Red-breasted Merganser, Common Goldeneye, or even Red-throated Loon.

> Mud Bay

From Serpentine Fen, return to the King George Boulevard, then turn left (north) and drive for 1.2 kilometres before exiting right for Colebrook Road. Turn left on Colebrook and proceed under the highway, heading west for 3.8 kilometres. If the fields along Colebrook are flooded, it may be worth stopping to scan for shorebirds and ducks. After 3.8 kilometres, turn left (south) on 127A Street/Railway Road, following signs for **Mud Bay Park**. From the parking area, walk the trails around the nearby marshes and fields and then out to the dyke along Boundary Bay. The best times to visit this area are in winter

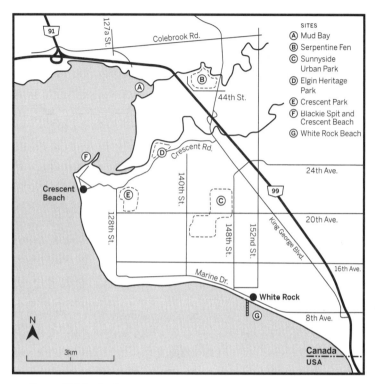

13 Surrey/White Rock

and during spring and fall migration, when thousands of shorebirds and ducks can be seen along the foreshore. Tides will be a
factor in determining the mix of birds seen (for example, high
tide is best for waterfowl to be in close, whereas shorebirds
need some exposed mud to forage on). In winter, several Eurasian Wigeon (as many as fifty) can be seen among the massive
flocks of American Wigeon, Mallards, Northern Pintail, and
Green-winged Teal. Be sure to look through the teal for the rare
but regular Eurasian "Common" Teal, which sports a horizon-
tal white bar above the flanks, instead of the vertical spur on
American Green-wings.

> Sunnyside Woods

Right in the middle of South Surrey is the little-known **Sunnyside Acres Urban Forest Park**. Look for parking along 24th Avenue in South Surrey (west of Hwy. 99A/King George Boulevard), where the road passes the park. The woods will be obvious, as there are few large patches of Douglas-fir forest in South Surrey. The signed Chickadee Loop and Douglas-fir Trail are two of the birdiest trails in the section north of 24th Avenue. In late spring and early summer, birders can expect not only many western specialties, such as Pacific-slope Flycatcher, Pacific Wren, Bewick's Wren, Anna's Hummingbird, Bushtit, and Chestnut-backed Chickadee, but also a variety of other forest birds, such as Pileated and Hairy Woodpeckers, Golden-crowned Kinglets, Olive-sided Flycatcher, and Hermit Thrush.

> Elgin Pond and Elgin Heritage Park

From the King George Boulevard (99A), head west on Crescent Road; after 1.7 kilometres, you will see a sign for **Elgin Heritage Park** on the right (north) side. You can either turn in here and park or proceed another 350 metres to the main parking lot for **Elgin Pond** (essentially the western extension of Elgin Heritage Park). Most birders park near the main pond at the west end of the park, but since both ends are connected by a footpath, it doesn't really matter. Elgin Pond itself is a prime spot to see waders such as yellowlegs and dowitchers up close (in season), especially during high tide. Other freshwater shorebirds such as Pectoral Sandpiper, Sharp-tailed Sandpiper, and Stilt Sandpiper occasionally occur, and Green Herons are sometimes present in late summer. Virginia Rail and Sora, as well as Marsh Wren and Common Yellowthroat, can be found in the nearby marshy areas. The neighbouring Nicomekl River can be a good spot for grebes and waterfowl, especially in winter—check the flocks of

Green-winged Teal for the Eurasian "Common" form, a rare but regular winter visitor. The surrounding deciduous trees and coniferous forest can harbour large numbers of migrants in spring and fall and many others year round, such as Chestnut-backed Chickadee, Steller's Jay, and Purple Finch.

> Crescent Park

Crescent Park (signed off Crescent Road, 1.7 kilometres west of Elgin Pond) is perfect for a leisurely stroll or a picnic lunch—and the birding is good, too! It is especially attractive to visiting birders, as it boasts a mix of Pacific Northwest birds that can be found among stands of towering Douglas-fir and Western Red Cedar. Band-tailed Pigeon, Hutton's Vireo, Bewick's Wren, Pacific Wren, Chestnut-backed Chickadee, and Spotted Towhee are present most of the year, and Pacific-slope Flycatcher, Cassin's Vireo, and Black-throated Gray Warbler are some of the specialty summer breeders. Many other forest species are present throughout the year, so take your time along the trails and enjoy this small patch of old-growth forest.

> Blackie Spit and Crescent Beach

Like Iona Island and Reifel Refuge, **Blackie Spit** is a very popular birding site—and for good reason. Follow Crescent Road west into the community of Crescent Beach (stay right on Sullivan Street after crossing the railroad tracks). Turn right on McBride Avenue and drive all the way to the end until you come to an obvious parking lot at the entrance to Blackie Spit Park. It's usually best to visit at or near high tide, since many of the water birds will be closer to shore. In most winters, a Long-billed Curlew and several Marbled Godwits can be found in and around the spit, so inspect the shoreline carefully. Small flocks of Whimbrel pass through in spring and fall, and the occasional Willet has been found. For the most part, however, Black-bellied Plovers, dowitchers, and yellowlegs are the most regular shorebirds, and a variety of peeps occur mainly in migration season. In addition to checking Blackie Spit itself, scan for shorebirds and other roosting water birds on the hummocky islands and banks across the water to the northeast (a scope is handy for this). From fall until early spring, large numbers of dabbling ducks can be seen around Blackie Spit—mainly Northern Pintail, American Wigeon, and Green-winged Teal, with a few Eurasian Wigeon mixed in. At high tide, many loons and grebes can be seen off the west side of the spit (outside of summer), and Caspian Terns are common during the breeding season.

After walking the spit itself, take some time to walk the trails leading southeast along the edge of the estuary. This is a fantastic area for shorebirds and waterfowl, and the mixed scrub and trees can be good places for songbirds, especially during migration periods. Purple Martins nest in the boxes provided for them on the pilings along the Nicomekl River and are present from April through August. You can walk along the dyke toward the railway bridge, then turn southwest after crossing the small channel, and enter the **Dunsmuir Community Gardens** to find sparrows and other migrants. From there, you can either retrace your steps or head back via Sullivan Street and Dunsmuir Road.

Crescent Beach itself (many access points along the northwest and western edge of town) can be worth a look as well, especially in spring and fall, when gulls, terns, loons, and scoters are passing through. Large numbers of sea ducks and other water birds are present throughout the winter, including Common, Pacific, and Red-throated Loons.

> White Rock Beach

The waterfront along Marine Drive in White Rock, particularly in and around the main **White Rock pier**, is often full of loons, sea ducks, gulls, and shorebirds. Although migration season is always a great time to visit this area, it's probably most noted for its winter residents. All three species of scoter can be reliably found here in winter (Black Scoter being very scarce elsewhere in the Vancouver area), along with several Long-tailed Ducks. Rare elsewhere around Vancouver, both Eared Grebe and Ruddy Duck are present in most winters—usually close to the pier. The three regular species of loons are around through the winter, as well as large numbers of Horned, Red-necked, and Western Grebes. It may also be worthwhile to check the gull flocks that loaf along the beach and grassy areas; Glaucous-winged and Mew are most common in winter, but California and Bonaparte's pass through in large numbers, and the occasional Western, Herring, and Thayer's Gull can be found in winter.

> ## Campbell Valley Regional Park

Located south of Langley and east of White Rock, **Campbell Valley Regional Park** provides an oasis for birds and birders alike. Surrounded by farmland and the expanding urban centre of Langley, this large patch of riparian woodland and marshes is a great spot to see a variety of birds at any time of year. Late spring through early summer is the best period to visit the park, when breeding species are all back and singing vigorously.

To reach the main parking area from White Rock, proceed east on 16th Avenue, then turn right into the signed parking lot after passing 200th Street/Carvoth Road. If you're approaching from Langley, head south on 200th Street then turn left (east) onto 16th Avenue. There is also parking along the west side of the park, off 8th Avenue. In spring and summer, listen for Black-throated Gray Warblers in the maple and cottonwood trees right beside the parking lot, then proceed into the trail system that passes through mixed forests and wetlands. This is a fantastic spot to get a cross-section of Pacific Northwest breeding passerines. Between May and July, look and listen for Rufous Hummingbird, Olive-sided Flycatcher, Western Wood-Pewee, Pacific-slope Flycatcher, Hutton's Vireo, Cassin's Vireo, Warbling Vireo, Red-eyed Vireo (local), Swainson's Thrush, Townsend's Warbler, Wilson's Warbler, Spotted Towhee, Black-headed Grosbeak, and Western Tanager (all during spring and summer). Anna's Hummingbird and Downy, Hairy, and Pileated Woodpeckers are present year round, along with Steller's Jay, Bewick's Wren, Pacific Wren, Marsh Wren, Brown Creeper, and Dark-eyed Juncos. Varied Thrush might be seen at any time of year but are most common in winter.

BURNABY AND COQUITLAM

> Burnaby Mountain Conservation Area

Around 5 kilometres east of the PNE fairgrounds (and Hwy. 1 overpass), East Hastings Street turns into Burnaby Mountain Parkway. Here the road leaves the suburbs of Burnaby and enters a forested area. Look for Centennial Way on the left side of the road and take it all the way up to the Horizons Restaurant parking lot. If you're approaching from the east or perhaps points south, take the Gaglardi Way exit north off either Hwy. 1 or the Lougheed Highway (Hwy. 7); this will soon merge into the Burnaby Mountain Parkway (as long as you don't go up to the university). Turn north at Centennial Way and park at the end. If the gate is closed, park on the west side of Centennial Way, 200 metres before the restaurant.

Burnaby Mountain can be a pleasant place to bird at any time of year, especially on clear days when you can get a fantastic view of Burrard Inlet and Greater Vancouver. Spring is usually the best time to visit, as many of the local breeders, such as Swainson's Thrush, Pacific-slope Flycatcher, Olive-sided Flycatcher, Hutton's Vireo, Black-throated Gray Warbler, Wilson's Warbler,

Northwestern Crow

and Spotted Towhee, are singing. Because Burnaby Mountain is a high point of land, covered in mature forest habitat and surrounded by urban sprawl, it is a natural "migrant trap," when northerly winds or heavy rains push migrants down out of the sky in April and May. During these times, hundreds of songbirds, including flycatchers, vireos, thrushes, and warblers, can sometimes be seen in the trees and shrubs near the restaurant. With these fall-outs comes the occasional rarity, such as Hermit Warbler or Flammulated Owl—so be vigilant. Once up there, you'll see that there is plenty of room to branch out and explore. Perhaps the most productive trail for flocking birds is right at the top of the ridge behind the restaurant. This section of the Trans-Canada Trail passes by a large water tank and eventually ends up at the Simon Fraser University campus. Another bird to look out for here, particularly from March to June, is Sooty Grouse. In the Vancouver area, this is the only place south of Burrard Inlet where Sooty Grouse can still be found. Listen for the low-pitched display hoots of the male in spring, and with some luck, you may bump into him in the middle of the trail! Early morning is best, before too many people have been on the upper trail.

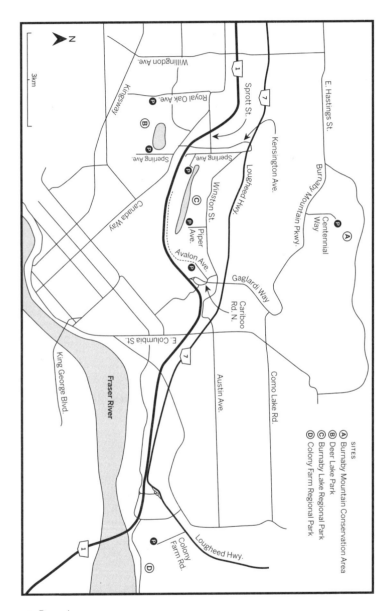

N

3km

Willingdon Ave.

Kingsway

Royal Oak Ave.

Sprott St.

1

7

Kensington Ave.

E. Hastings St.

Sperling Ave.

Sperling Ave.

Winston St.

Lougheed Hwy.

Burnaby Mountain Pkwy.

Centennial Way

Ⓐ

Canada Way

Ⓒ

Piper Ave.

Avalon Ave.

Gaglardi Way

Cariboo Rd. N.

E. Columbia St.

7

King George Blvd.

Fraser River

Austin Ave.

Como Lake Rd.

1

Colony Farm Rd.

Lougheed Hwy.

Ⓓ

SITES

Ⓐ Burnaby Mountain Conservation Area
Ⓑ Deer Lake Park
Ⓒ Burnaby Lake Regional Park
Ⓓ Colony Farm Regional Park

⟩ Burnaby Lake Regional Park

There are three main access points to this elongated park. At the east end, the Avalon Entrance is off Gaglardi Way (south from Lougheed Hwy.). Turn right onto Cariboo Road North, then left onto Avalon Street (signed for the Burnaby Equestrian Club), which dead-ends at a large parking area. On the north side, and the most popular area with birders and the public, is Piper Spit at the south end of Piper Avenue. Access Piper Avenue by turning south off Winston Street. Drive to the end of Piper Avenue, parking either in front of the Nature House or on the west side of Piper, just before the Nature House turnaround. The most westerly entrance, the Burnaby Lake Pavilion, is off Sperling Avenue on Roberts Street, accessed from Kensington Avenue via Sprott Street. Drive south on Sperling Avenue, past the rugby fields, turn east onto Roberts Street, and continue to the parking at the end of the road.

If this is your first visit to Burnaby Lake, we recommend that you park at the main entrance near **Piper Spit**. There is a feeder beside the park headquarters that between fall and spring regularly attracts Spotted Towhee, Golden-crowned Sparrow, White-crowned Sparrow, Fox Sparrow, Song Sparrow, and Dark-eyed Junco. There is a boardwalk that leads out to the spit itself. This is usually a popular duck-feeding area—mostly for Mallards—but throughout most of the year, there are also many Wood Duck and Green-winged Teal that have grown accustomed to people, allowing for fantastic views of these otherwise cagey species. During migration season, shorebirds are often seen feeding on exposed muddy areas east of the boardwalk. Long-billed Dowitcher, Greater and Lesser Yellowlegs, and Least and Spotted Sandpipers are probably the most common species, but many others have been recorded over the years. Scan the lake for Pied-billed Grebe, Horned Grebe (in fall and winter), Double-crested Cormorant, Hooded Merganser, and a variety of other duck species (depending on the season). Common Yellowthroat, Marsh Wren, and Willow Flycatcher are all common breeding species along the fringes of the lake, and the walking trails surrounding the lake offer an appealing mix of coniferous and deciduous-loving species, from woodpeckers and hawks to kinglets and chickadees.

Another part of the lake where you might pick up a few additional species is at the west end (mentioned above) off Sperling Avenue. This takes you to the parking area for the **Burnaby Lake Rowing Club**. There are walking trails from here, but we recommend walking up onto the rowing club wharf and scanning the lake and surrounding shoreline. Check any exposed mud on the far side for migrating shorebirds. Virtually all the species mentioned from the Piper Spit area can also be found here—you just have to check.

> Deer Lake Park

If you're coming from either the Grandview Highway or the North Shore, take Exit 29A for Willingdon Avenue South; merge onto Willingdon then turn left on Canada Way, and after 1.5 kilometres, turn right on Royal Oak Avenue. After passing Deer Lake Parkway, Royal Oak Avenue goes up a hill; you will have to head up the hill and turn around where possible, as the parking area for the west end of **Deer Lake Park** is only accessible by northbound traffic. As you head back north, look for an unmarked parking lot on the right side, 200 metres south of Deer Lake Parkway. From this location, walk west. There are park maps at several kiosks in the area.

The main draw of this park is the open meadows west of the lake. This is one of the few areas in urban Greater Vancouver where Northern Harriers and Ring-necked Pheasants breed. Lazuli Buntings are uncommon but regular in spring and may breed in some years. Common Yellowthroats and both Sora and Virginia Rails can be heard and sometimes seen in the wet areas, and in fall and winter, look through flocks of juncos and Song Sparrows for rarities such as Swamp and Harris's Sparrow. Locals put out seed along many of the forest trails in this area, which attracts Spotted Towhees, Fox Sparrows, Dark-eyed Juncos, and Song Sparrows. The forest itself can showcase all of the typical species mentioned at Burnaby Lake, including Hutton's Vireo and Black-headed Grosbeak.

The other principal way to access the park is from the east side of the lake at the children's playground along Sperling Avenue, south off Canada Way (see Map 14). In fall and winter, this is a great spot to work on your gull ID skills. Ring-billed Gulls are usually most numerous, followed by Glaucous-winged Gulls and various Glaucous-winged x Western x Herring hybrids. Thayer's, Herring, California, and Mew Gulls are also regular in small numbers. The gulls are here partly because of all the duck feeders, so expect a few ducks, too. Mallards are most common, but outside of summer, expect Gadwall, Green-winged Teal, and Northern Shoveler in the area. By scanning the lake and the lily pads along the shoreline, you may see divers such as Hooded and Common Merganser, as well as Bufflehead, Ring-necked Duck, and Lesser Scaup (all are most regular from fall to spring). More trails lead from this point to the forest on both sides of the lake.

> Colony Farm Regional Park

Colony Farm was set aside in 1996 as a designated site for extensive wildlife habitat enhancement projects, including tree and hedgerow planting and wetland creation. Habitat management programs have helped to control invasive plants and allow for better habitat for migrating and nesting birds. From Hwy. 1, take Exit 44 and follow signs to Lougheed Highway (Hwy. 7) east. Continue travelling east on Lougheed Highway to the traffic light at Colony Farm Road. Turn right and continue 1 kilometre to the main parking lot. From the east along Lougheed, travel through Coquitlam past the lights at Pitt River Road and Riverview Hospital. Turn left at the traffic lights at Colony Farm Road; the parking lot is on your left, about 1 kilometre from Hwy. 7. There are several other places to park to access different sections of the park. For a detailed trail map, visit metrovancouver.org, then follow the following links: Services > Regional Parks & Seymour Conservation Reserve > Regional Parks > Colony Farm.

There are 8.7 kilometres of walking trails through a mix of wetlands, grassy meadows, shrub land, and riparian forest. Colony Farm can be a great place to bird at any time of year, but spring and fall, when migrant songbirds are passing through, are probably the most exciting times. The Vancouver Avian Research Centre operates a migration monitoring station in the park and welcomes volunteers (for more information, visit birdvancouver. com/visit.html).

In addition to the usual mix of lowland Vancouver species (Downy Woodpecker, Northwestern Crow, Bushtit, Spotted Towhee), Colony Farm (like Pitt Meadows) harbours a few species more typical of the Interior. These include Lazuli Bunting (open brushy country), Gray Catbird (dense thickets), and Eastern Kingbird (same habitat as the bunting). Numbers are small enough that none of these species is guaranteed on a short visit, but with luck and patience, you may be rewarded. Other regular rarities (not seen every year) include Yellow-breasted Chat and Indigo Bunting.

PITT MEADOWS AND HARRISON

For those travelling from Vancouver to Hope and points eastward, Hwy. 7 provides a pleasant alternate route that stays north of the Fraser and straddles the foothills of the Coast Mountains. Despite a long history of farming in the area, there remains a large portion of healthy riparian and marshland habitat that hosts a mix of birds in all seasons. As a result, you can find several breeding species that are quite rare closer to Vancouver and the Fraser Delta. These include Green Heron, Least Flycatcher, Eastern Kingbird, Gray Catbird, and American Redstart. Despite its fantastic natural value, this area is relatively under-birded. So whether you're looking for a slower-paced "scenic route" to the Interior or a new patch to bird in the Lower Mainland, we highly recommend exploring this area—both at the specific locales we outline and beyond.

> Grant Narrows

Your best bet to see some of the specialties mentioned above are the marshy thickets of the **Grand Narrows** area, now managed by the province and the Katzie First Nation. From Hwy. 1, take Exit 58 for 200 Street, following signs for the Golden Ears Bridge and Pitt Meadows/Maple Ridge. After crossing the bridge, stay on Golden Ears Way to the intersection with 203 Street (about 1.7 kilometres after the Hwy. 7 overpass). Turn left and proceed to the first stop sign at the intersection with Dewdney Trunk Road. To make life difficult, there are two Dewdney Trunk Roads in Maple Ridge: one just 200 metres north of Hwy. 7 and the one you want—2.3 kilometres north of Hwy. 7, often called Old Dewdney Trunk Road. Turn right onto Dewdney Trunk Road and proceed 0.8 kilometres to Neaves Road, where you will turn left and proceed north. If you're approaching from the west (Hwy. 7 from Port Coquitlam), take Hwy. 7 to the intersection of Harris Road (there is a McDonald's on the southwest corner), turn left, and proceed to the first stop sign. Turn right onto Dewdney Trunk Road, then travel about 3.3 kilometres to Neaves Road (there is a large white house on the northwest corner). Turn left onto Neaves. And finally, if you're travelling from points east (Maple Ridge or Mission), head west along Hwy. 7 to 203 Street, turn right on 203 Street, and proceed north to (Old) Dewdney Trunk Road. Directions from here are the same as above.

From the beginning of **Neaves Road**, drive north for 4.1 kilometres. This stretch of road used to be home to open-country species such as raptors and sparrows, but because of widespread conversion from dairy farming to berry production, a lot of this area has lost its birding value. In winter, it is worthwhile to head west on **McNeil Road** or east on **Thompson Road**, as there are still some old fields to check for hawks, harriers, falcons, and shrikes. If you're visiting during the breeding season, try the end of Thompson Road for Least Flycatcher. Otherwise, proceed north along **Rannie Road** for 1.8 kilometres to where it crosses **Sturgeon Slough**. Eastern Kingbirds are usually present here in summer, and the slough can host waterfowl between fall and spring. Great Blue Herons are ever present, whereas American Bitterns and Green Herons are sometimes spotted by sharp-eyed or lucky birders. Continue up Rannie Road and after 2.3 kilometres you will come alongside the **Pitt Polder Sandhill Crane Reserve**. Drive straight to where the road turns to the right. For the next 2 kilometres or more, the wetland area on the left-hand side (river side) is known as **Catbird Slough**—home to, you guessed it: Gray Catbirds! About 1.3 kilometres from the right turn there is a thicker patch of trees and shrubs along Catbird Slough where American Redstarts occasionally nest. After checking this area carefully, proceed to the parking lot at **Grant Narrows**, where the **Pitt River** flows out of **Pitt Lake**; it's always worth scanning this area for water birds. Then cross the road and walk down the "**Nature Dyke**" that heads southeast along a narrow slough. The riparian thickets along this trail provide the best chance at finding American Redstarts and Least Flycatchers, as well as the more common

Eastern Kingbirds, Willow Flycatchers, Yellow Warblers, and Marsh Wrens. In spring and fall, it may be worthwhile to scour the southern edge of Pitt Lake, from Grant Narrows east to the end of the gravel dyke at the base of the mountains. Snow Buntings, Lapland Longspurs, and Vesper Sparrows have all been reported along this stretch.

> Chehalis Flats

As you travel along Hwy. 7 between Maple Ridge and Harrison, you will pass countless sloughs, oxbows, and flooded fields, all with the potential for an assortment of waterfowl—particularly in winter and early spring. There are too many locations to cover in this entry, and they can all be productive. Stop wherever you like, as long as it's safe to pull off. In addition to the wintering geese, swans, and ducks, this area is also famous for its Bald Eagle concentrations. Each year in late fall and early winter, these large scavengers gather in huge numbers, sometimes in the thousands, to feast on the carcasses of salmon that are left over from the spawning season.

One of the best areas to see these big numbers is at **Eagle Point** overlooking **Chehalis Flats**. Approximately 30 kilometres east of Mission, turn left (northeast) on Morris Valley Road, just after passing a large eddy in the Harrison River. If you're coming from the east, turn right onto this road, just after crossing over the Harrison River (about 15 kilometres from Agassiz). Drive north along Morris Valley Road for more than 1 kilometre until you get to a new subdivision. Park at the mailboxes, then walk down the straight gravel trail toward the flats. You will reach a trail that parallels the river channels and turning right will take you to a raised platform from which you can scan for eagles and other species. In the summer of 2010, a Great Egret was found here; then later on that same year, a Boreal Owl was found roosting in a nearby cedar tree.

> Harrison Lake

As much as it is a tourist destination, the waterfront of **Harrison Hot Springs** is also a great place to go birding. Increased coverage in recent years has shown that the south end of the lake is an important staging area for both waterfowl and gull migration. Therefore, spring and fall are the best times to visit, and if the weather is clear, the azure lake complemented by the surrounding snow-covered peaks can be breathtaking. The waterfront can also be a rarity trap—particularly around the lagoon and near the boat launch. Both Northern Mockingbird and Sage Thrasher have been recorded in recent years, and Gray-crowned Rosy-Finch and Snow Bunting are becoming annual in fall and winter, now that people are looking. Say's Phoebe, Mountain Bluebird, and Vesper Sparrows are also regular during migration.

ABBOTSFORD AND CHILLIWACK

> Mill Lake

Located in the heart of Abbotsford, this small lake is an excellent local spot to observe waterfowl in winter and spring, as well as a few songbird migrants in spring and fall. From Hwy. 1, take Exit 90 for McCallum Road (north). Continue north past Marshall Avenue, make a left on Cannon Avenue, then stay left on Bevan Avenue. Follow Bevan through the S-bend, then turn into the parking lot on the right side, 400 metres past Ware Street.

Virtually all the freshwater ducks can be seen here in spring migration, including locally uncommon or rare species such as Blue-winged and Cinnamon Teal, Canvasback, Redhead, and Ruddy Duck. As many as thirty Ruddy Ducks can be seen here in March, when migrants start to pass through. Green Herons are sometimes encountered in summer, and a few other breeders that visitors might be interested in are Anna's Hummingbird, Violet-green Swallow, Bushtit, Bewick's Wren, and

Spotted Towhee. It's possible to see both Pacific Wren and Varied Thrush outside of summer.

> ## Sumas Prairie

Between the city of Abbotsford and the Vedder Canal (just west of Chilliwack), lies a flat, fertile plain known as **Sumas Prairie**. This is the former site of Sumas Lake, a huge wetland that was drained in 1924 to create more arable farmland and to control mosquito numbers in the area. Historically, Sumas Lake was one of the most important wetland complexes in the province for breeding, migrating, and wintering water birds. Although the habitat has changed dramatically, this area is still a great place to observe waterfowl and raptors in winter and during migration season, as well as shorebirds in spring and fall. March to early May is the best time to see waterfowl, whereas April (and sometimes fall, depending on water levels) is best for shorebirds. The key factor for the water birds is, of course, water. After heavy rains, the fields become flooded and this is when high numbers of swans, geese, ducks, herons, gulls, and shorebirds move in to feed.

From Hwy. 1, take Exit 92 (southbound) for Sumas Way (Hwy. 11), then turn left on Vye Road and continue straight for 5.9 kilometres to the junction of Vye and Coal Roads. From this junction, you can do a basic 17-kilometre-long loop. Winter and spring are the best times to bird this area, but if the fields are flooded, late summer and fall can be good, too. From this junction, continue east on Vye to Powerhouse Road, where you will turn left. At Wells Line Road turn right, then follow the road as it bends to the north and meets Campbell Road, where you will turn left and return to Coal Road, which will take you back south to Vye Road. If you want, there are plenty of other roads to explore in the area. If you're visiting in winter, expect to find flocks of Trumpeter Swans, various geese, and Glaucous-winged, Ring-billed, and Mew Gulls, as well as a selection of raptors, including Bald Eagle, Red-tailed Hawk, Rough-legged Hawk, Peregrine Falcon, Merlin, and American Kestrel. In recent winters, a Gyrfalcon has been seen regularly.

> Great Blue Heron Nature Reserve

This reserve is named for the large colony of Great Blue Herons located within it. An interpretive centre provides information about the breeding biology of these majestic yet sometimes awkward fish nabbers. From Hwy. 1, take Exit 109 for Yale Road West (eastbound). Once on Yale Road, take the second right onto Chadsey Road. Follow Chadsey Road for 3.1 kilometres, then when you get to a T-junction at Keith Wilson Road, turn left and head east for 1.6 kilometres, then turn right on Sumas Prairie Road, follow this to the end, and park at the reserve headquarters. In addition to the herons, expect a variety of waterfowl at any time of year, including Wood Duck, Common and Hooded Mergansers, Pied-billed Grebe, and American Coot (among many others). There are plenty of other species present, depending on the time of year—particularly marsh specialties such as Virginia Rail, Marsh Wren, Common Yellowthroat, and Willow Flycatcher. With birds like Eurasian Wigeon, Black-and-White Warbler, and Western Scrub-Jay on the checklist, the possibilities are wide open.

> Sardis Pond

Like Mill Lake, Sardis Pond is conveniently located (just across Hwy. 1 from downtown Chilliwack) and is a nice little spot for waterfowl and migrant songbirds. From Hwy. 1, take Exit 119 for Vedder Road (southbound). Once on Vedder, proceed south for nearly 2 kilometres before turning left (east) on Manual Road. The parking lot for **Sardis Park** will be obvious where the road curves to the right. From the heron reserve, head west on Keith

Wilson Road, turn left (north) onto Vedder Road, then follow the same instructions.

The main attraction here in winter is the high numbers of Cackling Geese that frequent the pond between feeding sessions out in the fields. Since the mid-2000s, the wintering population in the Fraser Valley has swelled into the thousands, and up to two hundred can be seen at a time, bathing in Sardis Pond. Canada Geese are, of course, common as well (there should be a mix of subspecies to study), and Greater White-fronted Geese and the odd Snow Goose may also turn up in migration season or winter. In April 2005, a lone Brant was found here! In addition to the geese, there is usually a variety of duck species present in spring, fall, and winter, and gulls also use the pond to bathe. Glaucous-winged is the dominant gull species throughout most of the year, but at least seven other species have been recorded, including an adult Iceland Gull that appeared in February 2008. As with many coastal areas, summer is a relatively quiet time for birding; however, there are still a few nice birds around, including Green Heron, Rufous Hummingbird, Bushtit, Yellow Warbler, and the odd Black-throated Gray Warbler.

> Cultus Lake

Cultus Lake Provincial Park is well-signed off Hwy. 1 and is the same exit you would take for Sardis Pond (Exit 119, Vedder Road). It's a lovely spot for fishing and can provide visiting birders with a mix of forest birds, such as woodpeckers, Hammond's Flycatcher, Hutton's Vireo (getting sparse this far east), Cassin's Vireo, Townsend's and Black-throated Gray Warblers, Western Tanager, and Pine Siskin. During migration and in winter, a few water birds can be expected out on the lake. In winter, it is often worthwhile to visit the lake an hour before dusk, when thousands of gulls come in from around the Fraser Valley to bathe and roost. Among the numerous

Glaucous-wings, look for Thayer's, Herring, Western, and Glaucous—or perhaps something unexpected.

> Mount Cheam

For the best views of the Fraser Valley and a chance to find alpine species such as White-tailed Ptarmigan and Gray-crowned Rosy-Finch, driving and hiking up the prominent peak of **Mount Cheam** southeast of Chilliwack is a fantastic way to spend a sunny day in summer or fall. To get there, take Exit 119 off Hwy. 1 for Vedder Road (southbound). Drive all the way to the Vedder River, then turn left on Chilliwack Lake Road (before crossing the bridge). Zero your odometer at the beginning of the Chilliwack Lake Road, then turn left at 26.7 kilometres onto the Foley Forest Service Road. Zero your odometer again and drive 2 kilometres, cross the bridge over Foley Creek, then turn left at the T-junction. After 2 kilometres more, cross the Chipmunk Creek Bridge and take the next right uphill (passing the gravel pit on your left) on Chipmunk Creek Forest Service Road. This is a rough road with many water bars (the culverts have been dug out) but not very steep for the first 7 kilometres. Keep right after crossing Chipmunk Creek. The road is rougher and steeper (four-wheel drive and good clearance are recommended) for the final 4 kilometres to the parking area. Orange squares mark the hiking route (9.5 kilometres round trip).

July to September is by far the easiest time to hike to the summit (2,112 metres/6,929 feet), since snow levels will be minimal. Bird diversity is high but, unfortunately, so is people traffic. We recommend that you avoid weekends, particularly in August and early September, when there can be as many as fifty hikers plus dogs along the route. Starting early will greatly enhance your chances of seeing the most birds. If you drive up just before dawn, you have a decent chance of seeing Barred Owls hunting along the roadside. Also watch for Ruffed Grouse on the road up, then Sooty Grouse along the upper reaches of the road and farther up the hiking route. Northern Pygmy-Owl and Northern Goshawk have both been seen near the parking area, along with the usual mix of forest species, including Olive-sided Flycatcher, Varied Thrush, Red-breasted Nuthatch, both kinglet species, several warblers, Dark-eyed Junco, Evening Grosbeak, Pine Siskin, Red Crossbill, and occasionally White-winged Crossbill. American Dippers have been seen in the stream 1 kilometre into the hike.

The real attraction of this mountain is, of course, the alpine birds. Once above treeline, look and listen for Horned Larks and American Pipits during the breeding season, and watch for Gray-crowned Rosy-Finches on or near the remaining patches of snow (this species is nearly guaranteed as long as there are still some snow fields around). Golden Eagles nest somewhere in the area, along with one of their top preys: ptarmigan! Rock Ptarmigan have been recorded on a few occasions (and have bred), but the most likely species is White-tailed. It seems that sightings are more frequent earlier in the season, which could have something to do with the increase in people traffic later on in the summer (possibly pushing the ptarmies to nearby Lady and Knight Peaks). If you visit in June or early July, be prepared to hike through much more snow to reach the top—but at least it will increase your chances of seeing both ptarmigan and Rosy-Finches. Regardless, the views from the top are spectacular on clear days and are worth the trip on their own. In berry season, watch out for Black Bears along the trail.

Note: For a less busy but equally stunning site for White-tailed Ptarmigan, you may want to try Needle Peak, described at the end of the Hope section below.

> Island 22 Regional Park

Along with the Hope Airport, **Island 22** north of Chilliwack is considered one of the Fraser Valley's premier migrant traps. From Hwy. 1, take Exit 119 for Vedder Road (northbound), which will merge into Yale Road West. After 3.1 kilometres, turn left on Young Road and follow this for 2.5 kilometres before turning left on Cartmell Road, following signs for Island 22 Regional Park.

The best times to visit are in May and from August to September, when songbird migration is in full swing, but the park can be a productive site both in winter also. Breeding species here include Ruffed Grouse; Great Horned Owl; Downy, Hairy, and Pileated Woodpeckers; Western Wood-Pewee; Willow Flycatcher; Red-eyed Vireo; Northwestern Crow; Tree and Violet-green Swallows; Black-capped Chickadee; Bushtit; Bewick's Wren; Swainson's Thrush; Yellow Warbler; Black-headed Grosbeak; and Red-winged Blackbird. Lazuli Buntings nest in open areas at both ends of the park, and American Redstarts will often show up in June to set up territories but usually don't stay. Most of the park's rarities have shown up during fall migration, which is the time when you can find the greatest variety of songbirds in the park (August to November). These include Philadelphia Vireo, Northern Mockingbird, Tennessee Warbler, Blackpoll Warbler, and Chestnut-sided Warbler. There is a pond near the entrance gate that can host a variety of waterfowl. It's worth checking out the boat-launch area and the gravel bars out in the river, where most of the park's shorebirds have been recorded.

> East Chilliwack Farm Fields and Promontory Landfill

The farmlands of **East Chilliwack** are similar to Sumas Prairie in that waterfowl and shorebird numbers and diversity can be eye popping after periods of rain. March to May is best, but fall and winter can also produce a large bounty of mud- and grass-loving water birds, and raptor numbers in winter and during migration can be impressive, too. To check out some of the best roads during these peak periods, take Exit 123 south on Prest Road. Turn left on Prairie Central Road, then proceed east before turning down either Banford or Gibson Roads. McGuire Road runs parallel to Prairie Central below these roads. In spring and fall, the key is to look for the flooded fields, then scan closely for shorebirds. Large flocks of waterfowl should be obvious (when present), both during migration and in winter, when large groups of Trumpeter Swans and Cackling Geese also join in the fun. Look for concentrations of gulls, too, that may contain something out of the ordinary (Slaty-backed Gull has been recorded). You would be surprised how many species of shorebirds have been recorded in this area; you just need to hit it on the right day under ideal conditions. Ferruginous Hawk, Prairie Falcon, Black-necked Stilt, American Golden-Plover, and Buff-breasted Sandpiper are some of the rarities that have turned up in the area over recent years.

For some good winter gulling, a quick check of the **Promontory Landfill** may be worthwhile. Head to the south end of Prest Road, and 950 metres after passing Bailey Road (as you drive up a hill), there is a small pull-off area near some barricades. From here, you can walk to the edge of the hill and look down onto the landfill. Thousands of Glaucous-winged Gulls use this dump in the winter. Among them are usually a few Herring, Thayer's, Western (scarce but always a couple around), and Glaucous Gulls (rare). If you're lucky, you might pick out something more unusual, such as a Slaty-backed or Iceland Gull.

➤ Cheam Lake Wetlands Regional Park
From Hwy. 1, take Exit 135 north for Hwy. 9 to Agassiz. At the traffic circle, turn right on Yale Road then continue onto

Popkum Road North. The turnoff to the park should be signed on the left side, 2.8 kilometres from the traffic circle. With close to two hundred species recorded in the park, the **Cheam Lake Wetlands** is a terrific place to bird at any time of year. The busiest time is between spring and early fall, when migrants are joined by a bounty of summer breeders. Some of the notable nesters here include Virginia Rail, Osprey, Western Wood-Pewee, Least Flycatcher (uncommon), Eastern Kingbird, Red-eyed Vireo, Marsh Wren, Gray Catbird (uncommon), Yellow Warbler, Common Yellowthroat, Black-headed Grosbeak, and Bullock's Oriole. Green Herons are often present post-breeding in late summer, and hawking swallows and both Vaux's and Black Swifts fly overhead between May and September. Solitary Sandpipers migrate through in mid-August. Like Island 22 and the Hope Airport, this spot has yielded rarities in migration season, despite low coverage. A short list of highlights boasts Chestnut-sided Warbler, Scarlet Tanager, and Indigo Bunting. Things tend to quiet down in winter, other than a mix of waterfowl out on the lake. A daily highlight between late October and early March is the late afternoon arrival of hundreds of Trumpeter Swans that spend the night on the lake, leaving for local fields in the early morning. In most years, a handful of Tundra Swans are mixed in with the Trumpeters.

HOPE

› Hunter Creek Rest Area

This is a nice pit stop on your way to or from Vancouver (signed off Hwy. 1 just west of Hope). In summer, breeding specialties here include Pacific-slope Flycatcher, Black-throated Gray Warbler, and Black-headed Grosbeak. Watch for Band-tailed

Pigeons and Steller's Jays flying across the highway between here and Hope.

> ➤ Skagit Valley and Ross Lake

The Canadian section of the Skagit Valley is another area that is fantastic for birding but gets very little coverage. Exit off Hwy. 1 just west of Hope (Exit 168), then get onto **Silver-Skagit Road**, which heads south for about 60 kilometres before reaching the U.S. border. As a transition zone between coastal and Interior habitats, there are several species found along this valley, during both the migration and breeding seasons, that are uncommon or quite rare farther west toward Vancouver. For instance, Veery, American Redstart, Northern Waterthrush, and Vesper Sparrow are all relatively common in May and early June, and sometimes a few stick around to breed. Dusky Flycatcher, Nashville Warbler, and Chipping Sparrow nest in the mixed forests higher up, and Least Flycatcher is a local breeder that is often heard calling from aspen stands toward the south end of the road. Both Red-breasted and Red-naped Sapsucker occur in the valley (Red-breasted being more common at the north end), and hybrids have also been observed. Historically, the now-endangered Spotted Owl used to reside in the old-growth fir and cedar forest here but is now probably extirpated. It is hypothetically possible, however, that the odd individual has hung on, so it can't hurt to be vigilant. More common species along the road include Pacific-slope Flycatcher, Hammond's Flycatcher, Red-eyed Vireo, Cassin's Vireo, Warbling Vireo, Brown Creeper, Red-breasted Nuthatch, Pacific Wren, American Dipper, Swainson's Thrush, Varied Thrush, American Robin, Townsend's Warbler, Black-throated Gray Warbler, MacGillivray's Warbler, Western Tanager, and Dark-eyed Junco.

After 8 kilometres, you will reach **Silver Lake** on the right (west) side. Look for migrant waterfowl in season, including the odd group of scoters. During summer, a visit here near dusk or before a storm can yield huge numbers of Vaux's Swifts as well as a few Black Swifts. The end of the Canadian section of the Skagit Valley is at the north end of **Ross Lake**. There is a campground here with all the amenities, and although the birding is often quite good, the mosquitoes can be dreadful in summer! American White-Pelican (rare on the coast) are nearly annual in early September, and a pair of Lewis's Woodpeckers were suspected of nesting near the campground in 2010, so be on the lookout for them. Winter birding in the Skagit Valley can also be rewarding, as the area is usually host to Northern Pygmy-Owl and forest finches such as Red Crossbill, Pine Siskin, and, in some years, Pine Grosbeak, White-winged Crossbill, and Common Redpoll.

Note: Outside of summer, the condition of this gravel road can be quite poor, so we advise those with low-clearance vehicles to wait until springtime grading before venturing into the area.

> Hope Airport

Between Chilliwack and Hope, the Fraser Valley narrows considerably as it approaches the Cascade Mountains. Consequently, this is the most easterly extent for several Pacific coastal bird species, such as Northwestern Crow, Bushtit, and Black-throated Gray Warbler. The bottlenecking of the valley also has a great effect on migrating birds, since foul weather can force birds down into the narrow valley bottom, where there is little choice of habitats. The **Hope Airport** is an ideal place for birding, since it offers a variety of habitats, from expansive grassy areas to mixed woodland, in an otherwise heavily forested area. Interior species such as Say's Phoebe, Mountain Bluebird, Vesper Sparrow, and even Lewis's Woodpecker are seen regularly each year, and coastal rarities such as Western Kingbird and Dusky Flycatcher occur with a much greater frequency than farther west in Vancouver.

To bird the airport, take either the Flood Hope Road exit off Hwy. 1 (Exit 165 if you're coming from the west; Exit 168 from the east), cross over to the north side of the highway, and then follow airport signs on Floods Road and Old Yale Road (it's fairly straightforward—just look for a grassy runway). Old Yale Road passes the runway along the south perimeter, and Airport Road follows the west and north sides of the runway—this is the most popular stretch for birders, as it offers the best views. Raptors such as Red-tailed Hawk, Bald Eagle, and American Kestrel (uncommon) are found throughout the year, Rough-legged Hawks are around in some winters, and Short-eared Owls are sighted during migration. Among the local breeders, showy-looking Lazuli Buntings and Black-headed Grosbeaks can be found in the surrounding area in spring and summer, and Band-tailed Pigeons also nest here (watch for roosting flocks around dawn and dusk around the big trees at the southeast corner of the airport). During migration season, impressive numbers of migrants can sometimes be found out in the open grassy areas or along the brushy borders of the runway—rarities here include two Scissor-tailed Flycatchers, Gray Flycatcher, Yellow-breasted Chat, Brewer's Sparrow, Lark Sparrow, Black-throated Sparrow, Chestnut-collared Longspur, and Rustic Bunting.

At the northeast corner of the airport, you may want to check out **Bristol Slough** (via Bristol Slough Road). This back channel of the Fraser River can sometimes yield a variety of waterfowl and the occasional shorebird.

> Needle Peak

With a little effort, this hiking route provides the opportunity to search for White-tailed Ptarmigan and other alpine species in a day trip from the Lower Mainland, making a day trip to the alpine a likely possibility. Unlike the Mount Cheam trail, you do not need a four-wheel-drive vehicle to reach the trailhead—you just pull off the highway. This trail is accessible throughout the year, and White-tailed Ptarmigan have been seen during all seasons, but is appropriate for hiking only from July through October because of snow conditions in winter.

To reach the trailhead, drive east of Hope on the Coquihalla Highway (Hwy. 5), following signs for Merritt and Kelowna. Zero your odometer after you pass the turnoff for Hwy. 3 (stay on the Coquihalla Highway). Pull off on the right-hand side 38.2 kilometres after passing this junction and park below a highway maintenance shed. The impressive granite slabs of Yak Peak will be above you on the other side of the highway. From the trailhead (signed off the side road where you park), it takes about an hour of strenuous switchback hiking to reach the saddle just west of the domed peak. From here, there is a T-junction where you can either turn left to scramble up **Needle Peak** itself or turn right to arrive at a small alpine lake surrounded by lichen-covered rock and alpine meadows. White-tailed Ptarmigan can be found along both routes, but they seem to be more reliable around the lake and farther up the slope from the lake. It is, of course, possible to do both trails in a day, but be sure to watch your time for the return trip. It's possible to see all of the species mentioned for Mount Cheam here, as well as American Three-toed Woodpecker (in the forest during the first section of the hike).

➤ Fraser Canyon

From Hope to Lytton, the Trans-Canada Highway (Hwy. 1) hugs the side of the historic Fraser Canyon, following the course of the Fraser River as it roars downstream the other way. The route begins in the rainforests of Hope and ends in the desert grass and pines of Lytton, travelling through one of the most abrupt climatic changes on the continent. This precarious route was first established by prospectors headed to gold fields east of Quesnel. There are very few places to pull off safely, and birding is difficult because of the steep slopes of the valley, but the following sites may be of interest.

Slightly more than 2 kilometres north of Yale there is a small pull-off on the right (east) side. From here, you can over look the river and across to the little-known **Yale Garry Oak Ecological Reserve**. You probably won't see many birds here, but it's another illustration of how diverse British Columbia is. The reserve features the easternmost stands of Garry Oak in British Columbia, some 160 kilometres away from their main distribution along the coast. Look for them on both sides of the railway tracks, fairly close to the river. As you drive north along the Fraser River, watch the vegetative habitat change as you pass through this "transition zone" and think about how British Columbia's tremendous bird diversity has been shaped by its dramatic topography.

Continuing north, pull into **Alexandra Bridge Provincial Park** (about 2 kilometres north of Spuzzum). This small historic park is perfect for a picnic or a pit stop. In spring and summer, it has an attractive mix of nesting forest species, including Band-tailed Pigeon, Vaux's Swift, Rufous Hummingbird, Red-breasted Sapsucker, Western Wood-Pewee, Hammond's Flycatcher, Cassin's Vireo, Steller's Jay, Chestnut-backed Chickadee, Pacific Wren, MacGillivray's Warbler, Black-throated Gray Warbler, Townsend's Warbler, and Black-headed Grosbeak.

For those planning to take the famous Airtram tour of **Hell's Gate** across the boiling river rapids, you will be happy to know that there are usually a few interesting birds in the area. Scan above you for Golden Eagles, Vaux's Swifts, and Band-tailed Pigeons. Once you take the tram to the restaurant area across the river, there are usually some well-stocked feeders set up that can be attractive to local breeders such as Lazuli Bunting and

Black-headed Grosbeaks; a male Indigo Bunting was seen in the summer of 2010.

Soon after passing Lytton (continuing along Hwy. 1), watch for signs indicating **Skihist Provincial Park**. This is a pleasant place to camp and a good spot to kick off your Interior birding. In the Ponderosa Pine woodlands here, expect a mix of Interior species such as Dusky Grouse, Black-billed Magpie, Clark's Nutcracker, American Crow, Mountain Chickadee, all three nuthatch species, Townsend's Solitaire, Nashville Warbler, and Cassin's Finch.

SUNSHINE COAST

Contributed in part by Tony Greenfield and Alexis Harrington

Noted for its laid-back, "island feel," the Sunshine Coast is a great place to get away from Vancouver traffic and see some West Coast birds in wonderful West Coast environments. Although some birds closely associated with the Nanaimo and Parksville area (just across Georgia Strait) are surprisingly scarce here, such as Brant, Red-throated Loon, and Thayer's Gull, there are also several species that are much more reliable on this side of the water. Most notable is the Rock Sandpiper, which occurs in small numbers from late fall into early spring. Although it is technically part of the mainland, this lovely corner of British Columbia is accessed by ferries running from Horseshoe Bay (in West Vancouver) to Langdale. The ferries run every hour or two and the crossing takes about forty minutes (consult bcferries.com for a complete schedule).

➤ Gibsons

From Langdale, take a left turn at the light directly out of the ferry terminal to follow Marine Drive along the Granthams Landing waterfront into the town of Gibsons, then continue along Gower Point Road along the **Gibsons waterfront**. At any time of year (especially winter), a mix of ducks, grebes, and loons can be found in and around the marina, and during spring and fall, the nearby willows can house mixed warbler flocks. If you continue straight past Prowse Road (which leads down to the marina), the road turns into Dougall Road. Then after 140 metres, turn right on Trueman Road, and after 130 metres, the small **Arrowhead Park** should be noticeable on the left side. This thin strip of riparian habitat is surrounded by houses but can be an excellent spot for birdfinding at any time of year. In winter, plenty of sparrows should be present, attracted by local birdfeeders and the sufficient cover provided by the park. In spring and fall, look out for migrant flycatchers, vireos, and warblers.

From Trueman Road head south on either Burns or Cochrane Road, which will both quickly lead to Franklin Road where you will turn right (west) to rejoin Gower Point Road. Turn left and continue south on Gower Point Road for 450 metres, then park at the small oceanside pull-off near **Gospel Rock**. This is a beautiful place to scan the waters around Keats Island and the mouth of Howe Sound, but do not leave the road area as the land is private property. All three scoter species can be found outside of summer, as well as many other sea ducks, cormorants, grebes, and loons. Common Murres, Marbled Murrelets, and Pigeon Guillemots are a regular sight, whereas Rhinoceros Auklets are usually scarce but almost always present in some numbers (especially during migration periods). Late fall to early winter is the best time to see groups of Ancient Murrelets passing through, and Pacific Loons and Long-tailed Ducks are particularly numerous in winter.

> Chaster Beach

To reach **Chaster Beach**, continue to the end of Gower Point Road, where it drops down to the beach and meets Ocean Beach Esplanade. Here Chaster Creek empties into the Georgia Strait at the

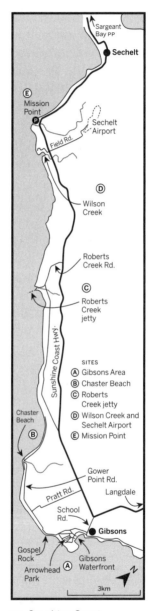

Sargeant
Bay PP

Sechelt

Ⓔ
Mission
Point

Ⓟ

Sechelt
Airport

Field Rd.

Ⓓ
Wilson
Creek

Roberts
Creek Rd.

Ⓒ
Roberts
Creek
jetty

SITES
Ⓐ Gibsons Area
Ⓑ Chaster Beach
Ⓒ Roberts
Creek jetty
Ⓓ Wilson Creek and
Sechelt Airport
Ⓔ Mission Point

Sunshine Coast Hwy.

Chaster
Beach
Ⓑ

Gower
Point Rd.

Langdale

Pratt Rd.

School
Rd.

Gibsons

Gospel
Rock

Arrowhead
Park

Ⓐ

Gibsons
Waterfront

N

3km

15 Sunshine Coast

historic Chaster House. Like Gospel Rock, this is a fantastic place to scope for seabirds passing by offshore, including scoters, cormorants, loons, and alcids. See the Gospel Rock entry for possible alcid species but also look out for more unusual birds, such as Cassin's Auklet and Fork-tailed Storm-Petrel—both of which have been recorded here in fall. Even more unusual—a probable Kittlitz's Murrelet was seen here in December 2010. Continue northwest along Ocean Beach Esplanade to look for more inshore species, such as Black Oystercatcher, Black Turnstone, and other shorebirds (in season), as well as all three scoter species, Harlequin Duck, and Long-tailed Duck (winter is best for waterfowl numbers). The trees and gardens along this road often host a variety of western specialties, such as Hutton's Vireo, Chestnut-backed Chickadee, Pacific Wren, Spotted Towhee, "Sooty" Fox Sparrow, and Golden-crowned Sparrow (the latter two are only seen outside of summer).

To return to the Sunshine Coast Highway (Hwy. 101) for Sechelt and other destinations, retrace your route along Gower Point Road, then turn left (north) on Pratt Road, and take this straight up to the highway (with a minor dog-leg right at Grandview Road).

> ## Roberts Creek jetty

Turn off south from the Sunshine Coast Highway at Roberts Creek Road (about a ten-minute drive west of Gibsons) and take this all the way down to the bottom, where there is a parking area at the mouth of Roberts Creek (keep right once you reach the small "town," then head straight past the next stop sign). From the parking area, you can walk out onto the **Roberts Creek jetty**, where all of the sea watching possibilities discussed in the previous entries are available and sometimes more. Of the many exciting birds that have been seen here, Roberts Creek's claim to fame is the world record for Ancient

Murrelets seen on a Christmas Bird Count. On December 17, 2011, six observers estimated that more than 21,000 of these buzzy-winged alcids passed the jetty in the span of 1.5 hours! Although you probably won't witness something like that during your visit, a trip in October to December should give you a chance at seeing a few Ancients passing by, if conditions are good and you have a decent scope.

In addition to the seabirds passing by offshore (time of year, weather, and food availability will be factors), check out the gravel bars around the mouth of the creek for shorebirds and loafing gulls. Depending on the tides, there can sometimes be large numbers of Black Oystercatchers, turnstones, Dunlin, and other species (depending on the season), along with the abundant Glaucous-winged (and its various hybrid combos), Mew, and California Gulls (the latter being scarce in winter). Herring, Thayer's, Ring-billed, and Bonaparte's Gulls are all regular at times but in low numbers. Parasitic Jaegers are annual in late summer and fall, and the other two jaeger species are possible but rare. Look for American Dippers, dipping for fish eggs in the creek, and for Belted Kingfishers flying by or sitting on prominent perches nearby.

> Wilson Creek and the Sechelt Airport
Note: The rewarding birding habitat (the scrubby vacant lot) around the Wilson Creek Estuary is on private property. Birders have always been tolerated, but this may change in the future. Respect any Private Property signs.

Almost 5 kilometres west of the Roberts Creek turnoff, turn left (south) at Field Road, then park in the allotted spaces beside the **Wilson Creek Estuary.** Formerly, this was one of the Sunshine Coast's premier birding locations, but recent development around the estuary and tampering with the estuary itself have diminished its importance. The estuary is tiny but encompasses the only real mud flat on the mainland side of the Strait of Georgia between Pender Harbour and the Fraser Delta. Consequently, in spring, summer, and fall, it attracts a regular flow of migrant shorebirds, and more than twenty species of shorebirds have been recorded here. In spring, fall, and winter, the estuary is home to a variety of water birds, from diving ducks and dabblers to Great Blue Herons and Bald Eagles. In spring and summer, walk carefully because a pair of Killdeer often nests in the open gravel patches here. The beaches, gravel flats, and scrubby vegetation surrounding the estuary were formerly the single best location on the Sunshine Coast for rare passerines. The potential for rarities is now diminished, but amazing birds do still appear (a Sage Thrasher on April 21, 2001). This proves the powerful attraction that estuaries hold for migrant birds, and the area is always worth visiting. Some of the other outstanding species that have been recorded here over the years include Ash-throated Flycatcher, Say's Phoebe, Western Kingbird, Eastern Kingbird, Horned Lark, Rock Wren, Mountain Bluebird, Green-tailed Towhee, Snow Bunting, and Lesser Goldfinch.

After birding the estuary, cross the highway and continue up Field Road to the **Sechelt Airport**, which has become a favoured location for local birders. As with many other airports around British Columbia, the short-grass habitat amid the coniferous forest is attractive to a variety of birds. Access to the runways is not permitted, but careful use of a scope allows you to scan all areas. Rarer raptors noted here include Northern Harrier, Short-eared Owl, and Pygmy Owl in fall and early winter. Wilson's Snipe are regular in wetter areas, whereas in open areas with brush, Mountain Bluebirds and Townsend's Solitaires have appeared in winter and especially during spring migration. American Pipits are abundant migrants, and twelve species of sparrow have been recorded, including rarities such as American Tree-Sparrow, Vesper Sparrow, and Lark Sparrow. This has also

Rock Sandpiper

been the only reliable location on the Sunshine Coast for Chipping Sparrows. Willow Flycatchers and Black-headed Grosbeaks breed here, along with Hutton's Vireos and Bewick's Wrens (very local on the Sunshine Coast), and Bushtits have been regular in recent years. Western Meadowlarks are regular in fall and early winter. In 1999, a major West Coast rarity, a Hooded Warbler, was present for a few days and seen by many. In the fall of 2003–04, a banding project was conducted at the airport that produced three species new to the Sunshine Coast: Dusky Flycatcher, Tennessee Warbler, and Palm Warbler. Other rare species banded were House Wren and Nashville Warbler.

> Mission Point/Chapman Creek

The mouth of Chapman Creek at Mission Point is considered by many to be the most important birding site on the Sunshine Coast. First and foremost, it is the most reliable site in mainland British Columbia (and Canada, for that matter) to see Rock Sandpiper (November to early April). Therefore, many birding visitors to the Sunshine Coast come with high hopes of seeing this specialty. If this happens to be you, it is important to know how and when to search them out.

To reach **Mission Point**, continue west from Field Road (access to Wilson Creek and the Sechelt Airport) along the highway. In 900 metres you will cross over **Chapman Creek**, then soon after, a parking area and beach will come up on the left. A flock of around ten to thirty Rock Sandpipers regularly winters in the area and is usually associated with a larger mixed flock of Black Turnstones and Surfbirds. Arrival and departure dates will vary year to year, but if you arrive between November and early April, you should have a chance of seeing the Rocks. Try to arrive at the first dropping tide of the day, when a couple of small spits form where all the action will focus. At low tide you still have a chance to find the birds, but they will be spread out and may not be at Mission Point at all. At high tide, the rock-piper flocks are usually offshore on Whyte Islet and thus inaccessible to birders without a boat. If the tide is low and the birds aren't there, just sit and wait, because the main flock moves around quite a bit but almost always returns to Mission Point on a daily basis. If you grow impatient, check out a few nearby locations, such as Roberts Creek or the mouth of Wakefield Creek—two places where turnstone flocks often turn up. But, really, your best bet is to just be patient and keep watch at Mission Point.

Even if the shorebirds aren't co-operating, there should be plenty to look at—large numbers of gulls (fifteen species of larids have been recorded at this site!), as well as a variety of waterfowl and other seabirds, from Caspian Terns (summer) to Rhinoceros Auklets. Even though the Rock Sandpipers are only present in winter and early spring, Black Oystercatchers are present year round, and the turnstones and surfbirds start arriving in mid-July, so there should still be a few Pacific specialty shorebirds to gawk at. The gull flock is usually composed mostly of Glaucous-winged Gulls and hybrids, but Mew Gull numbers are also high between fall and spring, and both California and Bonaparte's Gulls move through during migration periods. Despite being fairly common (in season) on the other side of the strait, both Herring and Thayer's Gulls are decidedly rare on the Sunshine Coast, but there are usually one or two of each in the main flock at Mission Point each winter. Caspian Terns are fairly common in summer. In late summer, look out for streaking Parasitic Jaegers that might try to steal a meal from the mingling gulls and terns. In addition to the birds, it is also possible to rack up a few marine mammals from shore, including Gray Whale, Killer Whale, Pacific White-sided Dolphin, Harbour Porpoise, Dall's Porpoise, Steller's Sea Lion, Harbour Seal, and River Otter.

> Sechelt

The beachfront community of **Sechelt** lies at the heart of the Lower Sunshine Coast and is a fantastic place to base your birding operation in the region or to simply enjoy a summery week away from the hustle-bustle of Vancouver. There are seawalls along Davis Bay (just north of Mission Point) and the Sechelt waterfront, where one can enjoy an easy stroll and look for ducks, loons, and grebes. Winter is the best time for waterfowl variety, when all three scoter species can be seen (White-winged being the toughest), along with showy Harlequin and Long-tailed Ducks. Summer can be a quiet time for waterfowl, but at least the weather is nice!

If you're in Sechelt, you might as will visit the small but often very productive **Sechelt Marsh**. This tiny reserve is found by turning north on Wharf Avenue in the centre of town, then turning left (west) onto Ebbtide Street. The marsh access will be on the right side of the street—park along Ebbtide Street then walk in. Despite its small size, Sechelt Marsh has produced a large number of local rarities in recent years, including Redhead, Tufted Duck, Green Heron, Gray Catbird, and Rusty Blackbird. Mallards are present in substantial numbers year round, whereas other

dabblers, such as American Wigeon, Northern Pintail, and Gadwall, occur in smaller numbers—particularly during migration
and in winter. Both Cinnamon and Blue-winged Teals show up in
May but don't stick around to nest. A pair of Bald Eagle nests in
the trees overlooking the marsh, and this is one of the best areas
on the Sunshine Coast to see Black-capped Chickadees, which
have only recently begun to colonize the area. The northwest corner of the reserve is a hot spot for sparrows, including such local
rarities as White-throated Sparrow and American Tree-Sparrow.
At the northeast end of the marsh, cross Wharf Avenue and scan
the southern section of **Porpoise Bay** for waterfowl and shorebirds (in season, when mud flats are exposed).

For access to some nearby forest habitat and to see another
portion of Porpoise Bay, return to your vehicle and proceed
northeast on Ebbtide Street. This will turn into Sechelt Inlet
Road, and the access road to **Porpoise Bay Provincial Park** will be
on the left side, 3.4 kilometres from where you crossed Wharf
Avenue. There is a parking lot near the entrance. From here, you
can walk down **Angus Creek** through the woods to the estuary. A
variety of western coniferous forest specialties can be expected
here in spring and summer, including Pileated Woodpecker, Red-
breasted Sapsucker, Chestnut-backed Chickadee, Pacific Wren,
Varied Thrush (most common in winter), MacGillivray's Warbler, Townsend's Warbler, and Western Tanager. At the creek
mouth there is some marshy habitat that may net you some
equally marshy birds, such as Common Yellowthroat and Virginia Rail. In winter, American Dippers are common along the
creek, and the grassy fringes of the estuary and bay shoreline can
be great for sparrows and even the odd Lapland Longspur in fall.
Camping and picnicking facilities are provided here, and there is
another parking area closer to the bay.

Another spot that is always worth a quick look is the mouth
of **Wakefield Creek**. Drive slightly more than 3 kilometres west

of downtown Sechelt (along the Sunshine Coast Highway), then turn left on Wakefield Road, which terminates at a small beach. Many of the same species outlined at Mission Point occur here, usually in smaller numbers—but not always. Inshore alcids such as Pigeon Guillemot and Marbled Murrelets are often found in large numbers, and occasionally workups of food will attract large feeding frenzies of cormorants, terns, and gulls into the waters between Wakefield Creek and the Trail Islets.

> Tetrahedron Provincial Park

For those wanting to find upper-elevation species—including the Holy Grail of mountain birding: ptarmigan—a day hike or overnight camping in **Tetrahedron Provincial Park** may prove worthwhile. Located 10 kilometres northeast of Sechelt, access involves driving on logging roads, then hiking a series of trails that lead above treeline, so you should get detailed access and weather information from a local tourist information centre. The trails begin at about the 1,000-metre level, so it's possible to find high-elevation forest species such as Northern Goshawk, Three-toed Woodpecker, Gray Jay, Pine Grosbeak, and White-winged Crossbill. A trail leads above treeline on **Mount Steele**, and in this true alpine habitat, Rock Ptarmigan have bred and White-tailed Ptarmigan are also a possibility. American Pipits are regular breeders, and at the very peak of the mountain, around the snow fields, Gray-crowned Rosy-Finches are regular. Similar habitat and species occur on both Panther Peak and Mount Tetrahedron, but they are more difficult to access. As with nearly all of British Columbia's high peaks, summer and early fall are the best times to visit, when snow levels are at a minimum.

> Sargeant Bay Provincial Park

From Wakefield Road, continue west for 3.2 kilometres then turn left onto Redroofs Road. After 1.8 kilometres, turn left down a gravel road to access **Sargeant Bay**. You can scan the bay for oceangoing waterfowl, but the real attraction in this spot is the freshwater cattails of Colvin Lake (more of a pond!). Virginia Rail is present year round, Common Yellowthroat and Red-winged Blackbird are plentiful during the breeding season, and Sora is an uncommon breeder. Although these species may be widespread and common in other parts of the province, there is scant freshwater marsh habitat along the Sunshine Coast, so a location like this is valuable. There are also a series of woodland trails on the other side of Redroofs Road that can produce a variety of forest species, such as Hammond's Flycatcher, Pacific-slope Flycatcher, Warbling Vireo, Black-headed Grosbeak, and Western Tanager (all in spring and summer), whereas Red-breasted Sapsucker, Pacific Wren, and Varied Thrush are possible year round.

> ➤ Caren Range/Spipiyus Provincial Park

The other accessible mountain area on the Sunshine Coast is the **Caren Range**. This area achieved fame twice in the early 1990s. Firstly, when some of the oldest known trees in Canada were found here, including a Yellow Cedar stump with 1,736 rings—thus, the area is referred to as "the oldest known forest in Canada." Secondly, after an intensive research project, the remnant stand of old-growth trees yielded the first ever nest of a Marbled Murrelet in Canada. In midsummer, the murrelets are very active from about 4:15 to 6 A M as they fly in with food for their nestlings and announce their presence with a *keer-keer* call. Eventually, the ancient stand of trees was protected and given park status with the name **Spipiyus**, the Sechelt First Nations name for the Marbled Murrelet. Other species to look for along this ridge include Sooty Grouse, American Three-toed Woodpecker, Gray Jay, and both Black and Vaux's Swifts.

To reach the park, drive about 11 kilometres northwest of Sechelt along the Sunshine Coast Highway, then turn right on

Trout Lake Road about 2 kilometres east of Halfmoon Bay. Proceed up this logging road, then take the left fork at the main junction at kilometre 12. Continue to kilometre 19.5 and walk from there.

> ## Smuggler's Cove Provincial Park

This picturesque marine park is located between the communities of Halfmoon Bay and Secret Cove, 16 kilometres along the Sunshine Coast Highway (Hwy. 101) from Sechelt. It is a wonderful area for hiking and wilderness camping and can produce a mix of forest species, such as Hammond's Flycatcher, Hutton's Vireo, Townsend's Warbler, and Black-throated Gray Warbler, as well as marine birds such as Surf Scoter, Black Oystercatcher, Black Turnstone, Surfbird, Pigeon Guillemot, and Marbled Murrelet.

> ## Pender Harbour

The area known to local birders as **Pender Harbour** ("The Venice of Canada," or so they say) refers to the large complex of coves and harbours that comprise the communities of Madeira Park, Garden Bay, and Irvines Landing. Most of the birding hot spots here centre around bodies of water, but visiting birders will also be able to see a mix of forest birds.

The first spot to check is **Lily Lake**—located beside the highway (west side), just as you get into Madeira Park. Common Loons nest here in the summer, and a variety of other waterfowl species can be found throughout the year. Continue past the community of Madeira Park/Pender Harbour, and turn left after nearly 5 kilometres onto Garden Bay Road, which turns into Irvines Landing Road. Along this road, you will pass four freshwater lakes (Garden Bay, Katherine, Mixal, and Hotel), all of which can present breeding and migrating waterfowl, including Ring-necked Duck, Lesser Scaup, Hooded and Common Mergansers, and Pied-billed Grebe. After passing Garden Bay Lake, you can either turn left down

Garden Bay Road to the community of Garden Bay (north side of Pender Harbour) or head straight onto Irvines Landing Road, which turns into Lee Road at **Lee Bay**. From here, you can scope the mouth of Pender Harbour and the open waters of the Georgia Strait for scoters, loons, and grebes. From Lee Bay, continue along Lee Road northward for 1.3 kilometres, then turn left on Sakinaw Road. From this road, you have a good vantage point over the mouth of **Agamemnon Channel**, where large flocks of Long-tailed Ducks and Common Murres congregate in winter.

> ## Ruby Lake Lagoon

From the Garden Bay turnoff, drive north along the Sunshine Coast Highway (Hwy. 101) for 9.2 kilometres, then look for signs for **Ruby Lake Resort** and the **Iris Griffith Field Studies and Interpretive Centre** (two different sites adjacent to one another). Thanks to Aldo Cogrossi, the bird-loving proprietor of the Ruby Lake Resort who spends a small fortune feeding the birds and conserving habitat, the Ruby Lake Lagoon is an excellent place to observe many water birds. The lagoon is now famous for its large breeding population of Wood Ducks. During the winter months, many ducks of numerous species are present, and this is the only reliable site on the Sunshine Coast for American Coot. Aldo also maintains numerous nest boxes that are home to various swallows in summer. Bald Eagles and Turkey Vultures (summer) are common. For more information, visit rubylakeresort.com.

> ## Powell River

Birding in Powell River is centred primarily on the seashores around town. Visit the beach at **Willingdon Park**, where McGuffie Creek flows into the ocean (along Hwy. 101 just north of Alberni Street), to look for scoters, Harlequin Ducks, gulls, Black Turnstones, and occasionally other shorebirds. **Myrtle Point** is another good spot; check the pilings for Purple Martins through summer. Access to the point is via the beach from a pull-off on Hwy. 101 about 200 metres south of the Maris Street intersection. For freshwater birding, check out **Cranberry Lake** from the Lindsay Park access. There are several ways to get to Lindsay Park from Hwy. 101, one of the more straightforward ones is to turn east onto Hawthorn Street (near the south end of the pulp mill area); this turns into Timberlane Avenue and then into Dieppe Avenue. When you reach Cranberry Street, turn right and travel east for 1.3 kilometres; the park and lake will be on your right. In winter, Cranberry Lake usually has a few Trumpeter Swans and plenty of Ring-necked Ducks, among other assorted waterfowl.

SQUAMISH AND WHISTLER

> Squamish River Estuary

The **Squamish River training dyke** gives access to the best variety of birding habitats in the area, from flood plain forests, main river channels, oxbows, and grassy marshlands to open views of Howe Sound and the surrounding mountains.

If you're approaching from the south (Vancouver), turn left (west) off Hwy. 99 at Industrial Way, then right (north) on Queens Way, which will swing left (west) and turn into Government Road. Follow Government Road southwest past the B.C. Railway Museum and turn right (west) onto the gravel dyke road, and then left (south) toward the windsurfing area at the end of the dyke. *Note: A checklist of Squamish birds and a brochure showing the trails and access points to the Squamish River estuary are available from the Adventure Centre near the entrance to Squamish.*

The forested Woodpecker Trail is on the left (500 metres from where you first drive up onto the dyke) and is home to Pacific Wren, Red-breasted Nuthatch, Black-capped and

Bald Eagle

Chestnut-backed Chickadees, as well as five species of wood-peckers year round (Red-breasted Sapsucker, Flicker, Hairy, Downy, and Pileated). During summer Warbling, Red-eyed, and Cassin's Vireos can be found here, along with Yellow-rumped, Townsend's, and Black-throated Gray Warblers.

Along the dyke road 2.5 kilometres in, a trail on the left will take you through a grasslands area and then out along the Squamish River training dyke. During winter, there should be a variety of dabbling ducks in the sloughs and marshland and perhaps a few Western Meadowlarks and Northern Shrikes in the grassland areas. Winter is a good time to see raptors, such as Red-tailed Hawk, Coopers and Sharp-shinned Hawks, Peregrine Falcon and many Bald Eagles. Along the training dyke, scan the Squamish River and its side channels for grebes, loons, and waterfowl, including Bufflehead and both Common and Barrow's Goldeneyes. During summer, expect to see Red-winged Blackbird, Common Yellowthroat, White-crowned Sparrow, Song Sparrow, Savannah Sparrow, Osprey, Turkey Vulture, Spotted Sandpiper, and Killdeer in the same area.

Not surprisingly, the Squamish Estuary has turned up its fair share of local rarities. Lewis's Woodpeckers have showed up in September three years in a row (2009–11), Green Herons bred for the first time in 2011, both Great and Cattle Egrets have appeared in the last decade, and Yellow-billed Loons have occurred at least three times since 2002.

> Brackendale

The Squamish River Valley has long been recognized as one of the most significant areas of wintering Bald Eagles in North America. In 1994, Squamish set a world record with 3,769 eagles counted in one day! The prolific runs of chum salmon in the Squamish, Cheakamus, and Mamquam Rivers attract eagles from all over the Pacific Northwest from November to February each year, and the adjacent riparian area provides suitable habitat for roosting, perching, and feeding. December to January is usually peak season.

From Hwy. 99 turn left (west) at Garibaldi Way (near the Burger King), then right onto Government Road, and drive to the eagle-viewing kiosk located on the Squamish River dyke opposite the Easter Seals Camp near **Brackendale**. Eagle Watch volunteers provide information and spotting scopes at the kiosk.

> Garibaldi Provincial Park

Garibaldi Provincial Park is both a good mountain-birding area and a region of unparalleled beauty and geological wonder. Mount Garibaldi is the northernmost of the recently active (in the last few thousand years) Cascade volcanoes, but there are many other volcanic features around the large park. There are two main access points to the park, both involving hiking.

The **Diamond Head** area is the southern part of **Garibaldi Provincial Park** and provides an opportunity for high-elevation hiking and birding as a day trip from Vancouver—a day trip with exquisite scenery as well as birds. July through September is the best time for birds (expect snow on the ground from November through June), but the trails are popular with cross-country skiers in winter. From Hwy. 99 in Squamish, drive 4 kilometres north and turn right (east) onto Mamquam Road. Past the golf course, take the logging road just past the Mashiter Creek Bridge and drive for about 16 kilometres to the trailhead. The trail climbs fairly steeply at first to Red Heather Meadows (3.5 kilometres one way), then reaches Paul Ridge in about another 3 kilometres. For a truly memorable hike, continue on to **Elfin Lakes** (11 kilometres one way), where there is a hut for overnight camping. At any time of year, you could see Sooty Grouse, Northern Pygmy-Owl, Gray Jay, and Chestnut-backed Chickadee along this trail.

Garibaldi Lake is an even better destination for summer and early fall birding but requires an overnight hike to take full advantage of its geography. The usual way to access the Garibaldi Lake area is to drive 32 kilometres north of Squamish on Hwy. 99, then turn right, following the Garibaldi Provincial Park signs. Follow the access road for a couple of kilometres to the trailhead. The trail, like most mountain trails, goes up for most of its length, but keep in mind the views and birds that you'll see at the top. After about 6 kilometres, you will reach a junction; the right-hand trail takes you to Garibaldi Lake, where you can set up camp and enjoy the view of the Sphinx Glacier beyond the powder-blue waters of the lake. The lake is set in subalpine forests, with birds typical to such an area, including Gray Jay, Mountain and Chestnut-backed Chickadees, Hermit Thrush, and Fox Sparrow; Common Loons and Ospreys are seen around the lake as well.

Alternatively, you can turn left and keep climbing to Taylor Meadows, where there is another wilderness campsite. From here, you can explore the Helm Lake valley to the east; Barrow's

Goldeneyes nest at the lake and small numbers of shorebirds can stop by in late summer. Northern Hawk Owls have occasionally been seen in this area. If you want to get into the true alpine for a chance at White-tailed Ptarmigan, Horned Lark, American Pipit, and Gray-crowned Rosy-Finch, take the trail up Panorama Ridge; this is perhaps best done as a full-day hike from one of the campgrounds.

> Whistler Blackcomb

As a world-famous ski resort, **Whistler Blackcomb** is crowded with people year round—whether they're skiers, riders, bikers, or simply taking part in the spectacle that is Whistler. Thanks to the abundant infrastructure, birders can also cash in on the beauty and splendour of the surrounding mountains and lakes and the birds that inhabit them. Obviously, upper-elevation species such as American Three-toed Woodpecker, Pine Grosbeak, and White-tailed Ptarmigan are the specialties, but down in the valley bottom, there are several areas where one can enjoy a mix of waterfowl and songbirds outside of winter.

Ski lifts give access to the alpine areas of Whistler and Blackcomb, where you can find White-tailed Ptarmigan, Horned Lark, and Gray-crowned Rosy-Finches; Clark's Nutcrackers and Gray Jays are fairly easy to spot year round. In summer, the subalpine forests of these mountains have Sooty Grouse, Hermit and Varied Thrush, American Pipit, Yellow-rumped Warbler, and Ruby-crowned Kinglet. White-tailed Ptarmigan are usually found on the rocky slopes near the top, whereas rosy-finches are seen either flying over or foraging along snow fields on steep slopes.

To access a paved path with views of **Alta Lake**, turn northwest off Hwy. 99 onto Lorimer Road (at the main intersection in Whistler). This means you will be on the opposite side of the highway from the main ski hills. Park at the end of Lorimer Road; from here, you can access the 2-kilometre **Valley Trail** to Rainbow Park. Partway along, there is an observation platform for viewing Alta Lake. **Rainbow Park** can also be reached from Alta Lake Road on the west side of Alta Lake. The birding here is best between spring and fall, when you can expect to see Canada Geese, Mallards, Ring-necked Ducks, Bufflehead, Surf and White-winged Scoters (migration only), Hooded Mergansers, and a few loons and grebes out on the lake. Corvids, woodpeckers, chickadees, and forest finches such as Pine Siskin are present year round, and summertime breeders include Orange-crowned, MacGillivray's, Yellow-rumped, and Yellow Warblers, along with White-crowned Sparrow, Song Sparrow, and the abundant Dark-eyed (Oregon) Juncos.

Another spot to check out with similar attributes to Alta Lake is the larger **Green Lake**. Drive north along Hwy. 99 from the main Whistler Village, then 450 metres after crossing the railway line, make the first right on Nicklaus North Boulevard, followed by a left onto Golden Bear Place. At the end of Golden Bear Place, you can park and access another section of Valley Trail. Walk east along the edge of Green Lake to the mouth of **Fitzsimmons Creek**. Not surprisingly, both Green Lake and Alta Lake usually freeze in winter, but many of the creeks and rivers will be partially open, so you never know what you might find in these brushy areas near water.

> Pemberton

A convenient place to start birding in Pemberton is **One Mile Lake**. If you're approaching from the south along Hwy. 99, the lake will be on the right (west) side, just before you get to the town. Park at the tourist information centre or the swimming beach at the south end of the lake, then walk the 2 kilometres of trails around the lake and on the dyke along Pemberton Creek. Scan the skies in spring and summer for soaring raptors, such as Osprey, Peregrine Falcon, and Turkey Vulture. Marshy areas may produce both Virginia Rail and Sora, and the forest here can be great during the breeding season for Veery, Western Tanager, American Redstart, and a variety of other warblers.

The **Pemberton Meadows Road** is a 27-kilometre-long flat, paved road that takes you through a mix of farmland and valley-bottom forest habitat. From the main intersection in town, head northwest on Portage Road, continue on Portage by turning left at the traffic circle, then make an immediate right onto Prospect Street. Follow Prospect to a T-junction, then turn left to follow Pemberton Meadows Road. If it's a clear day, your views of the surrounding mountains should be fantastic. This road can be a productive site at any time of year. In winter, raptors are the main attraction. Red-tailed Hawks and Northern Harriers are fairly common, and both Northern Shrikes and Northern Pygmy-Owls are seen regularly. In spring and summer, look for Lazuli Buntings sitting up on fence posts and along the telephone wires; a variety of sparrows may be present along the hedgerows, especially in migration. Trumpeter Swans frequent the area outside of the breeding season, and Eurasian Collared-Doves are now a common sight.

> Joffre Lakes Provincial Park

The section of Hwy. 99 between Pemberton and Lillooet is called the **Duffy Lake Road**, known for its scenery and hazardous driving conditions in winter. If you are passing through in summer and looking for a nice hike to break up a drive, or simply want to have a look for some mountain birds, stop at the parking lot for **Joffre Lakes Provincial Park** (near Cayoosh Summit, about 30 kilometres east of Pemberton). A marked trail leads to the nearby Lower Joffre Lake then climbs to two more lakes (Middle and Upper) along a steep but well-maintained 5-kilometre-long trail. Spotted Sandpipers breed along the lakeshore, and American Dippers are sometimes seen flying up and down the creeks. Gray Jay, Clark's Nutcracker, American Three-toed Woodpecker, Red-breasted Nuthatch, and both species of crossbill are possible year round, whereas Hermit Thrush, Townsend's Warbler, Yellow-rumped Warbler, and Dark-eyed Juncos are some of the common species nesting in summer.

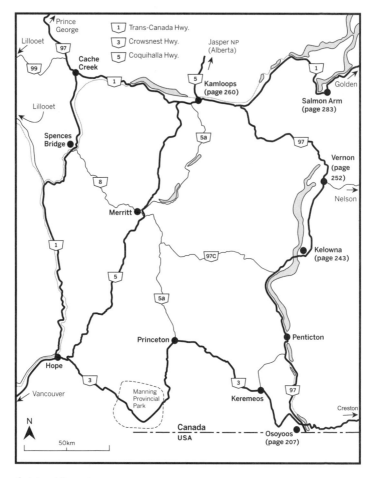

16 Inland Overview

OKANAGAN
AND
SIMILKAMEEN

MANNING PARK

E.C. Manning Provincial Park is one of British Columbia's most popular destinations for mountain hiking and a great access to high elevations for finding mountain birds. The park straddles the crest of the Cascade Mountains, extending from the low-elevation coastal forests along the Sumallo River just east of Hope to the dry pine forests of the Interior, about forty minutes west of Princeton. In between is a wide variety of mountain forests, lakes, subalpine meadows, and high rocky peaks. There are four campgrounds in the park; Lightning Lake Campground is best for birding purposes. Manning Park Lodge, in the centre of the park on Hwy. 3, provides lodging and restaurant facilities.

Coming from the west, you enter the park about 23 kilometres west of Hope. A large statue of a Hoary Marmot adorns the park entrance sign at the **West Gate.** You are travelling along the Sumallo River here as it winds through willow beds in a narrow valley. Watch for Harlequin Ducks along the river in spring and summer and American Dippers in all seasons. In summer, Black-throated Gray Warblers are uncommon in the riverside forests, and Northern Waterthrushes can be heard singing from the willows. About 10 kilometres from the West Gate, you come to the entrance (on the southwest side of the highway) of the **Sumallo Grove picnic area**. This is a must stop, if only to enjoy the magnificent old-growth stand of Western Red Cedars and Douglas-firs. A short nature trail loops through the forest, and a longer trail strikes off to the junction of the Sumallo and Skagit Rivers, then proceeds down the Skagit Valley for many kilometres. Watch and listen for Vaux's Swifts, Red-breasted Sapsuckers, Pacific-slope Flycatchers, Chestnut-backed Chickadees, and Brown Creepers in the forest. These species can also be found along the Skagit River trail, as well as MacGillivray's Warblers in shrubby tangles.

In the centre of the park, a pit stop at **Manning Park Lodge** could yield Clark's Nutcrackers and Gray Jays at any time of year. If you turn northeast (left if travelling east) at the lodge, you will find yourself on the Alpine Meadows Road, open only in summer. Watch for Sooty Grouse on the roadside as you climb. After about 8 kilometres, you reach the **Cascade Lookout**, always worth a stop for spectacular views, especially when the weather is fine. Clark's Nutcrackers are almost guaranteed at the lookout; in fact, they will steal your lunch if you give them the chance. Continuing up the road, keep watching for grouse on the roadside—Sooty Grouse is the most likely species, but this is the boundary between it and its Interior counterpart, the Dusky Grouse. Check the tail tips of the birds—Sooty Grouse have a pale grey band across the tip of the tail, whereas Dusky Grouse have all-black tails or, at most, only a shadow of a band. Spruce Grouse are also common here.

After another 6 kilometres, you will see the trailhead for the **Heather Trail** on the left; the road ends at a picnic area about a kilometre farther on. The Heather Trail provides relatively easy

Clark's Nutcracker

walking access to various alpine habitats. A few hours of birding on this trail will likely produce Sooty and Spruce Grouse, Mountain Chickadees, Boreal Chickadee, Pacific Wren, Townsend's Solitaire, Hermit Thrush, Varied Thrush, Townsend's Warbler, Fox Sparrow, and White-crowned Sparrow. Northern Goshawks are uncommon, and White-winged Crossbills are common only in certain years. Northern Hawk Owls have nested in the old burn about 6 kilometres along the trail. If you do a long day hike (about 20 kilometres return) you can reach the First Brother, the highest peak along the trail; White-tailed Ptarmigan nest on this peak but are very difficult to find. In the alpine meadows, you will likely see Horned Larks and American Pipits. There are three hike-in campsites along the Heather Trail, if you'd like to explore this beautiful area more thoroughly.

Returning to the lodge area, cross the highway and drive southwest to **Lightning Lake**. There is a large picnic area at the east end of the lake, but the right hand branch of the road will take you past the campground and the turnoff to **Spruce Bay Beach**. The latter is the best place to park for a quick birding walk in the valley, or you can take more time and walk around the entire lake (9 kilometres return) or all the way to Thunder Lake (20 kilometres return). The old spruce forest is a beautiful place for Red-breasted and Red-naped Sapsuckers (you are right in the middle of the hybrid zone for these two species—you might even see a mixed pair!). Also here are Chestnut-backed Chickadees, Mountain Chickadees, Brown Creepers, and Townsend's Warblers. Barrow's Goldeneyes and Common Loons nest on the lake. If you camp overnight at Lightning Lake, listen for Barred Owls at night and the slow, soft toots of Northern Pygmy-Owl in the morning and evening. If you continue west on the road past Lightning Lake, you will come to **Strawberry Flats**. A gate blocks the road beyond this point in summer (it leads to the winter ski area), but birding is good along the trail through the flats on the left. The patchy meadows have become even more open because of recent beetle epidemics, and American Three-toed Woodpeckers are often found here—listen for their quiet tapping as they flake bark off infested trees. Boreal and Chestnut-backed Chickadees can also be found, along with the common Mountain Chickadees and Pine Grosbeaks. Spruce and Sooty Grouse are common but often difficult to see.

Back on Hwy. 3, turn right (east) and drive 1.5 kilometres to the **Beaver Pond** (entrance on the right/south). This traditional stopping point for birders and naturalists is almost always worth a quick stop, though highway widening has made it somewhat noisier. Virginia Rails, Sora, Olive-sided Flycatchers, and Pine Grosbeaks are found here, and the common nesting songbirds are Tree Swallow, Yellow Warbler, Common Yellowthroat, Song Sparrow, and Lincoln's Sparrow. Continuing east (and watching the Similkameen River for Harlequin Ducks and American Dippers as you go), you will reach the **East Gate** of the park, about 16 kilometres from the lodge. Erosion from the Similkameen River has closed the McDiarmid Meadows picnic area, but you can pull off on the southeast side of the road just west of the park entrance sign. A stroll through the shrubby meadows in late spring or summer could produce a good list, including Red-naped Sapsucker, Hammond's Flycatcher, Orange-crowned Warbler, American Redstart, and Northern Waterthrush. Dusky Flycatchers can be found in the drier forests on the hillsides across the highway.

PRINCETON

Long underappreciated in the birding world, the **Princeton** area is now known to be an exciting place to explore, either as a destination itself or as a lengthy stop on a trip between the coast and the Okanagan Valley. Around town, look for American Dippers (October to March) and Harlequin Ducks (April to May) in the Similkameen and Tulameen Rivers; in winter, the residential areas (especially those around the hospital) are good spots for Bohemian Waxwings and Pine Grosbeaks. Mountain Bluebirds are commonly seen along fence lines outside the town, from March through October. **Swan Lake Bird Sanctuary** on the north side of town is a wonderful place for a walk, from spring through fall; follow directions for Osprey Lake Road (see below), then stop between the racetrack and MacNamara Road, where the trail to the lake goes west for about 750 metres through the grasslands and down into a bowl-shaped valley. The grasslands have Dusky Grouse, Mountain Bluebirds, Vesper Sparrows, and Western Meadowlarks, and the open pine woodlands have Clark's Nutcrackers, Mountain Chickadees, and all three nuthatch species. Two blinds overlook the lake and its marshes, where you could see a variety of waterfowl, including Ruddy Ducks.

› Darcy Mountain Road and August Lake

An excellent place to start birding around Princeton is **Darcy Mountain Road**, which turns south off Hwy. 3 about 2.5

kilometres west of the Similkameen River Bridge in Princeton. Only 200 metres along this road, a left turn will take you onto a gravel track that parallels the local sewage lagoons (you might have to scramble up a gravel slope for the best view), which are good for birding at any time of year, especially for waterfowl. The lagoons are about 1 kilometre long, so a few stops are necessary to cover them thoroughly. In spring and early summer, the ponds have a variety of ducks, including Wood Duck, Northern Shoveler, all three teal species, Lesser Scaup, Barrow's Goldeneye, and Ruddy Duck. Their steep shorelines are not attractive to large numbers of shorebirds, but Solitary Sandpipers are seen regularly in migration. In winter, the diversity is lower, but the ponds can still be worth a stop.

Continue along Darcy Mountain Road, travel through the golf course, then swing south again to climb into the hills. After about 5 kilometres, you will reach a large, round pond on the left; this is **August Lake**. The huge Ponderosa Pines around the lake, especially at the north end, have been ravaged by pine beetles and salvage logging but can still be worth checking for Williamson's Sapsucker (best in late March and April, when they are noisily drumming), White-breasted Nuthatch, Pygmy Nuthatch (both year round), and Cassin's Finch (April to June). Check the lake for a variety of ducks and grebes from spring through fall.

> Copper Mountain Road

Copper Mountain Road leaves Hwy. 3 about 500 metres east of the Similkameen bridge. It travels through open coniferous forests for about 20 kilometres before reaching a large copper mine and dispersing into a myriad of logging roads. The small wetlands between kilometres 5 and 10 are surrounded by diverse woodlands, and a satisfying list of birds can be found here in spring and early summer; for instance, Williamson's Sapsuckers have nested in aspen stands here. This is all private land,

*Calliope
Hummingbirds*

however, so please stay on the road while birding. Bird diversity drops dramatically after the road climbs out of a valley and up to the mine turnoff and logging roads, so it's best to retrace your route to the highway at that point. This road is very busy during shift changes at the mine.

› Osprey Lake Road

Osprey Lake Road (also known as Princeton-Summerland Road) can be either a rewarding day trip out of Princeton or an alternate route to the Okanagan Valley. The road is paved from Princeton to Osprey Lake and has an even gravel surface from there to Summerland. Turn north off Hwy. 3 onto Hwy. 5A in downtown Princeton and follow that road across the bridge over the Tulameen River (watch for Harlequin Ducks in the river in spring). Take the first right after the bridge, then keep left at the Y-intersection 200 metres beyond that, where the Old Hedley Road goes off to the right. About 6 kilometres from the highway turnoff, you'll see a small, marshy pond immediately west of the road; this is **Wayne Lake**, a perfect place to stop whenever it is ice free. Common ducks here include Cinnamon

Teal, Ring-necked Duck, and Ruddy Duck; Yellow-headed Blackbirds nest in the cattails.

About 2 kilometres past Wayne Lake, you will see **Separation Lake** on the right (southeast). This lake has shrunk dramatically in size over the past decade, so it's not very attractive to birds at the moment but still good for shorebirds in spring and late summer and a variety of waterfowl from March through October. From there, the road drops into the **Hayes Creek Valley** and gradually climbs past three small mountain lakes: Chain, Link, and Osprey. Watch for Barrow's Goldeneyes, Ospreys, Red-necked Grebes, Common Loons, and Northern Waterthrush on and around these lakes in summer; the forests have subalpine species such as American Three-toed Woodpecker, Gray Jay, Mountain Chickadee, and Golden-crowned Kinglet. There is a variety of campsites and cabins in the area, including Tellier's Fisherman's Cove at Osprey Lake—owned and operated by birders.

> Keremeos and Cawston

The small fruit-growing communities of Keremeos and Cawston are not well-known to many birders, despite being nestled in the Lower Similkameen Valley, which boasts nearly all of the same bird specialties found in the adjacent Okanagan Valley. Because there are much fewer people living in this area (no beaches), it can almost be like seeing what the Okanagan was like in the 1970s. Whether you are passing through from Vancouver to either Penticton or Osoyoos, there are many little spots just off the road that can show some lovely birds.

For those taking Hwy. 3A north from Keremeos to Penticton, look for the Keremeos Cemetery on the right (east) side of the road, roughly 3.3 kilometres north of Keremeos. Turn on this road (Lindicoat Road), and proceed to the bottom of a gated gravel road heading uphill. Depending on your preference, you can either park here and walk up the track or open the gate

Evening Grosbeak

and continue up the rough road (high-clearance vehicle recommended). This is the road to the **Keremeos Columns** (neat
geological formations), as well as a summer grazing area for cattle. In spring and summer, driving this road at dawn will give
you a chance of seeing both Chukar and Gray Partridge, which
gather on the roads in groups of up to thirty. After roughly 3
kilometres, there is a fork in the main road. Left will take you to
the columns, and right will take you higher into the sagebrush
country, as well as to two creek crossings with nice riparian habitat. There are several colonies of Brewer's Sparrows
in the sage in this area, and Vesper Sparrows are widespread
and common. Sage Thrashers have bred in this area on several occasions, and the showy Lark Sparrow is a regular nester
(study your sparrow songs). The forest along the shaded creeks
produce Calliope Hummingbird, Pacific-slope Flycatcher, Hammond's Flycatcher, Cassin's Vireo, Nashville Warbler, Western
Tanager, Lazuli Bunting, Black-headed Grosbeak, and Cassin's
Finch. Before reaching the junction, there is a rocky hump with
a radio tower on top—this hill often has Rock Wrens nesting in
spring and summer.

To reach Cawston, head southeast on Hwy. 3 from Keremeos, following signs for Osoyoos. Once you reach the main intersection in Cawston (indicated by a flashing amber traffic light), turn right (southwest) onto Coulthard Avenue and take this all the way to the end. This is **Kobau Park**, a lovely spot for a picnic. All three nuthatch species are found in the tall pine trees surrounding the park; there are walking trails that lead along the Similkameen River and up a small creek just on the other side of the playing fields. Scan the cliffs across the river and the skies above for soaring Golden Eagles. Canyon Wrens can often be heard, calling or singing, from across the river, and outside of summer, expect to find an American Dipper or two bouncing up and down on exposed rocks along the river. Harlequin Ducks are sometimes seen here during migration, but Common Mergansers are usually the most usual species, along with Common Goldeneye (in winter). Belted Kingfishers can often be seen patrolling the area for fish, and the thickets along the small creek can be full of songbirds at any time of year.

From Kobau Park, return on Coulthard Road to Wooden Road then turn right. After passing VLA Road, this road will pass a small oxbow slough before reaching the main portion of **Ginty's Pond** (signed). The birding here can be rewarding throughout the year, but early to mid-May is best, when migrants are moving through the thick riparian thickets and nesting birds are in full song. All three species of teal nest here, and Wood Ducks are often seen perched on the logs in the small oxbow. Both Red-winged and Yellow-headed Blackbirds nest in the cattails around Ginty's Pond, and Marsh Wrens, American Coots, Virginia Rails, Soras, and Mallards round out some of the marsh breeders. Because of recent low water levels, the pond is being taken over by reeds, so it can be hard to see any open water. In spring and summer, expect to hear the songs of Cassin's, Warbling, and

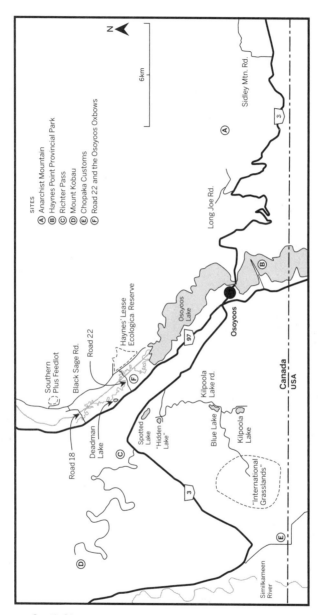

SITES
Ⓐ Anarchist Mountain
Ⓑ Haynes Point Provincial Park
Ⓒ Richter Pass
Ⓓ Mount Kobau
Ⓔ Chopaka Customs
Ⓕ Road 22 and the Osoyoos Oxbows

6km

Sidley Mtn. Rd.

Long Joe Rd.

Ⓐ

Ⓑ

Osoyoos
Lake

Osoyoos

97

Canada
USA

Haynes' Lease
Ecologica Reserve

Southern
Plus Feedlot

Black Sage Rd.

Road 22

Ⓕ

Deadman
Lake

Road 18

Ⓒ

Spotted
Lake

"Hidden
Lake"

Kilpoola
Lake rd.

Blue Lake

Kilpoola
Lake

"International
Grasslands"

3

Ⓔ

Ⓓ

Similkameen
River

17 South Okanagan

Red-eyed Vireos cascading from nearby cottonwoods, along with the meows of Gray Catbirds and the beautiful melodies of Veeries and Yellow Warblers. Return to VLA Road and turn right. Along this stretch of road, you will probably see a few Eurasian Collared-Doves. Now locally common in many of British Columbia's towns, this neighbourhood used to be the only reliable place in the province to find them. Just before reaching Main Street in the village of Cawston, VLA Road passes another slough (part of the same complex as Ginty's Pond). In migration, this pond can host a wide variety of waterfowl. Turn right on Main Street, then left on Pitt Road to rejoin Hwy. 3.

Slightly more than 1 kilometre down the highway from Pitt Road, a large expanse of pastureland will come up on the right (southwest) side of the road. This is the most reliable area in the Okanagan-Similkameen for nesting Long-billed Curlew, with about ten pairs annually. Find a safe place to pull off, then scan the grassy flats for cinnamon-coloured shorebirds. They can be found easily in April, when they are noisy and the vegetation is low, but with a bit of patience, you can usually find some any time, from March to mid-July, when they migrate south. As you continue south along the highway, feel free to stop wherever looks good. A few small colonies of Bobolinks are scattered throughout these meadow areas on the Lower Similkameen First Nation reserve. Ring-necked Pheasants are also frequently spotted.

OSOYOOS

> Anarchist Mountain

This high ridge, which forms the east wall of the Okanagan Valley at Osoyoos, was apparently named after Richard Sidley, an Irish anarchist who ran an archetypal border town called, appropriately enough, Sidley, on the broad plateau forming this mountain's southern slope. Hwy. 3, hemmed in by the

*White-headed
Woodpecker*

international boundary, is forced to ascend its slopes, giving birders access to a multitude of habitats.

Starting at the Hwy. 97 junction, travel east on Hwy. 3 through downtown Osoyoos and cross the bridge over the lake narrows. The pull-off on the east side of the bridge is a prime spot to scan the lake, especially in fall, winter, and early spring, when waterfowl are common and speedboats are not. Hwy. 3 soon begins winding up through orchards and vineyards and then through semi-desert grassland. The rock bluffs above the road are prime Chukar and Canyon Wren habitat; both species can be found with a bit of scrambling below the lookout at kilometre 11. Prairie Falcons have nested on the large cliff southeast of the lookout, and White-throated Swifts are common there in summer. Other species to watch for are Lewis's Woodpecker and Lazuli Bunting.

At kilometre 14.6, **Long Joe Road** branches off on the north side of the highway, providing access to some Ponderosa Pine and Douglas-fir habitat. White-headed Woodpeckers have been seen here, as well as along Hewitt Road a little farther on; other pine and fir forest birds such as Pygmy and White-breasted

Nuthatches are somewhat easier to find, and Dusky Grouse, Flammulated Owls (at night in May and June), and Northern Pygmy-Owls are distinct possibilities. The rest area at kilometre 19.6, as well as any of the side roads (part of the **Regal Ridge** development), can produce the typical Ponderosa Pine birds as well, including the very rare White-headed Woodpecker.

On the north side of the highway at kilometre 22.1, **Sidley Mountain Road** is a loop route through forest and farmland, and the branch to the north, 6 kilometres from the highway, ends in lower subalpine forest. Check the grove of mature Western Larch and Engelmann Spruce along **Wagon Wheel Road**, a short distance south of Sidley Mountain Road, for Williamson's Sapsuckers and, if you're really lucky—Great Gray Owl.

Watch for Swainson's Hawks in summer (Rough-legged Hawks replace them in winter) over the grasslands of Anarchist Mountain, especially eastward from the summit. In winter, the grasslands in this area often host large flocks of Common Redpolls and Snow Buntings. Johnstone Creek Provincial Park, past Bridesville at kilometre 45 is worth a stop or an overnight stay. Just before the Rock Creek Bridge at kilometre 50.3, Baldy Mountain Road branches off to the left (north); this makes an ideal day loop, returning to Oliver via the **Camp McKinney Road** (see page 217). The next good campground after Johnstone Creek is Kettle Valley Provincial Park, 6.4 kilometres north of Rock Creek, noted for its Barred Owls and Northern Pygmy-Owls. But we're well east of the Okanagan now, so let's return to Osoyoos.

> Haynes Point Provincial Park

Just before the Canada-U.S. border on Hwy. 97 there is a turn-off (east, 2.8 kilometres south of the Hwy. 3 junction) to **Haynes Point Provincial Park**. In spring and summer, the park is a busy camping and picnic area, but the birding can be rewarding all year. There are some marshes at the base of the spit that can be accessed by some well-signed trails. All three species of teal nest here, as well as Red-necked Grebe, American Bittern (rare), Virginia Rail, Sora, and Marsh Wren. Gray Catbird, Yellow Warbler, Common Yellowthroat, and Black-headed Grosbeak are some of the other local residents. Don't forget to check the lake. From late fall through spring, large numbers of grebes and loons are present (as long as it is not frozen), as well as Common and Red-breasted Mergansers—this is the best place in the southern Interior to find the latter species. In summer, the diversity of waterfowl drops off, but there is usually a small group of Western Grebes south of Haynes Point, and Caspian Terns are often seen resting on the beach with the local Ring-billed Gulls.

> Richter Pass, Mount Kobau, and Chopaka Customs

The drive west from Osoyoos on Hwy. 3 over Richter Pass to the Similkameen Valley offers a diversity of birding, primarily in sagebrush and marshy pond habitats. Starting at the Hwy. 97 junction, the road slowly climbs northwest through open country, with sage grassland to the south and vineyards to the north. At kilometre 5.2, there is a scenic viewpoint overlooking **Osoyoos Lake**; this is a beautiful spot to find Violet-green Swallows and Rock Wrens, as well as the ever-present flock of ravens attracted to the dump below. Look carefully through the ravens for Golden Eagles often soaring with them.

Kilpoola Lake road branches off to the south at kilometre 6.8. The signed road off the highway is Old Richter Pass Road. Follow that up the hill to a four-way junction. Before turning left (south) on Kruger Mountain Road (which turns into the Kilpoola Lake road), it's often worthwhile to check the small lake northwest of the junction. The best way to view it is by turning right (north) on Kruger Mountain Road. Depending on the time of year and water levels, Hidden Lake, as some birders call it, can be bursting with waterfowl and shorebirds. After a

Common Poorwill

satisfactory look, continue straight at the intersection on Kruger Mountain Road; soon the pavement turns to dirt, and this is the Kilpoola Lake road. In mid-winter, this is often about as far as most would wish to go in a two-wheel-drive vehicle; in spring and summer, the road is usually suitable for almost any vehicle. This is a very popular birding and picnicking destination in the south Okanagan, especially in spring and summer. The Kilpoola Lake road winds up the hills, passing several marshy ponds and small lakes in excellent open Ponderosa Pine and Douglas-fir forest. The first pond on the right, known as Turtle Pond, is an excellent place to take a stroll, looking for water birds and watching and listening for Pileated Woodpeckers, Red-naped Sapsuckers, or Northern Pygmy-Owls. The next wetland, Reed Lake, has breeding Ruddy Ducks, as well as both rail species and several other resident ducks. At night, the stretch of road leading up the hill past Reed Lake (past the cattle guard) can produce Common Poorwill (May to early September), Northern Saw-whet Owl, and Flammulated Owl (May to early July). **Blue Lake** is the first large lake you will reach (kilometre 4.3); it is well worth a detailed look and another walk. At kilometre 6.2, the road comes to a junction. To get to **Kilpoola Lake** and some quality sage brush habitat, turn left (south) by crossing over the cattle guard. Otherwise, continuing straight will eventually lead you to the "International Grasslands"—not advisable without a 4×4 vehicle and someone who knows the area well. Brewer's Sparrows are abundant in the sagebrush along the first stretch of road heading south toward Kilpoola Lake (before the gate). Sage Thrashers and Clay-colored Sparrow are also seen here in some years, whereas House Wrens and Red-naped Sapsuckers are usually evident in the aspen copses. After passing through the gate toward Kilpoola Lake itself, watch for both species of bluebird, Lark Sparrow, Chipping Sparrow, and with luck, you may hear the insect-like trill of a Grasshopper Sparrow. The lake can host a variety of ducks and often yields a few shorebirds in spring and late summer into fall.

If you return to Hwy. 3 and turn left (northwest), **Spotted Lake** (kilometre 8.3 from Osoyoos) is an interesting sight with its rings of magnesium sulphate but usually harbours few birds on its waters or shores. The sage-covered hills around it and the next two ponds, however, are terrific spots for Brewer's Sparrows and the occasional Sage Thrasher; a Black-throated Sparrow was seen here once.

Richter Pass is not very high (675 metres) and is quickly reached at kilometre 11.2. Here the road to the top of Mount Kobau branches off to the northwest. Watch for Western Bluebirds in the aspen copses and Chukar on the fence posts along the road as it descends to the southwest. Look for Lewis's Woodpeckers in the lone Ponderosa Pine south of the highway at kilometre 21.

The high ridge to the northwest of Richter Pass is **Mount Kobau**. A gravel road climbs 20 kilometres through sagebrush grasslands, Douglas-fir forests, Lodgepole Pine and subalpine fir forests to its peak at 1,800 metres. Kobau is probably not the best mountain for high-elevation bird diversity in the Okanagan, but it is certainly convenient and the views are magnificent. Over the first 3 kilometres, watch for Mountain Bluebirds nesting in nest boxes and Lewis's Woodpeckers in the big Douglas-fir snags. Frequent stops along the road should result in a long list of forest birds by the time you reach the top. One of the most appealing things about birding Kobau is the combination of sage and subalpine forest at the summit, where Brewer's Sparrows, Western Meadowlarks, and Lazuli Buntings sing alongside Hermit Thrushes and Fox Sparrows. There is a picnic site just below the summit.

As Hwy. 3 turns north toward Keremeos, a secondary highway branches off to the south at kilometre 21.6 and leads to Nighthawk, Washington. The 2.7-kilometre drive to the **Chopaka Customs** is a must for sagebrush birding. South of the farm fields to the east, both sides of the road are excellent places to find Western Kingbirds, Sage Thrashers (especially around the boulders near the entrance to the Elkink Ranch), Brewer's Sparrows, and Lark Sparrows from May through July; Long-billed Curlews, Horned Larks, and Grasshopper Sparrows are also occasionally seen (the curlews are most often found in the flat grasslands right along the border, east of the road). Mammal watching can be rewarding here as well; badgers are occasionally reported, and this is the last known site in British Columbia for White-tailed Jackrabbit (admittedly thirty years ago). The east side of the road is private land, so don't cross the fence on that side; the west side is Crown (public) land.

> Road 22

At the north end of Osoyoos Lake, the dykes along the Okanagan River channel provide access to public lands adjacent to the old river oxbows, amid lush pastures and arid benches. Nearby, the Haynes' Lease Ecological Reserve offers antelope-brush habitat at the base of towering rock cliffs. The proximity of such a wide variety of interesting bird habitats makes the **Road 22-Osoyoos oxbows** area one of the finest birding spots in Canada.

To reach this area, travel north on Hwy. 97 from the junction with Hwy. 3 (at the Husky gas station). At kilometre 5.4, you can scan the north end of Osoyoos Lake for waterfowl; Yellow-billed Loons are occasionally seen between September and May. At kilometre 7.7, turn right (east) at the No. 22 Road sign; if you're driving south from Oliver, take the first left after passing Road 21 at Deadmans Lake. The south end of **Deadmans Lake** is a prime location for waterfowl and shorebirds in spring and fall. The species diversity is often impressive in this small shallow lake, and if the water levels are right in April and May, or August and September, this can be the best place in the South Okanagan for shorebirds.

Immediately after crossing the cattle guard just off the highway, check the wet fields or marshes on either side of the road for marsh birds in spring. In summer, Wilson's Snipe, Soras, Marsh Wrens, and Yellow-headed Blackbirds are usually present. From mid-May through August, look for Bobolinks in the fields between the highway and the river; this is one of the best spots in British Columbia for this species. Long-billed Curlews also nest in these and other fields in the immediate area; they are most easily seen in April and May. Once you're at the bridge, you can drive south on the southeast dyke or park at the kiosk and continue on foot or by bicycle in any direction to explore the public lands on both sides of the river, or you can continue driving straight ahead to Black Sage Road. We recommend a drive to the south end of either dyke to scan the mouth of the **Okanagan River** for gulls, terns, or waterfowl. The birch woodlands along the old oxbows are excellent spots for migrants in spring and offer chances to see Great Horned and Long-eared Owls in winter and early spring before the leaves are out. Both species nest in old crow nests high in the birches; Northern Saw-whet Owls nest in the nest boxes provided for them. In summer, Gray Catbirds, Veeries, House Wrens, and Yellow Warblers are common in the birch groves, whereas Least Flycatchers and American Redstarts are annual but scarce. A few pairs of Yellow-breasted Chats nest in the rose thickets on the east side of the river. Wood Duck are also present in summer. You can walk or cycle north along the dykes all the way to Oliver, but the stretch north of Road 18 (the first road bridge north of Road 22) is not as productive. Turning left (west) at Road 18 brings you back to Hwy. 97, and turning right (east) will take you to Black Sage Road (see below), if you take another right at the first Y-junction.

If you continue past the Road 22 bridge, you soon come to a T-junction at some old ranch buildings; these are outbuildings from the historic Haynes Ranch, once the largest landholding in the Okanagan Valley, stretching from Penticton to the U.S. border. Barn Owls used to nest here, but lately only Barn Swallows, Rock Pigeons, Black-billed Magpies, and Say's Phoebes call it home. Turning left (north) puts you on **Black Sage Road** to Oliver.

Driving north along Black Sage Road, from the old barn, offers the best access to the **Haynes' Lease Ecological Reserve**. Take the paved road (Meadowlark Lane) up the hill to your right (east) on the south side of the southernmost vineyard. This short but steep road takes you to the north entrance to the reserve and is worth a trip at any time of year. Remember that camping, fires, and plant and animal collecting are not allowed in the reserve. Golden Eagles, Chukar, and Canyon Wrens are present year round on the rock cliffs and talus slopes of "The Throne," the large bluff forming the northeast corner of the reserve. In winter, watch for flocks of American Tree Sparrows in the antelope brush and the occasional Prairie Falcon overhead. In spring and summer, Turkey Vultures are often soaring overhead, and Rock Wrens, Lazuli Buntings, Cassin's Finches, and Lewis's Woodpeckers are singing and calling from the trees and bushes surround the cliffs. Lark Sparrows are common in the antelope brush, and a noisy pair of Peregrine Falcons nests on the cliffs.

Continuing north along Black Sage Road will lead eventually to Camp McKinney Road and Oliver (detailed in the next section). In winter, House Finches and Bohemian Waxwings are abundant in the vineyards along the way, and a worthwhile stop in that season is the **Southern Plus feedlot**, 5.3 kilometres north of Road 22. Turn right (east) up the hill until you get to the feedlots. In winter, this is usually the best spot in the south Okanagan to find Mourning Dove, Brewer's and Red-winged Blackbirds, and the occasional Western Meadowlark, Rusty Blackbird, Yellow-headed Blackbird, or Brown-headed Cowbird. Birders are usually permitted to drive between the stalls of the feedlots, but be sure to ask permission at the office. In recent winters, flocks of close to one hundred Eurasian Collared-Doves have been encountered.

OLIVER

The town of Oliver is a major crossroads for birders. Hwy. 97 passes straight through town, leading north to Vaseux Lake and, eventually, Penticton and south to Osoyoos. At the main intersection, you can also choose to head west on 350th Avenue, which will eventually turn into Fairview-White Lake Road, or east across the Okanagan River to the northern terminus of Black Sage Road and the start of our next recommended birding road.

› Camp McKinney Road and Mount Baldy

If you're turning off Hwy. 97, head east at the main lights in downtown Oliver (at the Esso/7-Eleven) and cross the bridge. Stay right at the Y-junction to continue east on 362nd Avenue past the Petro-Canada station *(Note: Since this gas station is on a First Nations reserve, gas is usually around 1 cent cheaper per litre)*. You will see Black Sage Road on your right (which leads south to Road 22), but you should continue straight onto **Camp**

Gray Flycatcher

McKinney Road if you're hankering for some sagebrush and pine forest birding. Note that for the first 9.5 kilometres, you are passing through the Oliver-Osoyoos Indian Reserve and are not permitted to leave the road. Just after kilometre 3, the road climbs onto a wide open plateau of sage and antelope brush known as Manuel's Flats. Long-billed Curlews are occasionally seen (mainly near the power lines), and Killdeer are annual nesters. Both Vesper and Lark Sparrows are common (the latter is most easily seen around the rock piles at the east end of the flats), and Sage Thrashers are reported sporadically. After leaving the flats, the road passes a couple of creek crossings with some riparian habitat, which is perfect for Nashville Warbler, Lazuli Bunting, Western Bluebird, and Calliope Hummingbird, to name a few. Once you get to kilometre 10, it's time to start looking out for one of McKinney's top attractions: Gray Flycatcher. The Canadian range of this pale grey *Empidonax* is limited to three or four reliable sites in the south Okanagan, and this is the most accessible. Listen for its *chilep-chilep* song coming from the pines near the cattle guard just past kilometre 10. Other features to look for include the black tip on its lower mandible and its habit of downward tail pumping. Be aware that similar-looking species such as Western Wood-Pewee, Dusky Flycatcher, and Hammond's Flycatcher also occur here. This area is also superb for open forest–loving birds, such as Clark's Nutcracker, three species of nuthatch, House Wren, Cassin's Finch, Red Crossbill, Townsend's Solitaire, and Chipping Sparrow.

At around kilometre 11.4 there is a pull-off on the left side and an inconspicuous sign that reads, Woody's Landing. This is the site of the famous White-headed Woodpecker of 2001 that many people managed to see. Although there have not been any reports of this rare cone lover at this site since that year, recent sightings less than a kilometre away suggest a small, persistent population in the area (at least two birds, that is!). Near kilometre 12, a gravel road turns off to the right (Old Camp McKinney Road), which leads to the site of the most recent White-headed Woodpecker reports (2010). Stay right at McCuddy Creek Road and head down the hill for a few hundred metres, passing a few small farms. Porcupine Place branches off to the right and if you drive all the way to the end, near an obvious gas line cut through the forest, you can park your car and continue on foot through a small gate to explore the pines to the north. This is another good area for Gray Flycatcher, as well as all the species mentioned around kilometres 9 and 10, and if you get really lucky, you'll find a White-headed Woodpecker. Check out Shrike Hill Road (continue down McCuddy Creek Road and make a quick left). There are a few ponds here that can yield a variety of ducks and shorebirds, and most of the forest around the first pond is public land.

For those who wish to continue up into higher elevation forests, Camp McKinney Road eventually leads to the **Mount Baldy ski area**. Near kilometre 33.6 (from the beginning of Camp McKinney Road near the Petro-Canada gas station), take a left at the junction and head up to the ski village. This is a prime area for subalpine species, such as Spruce Grouse, Northern Goshawk, Northern Pygmy-Owl, American Three-toed Woodpecker, Gray Jay, Boreal Chickadee, Pacific Wren, Pine Grosbeak, and White-winged Crossbill (numbers vary from year to year). From here, you can either return straight to Oliver or head southeast from the kilometre-33.6 junction, which connects with Hwy. 3 on Anarchist Mountain after around 17 kilometres (see page 208).

> Fairview-White Lake Road

From the main intersection in Oliver, head west on 350th Avenue/Fairview Road. Check the telephone wires for Eurasian Collared-Doves, especially along the first stretch of houses. There is a Bank Swallow colony on the left side of the road as it leaves the orchards and winds up through a gulley. After 4.3 kilometres, turn right (north) onto **Fairview-White Lake Road**. For the first 5 kilometres, this road winds through hills burned by a forest fire in 1970 and various rural properties; the best birding on this road is along the next stretch, where it travels through Ponderosa Pine forests and the course of Victoria Creek, marked by the growth of deciduous shrubs on the east side of the road. In spring, watch the dead branches atop these shrubs for male hummingbirds; the common species here are Black-chinned and Calliope. A few Least Flycatchers nest in the aspen copses. After about 7.5 kilometres, you will reach the junction for Secrest Road; you can turn right (east) here to join up with River Road (see below) or continue straight north to White Lake (see page 233). The pine forests immediately north of the intersection are public land and home to White-breasted and Pygmy Nuthatches year round and Western Bluebirds and Cassin's Finches in spring and early summer. Continuing north, you will reach the rural community of Willowbrook, and 4.5

kilometres north of the Secrest Road junction, you will reach the Green Lake Road junction on your left (see page 232). Turning east here will take you to Okanagan Falls; keeping straight north will take you to White Lake and on to Penticton.

> ## Secrest Road and River Road

If you're coming from Oliver on Fairview-White Lake Road, at kilometre 11.3 you can turn off on **Secrest Road**, which loops back to Hwy. 97 north of Oliver, and also **River Road**—another key birding spot (if you're coming from the north, it's the first left/east after the Green Lake Road turnoff). Along the first stretch of Secrest Road you will cross Park Rill, a small creek. Western Screech-Owl can sometimes be found here at nighttime; and in the daytime, many of the typical dry-forest specialties can be seen, such as Pygmy and White-breasted Nuthatch, Calliope Hummingbird, Western Bluebird, and House Wren. The terrain opens out into antelope brush and balsam root near Covert Farms, before heading down a steep hill to the valley bottom, where River Road turns off on the left (north side); continuing straight will lead you to the highway.

This first stretch of River Road (coming from Secrest Road) is sandy gravel and hugs the hillside until it turns into pavement and heads straight south to the highway (see Map 18). Birding can be excellent along this road. A pair of Say's Phoebes nests around the farm buildings at the Secrest end (April to August), and Great Horned Owls roost in the birches near the road. Ring-necked Pheasants and California Quail abound in the fields; raptors, swallows, and swifts patrol the skies overhead; and **Hack's Pond** (a small wetland beside the gravel portion of the road) is full of birds in spring and summer, including all three teal species, both rail species, Marsh Wren, House Wren, Willow Flycatcher, Yellow Warbler, Black-headed Grosbeak, Eastern Kingbird, and Gray Catbird. When you get back onto pavement at the north end of River Road, look for the male Black-chinned Hummingbird that reliably perches on the telephone wires above the street. If you're coming from the highway end of River Road, this spot is where River Road turns slightly to the left and about 200 metres south of where the road turns sharply left (west) onto the gravel portion. If you park near the entrance to a gravel road on the east side of River Road (at present this road is public land), look and listen for one of the skulky but vocal Yellow-breasted Chats that reside in the thick foliage to the east. There are several pairs here; thus, this site has become one of the more popular spots to view this species in Canada. Gray Catbird, Red-eyed Vireo, and Black-headed Grosbeak are also fairly common (May to August), and Bewick's Wrens have been found here year round in recent years.

› Inkaneep Provincial Park

From the junction of River Road and Hwy. 97, head east for 450 metres across the bridge, then turn right at the gas station on Tuc-ul-nuit Road. Continue south for 400 metres, then turn right (west) onto Campsite Road and park at the end. Although the park is no longer open to overnight campers (picnickers are welcome), it is still a great spot for birding at any time of year. In spring and fall, the thickets around the old camping loop, and the rich riparian habitat along the river, attract a diversity of migrants in early to mid-May. In summer, Yellow-breasted Chats, Gray Catbirds, Black-headed Grosbeaks, and Black-chinned Hummingbirds (and much more) breed, whereas in winter, the park is taken over by roving flocks of kinglets and chickadees (in November 2010, a Northern Parula was discovered in one of these groups!), as well as other locally uncommon winter birds, such as Pacific Wren and Spotted Towhee. At any time of year, watch and listen for the rare Bewick's Wren, a new arrival to the Okanagan.

After birding this spot, you may choose to re-park near the highway bridge and take a walk or bike ride down the paved pathway that overlooks the Okanagan River. The dyke is paved all the way to Oliver and takes you past some cottonwood stands and marshy oxbows. Otherwise, you may want to return to Hwy. 97 or continue south on Tuc-ul-nuit Road, which passes the small but sometimes productive **Tugulnuit Lake** (yes, it's spelled wrong on the road sign) and eventually links up with the northern end of Black Sage Road and the bottom of Camp McKinney Road (see Map 18).

OKANAGAN FALLS

Like Oliver, the small town of "Ok Falls" is an ideal place to begin an Okanagan birding adventure. Starting in town, you may want to scan for water birds on **Skaha Lake** (from the boat launch at the north end of Main Street, along the main beach, or from the old railway trestle at the northwest corner of town). Several pairs of Red-necked Grebes nest along the shoreline close by, as well as at the lagoon above the dam (visible from the highway bridge).

Okanagan Falls Provincial Park is a popular spot for birders and campers alike. To get there, turn south on Green Lake Road (immediately west of the highway bridge at the northwest corner of town), follow the river for about 100 metres, then turn into the park. The river usually sports river ducks such as goldeneye (both species), Bufflehead, and occasionally a Harlequin Duck or two. A pair of American Dippers nests on the dam itself, and in winter, ten to fifteen dippers can be counted between the dam and the south end of the park. Springtime is perhaps the best time to visit, as the deciduous trees around the camping area act as a magnet for migrating warblers, flycatchers, and other birds. High above, along cliffs, watch for White-throated and Vaux's Swifts, Golden Eagle, and the occasional Peregrine and Prairie

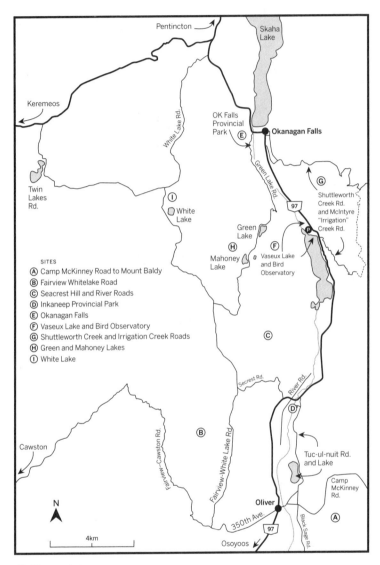

SITES
A Camp McKinney Road to Mount Baldy
B Fairview Whitelake Road
C Seacrest Hill and River Roads
D Inkaneep Provincial Park
E Okanagan Falls
F Vaseux Lake and Bird Observatory
G Shuttleworth Creek and Irrigation Creek Roads
H Green and Mahoney Lakes
I White Lake

18 Vaseux Lake

Falcon. Canyon Wrens are present year round but are often hard to hear because of the river sounds. On warm summer evenings, Common Nighthawks gather in swarms of hundreds and fly-catch low over the river, though numbers have been decreasing in recent years.

After exploring the town itself, it is now time to discover the other gems that lie nearby.

› Vaseux Lake

Only 5.5 kilometres south of Okanagan Falls (12 kilometres north of Oliver) is one of the Okanagan's most scenic and impor-tant natural areas: **Vaseux Lake**. This is the narrowest part of the Okanagan Valley and has been the focus of conservation efforts since the 1920s. Much of the land around the lake is part of the **Vaseux-Bighorn National Wildlife Area**. There is a small provin-cial park near the northeast corner, and several other properties around the lake are owned by the Nature Trust of B.C. It is no surprise that this area is a fantastic destination for bird lovers at any time of year. Large numbers of waterfowl can usually be found on the lake, especially during peak migration times in spring and fall. Both Tundra and Trumpeter Swans overwinter at the north end of the lake (unless it freezes completely), and substantial numbers of diving ducks are present throughout the year, with Redheads usually being the most prevalent. If you stop in at the gravel parking lot at the northeast end of the lake (signed off Hwy. 97 just north of the provincial park camp-grounds), a boardwalk will take you to a two-storey blind where you can get a closer look at some of the lake and marsh residents, such as Pied-billed Grebe, Marsh Wren, and Great Blue Heron. When water levels are low, a sandbar is exposed near the mouth of the Okanagan River (visible from the blind), where gulls, terns, and shorebirds occasionally congregate (scope needed). Along the boardwalk, you will pass several oxbows, where all three teal species can be found in spring and summer, as well as many other typical species, such as Belted Kingfisher and Virginia Rail. Veery, Gray Catbird, Yellow Warbler, Black-headed Grosbeak, and occasionally Yellow-breasted Chat can be heard singing from the thick brush. Remember to scan the cliffs to the east and west for Golden Eagle or Peregrine Falcon.

> ## Vaseux Cliffs and Irrigation Creek

To get a closer look at the cliffs and the birds associated with them, head south from the boardwalk area and turn east onto McIntyre Creek Road (known by local birders as **Irrigation Creek Road**, since that's the name of the creek that the road follows). Be sure to stop regularly along the lower sections of this gravel road, as this is one of the best places in Canada to see warm-cliff specialties such as Chukar, Canyon Wren, Rock Wren, and White-throated Swift. Large groups of California Bighorn Sheep can usually be seen either on the cliffs or down in the grasslands on the other side of the road, especially from October through April. About 800 metres up the road there is a sharp curve to the left. If you find a safe place to park here, it's worth a stop. This is a great place to find the formerly mentioned cliff birds and to overlook the lake and marvel at the views of McIntyre Bluff to the south. Lazuli Buntings, Vesper Sparrows, Western Meadowlarks, and Say's Phoebe can all be heard singing from the grasslands (and if you're lucky, you may spook a covey of Gray Partridge), while Western Kingbirds and American Kestrels watch for food from the high perches.

In addition to the cliff specialties, birders visit this road because it is one of the more reliable locations for Lewis's Woodpeckers. At least six pairs nest along the first 3.5 kilometres of the road; look for them around the large, burned snags or power poles. Although they are woodpeckers, these gorgeous green-and-pink birds fly like crows and have a diet consisting mainly of airborne insects and fruit. Since the fire of 2003 and subsequent logging, the upper reaches of this road are less hospitable for forest birds than they once were. Still, with a little bit of effort, all three species of nuthatches can be encountered in the live pines that remain, and other open forest species such as Cassin's Finch, Townsend's Solitaire, and Western Bluebird are also present for most of the year. After the first kilometre or so, the land on either side of the road is private, so stay on the road while birding. The road is gated after a Y-junction about 3 kilometres up; you can reach the upper parts of the left branch of this road via the Shuttleworth Creek forest road (see page 228).

> Vaseux Lake Bird Observatory

Another worthwhile but little-known spot for birders is the **Vaseux Lake Bird Observatory**, located exactly 1 kilometre north of the boardwalk parking lot (or roughly 4.5 kilometres from downtown Okanagan Falls). Park near the barbed-wire gate on the west side of the road and walk down the track. Every morning throughout August, September, and the first half of October, bird researchers use mist nets to capture and band migratory birds to gain a better understanding of bird population trends, dispersal patterns, and physiological attributes such as moult cycles and fat production. Simply put, it's a chance to see birds up close. Visitors (and volunteers) are welcome, so drop in. Outside of the banding season, this area is very under-visited but still fantastic for birds (especially during spring migration).

Once you're at the bottom of the short track, you can go south or north. South will take you along the main net lanes that border a long oxbow. Sora and Virginia Rail are common here, and Yellow Warbler, Gray Catbird, Willow Flycatcher, Veery, and Common Yellowthroat are some of the songbirds that nest here. In spring, Northern Waterthrush, MacGillivray's Warbler, and many others can be found in the low birches, and in the open areas, watch for fly-catching Eastern Kingbirds. Heading north will take you past another oxbow and through a thick stand of willows and birch, where both Long-eared and Barn Owls can be found roosting. Eventually, the trail leads onto the dyke, providing an excellent opportunity to check the Okanagan River and scan over the large marsh on the other side. You can walk south almost all the way to the lake, but going north ends at private property.

> ### Shuttleworth Creek and Venner Meadows

Like Vaseux Lake and Road 22, many birders consider **Shuttleworth Creek Road** (AKA 201 Road), a must on any trip to the Okanagan. The forest-bird diversity is hard to match—a productive morning along this logging road in mid-May could yield eighty species! To reach it from the centre of Okanagan Falls, head east at the main intersection (at the lone service station) on 9th Avenue for two blocks, then turn right (south) onto Maple Street. Continue along this road for 1.4 kilometres, then turn left (east) onto Commercial/Weyerhaeuser Road. Keep right at the first intersection, then skirt the old Weyerhaeuser lumber yards for 1 kilometre or so before reaching a T-junction. A pair of Mountain Bluebirds nests near that last bend in the road. Turn right at the T-junction and head east along Shuttleworth Creek— you are now on the Shuttleworth/201 logging road (note the yellow kilometre markers), and it's time to bird!

Note: Most birding groups start their birding from the top of the mountain and work their way down; this ensures that you're at the top for peak activity time for high-elevation targets such as Spruce Grouse, Williamson's Sapsucker, and Boreal Chickadee. For reasons of convenience, this guide explains the route from the bottom up, so we suggest taking note of each recommended stop as you ascend the road first thing in the morning, then birding it in reverse.

For the first two kilometres, the road passes through some creekside habitat, which is a good place for Veery, Yellow Warbler, Pacific-slope Flycatcher, and Cassin's Vireo. Once the road leaves the creek, look out for Lark Sparrows and Western Bluebirds, which favour the open, dry Ponderosa Pine and antelope-brush habitats, and listen for Nashville Warblers singing from shaded gullies. At kilometre 4.2, a hairpin turn marks a terrific place to pull over and enjoy the view, as well as a few birds. Rock Wrens, House Wrens, and Lazuli Buntings are usually conspicuous at this stop (spring and summer) as they fill the morning with energetic song. A pair of Lewis's Woodpeckers uses one of the large snags near the corner to nest each year, and Black-backed Woodpecker is a possibility in this old burn. Around kilometre 5.3, park at the top off Irrigation Creek Road (the unmarked track that heads off to the right). This is a great area for all three nuthatch species, Red Crossbill, Cassin's Finch, Evening Grosbeak, House Wren (spring and summer), and Clark's Nutcracker. Rock Wrens are usually calling from up on the rocky hillsides, and Spotted Towhees and Calliope Hummingbirds are also evident in the breeding season. It may be worthwhile to walk down the track for a kilometre or so in search of forest birds; the rare Gray Flycatcher can be found here in some years. This locally rare *Empidonax* used to be more regular, but the 2003 forest fire seems to have disturbed this once reliable site. Dusky Flycatchers still breed in large numbers, so be careful with your drab flycatcher identification. Knowing the vocalizations is probably the best ways of telling them apart.

After this stop, the main road continues through pine forest with similar species for another 2 kilometres. Between kilometres 8 and 12, birding is quiet because you're passing through young fir and larch forest. At kilometre 12.2, stop at the major junction of 201 and 200 Roads. Now you're high enough to start picking up subalpine specialties such as Gray Jay, Pine Grosbeak, and American Three-toed Woodpecker. This is also a likely spot for Williamson's Sapsucker; listen for its distinctive series of short, fast drum rolls. The Red-naped Sapsucker is more common at this location but has a continuous drum roll that slows at the end. Black-backed, Hairy, Downy, Pileated, and Northern Flickers round out the woodpecker possibilities for the area. In spring, the main songsters at this stop include Ruby-crowned Kinglet, American Robin, Swainson's and Hermit Thrush, Cassin's Vireo, Orange-crowned and MacGillivray's Warbler, Dark-eyed Junco, and Chipping Sparrow. Turning right at the junction onto 200 Road (known to birders as **Venner Meadows Road**), will lead to the largest stands of Western Larch—the best spot for Williamson's Sapsucker. The most reliable time to find sapsuckers is late March through early May, when they are drumming noisily.

Only a few hundred metres up this road, **Dutton Creek Road** branches off to the right. The aspen copse at the junction is a good spot for all woodpeckers, and Williamson's Sapsuckers have nested here in some years. Listen for Ruffed Grouse drumming in the forest, and always keep an ear out for the tooting of one of the resident Northern Pygmy-Owls. Between here and kilometre 15 on Venner Road, stop frequently in the larch forest, where many interesting birds can be found, including the sapsucker. *Note: Its call has a harsher more grating quality to it than the Red-naped, and its drum is characterized by a cascading series of double notes.* The start of **Browning Creek Road** (signed off to the right on the Venner Road near kilometre 15) is one of the more reliable spots for the sapsucker, as well as nesting Black-backed Woodpecker. Multiple sightings of Great Gray Owl during the breeding season suggest that this species is probably breeding in the area. You reach **Venner Meadows** itself at about kilometre 19; from here to kilometre 23, the road passes by several willow and sedge wetlands, where a variety of birds can be seen in spring and summer, including waterfowl, Sora, Wilson's Snipe, Willow

Flycatcher, Wilson's Warbler, Common Yellowthroat, Northern Waterthrush, White-crowned Sparrow, Lincoln's Sparrow, Song Sparrow, and Savannah Sparrow. Listen for Pine Grosbeaks and both crossbill species overhead and for the fading-machine-gun drum of the American Three-toed Woodpecker.

For the best chance at truly boreal specialties such as Spruce Grouse, American Three-toed Woodpecker, Boreal Chickadee, and White-winged Crossbill, return to the junction at kilometre 12.2 on the Shuttleworth Creek Road and turn right on **201 Road** (in fact, if these species are your main targets, you may want to cover this road first before moving on to Venner Meadows). For the first few kilometres, the habitat and thus the bird species are similar to the junction: Townsend's Warblers sing from high perches, Evening Grosbeaks and Pine Siskins call overhead, Red-naped Sapsuckers drum in the distance, and the songs of vireos, thrushes, and flycatchers fill the morning air. This starts to change around kilometre 19, where subalpine fir, Engelmann Spruce, and Lodgepole Pine take over from the larch and Douglas-fir. The most well-known place to stop is **Rabbit Lake** (accessed via an unmarked track that runs down to the left, just past the cattle guard at kilometres 22), where Hermit, Swainson's, and Varied Thrushes sing their hearts out each spring and summer. Common Loons, Ring-necked Ducks, and Barrow's Goldeneyes rear their young on the lake, and you should check the floating logs for a pair of Spotted Sandpipers. There is a chance to see Boreal Chickadee anywhere in this area, and White-winged Crossbills are possible any time of year. This spot has been reliable for Boreal Owls over the years, but finding them will require a nighttime visit. Across the road from Rabbit Lake, there is an inconspicuous trail that leads into the woods. If you follow this track for around 400 metres, you will reach the little-known Clark Lake, which boasts many of the same species found at Rabbit Lake and perhaps a greater diversity of water birds, including the occasional pair of Solitary Sandpipers. Spruce Grouse have also been seen along this trail.

Continuing north on 201 Road, the kilometre-24 sign marks "the most reliable Boreal Chickadee stop in the Okanagan" (according to Russell). Mixed chickadee flocks are often close to the road already, but you can also draw them in closer by imitating a Northern Pygmy-Owl or playing a recording (morning is best). Kilometre 25 is also a good spot, and the meadow on the downhill side of the road has many of the same breeding species found at Venner Meadows. If you are here at dawn in May or early June, you also have a great chance of hearing—and possibly seeing—a Spruce Grouse. They are present all year, but in the spring, males perform a unique double wing-clap display that can be heard from quite a distance. Stop periodically between kilometres 24 and 26 between 4:30 and 5:30 AM in late May and listen for the human-like *clap! clap!* Habitat for boreal species tails off around kilometre 28 because of logging patterns, but you can continue north on 201 Road all the way to about kilometre 37, where you can turn left on Carmi Road to reach Penticton.

> Green Lake and Mahoney Lake

From Okanagan Falls Provincial Park, continue south along Green Lake Road. There are several access point to the river, but the one about 2 kilometres south of the park is probably the most interesting. There is ample parking and from here you can walk either way along the dyke or explore the Ducks Unlimited wetlands (south of the parking area, on the west side of the river). From here, Green Lake Road heads up a steep hill to See Ya Later Ranch, then passes **Green Lake** itself. The pine forest between here and the White Lake Road junction is home to all three nuthatch species, Cassin's Finch, and all the other pine-loving birds.

On Green Lake, look for Ruddy Ducks, Bufflehead, and both gold-eneye species throughout the year.

The next lake along the road is **Mahoney Lake**, which is also a fantastic spot for forest birds and has had many White-headed Woodpecker sightings over the years. In spring and fall, check the lakeshore for migrant shorebirds. At night, listen along this stretch for Common Poorwill, Flammulated Owl, and Great Horned Owl. Soon after passing Mahoney Lake, the road reaches the small community of Willowbrook before hitting a T-junction. Turning right puts you at our next birding hot spot.

> White Lake

If you're travelling to White Lake from Penticton (Hwy. 97), take White Lake Road (right-hand turnoff 850 metres south of the Hwy. 3A turnoff), then follow these directions in reverse. About 5 kilometres north of the Green Lake Road–White Lake Road junction, there is a small parking area on the right (east) side of the road, where a gated track leads down toward **White Lake**. You're in a small bowl-shaped valley covered primarily in sagebrush grasslands. In spring and summer, watch for White-throated Swifts whizzing back and forth over the cliffs, and listen for Nashville Warbler, Lazuli Bunting, Chipping Sparrow, and Spotted Towhee singing from the vegetation near the base. Western Meadowlark, Vesper Sparrow, Black-billed Magpie, Mountain Bluebird, and Western Bluebird are some of the more common breeders, but you should always be alert for other goodies—both Chukar and Gray Partridge can be seen on this short walk (if you're lucky), and Golden Eagles are often seen soaring overhead.

About 1.3 kilometres north along White Lake Road from the first parking area, there is a pull-off on the left (west) side. This is a good vantage point from which to scope the lake, if water levels are favourable, and it's also another spot to start a walk. The land on both sides of the road is public (owned by the National Research Council and managed by the Nature Trust of B.C.), so public access is permitted (by foot only). At the pull-off there is a gate at the beginning of an overgrown track. By walking up the track then zigzagging up the hill, you have a decent chance of spooking up a Gray Partridge or two. In most years, a singing Grasshopper Sparrow can be found near the top of the closest rounded hill, but in peak years, this secretive species can be found throughout the White Lake basin—the key is to listen for its insect-like trill (not an easy task with all the beautiful and melodious meadowlarks distracting you!). Just past the pull-off as you continue north, the road starts to go up a hill. The sage on the right (east) side of the road, from the bottom of the hill to the top, is the epicentre of one of the largest Brewer's Sparrow colonies in Canada. Although some observers may dub it the "drabbest sparrow of them all," the rambunctious Brewer's Sparrow has one of the most varied songs. Between 5 and 8 AM each morning in spring and early summer, this patch of sage is overrun by the sound of miniature chainsaws—*buzz buzz buzz buzz, weeer weeer weeeer brrrrrrrrrsp!!!* In recent years, this stretch of road is also the most reliable area in Canada for Sage Thrasher. Although single males occasionally show up in May, the majority of our thrashers appear from mid-June into mid-July, perhaps to raise a second brood in Canada after raising one somewhere in the USA. Like the sparrow, this sage lover is best sought after in the morning, when temperatures are low and birdsong is at its peak.

After cresting the hill, the road comes to a T-junction. Left (north) will take you up **Twin Lakes Road**, which eventually (9 kilometres) leads to Hwy. 3A. Birding is good along this road, both in the sage and alongside the aspen copses, where House Wrens, Lark Sparrows, Lazuli Buntings, and the odd Least Flycatcher can be found. Otherwise, you can take White Lake Road east, then north, past the Dominion Radio Astrophysical Observatory. Between the observatory entrance (where Lark Sparrows can often be found) and the northern terminus of White Lake Road (at Hwy. 97 south of Penticton), you will pass through predominantly Ponderosa Pine habitat—a likely place for most of the pine specialties, such as Pygmy Nuthatch. Once you're out on the highway, you can continue north to Penticton, southwest to Keremeos, or south to Okanagan Falls.

PENTICTON

Nestled between two large lakes (Okanagan and Skaha), Penticton is more of a beach resort town than a birding mecca, especially in summer, when thousands of visitors crowd the lakeshore. Still, visiting birders often choose Penticton as a base of operations because of its proximity to the southern half of the valley, an availability of services, and an airport with regular commercial flights. If birding is not your reason for being in town but you're looking for a spot to spend an hour or two, the Okanagan lakeshore from the **SS Sicamous** (a retired sternwheeler) east to the **Penticton Yacht Club and Esplanade Trails** might be the ticket.

The *Sicamous* is a fairly easy landmark to find—at the north end of Riverside Drive where it turns into Lakeshore Drive. There is ample parking along the lakeshore or by the adjacent mini-golf complex. Between fall and spring, the sheltered cove behind the boat is usually occupied by several hundred coots that are often joined by mergansers, grebes, and diving ducks. If you walk past the rose gardens toward the dam, look downriver for American Dippers, Bufflehead, and Common Goldeneye. There is a rocky pier that juts out into the lake beside the *Sicamous*—this is a prime place to scope the southwest corner of the lake. Otherwise, head east on Lakeshore

Drive toward "The Peach" concession stand. In winter, this beach can host many gulls—mainly Ring-billed, California, Herring, and Glaucous-winged, but Mew and Thayer's are usually around in small numbers, and a Glaucous Gull or two will show up in some years. A longer wooden walking pier points north from the Lakeside Resort, which is usually a good place to see loons and grebes. Continue east along Lakeshore Drive until you reach a T-junction at the colourful Front Street bridge. Take a left here, then stay left on the roundabout, angling north toward the lake. Follow this road east until you reach the yacht club and tennis court parking lot. In winter, this marina has roosting gulls, and diving ducks if there is open water. From the parking lot, there are trails into the adjacent woods and brushy hillsides. In winter, Russian Olives attract frugivorous birds such as Bohemian and Cedar Waxwings, American Robin, Western Bluebird, and the occasional Hermit Thrush. For over a decade, a small flock of Yellow-rumped Warblers has overwintered, thanks to a diet of this introduced tree. Spring and fall give birders the highest numbers and greatest mix of birds, but summer features charismatic nesters like Calliope Hummingbird, Cassin's Vireo, Gray Catbird, Yellow Warbler, and Bullock's Oriole.

> Apex Mountain

As Penticton's nearest ski resort, Apex provides easy access (about a forty-five-minute drive on paved roads) to upper-elevation birds at any time of year. From the Channel Parkway (the Hwy. 97 route along the Okanagan River in Penticton), turn west at a set of traffic lights onto Green Mountain Road (called Fairview Road on the east side of the highway). Gray Jays, Stel-ler's Jays, Clark's Nutcrackers, and Common Ravens all abound throughout the year, and American Three-toed Woodpecker and Pine Grosbeaks can

usually be found with effort. If you're looking for Boreal Chickadees and can't find them around the ski village (Mountains are
the common chickadees here), drive up through the ski cabins
then continue on the main logging road to the northwest, following signs for the Nickel Plate Nordic ski area. The best place for
Boreals is at the sharp right-handed corner just before you reach
the Nickel Plate Nordic ski area. In summer, you can drive (vehicle
with decent clearance required) or hike to the top of **Apex Mountain** (the ski hill is on Mount Beaconsfield) for a chance to find
alpine species such as White-tailed Ptarmigan, Horned Lark, and
American Pipit. From the sharp corner mentioned above, head
east along the power line right-of-way for about 600 metres, then
turn right onto the old Apex Road (there should be a map posted
on a tree)—from there, it is 8 kilometres to the top.

› Carmi-Beaverdell Road

Another way to get up into the high country from Penticton is
via **Carmi-Beaverdell Road**. Head east on Carmi Avenue past the
hospital; soon it will start climbing, which provides spectacular views of the city below. After the Lost Moose Lodge, the road
turns to gravel. Stop where you like, but the true subalpine birding starts around kilometre 12 (yellow markers). The "real boreal"
habitat starts just beyond the yellow "KM 12" marker, where the
Ellis Reservoir is on the left (north) side. All the species mentioned in the Apex account are possible, as well as Boreal Owl. A
few more kilometres up the road, turn right at the junction with
the 201 Road to reach Rabbit Lake and points south (see Map 18).

› Naramata

As the only Okanagan town not located near a highway, **Naramata** is a quiet place to escape from the summer bustle. In
addition to the area's beautiful beaches, one of the highlights

California Quail

is the Kettle Valley Rail Trail, which provides spectacular views of Okanagan Lake and the surrounding countryside. To reach the most popular stretch of the KVR trail, drive north from Penticton along Naramata Road. About fifteen minutes from Penticton you will pass the Naramata Fire Hall on the left. Soon after this you will come to a Y-junction. Stay right at this junction to continue onto North Naramata Road. Take Smethurst Road on the right to the gravel parking area along the KVR. Walk north along the old railway line toward the "Little Tunnel" (4 kilometres one way). In the pines, look for all three nuthatch species, Cassin's Finch, Clark's Nutcracker, and Red Crossbill. Once you reach the tunnel, watch for White-throated Swifts, Violet-green Swallows, and Rock Wrens in spring and summer and Canyon Wren year round. If you strike out on either wren here, try around each rock cut on the way back and at "the big dip" just south of the Smethurst Road parking area, along the KVR trail (where there is also some riparian habitat). In summer, cool off after the long hike by heading down the hill into Naramata proper and jumping in the lake.

> Summerland and Peachland

Between Penticton and Kelowna, the steep hillsides of the Central Okanagan and the size of Okanagan Lake limit birding opportunities; however, there are a few key spots. The **Summerland Ornamental Gardens** (adjacent to the Pacific Agri-Food Research Centre, above Trout Creek Point) and **Okanagan Lake Provincial Park** (just south of Peachland) are both great places to visit during migratory periods (especially after rain-showers in April/May) and in summer for a nice mix of local breeding songbirds. Farther north, travelling birders might want to stop at **Hardy Falls** and **Antlers Beach**. Antlers Beach is signed on the right side, just as you come down the hill on Hwy. 97 into Peachland, and Hardy Street is a left-hand (west) turn nearly opposite the beach. From here, there is a short trail system that leads to a waterfall on Peachland Creek. Visit this spot during hot summer days or in fall, when the Kokanee Salmon are spawning. Western Screech-Owls and Vaux's Swifts nest in the large cottonwoods, and Veeries and Pacific-slope Flycatchers are prevalent songsters in spring and summer. A pair of American Dippers raises a brood along the creek each year, and in fall, look for loons and grebes floating just off the creek mouth.

KELOWNA

Despite rampant development in the past few decades, there are still a wide variety of excellent birding sites in and around the Okanagan's biggest city—you just need to know where to look!

> West Kelowna (Westbank)

Formerly known as Westbank, West Kelowna has some areas along the lakeshore that can be productive throughout the year. The **Gellatly Nut Farm Regional Park** and the mouth of **Powers**

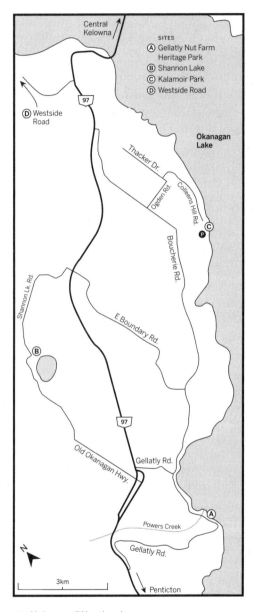

SITES
A Gellatly Nut Farm Heritage Park
B Shannon Lake
C Kalamoir Park
D Westside Road

Okanagan Lake

Central Kelowna

97

D Westside Road

Thacker Dr.

Ogden Rd.

Colleens Hill Rd.

C P

Boucherie Rd.

Shannon Lk. Rd.

B

E Boundary Rd.

97

Old Okanagan Hwy.

Gellatly Rd.

A

Powers Creek

Gellatly Rd.

N

3km

Penticton

19 Kelowna/Westbank

Creek are two spots to check out along Gellatly Road (turn south at the McDonald's), especially in fall, when gull and water bird numbers are high. **Kalamoir Park** is a charming place to take a walk at any time of year and offers a mix of birding habitat and lake access. To find it, turn onto Boucherie Road (south side of the highway close to the Kelowna Bridge), then right on Ogden Road, left on Thacker Drive, then right on Colleens Hill Road. Follow Colleens Hill Road into the park.

If you're spending some extra time in West Kelowna, you may also want to check out **Shannon Lake** (from downtown West Kelowna/Westbank, turn north on Old Okanagan Highway; this will turn into the Shannon Lake Road, and in slightly more than 3 kilometres you will see the small lake on the right side.) A variety of waterfowl is often present, and gulls frequently use it to drink and bathe, as the local dump is close by.

> Westside Road

Westside Road runs from West Kelowna all the way up to Vernon. Like most "scenic routes," it's a longer and windier way to travel to Vernon, but along the way there are some great areas to explore. Otherwise, many Kelowna birders simply visit the sites along the southern portion of the road before turning back to Kelowna. **Bear Creek Provincial Park** is the first hot spot (about 7 kilometres north of the Hwy. 97 bridge). Birding can be fun both on the lake side of the park and along the trails that skirt the impressive Bear Creek Canyon. Also, the log booms just south of Bear Creek are a favoured spot for diving ducks, mergansers, and grebes. You may, of course, stop wherever you like, but the next major stop of interest is **Fintry Point** (31 kilometres north of Hwy. 97). Like Bear Creek, there is a hiking trail that leads up Fintry Creek to some impressive waterfalls. A campground on the north side of the delta is a great place to swim or camp in summer, and a variety of forest habitats in the area can provide for some interesting birding. From here, Westside Road continues north through a mixture of pine and fir forest, old burn, grassland, and farmland before eventually reaching Vernon.

> ## Kelowna Waterfront

Outside of the busy summer months, when beachgoers crowd the lakeshore and water birds have dispersed into the hills and farther north, the Kelowna waterfront can be one of the most rewarding areas in the Okanagan for lake birds. Start the loop at **Sutherland Bay** at the north end of Ellis Street; this protected bay beside the Tolko Mill is a likely spot for waterfowl in fall, winter, and spring—particularly Tundra and Trumpeter Swan, diving ducks, and coots. From here, you can also head up **Knox Mountain** for forest birds and the best views of downtown. To continue the waterfront loop, head back south on Ellis Street, turn right (west) on Manhattan Drive, then left on Sunset Drive, and park along here. This is the access point to the **Rotary Marshes**, where a short boardwalk takes you around the man-made wetland and riparian area, then out to Okanagan Lake. A pair of Ospreys usually nests on the platform provided, and other water birds such as ducks, herons, and kingfishers are almost always conspicuous. If you wish, you can continue walking south along the lake into **Waterfront Park**, the **Kelowna Yacht Club**, and, eventually, **City Park**. Although this area may seem overly manicured and teeming with joggers and dogs, waterfowl are usually plentiful, and occasionally, large raptors such as Peregrine Falcon, Gyrfalcon (winter only), and Bald Eagle will come in and try to find lunch.

South of Hwy. 97/Harvey Avenue, cruise along Abbott Street and check out the various beach accesses. Diving ducks and grebes are usually in evidence from fall into spring, and a variety of gull species are usually present. At most times of year, the best place for gulls is the **Maude-Roxby Bird Sanctuary** (foot of

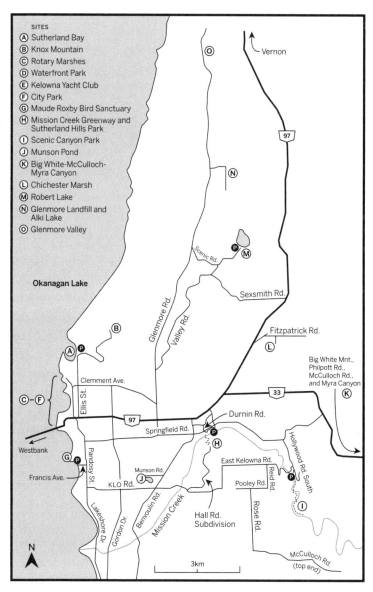

SITES

Ⓐ Sutherland Bay
Ⓑ Knox Mountain
Ⓒ Rotary Marshes
Ⓓ Waterfront Park
Ⓔ Kelowna Yacht Club
Ⓕ City Park
Ⓖ Maude Roxby Bird Sanctuary
Ⓗ Mission Creek Greenway and
   Sutherland Hills Park
Ⓘ Scenic Canyon Park
Ⓙ Munson Pond
Ⓚ Big White-McCulloch-
   Myra Canyon
Ⓛ Chichester Marsh
Ⓜ Robert Lake
Ⓝ Glenmore Landfill and
   Alki Lake
Ⓞ Glenmore Valley

Okanagan Lake

Vernon

97

Ⓞ

Ⓝ

Scenic Rd.

Ⓟ Ⓜ

Sexsmith Rd.

Glenmore Rd.

Valley Rd.

Fitzpatrick Rd.

Ⓑ

Ⓛ

Ⓐ Ⓟ

Big White Mnt.,
Philpott Rd.,
McCulloch Rd.,
and Myra Canyon

Clemment Ave.

Ⓒ–Ⓕ

Ellis St.

33

Ⓚ

Durnin Rd.

97

Springfield Rd.

Ⓟ

Ⓗ

Westbank

Ⓖ Ⓟ

Pandosy St.

Munson Rd.

East Kelowna Rd.

Hollywood Rd. South

Francis Ave.

KLO Rd.

Ⓙ

Pooley Rd.

Reid Rd.

Ⓟ

Lakeshore Dr.

Gordon Dr.

Benvoulin Rd.

Mission Creek

Hall Rd.
Subdivision

Rose Rd.

Ⓘ

McCulloch Rd.
(top end)

N

3km

Pygmy Nuthatch

Francis Avenue). Thirteen species of gulls have been recorded here, including a Lesser Black-backed and an apparently pure Western Gull. The best time is usually fall, when gull numbers are high because of migration and salmon spawning, and the water levels are low, which creates long sandbars out in the bay. Maude-Roxby can also be fantastic for a wide variety of waterfowl, and in spring and summer, check the wetland-boardwalk for marsh species and migrant passerines.

You can continue south on Lakeshore Drive all the way to **Okanagan Provincial Mountain Park.** There are many places to access the lake along this road, and there is always a chance of something wild and extraordinary (especially from August to November). If you do end up in Okanagan Mountain Provincial Park, look out for Northern Pygmy-Owl and Black-backed Woodpecker.

> Mission Creek Greenway and Sutherland Hills Park

Mission Creek is a convenient place for a quick walk, bike ride, or jog. Almost the entire stretch of creek within city limits has gravel or paved paths beside it. Access to these trails can be found at every road bridge over the creek, but the main parking area is behind the Orchard Park Shopping Centre (off Springfield Road, at the south end of Durnin Road). From the parking lot, we suggest you cross the footbridge over the creek to get away from the traffic noise. Also, if you head straight up the hill after crossing the bridge (instead of heading up or down the creek), you will enter the adjacent **Sutherland Hills Park**. This is an excellent area for birding, with its mixture of Ponderosa Pine, cottonwood, and shrubs. As a raised green area in the middle of a city, it often acts as a migrant trap in spring and fall, used by many warblers, vireos, flycatchers, and sparrows. Woodpeckers and nuthatches are present year round, and several local rarities have been recorded in the last couple of years alone, including Magnolia Warbler, Rusty Blackbird, and Ferruginous Hawk. The small ponds in the middle of the park are used frequently by Wood Ducks, teal, and other dabblers, as well as Hooded Mergansers. You can also enter this park from the south end via the **Hall Road subdivision** (turn north off KLO Road). In winter, the side streets around this neighbourhood can be full of birds—particularly waxwings, redpolls, and feeder birds. Check the upper end of Mission Creek, where it passes through **Scenic Canyon Regional Park**, for Western Screech-Owl at night.

> Munson's Pond

When open, **Munson's Pond** can be a fantastic place to look for waterfowl and other birds (spring and fall are best). Turn west on Munson's Road (signed but not obvious) off Benvoulin Road. The pond will be on the left side. There is no public access to the water's edge, but most of the pond is visible from various points of the road. Virtually every Interior duck species can be seen on this pond at some point during the year; of course, migration periods produce the highest numbers. Large flocks of migrating and resident geese use the pond to rest, bathe, and drink during certain parts of the day, before heading out into the orchards to graze. Canada Goose is the most prevalent species, but large numbers of Cackling are often present, and there are usually a couple of Greater White-fronts and Snows mixed in. A pair of Red-tailed Hawks nests in the trees near the road, and Great Horned Owls can sometimes be spotted on the opposite side of the pond. At the end of Munson's Road, there is a path heading west along a wet ditch. This trail connects with the south end of Burtch Road and is usually a great area for sparrows and finches and, in spring and fall, for migrants.

> Big White, McCulloch Lake, and Myra Canyon

Like Penticton and Vernon, the quickest way to the boreal forest from Kelowna is to head up to the ski hills. The road is paved and ploughed all the way up, and several side roads allow birders to get away from the sometimes busy skier traffic. The **Big White Ski Resort** is well-signed off Hwy. 33 east of Kelowna. On the drive up, scan the poles and fence lines along the Black Mountain rangelands for Swainson's Hawk in spring and summer and Rough-legged Hawk in winter. **Philpott Road** (on the left/north side) might be worth a stop for middle-elevation forest birds. It is one of the few places in the Okanagan where Chestnut-backed Chickadees are readily findable—meaning that on this trip up to Big White you have a chance at the "Chickadee Grand Slam" (four species)! There is no one particular spot that is best for birds once you turn onto Big White Road. The common strategy is to find safe pull-offs to listen for birds or explore the side roads and look for feeders around the village. Like Apex and Silver Star, the common year-round birds up here are Gray Jays, Common Ravens, Mountain Chickadees, and American Three-toed Woodpeckers. Pine Grosbeaks and White-winged Crossbills are often encountered, and in spring and summer, many more passerines will be present (mainly thrushes, sparrows, and kinglets).

Another (perhaps less busy) place to try for similar species is around the Nordic trails at **McCulloch Lake**. The turnoff is about 4.6 kilometres south of the Big White turnoff on Hwy. 33. Follow the signs for the cross-country trails and stop where suitable. In winter, there is usually a feeder near the warming hut that attracts nuthatches, nutcrackers, and chickadees. If you're visiting from spring to fall, the many lakes in the vicinity often hold a variety of breeding and migrant waterfowl. Outside of winter, it is worthwhile to head back to Kelowna via **McCulloch Road**, which continues down the hill past the lakes and ski trails. It's a steep and windy road, but it provides remarkable views of Kelowna and the peculiar Layer Cake Mountain, while taking you through a variety of productive birding habitat.

In spring and summer, the **Myra Canyon trestles** are a fantastic place to explore—for birds, scenery, and history. The Okanagan Mountain Provincial Park fire of 2003 destroyed the wooden behemoths, but they have since been restored. Black-backed Woodpecker, Rock Wrens, mountain goats, and pikas are a few of the summertime residents to look out for. This site is well-signed off McCulloch Road, though you may want to check a map carefully beforehand, as this part of Kelowna is quite a maze.

> Chichester Marsh

You wouldn't think that a small marsh surrounded by suburbia would be a great place to bird, but **Chichester Marsh** is just that. It's not as wild as it was even ten years ago, but the small park still attracts large numbers of marsh- and pond-loving birds throughout the year, while also acting as a sanctuary for migrant songbirds. If you're travelling from downtown Kelowna, take Hwy. 97 north and turn right (northeast) on Finns Road (this is the first right turn after the McCurdy Road intersection), then take a right (east) on Fitzpatrick Road, followed by a right (south) on Chichester Court. If you're approaching from north of Kelowna, turn left (east) at the Sexsmith/Old Vernon Road intersection and make an immediate right onto Rutland Road. Drive south on Rutland Road, turn right on Fitzpatrick Road, then turn left onto Chichester Court, and park at the end. Both Sora and Virginia Rail breed here, and male Virginias usually stay all winter. More than 180 species have been recorded in the park, demonstrating the outstanding birding possibilities, especially in spring and fall. Some of the rare finds include Upland Sandpiper (two records), Barn Owl, Tennessee Warbler, Lark Sparrow, and Rose-breasted Grosbeak.

> ### Robert Lake

If you're visiting Kelowna between late March and October, this is a must-see location. As long as it has water in it (which is not always the case in dry years), **Robert Lake** is a mecca for waterfowl, shorebirds, and gulls. To reach Robert Lake from downtown Kelowna, head east (northbound) on Hwy. 97 and turn left (north) on Spall Road, which will soon turn into Glenmore Road. After about 5 kilometres, turn right on Union Road, then left (northeast) on Valley Road, and continue on Valley all the way until you see an alkaline lake with a small parking area.

If you're travelling from Vernon, turn right (west) at the Sexsmith Road intersection, and after a couple of kilometres, turn right on Curtis Road, which will merge with Valley Road. In early spring, the lake is often packed with waterfowl, and from mid-April into May, be sure to look for various shorebirds, including American Avocet (several pairs breed here) and Black-necked Stilt. From mid-July into fall, large numbers of shorebirds are often present, if water levels are right.

> Glenmore Landfill and Alki Lake

The **Glenmore Landfill** services all the waste from the Kelowna region, and like most dumps, it attracts gulls, corvids, blackbirds, and starlings. What separates this facility from other similar operations, however, is that birders are welcome (as of 2011). The other advantage to this spot is that **Alki Lake**, an alkaline slough similar to Robert Lake, is right beside the dump. To reach the landfill, head north on Spall Road/Glenmore Road, past the turnoff to Robert Lake, and then it should be fairly obvious on the right-hand (east) side. You must first check in at the office and fill out a waiver form. From there, you can proceed to the active face (trash heap) or farther on to Alki Lake—it's best to ask the staff where you're allowed to go. For the greatest diversity of gulls, October to April is preferable. Herring is usually the most common species, followed by California, Glaucous-winged, and Ring-billed. In winter, Thayer's and Glaucous Gulls are regular sights, and a lone Lesser Black-backed Gull has been frequenting the dump for more than nine years. Mew Gull and Iceland (Kumlien's) Gull are rarer visitors, and Bonaparte's, Franklin's, and Sabine's Gull have all been recorded, either in the pond behind the office or around Alki Lake itself. In winter, be sure to check the blackbird and starling flocks for Rusty and Yellow-headed Blackbirds.

Unfortunately, Alki Lake is not what it once was. Over the years, it has been gradually filled in and deprived of its water source, and so in the summer, it is usually just a series of puddles. Even so, birds continue to visit the area in large numbers. The channel along the west perimeter road is usually a good spot for a variety of diving and dabbler ducks, whereas the inner ponds offer habitat for migrant shorebirds. At one point, more than thirty pairs of American Avocets bred here, but now (because of water levels) only a few pairs return each year. Along the east perimeter road, there is a small slough with bulrushes, where all three teal species and Yellow-headed Blackbirds are found in spring and summer. From the landfill, you can retrace your steps back to Kelowna or continue north into the narrow **Glenmore Valley** along Glenmore Road, which passes by some pine forest and several wetlands (Bubna Slough and Slater Pond), which often host ducks and shorebirds. Eventually, Glenmore Road reaches downtown Winfield and continues across Hwy. 97 to our next birding road.

> Beaver Lake Road

This is one of the favourite mountain roads among local birders, as it passes through a variety of habitats, reaches the boreal forest quickly, and is much less busy than Big White or Silver Star Roads. To find it, either continue north on Glenmore Road across the highway or head north from Kelowna on Hwy. 97, passing Ellison (Duck) Lake along the way, which is sometimes worth a quick scan. Then turn right (east) at the Glenmore Road/ Beaver Lake Road intersection. The first 6 kilometres of **Beaver Lake Road** pass through extensive grassland, where Swainson's Hawks, Western Bluebirds, Western Meadowlarks, and Vesper Sparrows are common in summer. In winter, this stretch hosts a variety of raptors. As the habitat here changes from open grassland to forest, the birds change accordingly. The first stretch of forest is a mixture of Ponderosa Pine and Douglas-fir. Here you should listen for all three species of nuthatch, Mountain Chickadee, and Cassin's Finch. A little farther along, the road passes through some patches of Western Red Cedar, where Varied Thrush and Golden-crowned Kinglets nest. During the breeding season, expect to find Red-naped Sapsuckers in patches of aspen and birch. In winter, these birches, as well as the roadside alders, are a favourite food source for Common Redpolls, and in some winters—the odd Hoary Redpell! Finally, as you get closer to the

Beaver Lake Lodge, Lodgepole Pine and subalpine fir take over as the dominant trees. American Three-toed Woodpecker is reliable up here, and both crossbill species are possible. Although Mountain is the most common chickadee here, Boreal Chickadees are possible, particularly along the first few kilometres of **Dee Lake Road** (continue left instead of heading to the Beaver Lake Lodge). Gray Jays and Pine Grosbeaks are usually around, and Northern Pygmy-Owl is often encountered. In spring and summer, birders can rack up quite a species total from top to bottom of the road, and if you want to find more high-elevation birds, you can continue north along Dee Lake Road all the way to Vernon.

VERNON

> Vernon Commonage

The **Vernon Commonage** is a grassy ridge between Kalamalka Lake and Okanagan Lake. Birding here is reminiscent of the prairie pothole country east of the Rockies, with soaring Swainson's Hawks, hordes of ducks, and the buzzing songs of Clay-colored Sparrows. In spring and fall, birds are everywhere—Red-tailed Hawks look down from above; an impressive diversity of waterfowl packs the lakes and ponds; and showy bluebirds, meadowlarks, and swallows sun themselves along the fence lines. If you're driving from the south, the main way to enter the commonage is by turning left on Bailey Road off Hwy. 97 (there is a large sign for Predator Ridge here). The first pond on the left is **Bailey Pond**. Despite its small size, a wide variety of ducks are usually present throughout the year. Just up the road at the T-junction, turning left will take you past **MacKay Reservoir** (another excellent spot for scoping water birds) and the Predator Ridge Golf Resort. The road continues

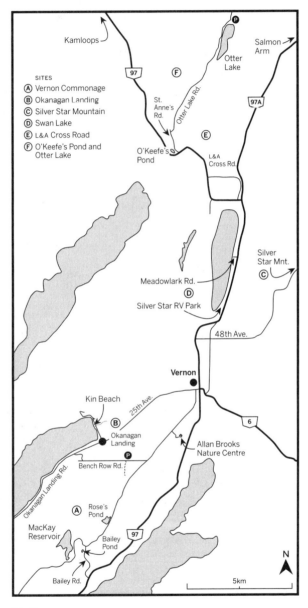

Kamloops

SITES
Ⓐ Vernon Commonage
Ⓑ Okanagan Landing
Ⓒ Silver Star Mountain
Ⓓ Swan Lake
Ⓔ L&A Cross Road
Ⓕ O'Keefe's Pond and Otter Lake

Ⓟ

97

Ⓕ

Otter Lake

Salmon Arm

St. Anne's Rd.

Otter Lake Rd.

97A

Ⓔ

O'Keefe's Pond

L&A Cross Rd.

Silver Star Mnt.
Ⓒ

Meadowlark Rd.

Ⓓ

Silver Star RV Park

48th Ave.

Vernon

Kin Beach

25th Ave.

Ⓑ

Okanagan Landing

Ⓟ

Bench Row Rd.

Allan Brooks Nature Centre

6

Okanagan Landing Rd.

Ⓐ Rose's Pond

MacKay Reservoir

Bailey Pond

97

Bailey Rd.

N

5km

21 Vernon

south all the way to Carr's Landing and eventually connects back to the highway near Winfield. South of Predator Ridge, it continues through beautiful mixed grassland and forest and passes by two small lakes—Tompson and Cochrane (both good for birding). Alternatively, a right-hand turn at the T-junction will eventually lead to Vernon.

We suggest checking MacKay Reservoir (and the other lakes, if you want), then doubling back and heading northeast along Commonage Road. The first interesting stop is the large **Rose's Pond**—great for waterfowl, including nesting Hooded Mergansers, but also good for shorebirds during migration. Continue north, stopping where you like, then just before the intersection with Bench Row Road (heading to the west), stop at the pillared gate on the right side of the road. From May to August, the rose bushes on the hillside behind this gate provide habitat for one of the few Clay-colored Sparrow colonies in the Okanagan.

If you're not here in season, turn left on **Bench Row Road** and continue west for almost 1 kilometre. Here you'll notice a sign for Vernon's experimental tree farm. There is a pull-off on the north side of the road; from here, you can walk through the old plantation and up along the hillside behind. Bird numbers are not always high in the plantation itself, but in winter, this can be a likely spot to look for wintering owls (concentrate your searches in the thick spruce and fir). Great Horned, Long-eared, and Short-eared Owls are present year round, and Barred, Northern Saw-whet, Northern Pygmy, and even Boreal Owl have also been recorded in the plantation in winter. From here, you can either continue westward on Bench Row Road, which will take you down to Okanagan Landing Road (our next location) or head back to Commonage Road and continue left (northeast) to downtown Vernon.

Before leaving the commonage grasslands you will pass the turnoff to the **Allan Brooks Nature Centre** (on the right). The centre is an interesting spot to learn about local ecosystems and one of North America's finest bird artists—Allan Brooks—who lived here from 1897 to 1945.

> Okanagan Landing

From downtown Vernon, take 25th Avenue west to Lakeshore Road and turn right. This road takes you to the mouth of Vernon Creek and **Kin Beach**—ideal for water birds, gulls, and swimming (in summer, of course). During winter, gulls congregate at the mouth of the creek (Lesser Black-backed and Iceland (Kumlien's) Gulls have both been recorded here on multiple occasions). Between fall and spring and to an extent in the summer, this arm of Okanagan Lake hosts large numbers of ducks, grebes, loons, and coots (a scope is recommended). For a bit of forest birding and more lake views, you can continue south on Okanagan Landing Road all the way to **Ellison Provincial Park** (10 kilometres one way, and you will have to return the same way).

> Silver Star

Vernon's ski hill provides easy access to subalpine forest birding at any time of year. To reach **Silver Star Mountain** from Vernon, head east on 48th Avenue/Silver Star Road (which runs east from Hwy. 97 near the north end of town). Follow this road (well signed) for about 20 kilometres up to the ski village. Just west of the main village is the road to the Sovereign Lake cross-country ski trails. At any time of year, it is possible to see upper-elevation specialties in both of these areas, including Spruce Grouse (watch the roadside ditches), Northern Goshawk, American Three-toed Woodpecker, Boreal Chickadee, White-winged Crossbill, and Pine Grosbeak (the latter two are more regular in winter). During the breeding season, Hermit Thrush, American Robin, Yellow-rumped Warbler, Orange-crowned Warbler, Townsend's Warbler,

White-crowned Sparrow, and Dark-eyed Junco are all common (morning is best, when birds are most active).

> ### Swan Lake

North of Vernon along Hwy. 97 lies **Swan Lake**. Virtually the entire shoreline is covered in bulrushes and natural vegetation, and so it is an attractive place for waterfowl, marsh birds, and birders alike. There are three main ways to view the lake.

Starting from the south, along Hwy. 97, the first access point to the lake is the **Silver Star RV Park**. Look for the yellow-and-black sign on the west side of the highway and cross carefully. Since this is a privately owned camping area, you should check in at the office before heading to the lakeshore to bird. From this site, you can scan the southern portion of the lake, which is almost always productive at any time of year, unless the lake is frozen. Spring and fall bring the highest variety of waterfowl, from Common Loon and Horned and Eared Grebes to flocks of Redheads, Ring-necked Ducks, and both Common and Hooded Mergansers. Large flocks of Bonaparte's Gulls pass through in late April and early May, then back again in late summer. Red-necked Phalaropes are also frequently found in spring and fall, usually spinning in circles out in the middle of the lake. Water bird numbers are a bit lower in summer, but you should be able to pick out some of the local breeders, including Cinnamon and Blue-winged Teal, Gadwall, Redhead, and both Pied-billed and Red-necked Grebes. Western Grebes used to nest here but are now only seen on migration or as non-breeders in the summer. Marsh Wrens, Common Yellowthroats, and both Red-winged and Yellow-headed Blackbirds are a common sight around the marshy fringes, and birders will often hear both Sora and Virginia Rails sounding off from deep within the cattails. Between May and August, swarms of midges attract large numbers of swallows and swifts. All six species of swallow are common, and both Vaux's and Black Swifts can be seen high overhead on most days.

For access to the middle section of the lake, continue north on Hwy. 97 for 2 kilometres, then turn left (west) onto **Meadowlark Road**, and park at the end. This is another great area for marsh birds in the bulrushes on both sides of the road and an excellent vantage point for lake watching during migration season.

Finally, you reach the north end of the lake by taking the exit for Kamloops, then making the first left (after passing under the highway) on Highland Road. Park near the trailer park, where you will have a superior view over the south end of the lake, and get out your scope. Chattering Bullock's Orioles can be seen frequently in spring and summer around the cottonwood trees at this end, and this is the good corner of the lake to hear pumping American Bitterns in spring.

› L&A Cross Road, O'Keefe's Pond, and Otter Lake

As you near the north end of Swan Lake (travelling northbound on Hwy. 97), take the exit for Kamloops; after driving due west parallel to the lake, the highway swings north again. The first road on the right (east) side is **L&A Cross Road**, which is often worth a stop in spring and fall. A pair of Long-billed Curlews can often be seen in one of the fields here (April to July), and the muddy pond just east of the farm buildings can be surprisingly productive. There is also a series of marshy reservoirs south of the farm buildings (access via the model aircraft gate). Although this property is managed by the model plane club, birders seem to be permitted to approach the pond as long as they stay out of the way. In spring, the fields around these reservoir cells often flood, which attracts a plethora of waterfowl and shorebirds; and in the evening, this is a wonderful place to watch for Black Swifts heading from the colonies near Enderby to feed over Swan Lake.

Continue north on Hwy. 97 (still toward Kamloops); when you reach a golf course on your left, look out for St. Anne's Road on the right side. Turn onto St. Anne's Road and park beside the small roadside pond. This is **O'Keefe's Pond**, and despite its diminutive size and proximity to a highway, it is one of the best waterfowl hot spots in the Okanagan. In spring and fall, the duck numbers and species change daily, and even in summer, you can expect to see more than a half-dozen species. Tufted Duck has been found here, as well as several Long-tailed Ducks (rare in the southern Interior).

Continue north up St. Anne's Road and turn right onto Otter Lake Road to reach **Otter Lake**. Park at the north end for a good view of the lake and the marsh below. The marsh and fields north of the lake often flood, especially in spring, making it a favourite spot for dabblers, geese, and shorebirds. From here, you can either continue north up Otter Lake Road to the town of Armstrong, where you can get back onto Hwy. 97A, or you can turn right on Otter Lake Crossing Road, which will lead you to Hwy. 97A south of Armstrong.

THOMPSON, NICOLA,

AND

LILLOOET

lthough many people might think of the Okanagan when they hear about desert grasslands in British Columbia, the Thompson Valley and surrounding areas have much more of this kind of habitat, and most of the birds to go with it, along with a strong mix of boreal species on the high plateaus. Pine beetle outbreaks in recent years have taken a heavy toll on the Ponderosa and Lodgepole Pine forests of the region, but pine specialists such as Pygmy and White-breasted Nuthatch are still present where live trees remain. The beetle epidemic has provided at least a short-term boon for woodpeckers, particularly Hairy, Black-backed, and American Three-toed, so if you find sites with newly infested trees (those that still have red needles), it is worth stopping to listen for the *tap-tap-tap* of feeding woodpeckers.

In many ways, the Thompson-Nicola region is a transition zone between the hot sagebrush country of the Great Basin and the pothole lakes, aspen groves, and mixed coniferous forests of the Cariboo Plateau. Here southern birds such as Williamson's Sapsuckers and Lewis's Woodpeckers mingle in the pine and fir forests with American Three-toed Woodpeckers and Gray Jays. Like the Okanagan, the breeding diversity is impressive, and keen birders can easily rack up more than 120 species in a single day in May. Sharp-tailed Grouse (extirpated from the Okanagan) breed in grasslands surrounding Kamloops and are often a top target for visiting birders. There are few Sharp-taileds left, however, and most leks (the grounds where males display in spring) are located on private land, where access is by permission only. Still, with patience it is possible to find these prairie dancers (particularly in winter), along with the large list of birds that also call the Thompson Valley home.

KAMLOOPS

The highest bird diversity of the area is found by exploring the many habitats surrounding Kamloops, but there are also areas of interest within the city. In winter, **Riverside Park** downtown can be a great place for water birds, such as geese, ducks, swans, Bald Eagle, and perhaps a Belted Kingfisher or Great Blue Heron. Great Horned Owls nest in the park and can be found roosting in the large conifers. For a chance to see Chukar, take a trip to the **Sun Rivers subdivision** (on the north side of the South Thompson River) early in the morning. Cross the river on Hwy. 5 (northbound), then turn right (east) at Shuswap Road before making a left on Sun Rivers Drive. This partridge, introduced from Eurasia, is notoriously difficult to find in most places, since they spend most of their day roaming steep, rocky hillsides, but in this neighbourhood they are often seen calling from atop the roofs of houses! On the way over to this area, you may want to have a quick look at **T'Kumlups Marsh**, located

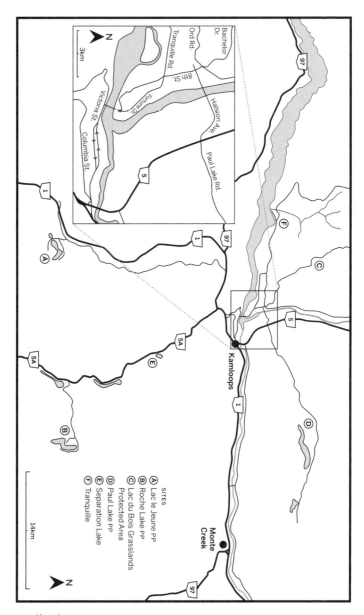

SITES

- (A) Lac le Jeune PP
- (B) Roche Lake PP
- (C) Lac du Bois Grasslands Protected Area
- (D) Paul Lake PP
- (E) Separation Lake
- (F) Tranquille

22 Kamloops

right beside Hwy. 5, just south of the intersection with Shuswap Road. To view the marsh closely, head west on Shuswap Road, then left down G&M Road to the pond. Unfortunately, the wetland has been fairly dry in recent years, but in spring, there is usually enough water to attract a mix of ducks, marsh birds, and a few shorebirds. On at least two occasions in the past, Black-necked Stilts have nested here.

> Paul Lake Provincial Park

Visit this park in spring and summer, when breeding forest birds are in full song. From Kamloops, head north on Hwy. 5 past T'Kumlups Marsh, then turn east following signs for **Paul Lake Provincial Park**. On the drive up you will pass through open country and shaded gullies fringed with aspen and cottonwood trees, until finally reaching the park in 17.9 kilometres. The riparian area along Paul Creek supports a variety of passerines and is the most productive deciduous creek bottom habitat anywhere in the vicinity. Look and listen for Calliope Hummingbird, Veery, Nashville Warbler, MacGillivray's Warbler, Spotted Towhee, and Lazuli Bunting down low in the brushy patches. The forests to the north of the lake are home to Flammulated Owls, as well as typical pine and fir forest species. After turning off at the park entrance, drive down to the lake and park near the far west end. Here there are several hiking trails that take off into the Douglas-fir forest, with some of the expected species being Downy, Hairy, and Pileated Woodpeckers; Northern Flicker; Red-naped Sapsucker; Steller's Jay; Dusky Flycatcher; Hammond's Flycatcher; Ruby-crowned Kinglet; Mountain Chickadee; and Evening Grosbeak. The lake can be hit or miss, but there are usually a few Barrow's Goldeneyes, Red-necked Grebes, and Common Loons. White-throated Swifts have been seen around the rock face known as Gibraltar Rock.

> Lac du Bois Grasslands

If you've ever had a hankering to see billions of Vesper Sparrows in one area, we recommend that you visit the **Lac du Bois
Grasslands** early in the morning in May or June. Okay, maybe not
billions, but there are a lot of Vesper Sparrows. Add that to high
numbers of Western Meadowlarks and you have a dawn chorus
to rival any place on earth. Spring mornings here are an absolute
joy. Lazuli Buntings and Mountain Bluebirds add some colour to
the day, and the cries of Long-billed Curlews and Sandhill Cranes
echo from far-off ridges. Happily, most of this area is conserved
in Lac du Bois Grasslands Protected Area, as well as a large property owned by the Nature Conservancy of Canada. The main way
of accessing this area is via **Lac du Bois Road**. From downtown
Kamloops, cross the river on Fortune Drive, then make a right
on 8th Street and follow it straight to the second set of lights at
Bachelor Drive, which will turn into Lac du Bois Road.

As you wind your way up through the grasslands, stop beside
roadside ponds that may hold migrant waterfowl and shorebirds
in spring and fall and can be attractive to local birds during hot
summer days. Essentially, all of the species mentioned above can
be found anywhere in the open grasslands. One species that is
a bit more localized is the Burrowing Owl. There is an ongoing
introductory effort in Lac du Bois, and with some luck and keen
eyes, it is possible to see several in one day without leaving the
road. About 4 kilometres past where the road turns from pavement to gravel, start scanning the west side of the road for lone
fence posts. These are favoured perches for the owls. If you turn
left on the first dirt road after the pavement ends, you may see
owls north of the old corral and farther along this road; you can
find Clay-colored Sparrows in the sage and, occasionally, Brewer's Sparrows. Around 8 kilometres from the start of the gravel
on the main road, look for a nondescript P sign indicating a

Horned Lark

small parking area on the right side of the road. Leave your car here and go for a bit of a hike. There are several trails that weave through the grasslands around **Long Lake** and a few other ponds. These lakes can have a variety of breeding and migrating ducks from spring through fall, and Sandhill Cranes are also possible. Look here for Sharp-tailed Grouse, but realistically, it's a needle-in-a-haystack scenario.

About 10.5 kilometres from the pavement, Lac du Bois Road will reach **Lac du Bois** (or "Lake of the Woods"). You can orient yourself at the Nature Conservancy of Canada kiosk on the east side of the road. Aspen groves around the lake support Least Flycatchers, which are locally scarce. From this point onward, the road follows a beautiful example of the Interior Douglas-fir ecotype. At night, listen for Common Poorwill (May to early September), Northern Saw-whet Owl (February to March), and the reclusive Flammulated Owl (late May to June). Many of the same species mentioned at Paul Lake are common here, but there will be a greater variety of waterfowl on the lakes beyond Lac du Bois (McQueen and Pass), as well as marsh species such as Virginia Rail, Sora, Marsh Wren, and Common Yellowthroat. Look for abundant Red-naped Sapsuckers here, and listen in the distance for the *quick-three-beers!* song of an Olive-sided Flycatcher.

The Lac du Bois Grasslands grow significantly quieter in winter, but the area can still be worth visiting. Predatory birds become the main focus, including Golden Eagle, Bald Eagle, Red-tailed Hawk, Rough-legged Hawk, Prairie Falcon (pretty rare indeed), Gyrfalcon (rare but regular), Northern Shrike, and Short-eared Owl.

> Tranquille

See Map 22 for reference: From 8th Street/Bachelor Drive, turn west on Ord Road, just north of Halston Avenue. Proceed west along Ord Road, which skirts a grassy hillside good for Say's Phoebe and Vesper Sparrow. Lark Sparrows have bred along here but have become scarce. In 3.6 kilometres, you will reach the start of **Rattlesnake Bluffs**—a series of small cliffs owned by the Nature Conservancy of Canada that provide nesting habitat for White-throated Swifts and Violet-green Swallows. Watch and listen for Chukar and Rock Wren. There is a short trail along the base of the bluffs and an interpretive kiosk. After passing the bluffs, turn left on Farm Road, then make an immediate right to drive west on Tranquille Road.

Considered by many to be the best birding area in Kamloops (especially in spring), **Tranquille** is a must-see location for visiting birders. Continue 2.6 kilometres from the Farm Road junction and Tranquille Road will take you alongside a larger area of grasslands and bluffs. Prairie Falcons (rare) nest near here and can sometimes be spotted perched high above on one of the rocky outcrops. Just before the road forks, there is usually a flooded area—**Tranquille Marsh**—on the south side that is fantastic in spring and early summer for waterfowl, shorebirds, and other migrants, such as American Pipit. If you take the left-hand road at the fork, there is a parking area immediately on the left from which you can also scan the area. The small trees and bushes here can be loaded with migrants in spring, since the riparian habitat is so limited in this valley. In spring and fall, you should take the time to bird the bushes all along this road to where it dead-ends near the mouth of **Tranquille Creek**. In November 2008, a Prairie Warbler was found in this area, and plenty of other goodies have turned up over the years. Spring and fall are the best times for variety, but there are also nice birds here in summer, including Downy Woodpecker, Western Wood-Pewee, Willow Flycatcher, Cassin's Vireo, Yellow Warbler, and Bullock's Oriole. At the end of this road there is a parking area; from there, you can walk down to the beach and scan Kamloops Lake. American White Pelicans are regular in spring and summer, whereas Double-crested Cormorants can be rare in some years and numerous the next. Common Merganser, Common Loon, and most of the grebe species are regular, and Bonaparte's Gulls move through in large numbers in late April and early May, then again in late summer and early fall.

For a pleasant walk up Tranquille Creek, return to the main junction near the marsh, then turn left and follow Red Lake Road across the railway tracks. Follow the road past the tracks for 1.2 kilometres, before turning right and driving to a small parking area. From here, a track follows the east side of the creek for about 1 kilometre to a picnic area and playground. Lewis's Woodpeckers can sometimes be seen around the old snags in this area, though in recent years European Starlings have started to take over. The main track ends a little way past the picnic area at a small dam structure. For those wishing to continue, you can either proceed up the east side of the creek or cross the dam and follow some cattle trails up past the old Chinese gold mine. Be wary of rattlesnakes in this area when scrambling over rocks.

> Knutsford

To reach the **Knutsford** area, head southeast from Kamloops on Hwy. 5A (alternate route to Merritt). Like Lac du Bois Road, the main attraction in this area is its open grassland, with a few aspen copses and mixed pine and fir forests on the fringes.

For the most reliable sites to find Sharp-tailed Grouse in winter, turn right onto **Long Lake Road** 1.8 kilometres after passing Aberdeen Drive (southbound on Hwy. 5A). In winter, the grouse will often gather in the aspen, willow, and rose thickets along the roadside, both for cover and to feed on buds. About 1.5 kilometres from the start of Long Lake Road, **Goose Lake Road** branches off to the right (west). The first 4.8 kilometres of this road can be worth checking for grouse, but the entirety of the road can produce a mix of birds at any time of year (similar to those found in the upper reaches of Lac du Bois Road). In winter, watch for Northern Pygmy-Owls perched on the telephone wires. Another spot for the grouse in winter is farther up Long Lake Road, past the Goose Lake Road junction. **Edith Lake Road** can be rewarding (turn right/west), as well as the rest of Long Lake Road (particularly the thicket just beyond the Edith Lake junction). In spring, you could easily spend a whole day exploring these roads.

Return to Hwy. 5A and proceed south for 1.6 kilometres, then turn left (east) on **Rose Hill Road**. In early spring, this is a great road for grassland birds such as Swainson's Hawk, Long-billed Curlew, Mountain Bluebird, Horned Lark, Vesper Sparrow, and Western Meadowlark. Snow Buntings pass through regularly in late fall and early spring; they also winter in the general area but have become scarce in recent years for unknown reasons. Snowy Owls (rare in the Interior) are nearly annual in winter. Grasslands in this area are also good places to hear Lapland Longspurs in migration, but seeing them is often a challenge. Commanding vistas from hilltops in this area make for excellent raptor viewing during spring and fall migrations. Land on either side of the road is private but unfenced in some areas, so please stick to the road.

From Rose Hill, continue south on Hwy. 5A for 3.4 kilometres and **Separation Lake** will appear on the left (east) side. If you're approaching from the south, Separation Lake is about 13 kilometres north of the Roche Lake turnoff. There is a dirt track at the north end of the lake, from which you can scope for shorebirds and waterfowl. April to May and August to October are the best times for variety, but Barrow's Goldeneye, Eared Grebes, and Wilson's Phalaropes are some of the highlights that stay to breed in most years. Western Kingbird, Say's Phoebe, Mountain Bluebird, Savannah, Vesper Sparrow, and Western Meadowlark all nest nearby, and there is a smaller pond just north of the lake (accessed via the same ranch road) that can produce a few extra water bird species. Swainson's Hawk, Red-tailed Hawk, Northern Harrier, and American Kestrel all breed in this area, whereas Rough-legged Hawk appears in winter, and Ferruginous Hawk (very rare) has been seen in the past. This is one of the best places in the Kamloops area to see migrating Sandhill Cranes by the thousands. Spring migration usually peaks around April 20; fall migration peaks during the last ten days of September.

> Roche Lake Provincial Park

For some of the best forest birding in the Kamloops area, head south from Separation Lake for about 13 kilometres, then turn left (east) onto Roche Lake Road. In addition to the main Roche Lake, there are several other smaller lakes in **Roche Lake Provincial Park** and in the surrounding areas that are all worth a visit. An impressive diversity of waterfowl nests on these lakes, along with Yellow-headed and Red-winged Blackbirds, Marsh Wrens, and Spotted and Solitary Sandpipers. The forests are dominated by Douglas-fir, where woodpeckers and flycatchers are numerous, along with Swainson's Thrush, American Robin, Townsend's Solitaire, Townsend's Warbler, Western Tanager, and Chipping Sparrow, just to name a few. The owling in this area can be satisfying as well, with Northern Saw-whet, Barred, and Great Horned being common, followed by Flammulated and Long-eared Owl, as well as Common Poorwill. Great Gray Owls nest annually in the area, but seeing them requires luck more than anything.

For the southern half of Hwy. 5A (to Merritt), see the Nicola Valley section.

> Logan Lake Area

If you're travelling from Merritt to Kamloops, there are several options for good birding along the way. One is to take Hwy. 5A past Nicola Lake, described in the Nicola Valley section. Another is to explore the Logan Lake area, which you can do in several ways. One is to take the Lac Le Jeune exit off Hwy. 5 and drive on Meadow Creek Road west to Logan Lake. If you like, you could first explore the **Lac Le Jeune** area as well, just a few kilometres in the other direction. There is a provincial park campground on Lac Le Jeune; if you have a small boat, the marshy west end is worth exploring for Yellow-headed Blackbirds and waterfowl. **Meadow Creek Road** travels through Douglas-fir and Lodgepole Pine forests and broad meadows. Mountain Bluebirds are common in summer, and the forests have American Three-toed Woodpeckers (especially in freshly dead pines), Pine Grosbeaks, and other species typical of high forests. You can also get to Logan Lake via Hwy. 97C, which leaves Hwy. 8 just west of Merritt and travels north via **Mamit Lake**. The latter could have interesting waterfowl during migration periods; a family of Whooper Swans was seen here in November 1999. **Logan Lake** is also worth a stop; it has a variety of breeding waterfowl, including nesting Canvasback. From Logan Lake, you can take Tunkwa Lake Road (at the junction of Hwy. 97C, west of Logan Lake) for 15 kilometres to **Tunkwa Lake,** and then down to Hwy. 1 at Savona. Tunkwa Lake has nesting Canvasbacks and Black Terns. Although Great Gray Owls could be seen anywhere on the plateau, the area around Tunkwa is one of the most reliable places to search.

NORTH THOMPSON

The North Thompson River drains the Monashee and Cariboo Mountains north of Kamloops, and Hwy. 5 follows it most of the way to the Rocky Mountain town of Valemount. Like many routes through mountain ranges in British Columbia, the North Thompson provides a relatively quick transect from the near-desert grasslands of Kamloops to the cool cedar and hemlock rainforests of the Rocky Mountain Trench. The town of Clearwater provides an ideal base from which to explore this valley and is a gateway to the magnificent wilderness of Wells Gray Provincial Park.

> Little Fort

The small town of **Little Fort** marks the northern limit of Ponderosa Pine forest along the North Thompson. A couple of side roads here are worth exploring. If you'd like a trip up into the subalpine forests, take Hwy. 24 west of town; this route climbs quickly to a rolling plateau dotted with small lakes. The forest has been heavily logged and much of it is beetle damaged, but a stop or two (for example, at the **Goose Lake recreation site** on the north side of the road about 20 kilometres from Little Fort) can produce such species as Gray Jay, Hermit Thrush, Varied Thrush, and Pine Grosbeak. About 9 kilometres north of Little Fort on Hwy. 5 is the **Roundtop Wildlife Area,** a beautiful mix of tree-lined oxbows and meadows accessible off Roundtop Road. Typical breeding species at Roundtop include Wood Duck, Least Flycatcher, Red-eyed Vireo, Veery, and Black-headed Grosbeak.

> Clearwater

North Thompson River Provincial Park, just south of Clearwater on Hwy. 5, provides camping facilities from spring through fall, as well as good forest birding. Breeding species in the park include Rufous Hummingbird, Red-naped Sapsucker, Pileated Woodpecker, Western Wood-pewee, and American Redstart. Slightly farther south, the community of **Blackpool** has a variety of back roads through a mix of agricultural, forested, and residential habitats, where you could see Calliope Hummingbird, Western Kingbird, Red-eyed Vireo, Veery, Gray Catbird, Lazuli Bunting, and Bullock's Oriole. Ospreys nest on the river by the Blackpool ferry, and Long-billed Curlews breed on grasslands adjacent to the Lacarya Golf Course. **Clearwater River Road** provides 38 kilometres of gravel-road access to forests along the Clearwater River north to its confluence with the Mahood River. Turn northwest off Hwy. 5 onto the Old North Thompson Highway (opposite the Wells Gray Inn in Clearwater). Immediately after crossing the Clearwater River, turn right, then take the second right (about 0.75 kilometres from the bridge you've just crossed), and you're on the road. Hammond's Flycatcher, Chestnut-backed Chickadee, Magnolia Warbler, and American Redstart are a few of the many species found along the river.

> Wells Gray Provincial Park

At the north end of Clearwater, Clearwater Valley Road goes north off Hwy. 5 to **Wells Gray Provincial Park**. There is a tourist information centre at the turnoff. The road climbs out of the North Thompson Valley into a broad valley above the Clearwater River. About 10 kilometres from Clearwater, you'll see signs on the left for **Spahats Falls**. This is one of several significant water-falls along this road and is well worth a stop. The forests of the Upper Clearwater Valley have typical montane species, such as American Three-toed Woodpecker, Hammond's Flycatchers, Mountain Chickadee, and Townsend's Warbler; in open mead-ows and aspen copses listen for Dusky and Least Flycatchers and Red-eyed Vireos. A stop at one of the wetlands in the val-ley might produce Alder Flycatcher, Veery, and Lincoln's Sparrow. After 42.5 kilometres you'll see signs on the left for **Helmcken Falls**; this is one of the most spectacular waterfalls you'll ever see (the fourth highest in Canada) and offers the chance (mid-April through August) of seeing White-throated Swifts at the north-ern edge of their range. The trail to **Ray Farm** leaves the road at kilometre 54.5; this short (1 kilometre return) walk is often good for birding in spring and summer. The mineral springs near the old farmhouse often attract birds, especially finches, such as Pine Grosbeaks, Red Crossbills, Pine Siskins, and Evening Gros-beaks. A few kilometres past Ray Farm you'll see the trailhead for **Bailey's Chute** on the right; the trail crosses the road and follows the river for 1 kilometre. American Dippers nest near the foot of the chute; if you take the walk in late summer or early fall, you might see huge Chinook Salmon leaping in vain at the falls. The road ends at **Clearwater Lake**, slightly more than 65 kilometres from Hwy. 5. There is a campground here if you'd like to stay overnight. Watch overhead for Black Swifts, listen for the shrill cries of nesting Merlins, and look for American Dippers at the falls on **Falls Creek** (aptly named Falls Falls).

NICOLA VALLEY

Like the Okanagan and Thompson Valleys, the Nicola is typified by dry grasslands and forests. It is a region of large ranches and farms and remains relatively undeveloped compared with its neighbours. Birding can be good at any time of year, but spring (late April to early May) and fall (September to early October) are probably best, since waterfowl and shorebird migration add exciting diversity to the local breeding populations. Merritt lies at the crossroads of six highways heading in every direction; thus, most travellers to the Interior will pass through this area.

> Merritt

The Coquihalla Highway (Hwy. 5) has made Merritt the gateway to the dry Interior for many coastal birders, and even a day trip from Vancouver can be exciting for birders more accustomed to rainforests and mud flats than grasslands and alkali ponds. **Lindley Creek Road** provides an introduction to Interior birding. Take the north exit off Hwy. 5 into Merritt (the second exit if you're coming from the south or west) and proceed into downtown Merritt along Voght Street. Carry on straight until the road crosses the Coldwater River; the main road then swings to the right (west) and turns into Lindley Creek Road. This road ultimately parallels the Nicola River for about 5.5 kilometres, then turns south up Lindley Creek and begins climbing into montane forests. Frequent stops along this road will produce a variety of birds, especially in spring and early summer (May to early July). It's possible to compile a list of fifty or more species in three to four hours, because of the wide variety of habitats along this road. Along the Nicola River and its oxbows watch for ducks, geese, Osprey, and Bald Eagle; in the coniferous and creekside forests expect species such as Hammond's and Dusky Flycatchers, Cassin's Vireo, Mountain Chickadee, Pygmy Nuthatch, and Cassin's Finch. Higher up, a variety of woodpeckers can be found; around aspen copses, watch for Red-naped Sapsucker (common) and Williamson's Sapsucker (uncommon and local). Northern Pygmy-Owls are a possibility anywhere along the road (active during the day), and

Flammulated Owl

Flammulated Owls call from the higher Ponderosa Pine forests on warm nights in late May and June. If you're driving through the pine forests on a warm night from May through early September, watch and listen for Common Poorwills.

If you're travelling from the coast through to the Okanagan and would like a short hit of grassland birding in the Nicola Valley, turn into the tourist information centre at the south highway exit, then turn east onto the old highway that goes up **Hamilton Hill**. This is a quieter road than Hwy. 5A; frequent stops in spring and summer should produce Mountain Bluebird, Vesper Sparrow, and Western Meadowlark, among other species. When you reach the main highway at the top of the hill, turn right and continue for 2 kilometres, then turn left onto **Lundbom Road**. Immediately off the highway to the right is the **Laurie Guichon Memorial Grasslands Interpretive Site**. Laurie Guichon was a Nicola Valley rancher whose passion was grassland conservation; a kiosk with signs and a short trail tell the story of grassland conservation in British Columbia. If you drive up the gravel road into the **Lundbom Commonage** for 3 kilometres, you will pass three lakes set in a mosaic of grassland and forest, the two largest lakes being Marquart and Lundbom. Both have picnic facilities. On the lakes, watch for Barrow's Goldeneye, Bufflehead, and other ducks; typical grassland birds here are Horned Lark, Mountain Bluebird, Brewer's Blackbird, and Western Meadowlark. The forests have species such as Cassin's Vireo, Golden-crowned, and Ruby-crowned Kinglets.

> Nicola Lake

Nicola Lake is about 8.5 kilometres east of Merritt on Hwy. 5A. It is a large lake—about 20 kilometres long—and can provide good birding at any time of year. Spring and fall (March to May, August to November) are best for water birds, but even in mid-winter, there are often ice-free areas on the lake. There are several spots where you can pull off the highway and scan for birds. The Nicola River flows out of the lake at the west end; there are usually a few (up to seven) American Dippers and many Barrow's Goldeneyes below the outlet dam and hundreds of dabbling ducks—mostly Mallards—in the shallows farther downstream. To check this out, turn off the highway onto **Nicola Cutoff Road** just above the small Nicola Lake dam and follow the road back down along the river to the start of the cattle feedlot about 500 metres downstream. The highway rest stop about 4 kilometres east of the outlet is a good place from fall through spring to scan the water for Trumpeter Swans and a variety of ducks, though the lake always freezes in winter in the shallow arm west of this point. It might be worth checking out the mouth of **Quilchena Creek**, just west of the Quilchena Hotel, where a sandbar juts into the lake, and the small bay at the base of **Pennask Lake Road**. The bay can be visited by driving down a short stretch of abandoned highway that closely approaches the lake and adjacent marshes; turn off 2 kilometres east of Quilchena.

The Nicola River flows into the lake about 13 kilometres farther east (about 1.5 kilometres north of the Douglas Lake Road junction). Check here in spring and fall for waterfowl, grebes, loons, and gulls; pull off just south of the bridge and scan the beach. American Tree Sparrows can be found in the shrubbery here in winter.

> ## Beaver Ranch Flats and Stump Lake

Just 3.5 kilometres north of Nicola Lake on Hwy. 5A is **Beaver Ranch Flats** (also known as Guichon Flats), a Ducks Unlimited project that is one of the finest birding spots in the province. There is a parking area on the west side of the highway. Birding is best from mid-March through November. Highlights include large colonies of Eared Grebes, Black Terns, and Yellow-headed Blackbirds. Also breeding here are many species of ducks, Wilson's Phalaropes, and sometimes American Avocets. In spring and fall, large numbers of water birds use the marsh as a staging area, including flocks of Tundra Swans, Sandhill Cranes, American White Pelicans, and a variety of shorebirds.

Watch for Lewis's Woodpeckers in the open pine woods along the highway between here and **Stump Lake** (about 9 kilometres north). Stump Lake is always worth a stop from spring through fall; the best pull-offs are at the south end and about halfway along the western lakeshore. This lake has particularly large numbers of ducks, grebes, and coots in fall migration.

> ## Kane Valley

The plateau south of Merritt is a rolling mosaic of montane forests, small lakes, and open grasslands. Perhaps the best birding spot in the area is the **Kane Valley**, a chain of marshy lakes set in diverse woodland. Turn west off Hwy. 97C/5A about twenty minutes south of Merritt (just north of Corbett Lake, if you're coming from Kelowna). The first 15 kilometres are the most diverse; after that the road winds down through woodlands for another 15 kilometres, goes under the Coquihalla Highway (Hwy. 5), and joins

Coldwater Road about 30 kilometres south of Merritt. The lakes in the chain (Chicken Ranch Lake, Harmon Lake, Kane Lakes, Harrison Lake, and others) have a diverse list of breeding water birds, such as Gadwall, Green-winged Teal, Blue-winged Teal, Cinnamon Teal, Ring-necked Duck, Pied-billed Grebe, Red-necked Grebe. Red-naped Sapsuckers are common, but watch and listen for Williamson's Sapsuckers around the Kane Lakes, where large aspens mix with spruce. Harrison Lake, the last lake in the chain, has a particularly long list of breeding birds in the woodlands bordering it, including Least Flycatchers in the aspen stands and Rusty Blackbirds in the lakeshore vegetation. Great Gray Owls are found in the valley year round but are usually elusive.

> Douglas Lake

The Douglas Lake plateau, a sea of grass in an ocean of trees, is one of the most storied places in the British Columbia Interior. It is dominated by the huge Douglas Lake Ranch, one of the largest ranches in the world. Extending almost 100 kilometres from Westwold to Princeton, the ranch has a herd of twenty thousand head of cattle ranging over a half million acres of land. It is an exciting place to watch birds, but because the land is either privately owned ranchland or First Nations reserve, please stay on the public roads throughout.

Take Hwy. 5A north from Merritt and turn left (east) onto **Pennask Lake Road**, just north of the Quilchena Hotel and golf course. This road travels through rolling grasslands with occasional pothole ponds. In spring and summer, the grasslands are alive with Horned Larks, Vesper Sparrows, and Western Meadowlarks, and Swainson's Hawk often soar overhead; in spring and fall migration, listen for the dry, rattling calls of Lapland Longspurs. Long-eared Owls nest in the aspen groves along this route—check for "ears" sticking out of all the crow's nests you can see in April (before the trees leaf out). The ponds can have a

Western Meadowlark

variety of waterfowl and are often home to shorebirds in spring (April to early May) and fall (July to early October). After about 20 kilometres, you reach **Minnie Lake**, which is just visible to the southeast but well off the road. Swainson's Hawks often concentrate around the Minnie Lake hayfields in spring, and Snowy Owls and Gyrfalcons have been seen there in winter. At kilometre 22, turn left (north) onto **Minnie Lake Road**, which travels through similar habitats for about 18 kilometres to **Douglas Lake**. American Avocets have nested on some of the alkali ponds along this stretch, and Sharp-tailed Grouse can be seen in the roadside shrubbery in winter. Turn right at the First Nations community of Spahomin onto Douglas Lake Road as it hugs the northwest shore of the lake. Douglas Lake can have good numbers of waterfowl during spring and fall migration, especially at the north and south ends. In summer, the lake has relatively few birds (Common Loon, Osprey, and Bald Eagle are some of the obvious summer residents), but there are a few spots to stop and scan for other possibilities.

The ranch headquarters are at the northeast end of the lake, set off from the road by the much smaller **Sanctuary Lake**. After a quick scan of Sanctuary Lake, continue east on Douglas Lake Road as it passes the airstrip then turns north to cross the Nicola River, here only a small creek. It might be worth stopping to scan the feedlots southeast of the bridge, especially in winter. From the bridge, the road continues north and east for 8 kilometres before reaching **Chapperon Lake**. If you stop at one place on this road, stop here and scan the lake. The birdlife on Chapperon Lake is outstanding from April through freeze-up in fall, with a tremendous diversity of nesting and migratory water birds, including Eared Grebe and Black Tern. Sandhill Cranes are common in migration (April and September to October), and a few breed locally. You might be lucky enough to see a flock of American White Pelicans en route to or from their colony at Stum Lake in the Chilcotin. About 3 kilometres past Chapperon Lake is marsh-bordered **Rush Lake**, again worth a stop, and equidistant past that is **Salmon Lake**. If you'd like to spend more time exploring this area, the Douglas Lake Ranch has cabins and a campground at Salmon Lake. Check the marshy west end of Salmon Lake for ducks and grebes. From Salmon Lake, the road follows the Salmon River—which will eventually flow into Shuswap Lake at Salmon Arm—through a gradient of habitats, from Douglas-fir and Engelmann Spruce forests through to the hot Ponderosa Pine woodlands at Westwold.

LILLOOET

The historic town of Lillooet is located along the Fraser River north of Lytton and east of Pemberton. The opening of the Duffy Lake section of Hwy. 99 between Pemberton and Lillooet has made the area an easy destination for coastal birders and it can be very rewarding. A walk down **Old Bridge Road** (starts opposite Old Mill Plaza along Main Street) to the old suspension bridge that crosses the Fraser River at the north end of town usually produces Osprey, Northern Rough-winged Swallow, Veery, and Lazuli Bunting in spring and early summer—and keep your ears open for the cackling call of Chukar, especially around the Ministry of Highways yard.

The **Powerhouse Restoration area** is another good place to start close to town. Take Hwy. 99 south out of town, crossing the bridge over the Seton River. Turn left onto Powerhouse Road about 200 metres south of the bridge, then turn into the parking area about 600 metres farther on. There is a series of trails through Ponderosa Pine woodlands, Black Cottonwood stands, willow thickets, and upland restoration zone. Birds to be expected (May to July) include Osprey (nesting), Western Kingbird, Nashville Warbler, Lazuli Bunting, and Bullock's Oriole. In late summer, watch the skies for Vaux's, Black, and White-throated Swifts, as well as Common Nighthawks.

Returning to Hwy. 99, turn left then take the first left onto **Texas Creek Road** (West Fraser Road). This road travels down the west side of the Fraser and even the first 10 kilometres or so provide an attractive sampling of the birds of Lillooet. This is all private land, however, so please remain on the road. Both Hammond's and Dusky Flycatchers are common, and the coastal-interior mix is evident with both Townsend's and Black-throated Gray Warblers present. A nocturnal trip down this road could produce a Western Screech-Owl (February to April, August to September).

Returning to Hwy. 99 and turning west (left) once again, drive 2.8 kilometres to the **Naxwit Picnic Area** on the Seton River. Veeries sing their beautiful downward-spiralling songs here in summer, and American Dippers are abundant along the river in winter—the Lillooet Christmas Bird Count holds the North American record for this species: 149 birds. Look carefully for Harlequin Ducks along the river in spring and summer. West of the picnic site, the highway crosses the Seton Canal (a reliable place for Harlequin Ducks), then makes a big switchback turn and climbs onto a bench where there is a scenic pull-off on the right with stunning views of Seton Lake. Park here and, after enjoying the view, walk across the highway and get onto the **B.C. Hydro campground trail system.** These trails wind through the Ponderosa Pine and Douglas-fir forests, where Cassin's Vireo, Red-breasted Nuthatch, and Western Tanager are common, and also go down to riparian habitats along Cayoosh Creek, where you can find Harlequin Duck, Spotted Sandpiper, American Dipper, and Black-throated Gray Warbler.

A longer, more adventurous trip, best done in a full day, is **West Pavilion Road.** Drive north on Main Street in Lillooet and turn left onto Hwy. 40 (Moha Road). This road crosses the Bridge River after about 8 kilometres; 250 metres past the bridge, turn sharply back to the right on West Pavilion Road. This route travels for more than 90 kilometres through spectacular country on the west side of the Fraser River, ending at the Big Bar ferry (on demand between 7 AM and 7 PM). You can explore the road at your leisure and simply return along the same route to Lillooet or make the crossing on the ferry and get onto Hwy. 97 north of Clinton. Along the way, watch for White-throated Swifts wheeling over the canyons of the Fraser; if you're out here on a late spring evening, listen for the soft hoots of Flammulated Owls in the pines.

> East of the Fraser River

Hwy. 99 travels north from Lillooet along the benchlands above the Fraser River. About 9 kilometres north of Lillooet, the highway swings around the north end of Fountain Ridge; there is a gravel pull-off here where you can stop and look for Lazuli Buntings (mid-May through July) and Calliope Hummingbirds (late April through June). About 14 kilometres north of Lillooet, you will pass **Fountain Valley Road** on the right (southeast) side of the highway. This makes a great side trip during migration (April to May, September to November), both for waterfowl and songbirds. The road travels for about 30 kilometres to the south and comes out on Hwy. 12 about 23 kilometres south of Lillooet. There are three main lakes in the Fountain Valley and all of them can sometimes have interesting water birds; breeding species include Ring-necked Duck, Barrow's Goldeneye, Ruddy Duck, Pied-billed Grebe, Horned Grebe, and Common Loon. Land on both sides of the road is private, so please bird from the road.

If you stay on Hwy. 99 north of the Fountain Valley junction, you will come to a logging road on the right (east) after 10 kilometres. This is the Tiffin forest service road, known locally as **Tom Cole Road**. It provides an exemplary altitudinal transect, starting in grasslands, then changing to Ponderosa Pine forest, and finally ending in subalpine forest. From the bottom of the road, scan the flats below for Lewis's Woodpecker; you may hear Long-billed Curlews calling from the fields as well. In the lower sections, listen for Vesper Sparrows (also found at higher elevation grasslands along this road) and watch for Chukar; White-breasted Nuthatches are fairly common in the Douglas-firs and Ponderosa Pines. Dusky Grouse and Mountain Bluebirds can be seen on the higher slopes, and species typical of subalpine forests, such as Olive-sided Flycatcher and Hermit Thrush, can be heard singing in early summer. If you drive up this road at night, listen for Flammulated Owls (late May to June) and watch for the glowing red eyes of Common Poorwill in your headlights (May to August).

SHUSWAP
AND
REVELSTOKE

SALMON ARM BAY

Located along the Trans-Canada Highway, Salmon Arm is a convenient birding stop for people travelling from the coast to the Rocky Mountains or for anyone wanting to see a variety of water birds. The annual Salmon Arm Grebe Festival is held each May to celebrate the large colony of Western Grebes that exists along the marshy shoreline of **Salmon Arm Bay**. In addition to the hundred or so pairs of Western Grebes, there are usually large numbers of Red-necked and Pied-billed Grebes breeding in the area, as well as one to three pairs of Clark's Grebes (the only place in British Columbia where this species regularly occurs). In spring and fall, it is usually possible to see a few Horned Grebes (also present in winter), as well as the odd Eared Grebe. No wonder they have a grebe fest!

The best place to view the grebes is from the **Salmon Arm public wharf** located at the end of Marine Park Drive. From Hwy. 1 turn north onto 4th Street (following the binocular signs); drive

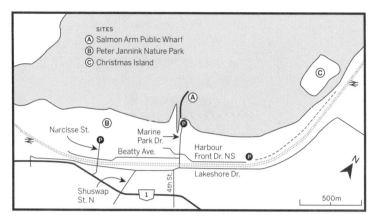

23 Salmon Arm

two blocks to Lakeshore Drive, turn right, then make an immediate left across the railway tracks onto Marine Park Drive. Parking will be on the right; then you can walk out onto the wharf. Unless the bay is frozen, there should be lots of waterfowl to look at. Spring and fall are usually best, but in summer, there is an abundance of young birds mucking about. Canada Goose, Wood Duck, Gadwall, American Wigeon, Mallard, all three teal species, and Northern Shoveler all breed here, and many diving duck species can also be seen throughout the year. The Western Grebes will be spread out to the east and west. To see a Clark's you will probably need a scope—look for a bird with pale silvery flanks, an all-white face with eyes distinctly separate from the cap, and a bright orange bill. During the breeding season, you will probably notice one or two of the local Osprey pairs nesting just west of the wharf, and in spring, scan to the west for resting flocks of American White Pelicans.

After the grebes, Salmon Arm's other claim to fame is its freshwater mud flats, which attract a bounty of shorebirds in late summer and early fall. When conditions are right, Salmon Arm

Western Grebe

Bay can be the best shorebirding spot in the Interior of British Columbia. Many species of shorebirds pass through in spring, but the water is often too high to expose enough foraging habitat. From late July into October, the entire shoreline of Salmon Arm Bay is worth checking (especially the southwest corner, where the Salmon River empties into the lake). At least thirty-three species of shorebird have been recorded in the bay, including local rarities such as Pacific Golden-Plover, Black Turnstone, Surfbird, Sharp-tailed Sandpiper, and Red Phalarope. The location of shorebird flocks can vary day to day. The wharf can be a good place to start, but here are two other spots that can be great not only for waders but for a variety of other birds.

> Peter Jannink Nature Park

From the Salmon Arm wharf parking area, head back along Marine Park Drive, then turn right (before reaching the railway tracks) on Beatty Avenue. Continue roughly westward for 600 metres, then turn right onto Narcisse Street. Park at the end of the road near the gate and walk in. There is a gazebo here that can be a lovely spot for a lunch break, and the brushy habitat on the west side of the park can be good for migrant songbirds in spring and fall. Straight out from the gazebo, you will be able to scope the lakeshore and an adjacent wetland to the east. Typical marsh species such as Sora, Wilson's Snipe, and both Yellow-headed and Red-winged Blackbirds can be seen here in summer, and the occasional American Bittern has been seen slinking through the reeds. There is a walking path that leads along the lakeshore back toward the wharf that can provide more views of the marshes. For those wanting closer looks at the shorebirds in fall, it is okay to walk out onto the shoreline, but bring your boots as it can be pretty mucky. Also, be sure to stay a respectable distance from the birds so as not to disturb them at this important staging time in their migration—and for the sake of other birders.

> Christmas Island

Located in the southeast corner of Salmon Arm Bay, **Christmas Island** (named after Eric Christmas, one of the key people involved in reserving the Salmon Arm foreshore as a bird sanctuary) is simply a fantastic place for birds. Perhaps the most conspicuous residents are the hundreds of Ring-billed Gulls, who have established British Columbia's largest Ring-billed Gull breeding colony here. A mix of waterfowl will usually be on show, as well as a number of different shorebirds in late summer and early fall. To get here from the public wharf, drive back toward the railway tracks but turn left (east) onto Harbour Front Drive and take this all the way to the end. Park in the small parking area and walk along the track to the north. The bushes and trees along the trail are great for migrants in spring and fall and have been particularly good for sparrows in September and October, with notable finds such as American Tree, Harris's, and Swamp Sparrows. Once out toward the "island" (accessible by foot unless water levels are high), you'll notice a couple of viewing platforms that can offer better looks at birds along the shoreline and out on the lake. In the past, Christmas Island was *the* place to see a variety of sandpipers, but lately it has been less productive in comparison with the western part of the bay. It still seems to be the best place to see the longer-legged shorebirds (both yellowlegs and dowitchers) and, for whatever reason, is also the best place to find a Hudsonian Godwit (rare but regular in August).

ADAMS RIVER AND
THE NORTH SHORE OF SHUSWAP LAKE

Between Shuswap Lake and Little Shuswap Lake, Squilax-Anglemont Road leaves Hwy. 1 on the south side, then crosses both the highway and the river and travels north. This road provides access to the Adams River area and the entire north shore of Shuswap Lake. About 3.5 kilometres from the highway, you cross the **Adams River**, famous around the world for its huge Sockeye Salmon run. Every fourth year features a dominant run (an easy way to remember the big years for Sockeye runs in the Adams River—they always occur in years with Winter Olympics), when about 2 million salmon swim up the Fraser and Thompson Rivers and enter the Adams River to spawn in late September and October. Even in off years, there are hundreds of thousands of salmon—and they attract a large congregation of fish-eating birds. Mergansers, loons, Bald Eagles, and gulls swarm the river's mouth. The best salmon viewing is had in Roderick Haig-Brown Provincial Park; the main entrance is about 1.5 kilometres beyond the Adams River Bridge.

Squilax-Anglemont Road continues east through the communities of Scotch Creek, Celista, and Anglemont, eventually reaching the end of Seymour Arm at the hamlet of Albas (the return trip would best be done in a full day). Perhaps the most interesting aspect of birding this road is the relatively rapid transition from the dry Ponderosa Pines of Squilax to the wet hemlock forests of Seymour Arm, a habitat change that involves a radical change in bird life as well. The Pygmy Nuthatches, Lazuli Buntings, and Lark Sparrows in the pines give way to Chestnut-backed Chickadees, Pacific Wrens, and Brown Creepers in Albas.

REVELSTOKE

› Mount Revelstoke National Park

Whether you're spending several days in the Revelstoke area or just passing through, a visit to **Mount Revelstoke National Park** is highly recommended. Although it is a relatively small park (260 square kilometres) in comparison with Glacier, Banff, and Jasper National Parks, Mount Revelstoke boasts a summit parkway, which allows summer visitors to climb 1,600 metres through a diverse mixture of forested habitats. At the top (26 kilometres one way), there are several easygoing interpretive trails that wind through the subalpine habitats. For the more serious hikers, there are much longer hikes that lead to several picturesque lakes and higher ridgelines, where alpine species such as White-tailed Ptarmigan, American Pipit, and Gray-crowned Rosy-Finch are a possibility.

To reach the summit parkway, follow signs for Revelstoke National Park: **Meadows in the Sky**, just east of the main highway junction in Revelstoke. The road will be on the north side of the highway. There is a daily fee for park use, but longer-term passes can be purchased as well, and all of these tickets are valid in any other Canadian national park. As you wind up the lower sections of the road, there are several viewpoints where you can pull off and marvel at both the scenery and the birds. Some common summer breeders in these lower-elevation woods include Hammond's Flycatcher, Warbling Vireo, Red-breasted

Black Swift

Nuthatch, Brown Creeper, and both Black-capped and Chestnut-backed Chickadees. In fact, all four species of chickadees can be seen along this road (Boreal and Mountain higher up), so with some luck, you may achieve the coveted "Chickadee Grand Slam." Western Tanager, Townsend's Warbler, Swainson's Thrush, and Townsend's Solitaire are also present in spring and summer; keep an eye on the sky for both Vaux's and Black Swifts, which routinely pass close by the viewing areas.

Once up at the top, park in one of the two designated parking areas and go for a walk. You can either do the short hike to the Revelstoke summit or hop on a shuttle bus that will take you to the start of the fire tower and Meadows in the Sky trails. Wildflowers typically peak in early August, but in years of prolonged snow cover, their time can be pushed back a bit. Golden-crowned Kinglets, Yellow-rumped Warblers, and Chipping Sparrows are perhaps the more noticeable birds along the interpretive trails, but it's possible to find many more upper-elevation specialties, including American Three-toed Woodpecker, Gray Jay, Boreal Chickadee, and Pine Grosbeak. In recent years, a Northern Hawk-Owl has been seen regularly along the road to the summit and near the fire tower. Look for this distinctive diurnal owl perched high in a subalpine spruce, scanning the meadows below for unwary rodents.

Another popular feature of Mount Revelstoke National Park is the **Skunk Cabbage Interpretive Trail**, located beside the Trans-Canada Highway (Hwy. 1) (about a fifteen-minute drive northeast of Revelstoke toward Golden). The trail is well-signed off the highway and is a fantastic spot to stop for lunch and marvel at the snow-capped Selkirk Mountains. There is also a 1.2-kilometre walking loop (hard-packed earth and boardwalks) that takes visitors through a rich riparian area loaded with Red-eyed Vireos, Least Flycatchers, American Redstarts, and MacGillivray's Warblers (to name but a few).

> Revelstoke Greenbelt

The **Revelstoke Greenbelt** wraps around the western and southern edges of town and provides pedestrians and cyclists with a roughly 3-kilometre-long paved path along the main dyke, as well as many other side trails. This is the easiest and most scenic way to get a sampling of the low-elevation species in the area. To reach the main parking area, exit the Trans-Canada Highway (Hwy 1.) onto Victoria Road (the main road that runs along the northeast edge of town), turn southwest onto Campbell Avenue and follow it straight past the community pool, down the hill, and just past the ball fields. From the parking lot, you will have a commanding view of the mighty Columbia River, where the water levels fluctuate throughout the year, depending on dam operations way down at the south end of Arrow Lake. Typically, the water starts rising in late May and peaks in early August before receding again. When the water is high, the northern section of the greenbelt becomes almost entirely flooded, leaving little to attract most bird species. But outside of this peak time, the willow and cottonwood habitats alongside the main path can be full of both migrating and breeding songbirds. Chipping Sparrows, Lazuli Buntings, and Yellow Warblers are some of the more conspicuous summer residents, and a wide variety of other flycatchers, warblers, and sparrows can be found in migration season.

As you walk from the main parking area around the back of the Downie mill, there are several ponds that can be fantastic places for waterfowl and shorebirds from spring through fall; in recent years, they have produced a few local rarities, including Black-necked Stilts and a Black-bellied Plover. As you pass the mill, you will notice the **Illecillewaet River** coming in from the east to join the Columbia. In spring and summer, you can see a pair of ospreys nesting on their designated platform; be sure to check the weedy fringes of a nearby outflow channel for lurking Wilson's Snipe or Solitary Sandpiper. As the path turns east and continues alongside the Illecillewaet River, the habitat changes from open willow and alder scrub to mixed riparian forest— mainly Black Cottonwood and Western Red Cedar. Red-eyed Vireo, Least Flycatcher, Veery, Gray Catbird, and American Redstart are all abundant here. Even when the reservoir is high, you should be able to take several side trails around this area that will take you through the rich riparian woodland and either up to the Illecillewaet Bridge or to a secondary parking lot at the south end of Edwards Street. A new footbridge over the Illecillewaet River now gives birders access to more bird habitat on the other side, including **Machete Island**—an isolated stand of cottonwood forest in the Columbia River flood plain that is often inaccessible in summer.

> South Road

South of Revelstoke, along the east side of the Columbia Valley, there is a series of wetlands and forested areas that will be of interest to out-of-town birders. From the main highway intersection at the northwest end of town, turn onto Victoria Road (the main access to Revelstoke city centre from the highway). Follow Victoria Road for 2.7 kilometres, then make a left (following the main flow of traffic) onto 4th Street, where you will cross a set of railroad tracks. After about 1 kilometre, the road reaches a bridge over the Illecillewaet River. On the left side, just before the bridge, there is a parking area where birders can pull off and access the Revelstoke Greenbelt (previous entry) by walking downstream underneath the bridge, following a series of well-marked paths.

If you've already checked out the greenbelt, continue south across the bridge and follow the main road for another 2.6 kilometres to where you'll see a sign on the left for **Williamson Lake**. This small lake is a popular swimming hole in the hot summer months, but it can also provide some good birding if there aren't too many people around. The best way to bird the lake is by turning around and heading about 150 metres back the way you came. Pull off on the right-hand side where there is plenty of space. You should see a trail leaving the road and heading down into a draw. This is the outflow of the Williamson Lake wetlands system into the larger marsh on the west side of the road. The main trail, as well as several side paths, will take you through a rich mixture of deciduous and coniferous trees with an abundance of breeding birds from May to August. Among these breeders are Red-eyed Vireo, Western Wood-Pewee, Hammond's and Least Flycatchers, Pacific Wren, Chestnut-backed and Black-capped Chickadees, Swainson's Thrush, Veery, MacGillivray's Warbler, and Dark-eyed (Oregon) Junco.

From the Williamson Lake turnoff, continue south along the road and you will come to the Revelstoke Airport. From the road, you should be able to find a spot to scan **Airport Marsh** (the wetlands on both sides of the runway) for waterfowl and other marsh species. If the reservoir waters are low, you can park at the base of the runway on the south side, where a small trail runs along its side. From this pull-off, you can continue another 2.3 kilometres down the road to **Montana Bay**. This marsh was originally a natural lake before the Columbia was dammed, but it still retains a unique character—the boggy islands in the middle of the bay are actually floating! A mix of waterfowl can be seen here in spring and fall, and in summer, you can expect to hear and/or see Wilson's Snipe, Willow Flycatcher, Cedar Waxwing, Yellow Warbler, Common Yellowthroat, and Song Sparrow.

From the south end of Montana Bay, where Montana Creek flows in, another 5.4 kilometres south will take you to **Nine Mile Point**. If the reservoir isn't high (usually anytime other than midsummer), you can walk or drive along this skinny westward-pointing spit. If you've birded for a little while now, you probably know that birds seem to like spits. In addition to small groups of shorebirds that touch down along the beach, small flocks of migrant songbirds can also be seen using the shrubs along the point, and Western Meadowlarks (locally rare) will often spend the summer here. Four species that are particularly fond of spits (and thus you should always keep an eye out for them in spring and fall) are Horned Lark, American Pipit, Lapland Longspur, and Snow Bunting. Three kilometres south of Nine Mile Point, the road turns to gravel near a fork. Take the right-hand road to continue along the valley bottom to where the road dead-ends at Drimmie Creek. This area at the end of the road is known as **12 Mile**. If the water is high, there won't be much to look at other than flooded willows, but in spring and fall, this can be a pleasant area to look for migrants. If you take the left-hand road (back at the fork), you will be on the Akolkolex Forest Service Road, which leads to **Echo Lake recreation site**—another nice swimming spot in the summer, with forest birds such as Northern Pygmy-Owl, Chestnut-backed Chickadee, Brown Creeper, and Townsend's Warbler.

KOOTENAYS

KETTLE VALLEY

The Kettle Valley of British Columbia, branded Boundary Country by local business people, offers a diverse mix of birds as the dry grasslands typical of the Okanagan Valley merge eastward with the wet forests of the Kootenays. It is one of those decidedly under-birded regions, so you may discover something special in your explorations. The valley bottoms of the Kettle River are characterized by magnificent stands of Black Cottonwood bordered by native grasslands. The **Kettle Valley Provincial Park**, 5 kilometres north of Rock Creek, has Ponderosa Pine forests (and yes, there has been a sighting of a White-headed Woodpecker here) mixed with old spruce and cottonwoods. If you camp, you're likely to hear Barred Owls calling at night, replaced by the mellow toots of the Northern Pygmy-Owl by day, especially in spring and fall. The pine forests have Mountain Chickadees, all three nuthatch species year round, and Cassin's Finches in the summer.

Just east of Rock Creek you can take **Rock Creek-Bridesville Road** on the south side of the highway. This road travels for about 14 kilometres though a mix of grasslands, aspen copses, and coniferous forests for very diverse birding. Watch for Great Gray Owls in the clearings along the western half of the road.

Boothman's Oxbow Provincial Park is an undeveloped park east of Grand Forks; watch for the small sign on the south side of Hwy. 3, leading to a parking spot 1 kilometre east of Collins Road. Walk down the track to the big marsh surrounded by riparian thickets. This can be an exciting place, with recent sightings of breeding Yellow-breasted Chats and breeding Bewick's Wrens, as well as the more usual Ring-necked Pheasants, Virginia Rails, Soras, Gray Catbirds, Bullock's Orioles, and Yellow-headed Blackbirds. **Gilpin Forest Service Road** goes off the north side of the highway 200 metres east of the Boothman's Oxbow turnoff; it provides a wonderful altitudinal transect through grasslands (House Wrens, Lazuli Buntings, Western Bluebirds, Western Meadowlarks), rocky cliffs (White-throated Swifts, Canyon and Rock Wrens) and Ponderosa Pine forests (all three nuthatches, Black-headed Grosbeaks, Northern Pygmy-Owls).

WEST KOOTENAYS

> Castlegar

At the junction of two of British Columbia's largest rivers—the Kootenay and the Columbia—Castlegar's birding spots centre on riverside habitats. **Waldie Island** has trails through thickets and woodland on the north bank of the Columbia River; to reach it, take the Nelson exit off Hwy. 3 on the east side of the Columbia and drive north about 3 kilometres until the highway crosses the Kootenay River on the Brilliant Bridge. Take the first exit on the right onto Robson Road and drive another 3 kilometres along the north shore of the Columbia until the road splits; take the left-hand turn (Broadwater Road), then take the first left onto Old Mill Road. This road curls left and dead-ends under the railway bridge, where you'll see the trail sign.

The trail is a loop about 1 kilometre long. It is a prime location for waterfowl throughout the year. Diving ducks can be found on the river and in the sewage lagoons in winter, whereas dabbling duck diversity is highest in summer. Watch for migrant Harlequin Ducks on the river in April and May and American Dippers in the winter. In spring and summer, the woods and shrubbery have breeding Willow Flycatchers, Red-eyed Vireos, Veeries, Gray Catbirds, Cedar Waxwings, Nashville Warblers, American Redstarts, and Bullock's Orioles. Spring and fall migration bring a much greater diversity.

Visit the **Syringa Creek Provincial Park** area year round to find Canyon Wrens, with Rock Wrens and White-throated Swifts as an added bonus from April to September. To get there from Waldie Island, turn left at the north end of Old Mill Road, then immediately turn right to get yourself back on Broadwater Road and going west to Robson Road. This road eventually goes by the Keenleyside Dam, the last dam on the Columbia system in Canada. About 17 kilometres from Old Mill Road you will reach Syringa Creek Provincial Park; drive beyond the campground and check the big cliffs above the road for the wrens and swifts.

The oxbow below **Selkirk College** is another productive spot year round. Take Hwy. 3 east across the Columbia River; after crossing the bridge, take the Hwy. 3A exit (follow signs for Nelson). Once you're on Hwy. 3A, take the first left to Selkirk College (opposite the right turn to the airport), then take the first right onto Rosedale Road. Almost 1 kilometre along, take the first left onto Campus Road and drive to the end of the road, turning sharply right onto Welsh Road and park at the end. Walk the trail to the left (west) above the large river oxbow that loops below the Kootenay River, just upstream from its confluence with the Columbia. From October through April, the oxbow and river have high concentrations of waterfowl. The numbers

Northern Pygmy Owl

of Barrow's Goldeneyes are especially noteworthy—the Castlegar Christmas Bird Count often reports more than eight hundred of these handsome ducks, one of the highest inland counts for the species on the continent. In summer, the nesting songbirds here include Gray Catbird, Spotted Towhee, and Bobolink (the latter in the fields east of the oxbow).

> Nelson

Birding around **Nelson** is focussed on Kootenay Lake and the Selkirk Mountains. From fall through spring, the lakeshore in front of the historic city (accessed easily at various points, such as the Chahko Mika shopping mall parking lot) has a variety of waterfowl, including Gadwall, American Wigeon, Redhead, Ring-necked Duck, Greater Scaup, Lesser Scaup (uncommon), Hooded Mergansers, and American Coots. Bald Eagles are common in winter (thanks to the ready supply of coots) but are largely replaced by Osprey in summer.

Kokanee Creek Provincial Park is one of the best year-round destinations for a day trip from Nelson. Drive across the bridge over the narrow arm of the lake at the north end of Nelson Avenue and continue along Hwy. 3A for about 20 kilometres until you reach the park. In spring and summer, the park is full of songbirds, especially riparian species, such as Willow Flycatcher, Red-eyed Vireo, and Gray Catbird. From August to early November, gulls gather at the creek mouth to take advantage of the Kokanee spawning run; Ring-billed, California, and Herring are the common species, but a few Bonaparte's can show up as well. Merlins nest in the park.

Kokanee Glacier Provincial Park provides an opportunity to find high-elevation species, especially if you're willing to do a bit of hiking. About 400 metres north of the entrance to Kokanee Creek Provincial Park, turn left (west) onto a forest service road. For the first 7 kilometres, this is an active logging road, so be alert for large trucks coming downhill. Follow signs for Gibson Lake and/or Kokanee Glacier; the road dead-ends at Gibson Lake about 16 kilometres from the highway. Gibson Lake is at 1,535 metres elevation, so expect typical subalpine species here, including Spruce Grouse, Gray Jay, Boreal Chickadee, Fox Sparrow (summer), and Pine Grosbeak. A trail that eventually leads to the glacier winds up the slope above the lake. To search areas above treeline for White-tailed Ptarmigan and Gray-crowned Rosy-Finch, it would be best to hike into one of the wilderness campsites or stay in one of the park cabins; call the Alpine Club of Canada at 403- 678-3200 for cabin reservations.

Another quick drive into subalpine forests is the road to the **Whitewater ski area.** Take Hwy. 3A east toward Salmo from Nelson for about 12 kilometres, then turn left onto Whitewater Road. You will reach the ski area after about 6 kilometres; it is at 1,630 metres elevation and the subalpine forests feature much the same species mentioned for the Gibson Lake area above. This is a reliable route for Boreal Owls—along the higher parts of the road, play recordings at night (February to April, September to November) and listen for the *skiew! moo-ah* or full song response from the owl.

> Trail

The city of **Trail** is the site of the historic Teck Cominco smelter, and at first glance, you might think it wouldn't hold much birding promise—but you'd be wrong. The most interesting birding in this part of the Kootenays is along the Columbia River southeast of town and along the Pend d'Oreille River that flows into the Columbia at **Waneta**. This is the driest part of the Interior Western Hemlock forests, so for the "Wet Kootenays" it holds some surprises.

To get to Waneta, cross to the east side of the Columbia River on Hwy. 3B, then about 6.5 kilometres from the bridge, turn south on the Waneta Highway (follow signs for the airport and the U.S. border). After 6 kilometres, turn left onto the Seven Mile Dam Road. As the road gets close to the mouth of the **Pend d'Oreille River** (flowing in from the east), take the gravel Waneta-Nelway Road on the left. This road travels through a mix of shrubby woodland, pastures, and dry forests; watch for Lewis's Woodpeckers around isolated large trees and Common Nighthawks foraging overhead. Yellow-breasted Chats have been found in dense thickets, particularly close to the confluence of the two rivers. You will travel through an area burned by a forest fire in 2007, where you can find Black-backed Woodpeckers at the moment, though over the years that species will likely drop off, whereas the Lewis's Woodpecker population will continue to prosper. If you'd like a somewhat adventurous loop trip, you can keep going on this road all the way to Nelway, the border crossing south of Salmo, and then continue your trip on Hwy. 3.

> Arrow Lakes

The **Arrow Lakes** were formerly two narrow lakes along the Columbia River north of Castlegar, but they were flooded by the Keenleyside Dam to form a single reservoir. The **Nakusp** area is a good base for exploration. Just 3 kilometres east of Nakusp on Hwy. 6, you can drive (or walk—it's only 6 kilometres) **Brouse Loop Road**, which goes south off the highway and loops back a little farther east. Bobolinks nest in the big field on the west side of the loop, and American Redstarts are common in the woods at the southeast corner. Willow Flycatchers, Hammond's Fly-catchers, Lazuli Buntings, and Savannah Sparrows are common as well. About 10 kilometres farther east on Hwy. 6 is **Summit Lake**—one of many lakes so-named in this mountainous prov-ince! This is one of the few places in the region where Magnolia Warblers nest, and there is often an Alder Flycatcher singing among the Willow Flycatchers at the southeast end of the lake. An old railway grade across the lake from the highway provides easy walking access to a variety of habitats.

South of Nakusp (about 35 kilometres) on Hwy. 6 is the vil-lage of **Burton**, and on the south side of the village, the highway crosses the delta of Caribou and Burton Creeks. You access the delta flats via Robazzo Road, which goes off to the west about 900 metres south of the bridge. Where this road makes a sharp turn back to the left, you can park and walk out onto the flats. During migration (April to May, August to October), watch for Horned Larks and Lapland Longspurs on the drier areas of the flats and shorebirds, well, along the shore. Although the Arrow Lakes are not a shorebird paradise, if you're going to see any shorebirds in the region, this is the place. Large numbers (500–1,500) of gulls gather at the creek mouth in fall (Septem-ber to October) to feed on spawning Kokanee. Most of these are California Gulls on their way to the coast from prairie breeding grounds, and the rest are mostly Herring Gulls—but scattered among them are usually a few individuals of other gull species, including the occasional Sabine's, Thayer's, Glaucous-winged, and (once) Lesser Black-backed. These flats, and other shoreline birding spots in the Arrow Lakes area, are significantly affected by water levels regulated at the Keenleyside Dam at Castlegar. In recent years, water levels have been kept relatively high, reducing the extent of the flats and thus the numbers of birds using them.

Burton is only 20 kilometres or so north of Fauquier (pronounced "folk-year") and the Needles ferry. This small (free!) cable ferry crosses the lake every thirty minutes on the hour and half hour, from 5 AM to 10 PM. It provides access to another Arrow Lakes birding spot: the **Edgewood** area. The highway climbs away from the lake west of Needles for slightly more than 8 kilometres before it reaches the idyllic Inonoaklin Valley. Turn south on Edgewood Road and drive the 10 kilometres to the village of Edgewood, stopping frequently to explore the side roads crossing the valley.

For a more detailed account on the Creston Valley, ask the staff at the nature centre about Linda Van Damme's Creston Valley birding booklet, which includes site information, as well as abundance bar-graphs for each species.

CRESTON

After two centuries of marsh clearing and draining, there are very few large wetland tracts left in British Columbia, particularly in a rather vertical province where fertile bottomlands are prized for both agriculture and urban developments. Fortunately, an insightful conservation initiative was undertaken in the Creston Valley when 7,000 hectares (17,000 acres) of cattail marshes, lakes, and riparian woodland were set aside as the **Creston Valley Wildlife Management Area**. The birding opportunities in the valley are fantastic year round, and visitors will be impressed with both the variety and sheer abundance of certain species. Breeding densities for riparian species are particularly high, as Creston

American Coot

has perhaps more Wood Ducks, American Coots, Gray Catbirds, Yellow Warblers, and Lazuli Buntings per capita than anywhere else in British Columbia! The only breeding site in the province for Forster's Tern is located at the south end of Duck Lake, along with British Columbia's second-largest Western Grebe colony. Spring and fall migration can bring waterfowl numbers to mind-boggling heights—most notable are the thousands of Tundra Swans that pass through each year, along with the hundreds (if not thousands) of Greater White-fronted Geese—the latter being considered a rare visitor throughout most of the other Interior valleys. Although the wetlands of the Creston Valley are extensive, there remains a significant amount of farmland as well, and this attracts a variety of other breeding, migrating, and wintering birds. Finally, the diverse coniferous forests of the surrounding foothills and mountains are not to be forgotten and can make for a well-rounded birding experience.

> Kootenay Pass and Stagleap Provincial Park

Most visitors to the Creston Valley arrive via Hwy. 3 and the 1,774-metre (5,820-feet) **Kootenay Pass**—the highest all-weather

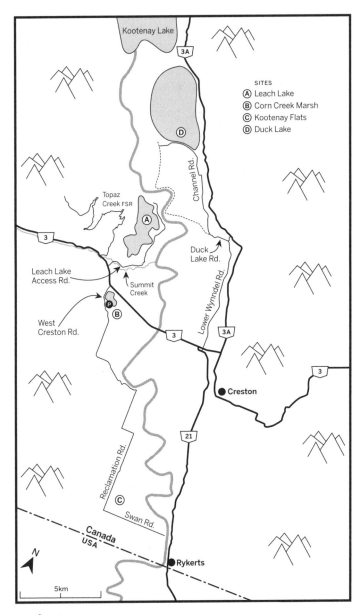

SITES
Ⓐ Leach Lake
Ⓑ Corn Creek Marsh
Ⓒ Kootenay Flats
Ⓓ Duck Lake

Kootenay Lake

Channel Rd.

Topaz
Creek FSR

Duck
Lake Rd.

Leach Lake
Access Rd.

Summit
Creek

Lower Wynndel Rd.

West
Creston Rd.

Creston

Reclamation Rd.

Swan Rd.

Canada
USA

N

Rykerts

5km

24 Creston

pass in Canada. Near the summit, pull off at the rest area beside the small but picturesque **Bridal Lake**. Here there are two trails that lead off into the subalpine habitat of **Stagleap Provincial Park**. Expected species in the breeding season include Spotted Sandpiper (along the lakeshore), Gray Jay, Steller's Jay, Mountain Chickadee, Red-breasted Nuthatch, both kinglet species, Varied Thrush, Yellow-rumped Warbler, and White-crowned Sparrow. For more high-elevation species, the decommissioned **Stagleap Forest Service Road** leads south off the highway, opposite the lake. More boreal species can be found along here, such as Boreal Chickadee, Hermit Thrush, Townsend's Warbler, and Chipping Sparrow. Boreal Owl nests in this area, but to hear or see this much sought-after species, you will need to visit between February and early May—and at night, of course. Not surprisingly, there are few birds to see in the winter, but keep an eye out for winter finches, such as Gray-crowned Rosy-Finch, Pine Grosbeak, Red and White-winged Crossbill, Pine Siskin, and Common Redpoll, all of which can be seen from time to time collecting grit along the roadsides during the snowy months.

> Leach Lake

Approximately 33 kilometres east of Kootenay Pass, the Crowsnest Highway (Hwy. 3) crosses a large bridge over Summit Creek. Six hundred metres after crossing the bridge, pull over on the left (north) side of the road (if you're approaching from Creston, this pull-off is 1.3 kilometres west of the wildlife centre turnoff at West Creston Road). This site used to be known as the Summit Creek Campground but is now just a day-use area and the principal way for birders to access **Leach Lake**. Bird diversity in the remnant old-growth cedar forest here is not particularly high, but the ambiance is refreshing and many new visitors to the area will probably not complain if they catch a glimpse of a few western specialties found here, including Vaux's Swift, Red-naped

Northern Saw-whet Owl

Sapsucker, Hammond's and Pacific-slope Flycatchers, Cassin's Vireo, Chestnut-backed Chickadee, and Townsend's Warbler. Barred Owls will often respond to hooting imitations or taped calls, and both Pileated and Hairy Woodpeckers may swoop in to investigate the ruckus.

Proceed northeast through the forest and cross the Bailey Bridge, stopping to look for American Dippers along Summit Creek and perhaps scanning the skies for swifts. Across the bridge there is a grassy trail that forks to the left and follows the old Dewdney Trail (somewhat overgrown in sections), but if you stay on the main roadway, it will lead you to the cattail marshes and cottonwood groves along the east side of Leach Lake. Water levels and your tolerance for mosquitoes will probably determine how long you spend out on these dyke trails, but it is possible to spend hours taking in this wonderful area. Look and listen for Least Flycatcher, Western Wood-Pewee, Black-billed Magpie, Yellow Warbler, Black-headed Grosbeak, and Bullock's Orioles in the tall stands of Black Cottonwoods; Common Yellowthroats, Lazuli Buntings, and Song Sparrows can be heard singing from the grassy and marshy meadows nearby. The main attraction of this location, however, is the marshland, with countless pairs of nesting dabbling ducks, coots, rails, Marsh Wrens, and the like. If you're lucky, you may flush an American Bittern or Sora rail, and in some years, Black Terns can be seen floating around the marsh. Double-crested Cormorants and American White-Pelicans summer here in the hundreds, and a few rare "spring overshoots" have popped up from time to time, such as Great Egret, White-faced Ibis, and Black-necked Stilt.

For an overview of the Leach Lake complex, return to your car and drive 800 metres back up the highway to the northwest. After crossing the bridge, make the first right onto the **Topaz Creek Forest Service Road.** This forestry road—usually well maintained—passes through a mixed forest of pine, fir, cedar, hemlock, larch, and maple and can produce a different mix of forest birds from the wetter cedar forest below. At kilometre 3, continue on the Newington Road. Several gaps in the trees will allow for views of Leach Lake, where outside of winter, there should be plenty of waterfowl to count. From February to April, listen for the monotonous whistles of the Northern Saw-whet Owl (at night), whereas the diurnal Northern Pygmy-Owl is a distinct possibility during the day—particularly in winter.

> Corn Creek Marsh

Nearly 2 kilometres southeast along Hwy. 3 from the Summit Creek Bridge is the well-signed turnoff to the **Creston Valley Wildlife Management and Interpretation Centre.** The red roofs of the buildings are easily visible on the left side of West Creston Road. At the centre, there is an array of indoor and outdoor interpretive displays, and the knowledgeable staff will be able to alert you to some of the recent bird sightings in the area. All three species of hummingbird (Calliope, Rufous, and

Black-chinned) can be seen at the feeders beside the building, and all six regular swallow species can be seen in spring and summer, hawking insects over the nearby ponds (Barn and Cliff nest on the buildings themselves). Interpretive walks and canoe tours are available, but visitors can also walk on their own the boardwalks and trails around Corn Creek Marsh, where all of the usual marsh species, from Great Blue Heron and Virginia Rail to Yellow-headed and Red-winged Blackbird, can be seen or heard. The winnowing sound of a displaying Wilson's Snipe is often heard in the morning and near dusk. Look carefully and perhaps you'll spot this pot-bellied shorebird way up in the sky. If you continue 2.1 kilometres south from the centre parking lot (along West Creston Road), you will reach a stand of mixed forest on the left (east) side—**Corn Creek Forest**. Here you will find several of the same species mentioned near Summit Creek.

> Kootenay Flats

Continue south along West Creston Road, until it curves to the east and parallels the Kootenay River, before making a 90-degree turn to the south (7 kilometres from the wildlife centre). From Hwy. 3, you can also head south along Nicks South Island Road, then make a left onto West Creston Road at the T-junction before reaching the sharp turn to the south. At this turn, the road becomes **Reclamation Road**. The wide open fields of Nicks Island and Reclamation Road can be fantastic in spring, when snowmelt floods the fields during peak waterfowl migration (March to April). Gull numbers can also be high; check the common Ring-billed, California, and Herring Gulls for rarer species such as Thayer's and Lesser Black-backed. Mid-May is a great time to visit, as most of the grassland breeders of **Kootenay Flats** will have returned—most notably, Long-billed Curlews and Bobolinks. Scan the alfalfa fields on both sides of Reclamation Road for curlews, Bobolinks, Western Meadowlarks, and

Savannah Sparrows. The Bobolinks are most often seen on the right (west) side of the road along this first straight stretch. If you don't see them at first, scan the far fence lines to the west. Curlews are a possibility on either side along this road, but the best place to see them is by pulling into the parking lot of the potato farm at the end of the straight stretch, then scanning the fields behind the buildings. For more fields, continue east then south from the potato farm along Reclamation Road for 5.7 kilometres, then turn left (east) onto Swan Road, which dead-ends at the river dyke. The dyke itself is private property, but from the end of the road, look and listen for singing Clay-colored Sparrows that nest in thickets of rose and snowberry.

In addition to the plethora of waterfowl, shorebirds, and songbirds that can be found along these open bottomlands, raptors too can be seen in big numbers—especially in winter during plentiful vole years. American Kestrel, Red-tailed Hawk, and Northern Harrier can be seen year round, Rough-legged Hawks are present in winter, and Turkey Vultures only in spring and summer. All three accipiter species are possible (goshawk mainly in winter), and more unusual species such as Peregrine Falcon (regular transient), Prairie Falcon, Short-eared Owl, and Snowy Owl (in irruption years) have all been recorded along these roads.

> Duck Lake

To reach the Creston Valley's most popular birding area, exit off Hwy. 3 south onto Hwy. 21 (for the U.S. border), then make an immediate left to go through the tunnel northward onto Lower Wynndel Road. Drive 6.8 kilometres north then turn left (west) onto Duck Lake Road—slow down, be ready for the turn, and observe caution for oncoming vehicles, as this is a bit of an awkward intersection. From Hwy. 3A (Creston to Kootenay Lake), you can turn west onto the other end of Lower Wynndel Road; Duck Lake Road will come up quickly on the right.

Once you're on Duck Lake Road, drive for slightly more than 1 kilometre, then make a right onto Channel Road after crossing a big slough. Between spring and fall, this channel is often filled with Wood Ducks, sometimes numbering in the hundreds! Many other ducks frequent this remnant course of the Old Goat River—the abundance and variety will depend on the time of year. From the start of Channel Road, it's nearly 6 kilometres to Duck Lake.

Along the way you may hear the perpetual summer song of Red-eyed Vireos somewhere high up in the cottonwoods, along with the chatter of Bullock's Orioles, the emphatic *chebek! chebek!* of a feisty Least Flycatcher, and the plaintive *peeeer* of the Western Wood-Pewee. In winter, keep an eye open for Northern Shrikes scanning the horizon from prominent perches on the left side of the road, and in early spring and late fall, you may be lucky enough to spot a flock of migrating Sandhill Cranes resting or feeding out in the fields.

As the road meets the south end of **Duck Lake**, it merges onto a dyke where there are several pull-offs from which to bird the lake and marshes on either side. There should be lots to look at no matter what time of year you visit, but March to April is the best time for the waterfowl migration spectacle. The most numerous species during this time are Northern Pintail, American Wigeon, and American Coot, each numbering in the thousands, followed by lesser but still impressive concentrations of other dabbling ducks, as well as divers, from loons and grebes to mergansers, Redhead, Ring-necked Ducks, and both scaup species. During the breeding season, scan the large summer flotilla of Western Grebes for any stray Clark's, though this can be a difficult task if the birds are far out. If there is any exposed mud between mid-April and May, large numbers of shorebirds can be seen. Common species include Killdeer; Least, Semipalmated,

Western, Pectoral, and Solitary Sandpipers; Greater and Lesser Yellowlegs; and Long-billed Dowitcher. It's possible to find many more species, including a few local rarities (in recent years), such as Willet, Marbled Godwit, Ruddy Turnstone, American Avocet, and Black-necked Stilt.

Between spring and early fall, look for Forster's Terns on both sides of the dyke. This is the only known breeding site in the province! If you arrive late in summer, after the young have fledged, and cannot see any nearby, try scanning along the far edges of Duck Lake, because the terns move around quite a bit. They will also move over to the south end of **Kootenay Lake** at times (to the north via Hwy. 3A). Like Leach Lake, birders can expect a bounty of marsh-loving species in this area, from the secretive Marsh Wren and American Bittern to the noisy blackbird sentinels. The willows along the dyke are well known for their rarities potential, so be vigilant and check any mixed migrant flocks that might be passing through. Among the long list of rarities, this patch has turned up multiple Sage Thrashers. In winter, the willows and reed beds on both sides are favourite haunts of a small flock of American Tree-Sparrows.

Road conditions can be muddy or snowy, depending on the time of year, so be careful when driving a small car. At the west end of the dyke (along the south side of Duck Lake), you will hit a T-junction. Turning right will take you north along the west side of the lake, through riparian habitat, before dead-ending in slightly more than 6 kilometres. It is usually possible to complete a loop by turning left at this junction, which will soon lead you to the western end of Duck Lake Road (which leads east back to the Channel Road junction). The mix of farmland, riparian thickets along the creek, and forest creates a diversity of birds, including Bobolinks in the hayfields and Gray Catbirds along the creek.

EAST KOOTENAYS

The East Kootenays are dominated by the Rocky Mountain Trench, a valley that cuts a wide, deep, and remarkably straight line between the Rocky Mountains to the east and the Purcell Mountains to the west. The region is known for its spectacular scenery and diverse natural history, with dry grasslands and Ponderosa Pine woodlands merging over short distances into the wet coniferous forests more typical of the West Kootenays. The broad valley bottom has the largest wetlands in the Interior of British Columbia, where the Kootenay and Columbia Rivers wind through marshes and sloughs. Birding is best here during the breeding season, but migration can produce exciting finds as well up and down the trench.

> Fernie and Elko

Fernie is best known for its skiing but has some good birding opportunities as well. Tucked into the narrow Elk Valley amid the western Rocky Mountains, Fernie has a definite mountain flavour. There is a bit of eastern spice as well; this is the only site west of the Continental Divide in British Columbia where Common Grackles can be easily found, and Tennessee Warblers are occasionally heard in summer. The best spot for grackles is along **Dicken Road**, which turns left (west) off Hwy. 3 about 1 kilometre north of the Elk River Bridge at the north end of Fernie—check the trailer park area about 1.5 kilometres from the highway. Also at the north end of town, behind the Extra Foods and Canadian Tire stores, is the artificial **Maiden Lake** and surrounding wetland, which is worth checking out from spring through fall. There is a small Great Blue Heron colony there. On the other end of town are the **West Fernie Wetlands**, located between the highway and the Elk River, across from the Super 8 motel. These wetlands can be very productive, especially during spring migration, when interesting birds occasionally pop in on their way through the mountains.

To get in some true mountain birding around Fernie, there are two easy options. One is to take the Timber Chairlift up the mountain at the **Fernie Alpine Resort** (open weekends and holidays in the summer). The resort also offers guided nature walks in the subalpine with a knowledgeable birding guide on summer weekends (call 250-423-2435 for details). Another option is to drive to the microwave station above Fernie on **Morrissey Ridge**. To access this road, turn east off the highway onto 4th Street (just north of the southern Elk River Bridge), then turn south (right) onto Pine Avenue, just after the railway tracks. Take the first left onto Coal Creek Road and drive for about 10 kilometres, until you see the Matheson Creek Road angling back to the right. Take this road for about 4 kilometres, then take the right fork where it crosses the creek. After another 5 kilometres or so, you will reach the top of the ridge (2,134 metres elevation). You might want to walk the last few hundred metres, both for your vehicle's sake and to enjoy the mountain scenery and birds. Subalpine specialties such as Spruce Grouse, Dusky Grouse, Boreal Chickadee, Fox Sparrow and Pine Grosbeak are all possible along this road.

About 16 kilometres south of Fernie, **Morrissey Road** turns left (east) off the highway. The road crosses the Elk River and a set of railway tracks; at the tracks is a pull-off for the **Ancient Cottonwood Trail**. The short trail accesses a property, owned by the Nature Conservancy of Canada, that protects the oldest stand of cottonwoods in the world—some are more than four hundred years old—and provides a scenic stroll where you can look for riparian woodland birds. Another 16 kilometres south and west of Morrissey Road on Hwy. 3 is the village of Elko, where Hwy. 93 branches off to the south, eventually crossing into Montana at Roosville. This highway traverses dry forests and some grasslands and may be worth a day trip out of Fernie. For the more adventurous, there is the road to **Wigwam Flats**, which is reached by taking the exit into Elko and driving south through town to Alexander Avenue. Turn left on Alexander and follow it as it swings south above the river, then turn left again on the logging road that crosses the river below the town. On the opposite side of the river, turn right at the Y-junction, then right again, and you're on your way to Wigwam Flats. The road parallels the river before reaching the flats in about 5 kilometres; the right-hand fork dead-ends at the Wigwam River a short distance farther on. This mix of woodlands and dry grasslands is home to Lewis's Woodpeckers, Mountain Bluebirds, Vesper Sparrows, and Western Meadowlarks; listen for Pacific-slope Flycatchers calling from shady cliffs and watch for Bald and Golden Eagles soaring overhead.

Another day trip is **Kikomun-Newgate Road**, which goes southwest off Hwy. 3 about 2 kilometres west of Elko. About 10 kilometres from Hwy. 3, the road crosses **Lake Koocanusa** (the reservoir of the dam at Libby, Montana, on the Kootenay River); you can scan the reservoir for waterfowl from a pull-off on the west side. Just 1 kilometre past the reservoir, Kikomun-Newgate Road turns off to the south (left). This is a good gravel road and goes for almost 40 kilometres through some Ponderosa Pine and Western Larch forests before reaching the border at Newgate (no facilities, no border crossing). Watch for Lewis's Woodpeckers in the open Ponderosa Pine woodlands; Williamson's Sapsuckers can be found around stands of large larch (easiest in early April). Flammulated Owls (late May to June) and Common Poorwills (May to August) can be heard calling near Newgate on warm nights.

> Cranbrook and Kimberley

Cranbrook and Kimberley are good bases for exploring the southern end of the East Kootenay region. One of the best places to

Bullock's Oriole

start is **Elizabeth Lake**, located at the west end of Cranbrook on Hwy. 3. In spring and summer, this large, marshy lake is alive with many species of waterfowl, including Wood Duck, Gadwall, Cinnamon Teal, Northern Shoveler, Ring-necked Duck, Lesser Scaup, Bufflehead, Common and Barrow's Goldeneyes, and Hooded Merganser. Eared Grebes nest here (mid-April to October), as do large numbers of Black Terns (May to July). The marsh is full of Marsh Wrens, Common Yellowthroats, Red-winged Blackbirds, and Yellow-headed Blackbirds. Small numbers of shorebirds can be seen in migration, and there are a few spring records of American Avocet and Black-necked Stilt.

Visit the irrigation fields east of Cranbrook to see waterfowl and shorebirds. Take Hwy. 3/95 northwest out of the city for about 6 kilometres, then turn right to stay on Hwy. 3. About 2 kilometres from that junction, watch for a road on the left (east). Recently, it hasn't had any official road signs, but it's the obvious road on the left at the bottom of the hill. This road provides access to the two large ponds that store treated effluent water for irrigation. Please stay on the gravel road—access to the ponds themselves is restricted, so you will need a scope to properly check the lower pond. A variety of waterfowl can be found here from spring through fall, and this is the best shorebird site in the area. It is also the best place near Cranbrook to find Bobolink (in the hayfields).

Nearby, you can also get a look at a larger reservoir that can be a good spot for waterfowl. Park just beyond the City of Cranbrook Irrigation Pump Station, then scramble up the bank to view the reservoir. The best view of the lower pond is just a little ways past the pump station, about 100 metres from the road. It is possible that a new pond will also be created close to the road by the time this book is published. In addition to the water birds, the open fields and pine forests along this road can provide a mix of birds during the breeding season, such as Pygmy Nuthatch, Western and Mountain Bluebirds, Vesper Sparrow, and Cassin's Finch.

Returning to Cranbrook, take the Kimberley Highway to the right (northwest) as you enter town. Immediately on your left are the **Cranbrook Sewage Lagoons**, worth a scan for waterfowl such as American Wigeon, Common and Barrow's Goldeneyes, and Ruddy Duck. These ponds are open in winter as well, so you can add a few aquatic species to your January list. About 1.5 kilometres from the junction, turn right onto Cranbrook-Mission Road. After about 5 kilometres you will reach the **St. Eugene Mission Resort**. Park at the golf course parking area and explore the trails through the shrubby meadows and woodlands on the north side of the resort. Almost two hundred species have been recorded here. All three hummingbirds—Black-chinned, Rufous, and Calliope—can be found; also watch for Lewis's Woodpecker, Willow and Least Flycatchers, Say's Phoebe, Clark's Nutcracker, Western and Mountain Bluebirds, Western Tanager, Black-headed Grosbeak, and Lazuli Bunting. There is also a small Great Blue Heron colony beside the golf course, and Cliff, Barn, and Violet-green Swallows all nest on or in the main resort building.

When leaving the resort, turn left onto Mission Road, then left again at the T-junction across the bridge over the river. You are now on **Mission-Wycliffe Road**, a quiet 11-kilometre drive through Ponderosa Pine forests and dry grasslands. Occasional stops could yield Lewis's Woodpecker, both White-breasted and Pygmy Nuthatches, and both Western and Mountain Bluebirds. The road crosses the airport access road then turns west and south to meet the Kimberley Highway; turn right here if you want to continue on to Kimberley.

The **Kimberley Nature Park** is a large (800-hectare) forested park with many trails; you can purchase a trail map for $5 at several outlets in Kimberley, including the Chamber of Commerce tourist information centre in the Platzl parking lot. The mixed conifer woodlands, particularly those with Western Larch, can have sought-after woodpeckers, such as Williamson's Sapsucker and American Three-toed Woodpecker, and a diversity of songbirds, including Chestnut-backed Chickadee and Townsend's Warbler.

> Fort Steele to Fairmont Hot Springs

Another good side road in the Cranbrook area is **Fenwick Road**. Take Hwy. 3 east to the Kootenay River Bridge and turn north onto Wardner-Fort Steele Road immediately after crossing the bridge. After about 5.5 kilometres, you will cross the Bull River; take the first left (west) after the bridge onto Fenwick Road. The road travels through a variety of forested and agricultural habitats for about 17 kilometres before rejoining the road to Fort Steele. Here you can either turn right to return to Hwy. 3 or turn left to reach Fort Steele and join Hwy. 93. In the grassy and shrubby areas, listen for the distinctive songs of Dusky Flycatcher, Clay-colored Sparrow, and Western Meadowlark; Red-naped Sapsucker and Pileated Woodpeckers are possibilities in the forests. Watch and listen for Great Gray Owls (rare) in the open forests.

Travelling north of Fort Steele on Hwy. 93, you will see a series of large marshes to the west along the eastern banks of the Kootenay River. The largest of these marshes is **Bummer's Flats**, accessible off North Star Landing on the west side of Hwy. 93, 9.6 kilometres north of Fort Steele. Watch for a dirt road that crosses the railway tracks and a Ducks Unlimited sign. Along with the usual marsh species, one can hope to see Sandhill Crane, Northern Harrier, and Short-eared Owls here during the breeding season. Just north of Bummer's Flats, you pass the **Wasa Sloughs**, a series of willow-lined ponds on the east side of the highway, always worth a stop, especially during migration periods. Just north of Wasa, the highway crosses the Kootenay River at Ta Ta Creek, meets up with the Kimberley Highway, and continues north along a series of flat benches. From 5.5 to 9 kilometres north of the junction, you cross **Skookumchuck Flats**, a large area covered with native grassland; this is an excellent spot in spring and summer to see Long-billed Curlews (April to June) and Lewis's Woodpeckers (look for isolated pine snags; May to August).

The highway crosses the Kootenay River again at Skookumchuck and begins to travel through young conifer forests on benchland east of the river. About 14 kilometres north of the bridge, on the east side of the road, there is a small lake with a single island; this usually has a variety of waterfowl on it from spring through fall. As it enters the town of Canal Flats, the highway crosses the Kootenay River for the final time; this is where the river emerges from the Rocky Mountains. **Canal Flats** marks the height of land between the Kootenay and the headwaters of the mighty river it will eventually flow into—the Columbia. You can stroll to the headwaters by taking the exit into the town of Canal Flats (Grainger Street) and driving north about 1.5 kilometres to Beatty Avenue. Turn left here and drive 1 kilometre west to Shaughnessy Street; turn right, then quickly left, and proceed until you come to an abandoned airstrip.

Drive north on the airstrip for half a kilometre, where you'll see a trailhead on the left (west). Walk these trails through the forest until it opens up into shrub land, which features a variety of songbirds, including the locally uncommon Calliope Hummingbird and Spotted Towhee.

Back on the highway, travelling north, you cross the railway as you leave Canal Flats and begin to climb a hill out of the valley bottom. If you want to scan Columbia Lake for waterfowl and shorebirds, stop at the pull-off on the right side of the road about half a kilometre north of the railway crossing. Scan the hills above for Lewis's Woodpeckers, especially above the intersection with Findlay Creek Road about 300 metres past the pull-off. Just north of Columbia Lake, the highway crosses Dutch Creek and turns sharply right (east) beneath a set of spectacular hoodoos. The **Dutch Creek Hoodoos** are the only site in the area where White-throated Swifts nest, so it's worth a quick stop from April through September.

> Invermere and Radium Hot Springs

North of Fairmont, the highway travels along hilly benches east of, and well above, the young Columbia River and then Lake Windermere. To explore this area and its fabulous wetlands, turn west and proceed down the hill and into the town of Invermere. Once you cross the railway tracks, turn north onto Panorama Drive and continue for slightly more than half a kilometre to Borden Street. Turn right here then left just before the railway tracks and follow a gravel road north, paralleling the tracks. This road takes you into the middle of the **Athalmer Sloughs**. Although there are No Trespassing signs along this road (more of a track paralleling a rail yard), birders are generally permitted to pass through at any time of year. As always, adhere to the wishes of any local officials who inform you otherwise. You can scan for birds on both sides of the tracks. There is a Great Blue Heron colony in the trees west of the road where it ends at the railway bridge over the Columbia River, and a pair of Great Horned Owls often nests in a large hole in the silt bluffs on the east side of the wetlands. Various species of waterfowl will be present year round, including a group of swans that overwinter here each year.

Some of the best of these Columbia River wetlands are protected in the **Wilmer National Wildlife Area**. To explore this jewel, return to Panorama Drive and turn right (west). Just beyond the Toby Creek Bridge turn right (north) onto Wilmer Road. Proceed into the village of Wilmer, turning right onto Main Avenue, which soon leaves town and becomes Westside Road. After about 2 kilometres on Westside Road, you will see a pull-off on the right (east) side of the road and National Wildlife Area signs. Follow the trail along the grassy slopes above spectacular silt bluffs. Grassland species such as American Kestrel and Vesper Sparrows are common here, and the views of the wetlands are exceptional (a spotting scope is recommended).

Returning to the highway, turn north to Radium Hot Springs. At the four-way stop (where turning right would take you into Kootenay National Park), turn left onto Forster's Landing Road. At the bottom of the hill, this road skirts the south side of the **Radium mill ponds**, a prime site for waterfowl, Yellow-headed Blackbirds, and Bullock's Orioles. It is very productive during spring and fall migration, but even in midsummer, nice birds such as Wood Duck and Hooded Merganser can be found. Return to the highway and drive about 30 kilometres north of Radium to the village of **Brisco**. Turn left (west) onto Brisco Road; the road turns north at a mill, then swings west to cross the wetlands. After crossing the river, the road turns sharply south, then sharply west. Immediately after this last corner, you will see two marshy ponds on either side of the road. These ponds, known locally as **Trescher's Ponds**, present species such as Sora (heard calling); check the hayfields on the south side of the road for Bobolinks.

> Golden

Formerly just a gas-station stop on the Trans-Canada Highway, Golden has become a tourist destination in its own right. On the south side of Golden on Hwy. 93, **Reflection Lake** is worth a scan for Ruddy Duck, Yellow-headed Blackbird, and other denizens of marshy ponds. If you'd like to get to high elevations for the chance to see White-tailed Ptarmigan or Gray-crowned Rosy-Finch, inquire at the Kicking Horse Mountain Resort about gondola rides and high elevation hiking (kickinghorseresort.com). The best birding spot in the area is **Moberly Marsh**, also known as **Burges and James Gadsden Provincial Park**. Moberly Marsh is a rich mix of woodland and marsh alongside the Columbia River, which you can access by driving north on Hwy. 1, about 15 kilometres from the Hwy. 93 junction, until you see Blaeberry River Road on the left (west). Park at the road entrance and walk along the south road to the hayfield, skirting around the north side of the field, then walk down the west side until you are on a dyke between the river and a rich marsh. Watch for Bobolinks in the field (June to July). The real attraction at Moberly Marsh is not so much the marsh itself but the riparian woodland and shrubbery beside it. The marsh is at or near the northern limit of several songbirds, including Gray Catbird, Black-headed Grosbeak, and Bullock's Oriole. The breeding ranges of Alder and Willow Flycatchers meet here, allowing close comparison of their songs. Watch for Purple Finches in the woodland—this species is replaced by Cassin's Finch farther south in the Rocky Mountain Trench.

ROCKY MOUNTAIN PARKS

The Canadian Rockies, with their unparalleled scenery and iconic landmarks, are on the itinerary of many visitors to British Columbia, as well as a vacation destination for local residents. These mountains are simply not to be missed, whether you are birding or not, and are quite frankly in a scenic class of their own when compared to the less rugged Rockies south of the U.S. border. Fortunately, much of the Canadian Rockies is preserved in a series of national and provincial parks. There are two national parks in the British Columbia Rockies—Yoho and Kootenay—and one large, easily accessible provincial park—Mount Robson. Please note that you need to purchase park permits (available at the park entrances) if you wish to stop and hike in the two national parks; no such permit is needed for Mount Robson Provincial Park.

YOHO NATIONAL PARK

The vast majority of visitors to **Yoho National Park** see it from the Trans-Canada Highway (Hwy. 1) as they're travelling to or from Alberta. Hwy. 1 follows the Kicking Horse Valley out of Golden, climbing into the western flank of the Rocky Mountains. After you enter Yoho National Park, the valley takes a sharp bend back to the left (northeast), and near this point you will see a side road going off to the south for **Wapta Falls**. The Wapta Falls road passes Leanchoil Marsh, where you can hear Wilson's Snipe winnowing and Lincoln's Sparrows singing. The trail to the falls is 2.4 kilometres long and goes through subalpine forests with Cassin's Vireo, Mountain Chickadee, Golden- and Ruby-crowned Kinglets, Townsend's Warblers, and other typical mountain species. The **Hoodoos Trail**, accessed from Hoodoos Creek Campground 2 kilometres along the highway from Wapta Falls, has similar species, though Hammond's Flycatcher may be more common here. About 20 kilometres northeast of Hoodoos Creek Campground there is a turnoff on the north side of the highway to **Emerald Lake**. This route, and the trail around the lake (the latter is about a one-hour walk), can be great for subalpine species, including American Three-toed Woodpecker, Olive-sided Flycatcher, Boreal Chickadee, Varied Thrush, Wilson's Warbler, and Pine Grosbeak. The lake is home to Barrow's Goldeneyes and Common Mergansers in summer. **Lake O'Hara** is even better for subalpine and alpine birding, but you must make a reservation on the daily shuttle (call Parks Canada at 250-343-6433) or make the 11-kilometre hike in on foot. The lake is at 2,000 metres elevation—close to treeline—and there is a myriad of trails leading into higher country, where you could see White-tailed Ptarmigan and Gray-crowned Rosy-Finch, as well as the subalpine species in the forests.

KOOTENAY NATIONAL PARK

From Radium Hot Springs you can take the road less travelled to Banff by turning west on Hwy. 93 and going through **Kootenay National Park**. A quick stop at **Olive Lake**, about 13 kilometres from Radium, should produce the common forest birds along the short nature trail, including Golden-crowned Kinglet and Townsend's Warbler. A longer trail to explore the forests, including those burned in the large fire that swept through the park in 2003, is the **Floe Lake Trail**, accessed from the trailhead about 9 kilometres north of Vermilion Crossing. The first 4 kilometres of the trail are quite gentle; if you're up for a more strenuous day hike you can go all the way to Floe Lake (10.7 kilometres one way). Watch for Northern Hawk Owls in the burned forest—they can be conspicuous from their snag-top perches. Shortly after the highway turns sharply east to climb to Vermilion Pass, you'll see a turnoff to **Marble Canyon**. This canyon is one of few sites in the world where Black Swift nests can be closely approached—the trick is to actually see the nests from the trail by looking into the narrow canyon. It's best to walk the trail in the evening in July or August and watch for the birds as they return to the nests.

MOUNT ROBSON PROVINCIAL PARK

Mount Robson Provincial Park is one of the most spectacular parks on the planet, offers exciting birding from fall through spring, and is much less crowded than its famous neighbour to the east—Jasper National Park. So now that you're in on the big secret, make sure you take some time to explore this gem.

> Kinney Lake and Berg Lake

The heart of Mount Robson Provincial Park is the trail to **Kinney Lake** and beyond to **Berg Lake**. You don't have to walk much to enjoy good birding on this route, since some of the best birding is along the access road to the trailhead, which leaves Hwy. 5 at the main visitor centre opposite Robson Meadows campground. In spring and early summer, the woods along this road are alive with warblers and other songbirds, including Western

Wood-Pewee, Orange-crowned Warbler, Tennessee Warbler, Northern Waterthrush, American Restart, Magnolia Warbler, Townsend's Warbler, Wilson's Warbler, Rusty Blackbird, and Purple Finch. If you'd like to add Blackpoll Warbler to the list, try the Robson River campground area, particularly the small spruces right along the river at the end of the campground. The trail to Kinney Lake (4.5 kilometres one way) goes through old-growth Western Red Cedar and Western Hemlock forests; common birds include Hammond's Flycatcher, Pacific-slope Flycatcher, Pacific Wren, and Swainson's Thrush. Beyond Kinney Lake, the trail climbs gently at first, then quite steeply to Berg Lake. This hike requires wilderness camping available on either end of Berg Lake. This is highly recommended, if only because Berg Lake is one of the iconic scenes of the Canadian wilderness. Easy day hikes from Berg Lake will put you into alpine habitats with White-tailed Ptarmigan and Gray-crowned Rosy-Finch or willow subalpine wetlands where Solitary Sandpipers and Golden-crowned Sparrows nest. Harlequin Ducks are often seen on the lake in spring and early summer.

› Moose Lake

If you're passing through Mount Robson on Hwy. 5, try to stop at **Moose Lake**, especially if you're travelling in spring (late April to May) or fall (September to October) migration. Interesting water birds here include scoters, Long-tailed Ducks, and Pacific Loons. The extensive marsh at the east end of the lake has breeding Greater Yellowlegs and Rusty Blackbirds; it is also notable as a site where both Alder and Willow Flycatchers breed side by side.

› Cranberry Marsh (Valemount)

If you're travelling to and from Mount Robson and Jasper via Kamloops, you will pass the small mountain town of Valemount (19 kilometres south of Tête Jaune Cache along Hwy. 5). At the south end of town, follow signs for Wildlife Viewing and park next to the Best Western Hotel. Here you will find the entrance to a network of trails that lead through the **R.W. Starratt Wildlife Refuge**. This is the official name for the refurbished wetland known to locals as Cranberry Marsh—a rich tract of cattail marsh surrounded by mixed second-growth forest. It's a fantastic birding area to break up a long drive, and give visitors a respite from boring old snow-capped mountain peaks! There are several interpretive signs that outline some of the wildlife, including the birds of the marsh, and these are fairly accurate with one major exception: American Black Ducks *do not* occur here. Don't believe everything you read! If you visit between May and September, you'll probably find a variety of waterfowl, such as Ring-necked and Ruddy Ducks, and a few dabblers, including Blue-winged Teal, American Wigeon, and the familiar Mallards. Sora and Virginia Rail are extremely common, so if you visit in the morning or evening, it is sometimes possible to hear ten to twenty Soras calling along your walk. Marsh Wrens and Common Yellowthroats are also abundant, and the trees and shrubs along the edges can net you a good mix as well, including Merlin, Dusky Flycatcher, Swainson's Thrush, Tennessee Warbler, American Redstart, Yellow-rumped Warbler, Chipping Sparrow, and Clay-colored Sparrow.

CARIBOO-CHILCOTIN

100 MILE HOUSE

There is a marsh in downtown 100 Mile House that is worth a stop anytime from May through October. Pull over at the tourist information centre (by the giant cross-country skis) to view the lake and marsh. Breeding species include Blue-winged and Cinnamon Teal, Northern Shoveler, Northern Pintail, Canvasback, Ring-necked Duck, Ruddy Duck, Pied-billed Grebe, Eared Grebe, and Black Tern. And in migration, the list of possible water birds is much longer. For good forest and woodland birding downtown, turn east off Hwy. 97 onto 4th Street just north of the tourist information centre, travel two blocks, make a right turn onto Cedar Avenue, then an immediate left. This takes you to a parking area for the 100 Mile **Centennial Park**, a small but wonderful mix of shrubby riparian and coniferous forest habitats. A series of trails goes along the stream, as well as up into the forest; species here in summer include Calliope Hummingbird, Red-naped Sapsucker, Hammond's Flycatcher, Dusky Flycatcher, Western Tanager, and Purple Finch.

WILLIAMS LAKE

The best birding spot in Williams Lake is **Scout Island Nature Centre**. Turn south off Hwy. 97 onto Hwy. 20, then immediately turn left onto Mackenzie Avenue and make two right turns: Borland Road then Scout Island Road. The centre is only about 1 kilometre from Hwy. 20. You reach the island along a narrow causeway through a marsh filled with Marsh Wrens, Yellow-headed Blackbirds, and other aquatic species. Check in at the nature centre for a bird checklist and recent sightings; walk the woodland trails for Veery, Gray Catbird, and Bullock's Oriole (you're close to the northern limit for these species), and scan the lake for waterfowl, loons, and grebes. If you're lucky, you might spot an American White Pelican on the lake or an American Bittern in the marsh.

ALKALI LAKE AND DOG CREEK ROAD

The road south from Williams Lake to Alkali Lake, then beyond to the arid benchlands of the Fraser River around Gang Ranch, can be one of the best birding routes in the British Columbia Interior, especially in spring. Take Hwy. 20 south out of Williams Lake; after 2.6 kilometres turn left (southeast) onto Dog Creek Road, following any signs for Springhouse or Alkali Lake. The road travels first through the rural outskirts of Williams Lake, then traverses typical plateau forest for 20 kilometres or so before reaching the marshy lakes of **Springhouse**. The first two lakes—Sorenson and Westwick—are well worth a scan for waterfowl and Eared Grebes. After passing the airstrip at Boitano Lake, it's about 25 kilometres to **Alkali Lake**, the must-see location on this route. From April through October, this lake features an assortment of water birds. Interesting migrants seen here include Tundra Swan, Eurasian Wigeon, Surf Scoter, and White-winged Scoter; in October 1950, local biologist Leo Jobin saw five Common Eiders on Alkali Lake, but thin ice prevented him from securing the specimen needed in those days to verify the sighting. American White Pelicans are a possibility here any time from mid-April through September; watch for Prairie and Peregrine Falcons checking out the ducks. Long-billed Curlews, Wilson's Snipe, and Wilson's Phalarope nest around the lake. Songbirds in the marshes and shrubby grasslands include Willow Flycatcher, Western Kingbird, Eastern Kingbird, Marsh Wren, Mountain Bluebird, Veery, Lazuli Bunting, and Bobolink.

South of Alkali Lake, the road emerges onto the highly scenic arid benches above the Fraser River—if you're used to the Fraser River as it flows through the dairy farms of Agassiz, this is like a different planet. On the **Dog Creek** benches, stop and look for Long-billed Curlews—this site has one of the best local populations of curlews in the province. You can see the outline of a triangular set of runways here, which were used to stage aircraft en route to Alaska during World War II. From the benches, the road passes under towering rock bluffs. There are Rock Wrens in the talus below the bluffs, and both Peregrine and Prairie Falcons nest here. The road descends steeply to Dog Creek, then continues south near the Fraser to a junction with Gang Ranch Road. If you have the time, you can cross the river here to Gang Ranch, then take the first left (south) onto Empire Valley Road. This quickly enters the Churn Creek Protected Area; the road goes for about 20 kilometres to the Empire Valley Ranch headquarters. This is a perfect area for dry grassland species, including Common Poorwill (at night) and Lark Sparrow. There is a campsite at Kenworthy Creek, about halfway to the headquarters.

CHILCOTIN PLATEAU

To the west of the Fraser River, in central British Columbia, lies the Chilcotin Plateau, a vast area of pine forests and grasslands. Flanked on the south and west by the rugged coast range, the plateau is largely a flat or rolling plain dotted with numerous lakes of all sizes. The forests have been devastated in recent years by the mountain pine beetle, but birding remains excellent. **Stum Lake**, north of Alexis Creek, is the site of British Columbia's only colony of American White Pelicans, and the waterfowl diversity across the plateau is outstanding. The southeastern corner of the Chilcotin, where the Chilcotin River meets the Fraser, is the northernmost outpost of many dry Interior species, such as Flammulated Owl, Common Poorwill, Lewis's Woodpecker, and Cassin's Finch, whereas the western rim of the plateau, particularly around the Itcha, Ilgachuz, and Rainbow Ranges, has produced records of breeding species with a subarctic flavour—Yellow Rail, American Golden-Plover, Semipalmated Plover, Arctic Tern, Bohemian Waxwing, and Gray-cheeked Thrush.

Hwy. 20 travels through the heart of the Chilcotin, from Williams Lake in the east to Bella Coola in the west. Turn west off Hwy. 97 in downtown Williams Lake (the same turn as for Springhouse and Alkali Lake) and continue south and west for about 25 kilometres. There the highway crosses the Fraser River in a steep-walled valley. It's often a good idea to stop briefly on the west side of the bridge and look and listen for Western Kingbirds and Lazuli Buntings—you won't be seeing these species after the highway climbs back onto the plateau.

> Riske Creek

After crossing the Fraser River, Hwy. 20 climbs to the plateau surface east of Riske Creek. If you have time, **Moon Road**

Golden Eagle

provides a pleasant back roads route through a variety of habitats; it goes south off Hwy. 20 about 2.5 kilometres west of the bridge over the Fraser. There are some old-growth Douglas-fir forests along this road, with a sizable breeding population of Flammulated Owls and Common Poorwills; watch for the latter sitting on the road at night from May through August. The owl is best sought by listening for its soft *boo-boot!* call in late May and early June. About 3 kilometres from the highway, Moon Road passes by **Doc English Bluff**, a large limestone bluff towering over the Fraser—watch for Golden Eagles and White-throated Swifts in front of the cliffs from April through August. The road is signed as private at the Deer Park Ranch, so it's best to retrace your route back to the highway. If you continue west on the highway, you'll travel through **Becher's Prairie**, a mix of forest and grassland dotted with numerous small lakes. The grasslands of Becher's Prairie are home to Sharp-tailed Grouse, Long-billed Curlew, Horned Larks, and Vesper Sparrows. This general area is the only site where Sprague's Pipits have bred in British Columbia (1991–92) and one of the few places where Upland Sandpiper occasionally nests.

Mountain Bluebird

Shortly after reaching the plateau, you'll see **McIntyre Lake** on your right; you can access the lake via Meldrum Creek Road immediately to the west—it warrants a quick scan for waterfowl or shorebirds. About 3.5 kilometres west of the Meldrum Creek junction, a small track goes north off the highway. If you have a vehicle with decent clearance, this track is well worth a drive, at least as far as **Rock Lake** (2.3 kilometres). Rock Lake is home to a large Eared Grebe colony and a diverse array of waterfowl. Beyond Rock Lake, the track enters a military training area; to travel there you need a permit—it might save the bother of being shelled by tanks—so it's probably best to get back to the highway the way you came.

Farwell Canyon Road is a highly recommended side trip that goes south from the highway at Riske Creek. This route winds through grasslands dotted with ponds for about 15 kilometres, then drops into the canyon of the Chilcotin River in a series of impressive switchbacks. At the top of this hill, a dirt track goes off to the left (east) into the **Junction Sheep Range Provincial Park**; here you can see Long-billed Curlew, Lewis's Woodpecker, and other grassland species. Watch for Bighorn Sheep in the steep slopes above both the Chilcotin and Fraser Rivers. If you're continuing along the main road, stop at the **Chilcotin River Bridge** to scan the sky for White-throated Swifts among the more common Violet-green Swallows; this is one of the northernmost outposts for the swift. Watch for heavily laden logging trucks along this road on weekdays—it is a major access point for the beetle-ravaged forests of the southeast Chilcotin.

> ➤ Central Chilcotin

Hwy. 20 continues west from Riske Creek, dropping into the Chilcotin Valley at Hanceville and Alexis Creek. The Anahim's Flat grasslands—just east of Alexis Creek—can be a good place to listen for songbirds in spring, but stay on the road as this is all private land or First Nations reserve.

If you're driving west to Bella Coola and have some time to spare (a few hours, a day, or even a week), turn south at Tatla Lake and drive 34 kilometres to **Tatlayoko Lake**. The scenery is simply spectacular, and the birding can be good as well. The Nature Conservancy of Canada runs a migration monitoring station there, the **Tatlayoko Lake Bird Observatory**. If you'd like to spend more time in this gorgeous spot, you can volunteer at the observatory. Check out their website for details (tatlayokobirds. wordpress.com). Nearby Eagle Lake has had breeding Arctic Terns in recent years.

The **Anahim Lake** area offers birding with a decidedly northern flavour. If you take Christensen Road out of Anahim Lake to the east and north, you'll pass through a sedge wetland and hayfield along a straight stretch about 6 kilometres from town. This wetland has Yellow Rails in some years (depending on water levels); unfortunately, the rails are usually well away from the road, but this is all private land, so try your luck from the road.

Lesser Yellowlegs nest in the area as well, at the southern end of their breeding range. Beyond Anahim Lake, the highway climbs gently to Heckman Pass, another area for exploration. Blackpoll Warblers are widespread in these spruce forests. After you enter **Tweedsmuir Provincial Park**, watch for the trailhead to the Rainbow Range on the right. Turn off the highway here and park at the trailhead—this is one of the few accessible and reliable places in the province for breeding Gray-cheeked Thrush. From here, the highway drops off the edge of the plateau down a spectacular hill known simply as The Hill. Make sure your brakes are in good order. Watch for loose breeding colonies of Bohemian Waxwings in the upper forests as you begin the descent, especially around Young Creek. Once down at the bottom of the hill, you are in coastal coniferous forests with all their usual species, including Sooty Grouse, Red-breasted Sapsucker, Pacific-slope Flycatcher, and MacGillivray's Warbler. At the eastern end of the valley near the Atnarko Campground you can hear Veeries in the riparian thickets and Nashville Warblers on the open, drier south-facing slopes. The Bella Coola estuary has little to attract the visiting birder, but it is nice to get there just to say you reached the Pacific after crossing the historic Chilcotin Plateau.

> Soda Creek

This is one of the favourite locales for birders from both Williams Lake and Quesnel, yet most outsiders have never heard of it. Slightly more than 30 kilometres north of Williams Lake, turn left onto Old Soda Creek Townsite Road, then wind down the hill before continuing west through the ranchlands of **Soda Creek**. If you reach a small marshy lake on the east side of the road (Duckworth Lake), you have gone too far north. Located along the Fraser River, the warm south-facing slopes around the old Soda Creek townsite and along Soda Creek-Macalister

Western Kingbird

Road produce a microclimate similar to the dry grasslands of the Fraser Canyon and Thompson region. As a result, several species found here are nearing the northern limits of their respective breeding ranges in British Columbia, or even North America. Some of these specialties include Turkey Vulture, Long-billed Curlew, Mourning Dove, Black-chinned Hummingbird, Lewis's Woodpecker (undetected since 2009), Western Kingbird, Willow Flycatcher, Veery, Gray Catbird, Lazuli Bunting, Western Meadowlark, and Bullock's Oriole. A singing male Lark Sparrow was found here in 2008. Winter can also be an interesting time to visit, when predators such as Golden Eagle, Rough-legged Hawk, and Northern Shrike move into the area, along with the possibility of a roving flock of Snow Buntings or Gray-crowned Rosy-Finches.

For those continuing north to Quesnel, there is an alternate route that you can take along the Fraser River (about 11 kilometres) to Macalister before rejoining Hwy. 97. Appropriately, this is **Soda Creek-Macalister Road**, which can be a fantastic place during waterfowl migration, since it passes by a series of sloughs and oxbows along the Fraser River. If you want to take this road from the Macalister side, it's the first road on the river side of Hwy. 97, just northwest of the railway overpass at Macalister. If you're approaching from Soda Creek, stay left at the fork about 3 kilometres north of where the road turns north along the river. In addition to the water birds along this road, it's possible to find many of the uncommon or rare species mentioned in the Soda Creek account above, as well as the more conspicuous breeders, such as American Kestrel, Red-tailed Hawk, Mountain Bluebird, Savannah Sparrow, Vesper Sparrow, and Brewer's Blackbird. The **Dunlevy Ranch** is the best spot along this road (where the Lark Sparrow was found). Another side road worth checking is **Edmunds Road**, which turns off from "Soda-Mac Road" and cuts north to Hwy. 97, passing an irrigation pond that attracts waterfowl and a few shorebirds.

› McLeese Lake

This medium-sized lake is located right alongside the highway and is a charming place for a pit stop. Like the other big lakes of central British Columbia, high numbers of ducks, loons, and grebes pass through in spring and fall, with only a few species present in summer. Some of these summer residents include Barrow's Goldeneye, Common Loon, and Red-necked Grebe. Both Osprey and Bald Eagles nest near the lake.

› Macalister to Quesnel

After passing McLeese Lake, Hwy. 97 heads west and meets the fertile banks of the Fraser River. From **Macalister** (the first community after McLeese Lake), the highway travels north, paralleling the river until reaching the outskirts of **Quesnel** at Dragon Lake. The wide open farming areas along this stretch provide habitat for the northernmost regularly occurring pairs of Western Meadowlark and Western Kingbird. Long-billed Curlew also nests in this area, and watch for Red-tailed Hawks and American Kestrels hunting from the power lines and poles along the drive. In spring and fall, flocks of Sandhill Cranes often use these fields, along with swans and geese. Dragon Lake itself is difficult to bird because of the lack of close access.

QUESNEL

Contributed in part by Adrian Leather

In addition to the specific location details below, there is plenty more to see in the Quesnel area. For an alternate route south to Williams Lake, we recommend checking out **West Fraser Road**— for a similar mix of birds mentioned for Soda Creek. There is also the **Nazko Highway** heading west and the **Barkerville Highway** to the east (for **Bowron Lakes**). Like Prince George, Quesnel offers no shortage of forest birding, but there are also plenty of wetlands and open country to explore. A back roads map is recommended for expeditions off the main highways.

> ### West Fraser Timber Park

Located close to downtown Quesnel, **West Fraser Timber Park** offers a convenient way to see a mix of local birds, whether you're passing through along Hwy. 97 or staying in town for a few days. If you're approaching Quesnel from the south (for example, from Williams Lake), exit onto North Star Road (southbound), just before crossing the first major bridge over the Quesnel River. Drive south along North Star Road past a McDonald's and a school, continue onto Johnston Avenue as the road swings to the right, follow this to a traffic circle where you will continue straight through along Johnston, and then make the first left to access the park. If you miss the North Star turnoff, simply turn left at the main T-junction at the river in downtown Quesnel (instead of following Hwy. 97 north to the right). Follow Front Street south underneath the Moffat Bridge, then east over to the Johnston Bridge, where you will turn right at the traffic circle, then left to access the park. If you're travelling from the north along Hwy. 97, continue straight along Front Street instead of making the left-hand turn in downtown Quesnel and follow the directions previously given.

The park includes the Nature Education and Resource Centre, which has public conveniences. A trail by the tennis courts leads to a pond and a few marshes then into some mixed woodland. The pond typically holds Ring-necked Duck, Bufflehead, Barrow's Goldeneye, and Blue-winged Teal (in spring and summer). Spotted Sandpipers are often present, and other shorebirds recorded include Greater Yellowlegs, Killdeer, Semipalmated Sandpiper, and Wilson's Phalarope. Riparian scrub and forest species can include Lincoln's Sparrow, Gray Catbird (locally rare), Bullock's Oriole (locally rare), and Alder Flycatcher. Typical marsh species present are Common Yellowthroat, Red-winged Blackbird, and Song Sparrow. Other species along the marsh trail could include Merlin, Sharp-shinned Hawk, Willow Flycatcher (locally rare, not annual), Sora, Wood Duck (locally rare), American Goldfinch, and Cedar Waxwing. Veery (locally rare) can be heard from the second marsh. The border between woodland and scrub has MacGillivray's Warbler, American Redstart, Northern Waterthrush, and both Calliope and Rufous Hummingbirds. The woods hold numerous Veery and are particularly good for flycatchers, including Pacific-slope, Hammond's, Dusky, Least, and Western Wood-Pewee. Regular migrants to this area are Eastern Kingbird, American Tree Sparrow (early spring and late fall), American Pipit, Tennessee Warbler, and Blackpoll Warbler.

CENTRAL
BRITISH COLUMBIA

PRINCE GEORGE

If you want to get acquainted with the typical birds of the northern forests, check out **Forests for the World**. This city park, accessed via Kueng Road (see Map 25), has more than 15 kilometres of beautiful trails through mixed spruce and deciduous forest. Breeding species include Magnolia Warbler, Least Flycatcher, Red-breasted Sapsucker, and Swainson's Thrush. **Shane Lake**, in the middle of the park, is easy to get to and is a great place for a picnic. Broad-winged Hawks have been discovered nesting in this area, so keep your eyes open. For more details on this park, you can pick up a park map at the Prince George Tourist Information Centre. There are also several trails behind the University of Northern British Columbia that lead north into Forests for the World.

Where Hwy. 97 crosses the Fraser River at the south end of town, there is an exit signed to Downtown via Queensway Street. If you take this exit, Queensway will cross **Hudson Slough**. Parking spots are located just before passing the slough; from there,

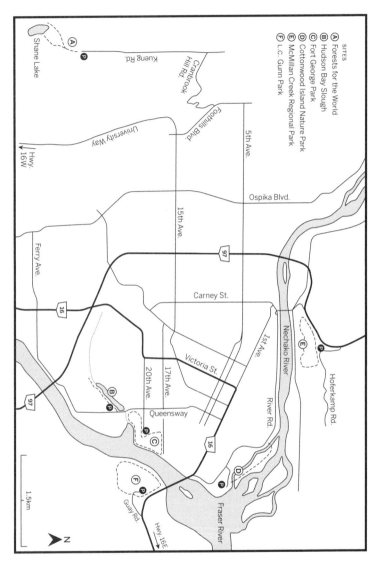

SITES
Ⓐ Forests for the World
Ⓑ Hudson Bay Slough
Ⓒ Fort George Park
Ⓓ Cottonwood Island Nature Park
Ⓔ McMillan Creek Regional Park
Ⓕ L.C. Gunn Park

25 Prince George

you can walk around the slough on the west side of Queensway Street or enter **Fort George Park** east of Queensway. These parks offer some nice birding in the city—both for water birds and riparian species.

Another fantastic spot is **Cottonwood Island Nature Park** (accessed from River Road). Located at the confluence of the Nechako and Fraser Rivers, the park is a natural spot for birds to congregate. Gulls and terns can often be seen out on the river during migration periods, and a variety of water birds can be found throughout the year. Some locally scarce species such as Wood Duck, Great Blue Heron, and Vaux's Sift can only be reliably found here. This is also a favoured spot by some of the recently arrived "eastern" White-breasted Nuthatches (except in summer). Unlike their conifer-loving brethren to the south, these birds prefer old-growth deciduous trees (they also sound different, giving *yank* calls instead of the western birds' whinny). Who knows? Perhaps one day they'll be split into two species. The big cottonwoods and rich undergrowth provide habitat for many songbirds in spring and summer, including Northern Waterthrush, American Redstart, and White-throated Sparrow.

McMillan Creek Regional Park and **L.C. Gunn Park** are also terrific spots to check out. You get to McMillan Creek Regional Park by taking the second right turn, onto Hoferkamp Road, after crossing the Nechako River and proceeding up the hill northbound on the John Hart Highway (Hwy. 97). To reach L.C. Gunn Park, take the first right turn, onto Guay Road, after crossing the Fraser River eastbound on the Yellowhead Highway (Hwy. 16). Both parks are ideal for short walks in mixed forest habitat with views of the city—L.C. Gunn Park is one of the most reliable spots in the Prince George area for Pacific-slope Flycatcher.

> Hwy. 16 East: Prince George to McBride

Note: Check your fuel before heading east as there are no service stations before McBride (about 200 kilometres away).

Only 5.4 kilometres east of Prince George is the **Prince George Airport**. Take the Yellowhead Highway (Hwy. 16) east, then turn right (south) onto the Old Cariboo Highway (Hwy. 97). At any time of year, the main and minor roads (Gunn, Giscome, Blackburn) around the airport can be great spots for hawks and owls. Diversity is highest in fall and winter, when northern owls such as Snowy, Great Gray, Short-eared, and Northern Hawk Owl move south. Short-eared Owls occasionally reside here throughout the year; be sure to scan for longspurs and migrant shorebirds around the nearby fields, as well as strays from the south such as Western Meadowlark and Western Kingbird.

Just over 4 kilometres east of the Old Cariboo Highway junction, turn left (north) on Shelley Road; 2.3 kilometres up this road, make a left onto an unsigned gravel road, which will take you to the **Shelley Sludge Lagoons**. This is Prince George's shorebird hot spot. If you can survive the smell and sometimes intense mosquitoes, these ponds can be very rewarding from spring through fall. In addition to all the regular Interior British Columbia wader migrants, several rarities have been found, including Hudsonian Godwit, Upland Sandpiper, Ruff, White-rumped Sandpiper, Buff-breasted Sandpiper, and Sharp-tailed Sandpiper. Throughout summer, more than ten species of ducks are present in the ponds, and Sora, Marsh Wren, and Red-winged Blackbirds nest in the cattails. A pair of Broad-winged Hawks nests in the area and are often seen soaring above the trees on sunny days or chasing Red-tailed Hawks.

Another 48 kilometres past the Shelley turnoff, Hwy. 16 reaches **Purden Lake Provincial Park**. This can be a delightful place for a pit stop between spring and fall. Typical boreal forest

Bohemian Waxwing

species such as Hermit Thrush, Varied Thrush, Ruby-crowned Kinglet, and Dark-eyed Juncos are abundant in the breeding season, and the lake can be a good spot for ducks (including scoters), loons, and grebes. Another 4.6 kilometres east along the highway is the turnoff to the **Purden Lake ski area**, where old cedar and hemlock trees provide favoured habitat for Pacific Wren, Chestnut-backed Chickadee, and Townsend's Warbler.

Take a trip down the **Bowron Forest Service Road** for the best chance at finding Yellow-bellied Flycatcher in the Prince George area. Watch for this turnoff 7.6 kilometres east of the Purden Lake ski area road. Turn right (south) then look for their favoured habitat. Throughout most of their range, Yellow-bellies are considered a bird of Black Spruce bogs and muskeg, but in the Rocky Mountain Trench area, they seem to like second-growth Lodgepole Pine with mossy understorey, often with other young trees and brush mixed in. The best time to look and listen is June and early July, as Yellow-bellies are a late-spring arrival here and one of the first species to depart. Be aware that the similar Hammond's, Dusky, and Least Flycatchers are also found along this road, so be sure to study up on your *Empidonax* calls. *Note: Although the similar-sounding Least Flycatcher usually sings from mid-height, giving its emphatic* chebek-chebek-chebek *notes, the Yellow-bellied Flycatcher seems to prefer prominent treetops to call from and usually only gives a single, weaker* che-lek *or* chebunk *note.*

For day hikes and overnight camping into the alpine, you may be interested in checking out **Sugarbowl-Grizzly Den Provincial Park**. About 28 kilometres past Purden Lake, look out for the Hungary Creek Bridge. Turn right onto Hungary Creek Road 300 metres past the bridge, and proceed for 11.5 kilometres to where you'll take the right fork and continue to a small side road on the left (it may be possible to drive up the last 250 metres, but parking here is fine, too). This is where the **Grizzly Den trail** starts. The **Raven Lake trail** starts 2.6 kilometres farther along Hungary Creek Road at a large parking lot. Both of these trails take a couple of hours to hike (Raven Lake is slightly shorter), and both will bring you into some fantastic subalpine habitat. American Three-toed Woodpecker, Varied Thrush, Hermit Thrush, Fox Sparrow, and Golden-crowned Sparrow are some of the breeders to look out for, and a hike above treeline into the alpine sometimes produces White-tailed Ptarmigan. Visitors are welcome in either the Grizzly Den or Raven Lake cabins, as long as they leave a donation in one of the envelopes provided and make sure that the firewood is well stocked. Watch out for Mountain Caribou in the area.

Returning to the highway, as you proceed east toward the Rocky Mountains, two "eastern" warblers become more common: Tennessee Warbler (mixed spruce and alder habitat) and Blackpoll Warbler (Black Spruce stands). Broad-winged Hawks are also a possibility anywhere between Prince George and McBride and all the way down the Rocky Mountain Trench to Golden.

> Fort George Canyon

A neat area to check out for all outdoors lovers, **Fort George Canyon** is especially attractive to birders from southern British Columbia because of its small Ovenbird population. This skulky cousin of the waterthrush, usually only found east of the Rocky Mountains, forages mostly on the ground in open aspen and birch woodland and is usually detected by the male's loud and emphatic song—*chur-TEE chur-TEE chur-TEE chur-TEE.* Many other forest birds are also prevalent in spring and summer, including Red-breasted Sapsucker, Least Flycatcher, Hammond's Flycatcher, MacGillivray's Warbler, American Redstart, Western Tanager, and White-throated Sparrow.

To reach this site, proceed west on Hwy. 16 out of Prince George; 9.4 kilometres west of the Hwy. 97 junction, turn south on Blackwater Road; drive 11.3 kilometres then turn left onto West Lake Road. Follow West Lake Road for 9.7 kilometres (pavement ends at 5 kilometres), passing by **West Lake Provincial Park** (a fantastic place to scope for grebes and waterfowl and have a picnic) and several other side roads to a major fork. Follow the left fork 1.9 kilometres uphill before turning left onto a narrow, old track. This track can be safely driven 1.8 kilometres to the trailhead parking lot. From there, the 4.6-kilometre trail heads off into the forest for a couple of kilometres before descending about 180 metres into the canyon.

> Hwy. 97 North: Prince George to Mackenzie

Between Prince George and Summit Lake, the highway passes through a mixture of second-growth forest and farm fields. In spring, look for Long-billed Curlews, Sandhill Cranes, and the odd Swainson's Hawk (Red-tails are abundant). The **Salmon River Bridge** is often worth a stop (24 kilometres north of Prince George) for both forest and river birds. From here to the Mackenzie junction, the highway becomes engulfed in seas of spruce and pine, with the odd lake thrown in. Most birders passing this way are aiming for either the Peace River or Alaska Highway, so they blitz through this area. If you have time and are interested in looking for more birds typical of the northern forests, try exploring a little. The **North Fraser Forest Service Road** is a great birding road (15 kilometres north of the Salmon River Bridge on the right/east side)—it is gravelled, usually well maintained, and passes through a mixture of riverside riparian and spruce forest. It follows the North Fraser River for about 30 kilometres before branching off farther into the bush. Be vigilant for logging vehicles on these roads, and use a radio if you have one. Back roads maps are always a good idea, and remember that this is bear country.

Another 6.6 kilometres north up the highway is **Summit Lake**, which has a few access roads and adjacent wetlands along the highway that can sometimes be productive. About 25 kilometres farther north is the small settlement of **Bear Lake** (with fuel service during business hours). Here, and at the nearby **Crooked River Provincial Park**, there are roads on both sides of the highway leading to a series of small wetlands and lakes near the highway, then farther off into the wilderness. The next point of interest is **Whiskers Point Provincial Park** on McLeod Lake (with camping and picnicking facilities). At the McLeod Lake settlement at the north end of the lake, you can take Carp Lake Road west for more forest birding if you haven't had your fix yet. From here, it's another 16 kilometres to the Mackenzie junction (see page 348 for Mackenzie).

VANDERHOOF

The town of Vanderhoof—"the geographical centre of British Columbia" (according to the sign)—is slightly more than an hour's drive west of Prince George on the Yellowhead Highway

(Hwy. 16). Whether you are passing through on your way to points west or looking for more birding options around Prince George, this area can be well worth the trip. Despite having relatively little birding coverage, the Vanderhoof/Fraser Lake/ Burns Lake area has turned up a stunning array of rarities over the years, from Scissor-tailed Flycatcher to Crested Caracara. Several wetlands in the area also attract breeding birds found nowhere else (reliably) in the Prince George checklist area, such as Redhead, Virginia Rail, and Yellow-headed Blackbird.

As you come down the hill toward the town centre (if you're driving from Prince George), look for Recreation Avenue on the right (northeast) side of the road. Proceed up this road for 650 metres, then turn right onto Stewart Street East. In a few hundred metres, the **Vanderhoof Sewage Lagoons** will be apparent. Check the lagoons in spring and late summer for migrant waterfowl, gulls, and phalaropes. Little Gull has been recorded on several occasions, when Bonaparte's Gull numbers were high.

Return to the highway and proceed west into Vanderhoof; look for the green sign for Kenny Dam and turn left (south) on Nechako Avenue; this turns into the Kenny Dam Road. After around 8 kilometres, continue straight south on Lakes District Road (instead of turning west on Kenny Dam Road to Stoney Creek Village). You will see a small marsh on the right-hand side 4.9 kilometres farther along (if you reach Stoney Creek Road, you've gone too far). This is **Wheeler's Slough** (AKA Nancy's Pond). Redhead, Eared Grebe, Black Tern, Marsh Wren, and Virginia Rail all nest here most years. Stay left at the Y-junction (continuing south) and the Ducks Unlimited project known as Ludwig Pond will be on the left (east) side of the road after about 1 kilometre. A scope might be necessary to check for waterfowl—in spring and fall the numbers can be impressive.

Return north to the Y-junction and turn left (west) this time, onto Stoney Creek Road. A large lake will be apparent on the west side—this is **Nulki Lake** (pronounced "noo-kye") and this viewing point is known by birders as Jaeger Beach. In fall (particularly September), Parasitic Jaegers are seen fairly regularly here, as well as migrant terns, gulls, and many species of waterfowl. American White Pelicans can also be seen on the lake throughout summer. Proceed along Stoney Creek Road to the village, then turn left (south) back onto Kenny Dam Road. This will take you past two more viewing points of the lake. *Note: Most of this land is private and/or First Nations reserve land, so be sure to check for No Trespassing signs.*

As you drive along the north shore of Nulki Lake, watch for signs advertising Tachick Lake Resort. Take the road north to the resort and park down by the boat launch. The owners of the resort are birder friendly, but it's always a good idea to call in advance just in case (250-567-4929). **Tachick Lake** is similar in many ways to Nulki and thus can be fabulous for lake watching in September and October. Ross's Gull (November 2007) has been the biggest find in recent years, but other species are proving to be less rare than previously thought (Franklin's Gull, Sabine's Gull, Parasitic Jaeger, Arctic Tern). All three species of jaeger are possible, so be sure to check all gull and tern flocks carefully!

Return to Vanderhoof and turn north on Burrard Avenue (main intersection). Continue north and look for signs to the **Nechako River Bird Sanctuary.** If you cross the bridge over the Nechako, you've gone too far. The sanctuary itself is mostly composed of a series of river islets in the middle of the Nechako, but a viewing tower near the parking area and playing fields provides a good view of this stretch of river. The birding here can be hit or miss—on some days waterfowl, gulls, and swallows are everywhere, then on others the river is barren. In spring and fall, it can be worthwhile to cross the river and follow Northside Road up past the airport to look for raptors, cranes, and Long-billed Curlews (April).

Turning left on Snell Road will take you west to Hwy. 27, where you can either return to Vanderhoof or turn north up to Fort St. James. The quickest way to Fort St. James from Vanderhoof is by continuing west on Hwy. 16, then turning north at the signed junction west of town. On the way out of Vanderhoof, you might see Black Terns circling around the roadside wetlands (May to August).

FORT ST. JAMES

From the signed junction six kilometres west of Vanderhoof, it's about a fifty-minute drive north to Fort St. James along Hwy 27. Just west of the main townsite, the highway crosses a bridge over the Stuart River. Stop here and check for water birds, as well as Barn and Cliff Swallows that nest under the bridge. Just west of the bridge, Sowchea Road heads off to the northwest and leads to **Paarens Beach Provincial Park** and the **Sowchea Marshes** (about 8 kilometres down the road). Uncommon local breeders such as Cinnamon Teal and Yellow-headed Blackbird can be found. Return to the highway and follow the main drag into Fort St. James, then turn left on Elm Street toward the lake, or turn left onto Stuart Drive in downtown, then follow the lakeshore north through town. **Cottonwood Park**, the main municipal beach at the northwest corner of town, is as good a place as any to scope the vast **Stuart Lake** for water birds. In spring and fall, almost anything is possible, with Red-throated and Yellow-billed Loons being regularly sighted among the more common species. Red-breasted Mergansers were discovered breeding here in 2007—one of the few central Interior summer records.

You can continue along the lakeshore northwest of town along Stones Bay Road—a trailhead parking lot for **Mount Pope** is only 4 kilometres down this road, offering birders a chance to hike the

6.5 kilometres to the peak. Here you might see several treeline species that are hard to find elsewhere in the area, including Dusky Grouse, Clark's Nutcracker, and Golden-crowned Sparrow (the latter two are rare). For forest birds, continue north on Hwy. 27, which will turn into a well-graded forestry road. Exploring for a few kilometres then returning to Fort St. James is one option; but for the adventurous, it is possible to drive all the way to McLeod Lake and/or Mackenzie (around three hours on a gravel road). A back roads map for the area is required, and a GPS and CB radio are strongly suggested. In summer, these roads are well maintained, but there are so many side roads that it can be easy to get disoriented. A variety of northern forest birds can be seen in the area, and there are several forestry campsites along the way. Gray-cheeked Thrushes are scattered throughout the area in mixed willow and spruce habitat (often with wet understorey). (See page 357 for Hwy. 16 west to Smithers and beyond).

MACKENZIE

Contributed in part by James Bradley

Just west of the Hwy. 37 (to Mackenzie) junction, check the **Parsnip River Bridge** for Eastern Phoebe—this species has been noted several times along the Parsnip at this location and farther south. Like other phoebes, it uses man-made structures for nesting habitat.

Mackenzie, on the banks of the massive Williston Reservoir, is a thirty-minute drive north of Hwy. 97 and can be a convenient place for an overnight stop or a couple of days of good birding. Among British Columbia birders, Mackenzie is well known for the migrant banding that takes place each fall at nearby Mugaha Marsh, which is a productive spot to visit anytime between May and September. A number of other locations are also worth visiting, each offering something a little different.

> ## ➤ Mugaha Marsh

To get to **Mugaha Marsh,** head north from the main intersection in Mackenzie for 7.5 kilometres until the pavement turns to hardpack. Continue 2 kilometres farther to a crossroads, proceeding straight ahead. After another 900 metres, bear left at an obvious junction and continue 3.6 kilometres to the marsh and banding station. Visitors are welcome at the banding station when it is running, but large groups should contact the station manager, Vi Lambie, beforehand through the Mackenzie Nature Observatory (MNO).

This is a rich natural marsh set back from Williston Lake, surrounded by a mixed forest of spruce, pine (many now dead from recent beetle outbreaks), poplars, and birch, and used by a variety of breeding and migratory birds. The causeway that bisects the marsh permits excellent viewing opportunities of open water and sedge meadow habitat, as does a viewing deck at the banding station. Swaths of regenerating willow add a further element to the variety of habitats represented here, which is reflected in the diversity of birds, combined with the surrounding mature mixed forests to add to the species richness. Breeding specialties around the marsh include Yellow-bellied Sapsucker, Eastern Kingbird, Swamp Sparrow, and Rusty Blackbird, whereas a foray deeper into the woods may yield Black-backed and American Three-toed Woodpeckers. During migration, a range of ducks and shorebirds use the marsh habitats, and the willows along the causeway can be full of passerines. Six *Empidonax* flycatcher species can be found here, four vireos, four chickadees, four *Spizella* sparrows, and both crossbills! Warblers are also well represented, with twelve species frequently banded and eastern specialties such as Ovenbird present in small numbers. Keep your eyes skyward in late August and early September, as flights of raptors can often occur and "Harlan's" Red-tailed Hawk is a regular feature. A host of rarities, including Great Egret, Canada

Warbler, and, to date, the northernmost record of Ash-throated Flycatcher in North America, complete the birding accolades of this top-notch site.

> ## Morfee Mountain

To get to **Morfee Mountain**, proceed north from the main intersection in Mackenzie for 2.9 kilometres before taking a right turn onto the dirt road that will take you all the way to the top, a further 14 kilometres. The road to Morfee Mountain offers an easy way to get into the alpine zone and search for some of the associated specialty birds. The road up is mostly decent to at least the subalpine zone, from where one can easily hike (or drive, if confident) to higher elevations above treeline. Both White-tailed and Willow Ptarmigan breed here, but numbers fluctuate from year to year, so they are never guaranteed. American Pipit and Horned Lark are also breeders, as are Say's Phoebe, which are often perched on the roadside barriers on the last stretch to the summit. Savannah Sparrows are widespread in open areas, and Golden-crowned Sparrows breed commonly in the dwarf birches and willows near treeline. Because of a string of summertime sightings, there is some speculation that a pair of Swainson's Hawk nests somewhere in the area, so keep an eye out when hiking the alpine. Don't forget to bird the forest on the access road, the subalpine zone near the ski hut being a good spot for Hermit Thrush, Boreal Chickadee, and Townsend's Warbler.

Note: This is Grizzly Bear country, so unless you're planning on staying close to your vehicle, make sure to take the appropriate precautions.

> ## Gagnon Culvert

To get to Gagnon Culvert, proceed south from the main intersection in Mackenzie back toward Hwy. 97 for 8.5 kilometres. Here take a right (a left after 20.5 kilometres, if you're coming northward from the Hwy. 97/Mackenzie Road junction) onto a small road that quickly joins a bigger logging road on the brow of the hill above Gagnon Creek. Take a right and continue for 500 metres to the culvert. Be sure to park well to the side of the road and stand on the upwind side so as to avoid being bathed in dust by the occasional passing truck.

Situated south of Mackenzie, this location constitutes a freshwater estuary of sorts, where **Gagnon Creek** enters **Williston Lake**. Depending on water levels in the lake, it may be flooded or comparatively dry, the latter situation providing the best birding opportunities. The road that crosses the creek and culvert makes for a suitable starting point. From here, one can either conduct a quick drive-by scan of the flats or carefully park and walk south or north along the water's edge. During low water years, especially in fall (but also May to June), the vegetated flats to the north of the road are often the most productive for a variety of water birds and shorebirds, as well as raptors and seed-eating passerines. Among the more common species, Greater White-fronted Goose, Canvasback, Peregrine, Short-billed Dowitcher, and Baird's Sandpiper are regularly observed, and this is a hospitable location for less common species, such as American Golden-Plover, which probably occurs annually. You should also make frequent scans of the surrounding sky, as raptors can be migrating high overhead here and Common Nighthawk often forage over the surrounding woodland in large numbers.

› Pine Pass

Soon after leaving the Mackenzie junction, the John Hart Highway (Hwy. 97) crosses through the Rockies over **Pine Pass** (elevation: 874 metres/2,868 feet) and follows the Pine River to Chetwynd. **Bijoux Falls Provincial Park** is located 32.8 kilometres past the Mackenzie turnoff and is a popular pit stop for birders and other tourists. A pair of American Dippers often builds a

Yellow-shafted Flicker

nest at the falls and can be heard and seen flying up and down the creek in the spring and early summer. Steller's Jays are also quite conspicuous here and often pose well for photographs, hoping for a peanut or two from travellers. The thundering rush of the falls makes "ear birding" difficult, but patient scanning of the treetops will often reveal Yellow-rumped Warblers (both Audubon and Myrtle types), Western Tanagers, Warbling Vireos, and several other species typical of this area.

Continuing north up the highway, you will soon pass Powder King Mountain Resort and the **Pine Pass Summit**, where high-elevation species such as Hermit Thrush, Boreal Chickadee, American Three-toed Woodpecker, and Pine Grosbeak can be found on occasion. As you follow the Pine River through the mountains and out the other side, you might notice that certain western species such as Townsend's Warbler and Pacific Wren start to dwindle and are replaced by their eastern counterparts: Black-throated Green Warbler and (eastern) Winter Wren respectively.

Once through the mountains, the highway straightens out and follows a rich band of cottonwoods that hug the **Pine River** and its meandering oxbows. If this is your first birding trip to the Peace River region, you may want to find some safe places to pull over along this stretch, since Peace specialties such as Blue-headed Vireo, Yellow-bellied Sapsucker, Tennessee Warbler, Black-and-White Warbler, and Rose-breasted Grosbeak are abundant in spring and summer. In some of the old spruce stands, you might be lucky enough to hear the high-pitched chiming of a Cape May Warbler or perhaps one of the more common conifer-loving warblers, such as Blackpoll or Black-throated Green. Ovenbirds are also fairly common in the open aspen and cottonwood copses, and Eastern Phoebes can be heard calling plaintively from perches overlooking the oxbows on the north side of the highway. Trumpeter Swans, Ring-necked Ducks, and both species of goldeneye also nest here.

NORTHWEST

Contributed in part by Rosamund Pojar

HWY. 16 WEST: FORT FRASER TO ROSE LAKE

› Fraser Lake

From the Stewart Highway (Hwy. 27) junction west of Vanderhoof, proceed west following signs for Smithers, Terrace, and Prince Rupert. After 30 kilometres, you will reach the community of Fort Fraser. Continue west for almost 3 kilometres until you see signs for **Beaumont Provincial Park** (turnoff is on the right/north side of the road). The park offers forty-nine campsites, as well as several picnic areas. Here you can expect many of the same forest species mentioned for the Prince George area, including Red-breasted Sapsucker, American Three-toed Woodpecker, Western Tanager, and White-throated Sparrow. There are several access points to the shoreline, where you can scan the east end of **Fraser Lake**. Like the lakes around Prince George, Vanderhoof, and Fort St. James, this lake can be fantastic during spring and fall migration.

Seventeen kilometres farther west from the Beaumont turnoff is the town of Fraser Lake—at the west end of the lake. Just past the main settlement, the highway turns north and crosses over the **Stellako River**. This can be a fantastic area for migrants—particularly waterfowl, such as diving ducks and swans in early spring and late fall (and parts of winter, as long as there is open water). Because of a lack of regular birder coverage, you never know what you might find by exploring the area a little bit.

> Burns Lake

Continue west from the Stellako River Bridge for 47 kilometres, when **Burns Lake** will become visible on the left (south) side of the highway. The eastern end of the lake is quite narrow and broken up by a series of islands and peninsulas. You can try scanning it from the east end, but the best way to bird the lake is to drive toward the town of Burns Lake (at the northwest end) and take François Lake Road (Hwy. 35) south. This road crosses over the lake, as well as **Gerow Island**, and allows for the best lake watching.

For those who want to explore more of the area, two more big lakes with great migrant potential lie just to the south along Hwy. 35—**Tchesinkut Lake** and **François Lake**. The latter has turned up a phenomenal amount of rarities over the years, including Whooping Crane (May 2007), Black Oystercatcher (May 2000), Lewis's Woodpecker, Northern Mockingbird, Cape May Warbler, Rose-breasted Grosbeak, Dickcissel, and Oriental Greenfinch (origin unconfirmed), just to name a few. Considering the lack of coverage in this area, this short list is simply amazing. Most of these records have come from the **Colleymount** area which is located along the northwest shore of the lake. Drive straight south to the village of François Lake, then head west along the lake for 30 kilometres on Colleymount Road.

> Rose Lake

Just west of the town of Burns Lake, Hwy. 16 passes yet another large lake—**Decker Lake**—and 11.6 kilometres west of Decker

Lake, you will see the small but productive **Rose Lake** on the left (south). As long as it's not frozen, this spot usually hosts a variety of waterfowl, as well as a diverse list of nesting songbirds between May and August. Just southwest of Rose Lake is Bulkley Lake, which marks the start of the Bulkley Valley.

BULKLEY VALLEY

> Topley

The small community of **Topley** is about a forty-minute drive west of Burns Lake. Nearly a kilometre west of Topley, there is a rest stop on the south side of the highway. There is a wetland here with breeding American Bittern (locally rare), Sora, Red-winged Blackbird, and the occasional Marsh Wren (scarce but regular), as well as a mix of nesting duck species. In the fields behind and beyond (north of) this rest stop, look for Sandhill Cranes in April and possibly through summer, as there may be one or two pairs nesting in the area.

> Tyhee Lake Provincial Park

After passing through Houston, the next significant settlement on Hwy. 16 is the village of Telkwa (about 13 kilometres southeast of Smithers). Once in Telkwa, look for the **Tyhee Lake Provincial Park** signed turnoff on the right (east). This turnoff is Telkwa High Road. Drive up the hill, make a right on Tyhee Road, and then follow this into the park. In addition to camping and picnic sites, there are walking trails along the lakeshore and through the woods. At the north end of the park, beside the lake, there is a viewing platform that provides views over an area of submerged and emergent vegetation favoured by ducks, grebes, loons, Bonaparte's Gulls, and more. Also expect close-up views of Common Yellowthroat and Red-winged Blackbirds in the nearby reeds, and be sure to scan the nearby willows and

snags for swallows, woodpeckers, Belted Kingfisher, and Eastern Kingbird. The aspen forests and alder thickets along the
shore and throughout the park are loaded with songbirds in
spring and summer, including Red-breasted Sapsucker, Rufous
Hummingbird, Dusky Flycatcher, Least Flycatcher, Cassin's and
Warbling Vireos, Black-capped Chickadee, Swainson's Thrush,
American Robin, American Redstart, Yellow Warbler, Yellow-
rumped Warbler, White-throated Sparrow, Song Sparrow, and
Lincoln's Sparrow. Bald Eagles and Osprey both nest along the
lake, whereas farther back in the coniferous forest, look and listen for Ruby-crowned Kinglet, Golden-crowned Kinglet, and
Red-breasted Nuthatch.

Just in case you need something to dream about—a single
Demoiselle Crane was photographed in this area in May 2002.
The origin of this bird will always be a mystery, but since it was
migrating north with a group of Sandhill Cranes, who knows?

> Smithers

For a lovely walk through mixed habitat to a great view, we recommend visiting **Malkow Lookout**. Access is off Hwy. 16, just
south of the bridge over the Bulkley River (southeast of town).
Turn northeast onto Old Babine Lake Road, and take this for
4.7 kilometres. After a sharp curve to the right, turn left (north)
on McCabe Road and follow this up for 1.6 kilometres, then
park in the designated lot opposite the driveway to the Logpile
Lodge. To hike to the lookout and back takes about two hours,
so we recommend taking drinking water and a few snacks.
This converted forestry road passes first through private
pastureland, then into mature aspen forest (loaded with songbirds—an absolute delight in May and June), before returning
to some hayfields where Lazuli Buntings are recorded in some
years. The trail then climbs up past a dry south-facing slope
covered in a mixture of conifers, stunted aspens, wildflowers,

and shrubbery, before reaching the lookout and its breathtaking 360-degree view of the Bulkley Valley. Near the top, be on the lookout for Dusky Grouse.

If you're in the Smithers area between late June and mid-September, a trip up **Hudson Bay Mountain** is recommended, as it provides easy access to alpine habitat (all three ptarmigan species, anyone?). July and August are probably the best months—the road should be clear of snow, the weather is decent, and the breeding birds are all present. Coming from the south, you can turn left at the first junction/traffic light (Tatlow Road), right onto Pacific Street, and then left onto Hudson Bay Mountain Road, which winds through a residential area and eventually climbs the mountain. No matter which direction you're coming from, there should be a sign off the highway for the ski area. Partway up the mountain, there is a Y-junction; you must take the right-hand road and then the left farther up— this takes you all the way up to the ski area. If you keep driving, you will see a sign at the bottom of one of the T-bar lifts that indicates the end of permitted motor-vehicle access. From here, trails take off to the right. You can go straight up the ski run, but it's usually best to take the left-hand side of the ski run that leads eventually to Crater Lake.

Lower down in the boreal forests, look and listen for Dusky Grouse; Ruffed Grouse; Spruce Grouse; Hammond's Flycatcher; American Three-toed and Black-backed Woodpeckers (especially in beetle-damaged patches); Gray Jay; Red-breasted Nuthatch; Boreal, Mountain, and Black-capped Chickadees; Varied Thrush; Swainson's Thrush; and both species of crossbill. As you climb up into alpine meadows, bordered by stunted subalpine firs, you should start picking up Hermit Thrush, Fox Sparrow, Lincoln's Sparrow, Dark-eyed Junco, and both Golden-crowned and White-crowned Sparrows. After leaving the last trees behind and reaching the true alpine habitat of the upper ridges, be alert for

American Pipits, Horned Larks, and Gray-crowned Rosy-Finches, since all three nest in the area. The three ptarmigan species are also possible on this hike: Willows down in the willow scrub, Rocks along the rugged slopes just below the ridge crest, and White-tailed up on the barren ridgetops near the summit. Despite their general habitat preferences, do not consider these guidelines "the rule" (that is, Willow Ptarmigan are fully capable of waddling up to the top if they want to).

HAZELTON

› Ross Lake Provincial Park

This is a favoured spot for local birders. The turnoff to **Ross Lake Provincial Park** is around 62 kilometres northwest of Smithers (along Hwy. 16) or 2.2 kilometres east of New Hazelton. From the highway, it's 2.8 kilometres to the park—a pleasant spot set up with picnic tables and toilets. If there is time, walk the trail around the lake (allow for a couple hours). The easiest way to find the trail is to go to the boat-launch area and follow the trail all the way around back to the picnic area. The trail passes though mature mixed forest, past willow-fringed wetlands, along dry south-facing slopes with aspen and many shrubs (often with basking garter snakes on sunny days), and back to mature conifer forest. There is a variety of birds here in migration and through breeding season, including Common Goldeneye, Common Loon, Spotted Sandpiper, Rufous Hummingbird, Olive-sided Flycatcher, Hammond's Flycatcher, Tree Swallow, Swainson's Thrush, Varied Thrush, Northern Waterthrush, Common Yellowthroat, American Redstart, and Song Sparrow.

› Hospital Lake

After passing the turnoff to Ross Lake, the first community you will reach along the highway is **New Hazelton**. Turn right after crossing the railway, following signs for **Old Hazelton** and the 'Ksan Historic Village. Follow this road over the Bulkley River, and continue along the main road as it curves to the southwest. Between Hazelton Secondary School and the Northwest Community College building, look for the trailhead to **Hospital Lake** on the right-hand side. This short walk will take you through mixed forest offering many of the same species found at Ross Lake. The lake itself is more marshy and muddy, so it can have a different mix of waterfowl and shorebirds (in migration) and is always worth a quick check.

> Seeley Lake Provincial Park

If you return to Hwy. 16 and continue toward Prince Rupert, **Seeley Lake Provincial Park** will be on your left-hand (southeast) side, a couple of kilometres south of South Hazelton. There are toilets, picnic tables, and a small campground. The birding here is not as good as at Ross or Hospital Lakes, but there can still be a variety of songbirds in breeding season and some waterfowl. The lake is overlooked by the flank of **Roche de Boule Mountain**, where mountain goats can often be seen through binoculars. Both Bald Eagles and Osprey nest nearby.

STEWART-CASSIAR HIGHWAY

Slightly more than 36 kilometres from South Hazelton, and 89 kilometres from Terrace, the **Stewart-Cassiar Highway** (Hwy. 37) splits off from Hwy. 16 and heads north. This highway is one of the two great northern roads of British Columbia, winding through 725 kilometres of mountain valleys and plateaus between the Skeena Valley and the Alaska Highway in southern Yukon. For much of its length, virtually half the length of the province, it is the only road traversing otherwise roadless wilderness. Northern wildlife is rich—moose and wolves may be seen, and Grizzly and Black Bears are especially abundant. The scenery is always astonishing among the Skeena and Cassiar Mountains.

Note: Service stations are few and far between on this highway, so be sure to plan accordingly. Carrying a gas can is a good idea.

> Snowbank Creek Wetlands

Just before reaching Ningunsaw Pass (265 kilometres north of Hwy. 16; 222 kilometres south of Dease Lake), the **Snowbank Creek Wetlands** should be apparent along the roadside. Waterfowl are abundant, particularly during migration, and Trumpeter Swans are present throughout most of the spring, summer, and fall.

> Kinaskan Lake Provincial Park

Located at the south end of Kinaskan Lake (365 kilometres north of Hwy. 16; 123 kilometres south of Dease Lake) and nestled between the Todagin Mountains to the east and the Klastline Plateau in the west, the scenic **Kinaskan Lake Provincial Park** offers camping and picnicking facilities—as well as good birding. At the far end of the campsite, there is a lovely trail that goes alongside the lake and ends in a spit near the creek that flows into the lake. Both Surf and White-winged Scoters frequent the lake in summer, and Spotted Sandpipers nest along the shore. Ruffed, Spruce, and Sooty Grouse are all possibilities in this area, and common summer songbirds around the camping area include Ruby-crowned Kinglet, Swainson's Thrush, American Robin, Orange-crowned Warbler, Yellow-rumped Warbler, Townsend's Warbler, and Dark-eyed Junco. Bohemian Waxwings are possible anytime between spring and fall but are never reliable. Gray Jays are a common sight throughout the year.

Blackpoll Warbler

> Tsaybahe Mountain Road

After leaving the village of Iskut and the Skeena Mountains behind, the highway climbs over a plateau-like pass at 40 Mile Flats. Near the top of the pass, watch on the right for the small, rough **Tsaybahe Mountain Road**, leading back to the east (about 12.5 kilometres north of Iskut; about 67 kilometres south of Dease Lake). If you have a vehicle with good clearance, you can make the journey into the alpine and be rewarded with a view of Mount Edziza to the southwest. Although we admittedly don't have any data on the birds here, all three ptarmigan species should be present in the alpine parts of this road, and if there are tundra habitats with low scrubby willows, look out for the elusive Smith's Longspur. In subalpine areas, watch and listen for Northern Shrike, Gray-cheeked Thrush, Blackpoll Warbler, American Tree Sparrow, and Fox Sparrow.

> Gnat Pass

Just south of **Gnat Pass** (462 kilometres north of Hwy. 16; 25.5 kilometres south of Dease Lake), there are some beautiful fens to check out close to **Upper and Lower Gnat Lakes**. In spring, there are early migrants in the area, because the water is open at the entry to Lower Gnat Lake. Waterfowl and shorebirds such as Solitary Sandpiper can be expected, and the mix of subalpine willow and Black Spruce through the pass has lots of songbirds, including Yellow-bellied Flycatcher, Bohemian Waxwing, Black-poll Warbler, and Pine Grosbeaks. There are many pull-outs and some gravel pits that you can camp in, if you so choose.

> Dease Lake

There is a set of little lakes with trails around them accessed from the town of **Dease Lake**. Turn left (west) off Hwy. 37 at the police station (between the police station and the restaurant), opposite the Arctic Divide Inn. Go down to the T-junction and turn left, then drive to the end of the road (less than one block). You can drive down to the lake, but the road is very steep and rough. If you're unsure, park and walk down. A trail takes off to the left side of the lake and passes through mature mixed forest and then into aspen. Between spring and fall, there should be a mix of waterfowl, shorebirds, raptors, woodpeckers, and songbirds in the area. In recent summers, White-winged Crossbills have been abundant here.

> Dease River

Driving north, after you pass the north end of Dease Lake (44 kilometres north of Dease Lake townsite), Hwy. 37 follows the meandering **Dease River** through a valley filled with rich marshlands and small lakes. For the next 40 kilometres, feel free to stop anywhere that looks appealing (and safe to pull over). Trumpeter Swans and Arctic Terns breed along this stretch, and there is often plenty more to see and hear. If you're approaching from the north, this productive stretch begins around 145 kilometres from the Yukon–British Columbia border.

› Boya Lake Provincial Park

Known for its colour and clarity, **Boya Lake** is a fantastic place to camp or have a picnic in summer. The turnoff to the provincial park is on the east side of Hwy. 37, 150 kilometres north of Dease Lake and around 82 kilometres south of the Yukon border. In summer, it's an absolute must for scenery, birds, and wildflowers; plus, it's one of the few lakes in northern British Columbia that is warm enough to swim in during summer. Arctic Terns and Osprey are common sights around the lake in summer, and depending on the time of year, there can also be a multitude of other water birds, including Mallard, American Wigeon, Ring-necked Duck, Bufflehead, both goldeneye species, Common Merganser, Common Loon, Bald Eagle, and Mew Gull. In the shorebird department, Spotted Sandpiper, Solitary Sandpiper, both Greater and Lesser Yellowlegs, and Wilson's Snipe all nest in the area. There is no shortage of forest birds around the camping area either, with Great Horned Owl, Black-backed Woodpecker, Varied Thrush, Northern Waterthrush, Townsend's Warbler, Lincoln's Sparrow, Pine Grosbeak, and Purple Finch being some of the notable species. Both Yellow-bellied and Red-breasted Sapsuckers have been reported in this area, so watch out for hybrids. Trails take off from both ends of the campsite: the south trail goes through wetlands where shorebirds are frequent, whereas the north trail goes through conifer and aspen stands. Both trails have orchids and primulas, as well as other wildflowers (in season).

SKEENA VALLEY

At 570 kilometres, the Skeena River is the second-longest river in British Columbia (after the Fraser). It originates on the Spatsizi Plateau before flowing southward to Hazelton. Here the

Yellowhead Highway (Hwy. 16) meets the Skeena and follows it for more than 200 kilometres to the sea.

TERRACE

As the retail and services hub for northwestern British Columbia, **Terrace** is a convenient place to stock up on supplies. It also has a few good birding spots. The first is **Ferry Island Campground**. Hwy. 16 uses this island to cross the Skeena River just east of downtown Terrace. Turn south off the highway, following signs for Ferry Island. The deciduous forest around the campground is a fantastic place to find local breeding birds in spring and summer. Woodpeckers, flycatchers, vireos, thrushes, and warblers are all well represented. Open from May to September, this campground is a lovely spot for a picnic or pit stop if you are just passing through.

With more than one hundred species recorded, **Lakelse Lake Provincial Park** is considered one of the Skeena region's finest birding locales. To reach it, exit off Hwy. 16 just east of Ferry Island/downtown Terrace, following signs for Kitimat (Hwy. 37 south). The north end of the lake is about 13.5 kilometres down this highway, but there are three different sections to choose from along the lake (all can be good for birding, and all have beach access).

As you leave Terrace (westbound on Hwy. 16 for Prince Rupert), pull off the highway at the rural community of **New Remo** (4.7 kilometres past the highway bridge over the Kitsumkalum River). The small oxbow sloughs and farm fields in this area are full of waterfowl, both in the breeding season and in migration. Wood Duck, Hooded Merganser, and American Coot are a few locally uncommon species that can be found here, along with other geese, ducks, and a mix of songbirds. After passing New Remo, the highway leaves civilization behind, and other than a few rest stops along the Skeena River, there will be no amenities until you reach Prince Rupert. Bird diversity is low along this stretch of highway, but the scenery is impressive (if it's not too cloudy), and a few stops here and there can still yield a few feathered treats for the visiting birder.

PRINCE RUPERT

With close to 2.5 metres of rain annually, **Prince Rupert** (affectionately called the City of Rainbows) has the dubious distinction of being Canada's wettest city. Because of its geography, pressed between the sea and mountains, there isn't a lot of choice when it comes to birding, but there can still be some nice birds to find. If you're driving into Prince Rupert from the east, stop off at **Oliver Lake** (signed off Hwy. 16, 8 kilometres before reaching the city). There won't be many birds along the trails near the lake, but visitors will probably be intrigued by the bonsai-like "Dwarf Forests" of this muskeg habitat.

The most productive birding in Prince Rupert is along the waterfront. At any time of year, check the waters around **Cow Bay** and **Rotary Waterfront Park** and farther northeast to the **Seal Cove Wharf**. Some of the common species present here year round include Common Merganser, Common Loon, Pelagic Cormorant, Double-crested Cormorant, Great Blue Heron, Bald Eagle, Glaucous-winged Gull, Pigeon Guillemot, and Belted Kingfisher. Diversity will be higher from fall into spring, when wintering birds such as Harlequin Duck, Surf and White-winged Scoter, Pacific Loon, Thayer's and Mew Gulls, Black-legged Kittiwakes, Rhinoceros Auklet, and Common Murre are frequently seen. In spring and fall, check the alders along **George Hills Way** (the main waterfront drive east of Cow Bay) for migrant flocks of songbirds. Varied Thrushes are also regular inhabitants in these woods (outside of summer).

For more gulls and a few rock-loving shorebirds, follow signs to the main ferry terminal south of town. Park near the terminal and scan the nearby log booms for gulls, cormorants, and shorebirds. The best area is just a little to the south, where there is a fish-processing plant, a few abandoned buildings, and a marina. Birders are generally welcome to walk around the docks near the marina, where at most times of year, there should be plenty of gulls to check through. Outside of the breeding season, there is usually a sizable flock of Black Turnstones in this area, so look and listen for them, and check the flock for Surfbirds, Ruddy Turnstones, and others that might be tagging along.

HAIDA GWAII (Queen Charlotte Islands)

As a remote archipelago, the almost mythic islands of Haida Gwaii hold a strong appeal to birders from across the continent. The islands are home to most of the world's breeding Ancient Murrelets, tiny seabirds that nest in underground burrows amid old-growth forests, their downy young tumbling to the shore to join their calling parents. Several of the islands' forest birds have evolved in isolation from their mainland cousins and now differ sufficiently to be designated as separate subspecies, giving the islands the moniker "Galapagos North." Subspecies of five bird species are largely or wholly restricted to Haida Gwaii: Northern Goshawk (also found on Vancouver Island), Northern Saw-whet Owl, Hairy Woodpecker, Steller's Jay, and Pine Grosbeak. Of these, the Haida Gwaii Saw-whet Owl is probably the most intriguing and may deserve full species status once sufficient research has been conducted. Their vocalizations are noticeably higher pitched than their mainland compatriots, and

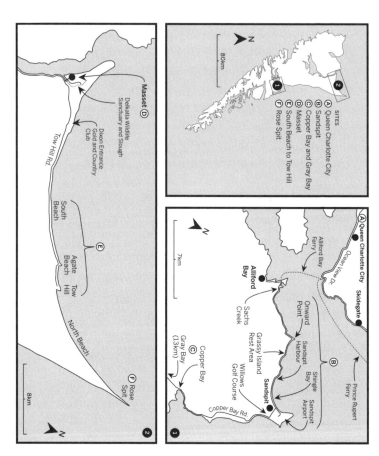

SITES

(A) Queen Charlotte City
(B) Sandspit
(C) Copper Bay and Gray Bay
(D) Masset
(E) South Beach to Tow Hill
(F) Rose Spit

80km

N

1

2

Masset (D)

Delkatla Wildlife
Sanctuary and Slough

Dixon Entrance
Gold and Country
Club

Tow Hill Rd.

South
Beach

(E)

Agate
Beach

Tow
Hill

North Beach

(F) Rose
Spit

8km

N

2

(A) Queen Charlotte City

Ocean View Dr.

Alliford Bay
Ferry

Skidegate

Alliford
Bay

Onward
Point

Sachs
Creek

Grassy Island
Rest Area

Sandspit
Harbour

Prince Rupert
Ferry

(B)

Shingle
Bay

Sandspit
Airport

Willows
Golf Course

Sandspit

(C)
Copper Bay

Gray Bay
(13km)

Copper Bay Rd.

7km

N

1

some of their contact calls seem completely different. Much of the white plumage typical of mainland birds is replaced on island birds by a rich tawny colour. Finding these birds is not difficult, as they are widespread in mature forest on both main islands— and can be called without much trouble between September and May. Beware that mainland saw-whets also reach Haida Gwaii during migration and in winter.

In addition to these unique forms, what is perhaps more notable is what species are not present. Graham Island alone covers about 6,500 square kilometres of mountains, coniferous forest, alder groves, bogs, inlets, and shoreline—and yet, there are NO Ruffed Grouse, NO Cooper's Hawks, NO Great Horned Owls, NO Western Screech-Owls, NO Northern Pygmy-Owls, NO Downy Woodpeckers, NO Black-capped Chickadees, NO Red-winged Blackbirds, NO House Finches, and NO House Sparrows! Only two species of swallow (Tree and Barn) and one flycatcher (Pacific-slope) occur regularly, and only three warbler species breed: Townsend's, Orange-crowned, and Wilson's (Yellow-rumped and Yellows are rare migrants, and there is only one record of Common Yellowthroat).

Many land mammals also never made it naturally to the islands. The Grizzly Bear, cougar, beaver, Red Squirrel, Sitka Mule Deer, and raccoon are not native to Haida Gwaii (though the latter four were successfully introduced by Europeans— along with rats). The endemic Dawson's Caribou is now extinct.

Outside of summer, the bird activity in the forests of Haida Gwaii is relatively quiet, but there is plenty of action along the shoreline and out to sea. Water bird migration in this part of the province can be spectacular in spring and fall, with various species of geese, sea ducks, loons, grebes, shorebirds, and alcids all being well represented. The best time to visit is August to September, when the weather is least volatile and migration is in full swing. The islands can act as a migrant trap, especially in fall, when you can expect the unexpected. Any time of year can yield its rewards, however, and there is plenty more to discover on this archipelago beyond birding.

> ### Hecate Strait Ferry (Prince Rupert to Skidegate)

The six-hour crossing of **Hecate Strait** between Prince Rupert on the British Columbia mainland and Skidegate (Haida Gwaii) provides a rare opportunity for birders to see a variety of pelagic species from the relative comfort of a large vessel. When swells pick up, the trip can be a bit bumpy, but this is the sacrifice for scoring Pacific seabird specialties for your life list! Be sure to book well ahead if you're making the trip in summer, and if you want to see any birds on the trip, be sure to reserve on a day when they're making the journey in daylight hours. There are two different vessels that run this route throughout the year; both offer ample viewing decks for birders, though unfortunately it is not possible to look straight ahead unless you can sweet-talk a crewmember into taking you onto the bridge. We recommend positioning yourself near the stern, as this protects you from the wind and gives you a view out both sides and of birds that might be following in the wake. Schedule and reservation information is available at the B.C. Ferries website (bcferries.com).

Once you leave the terminal in Prince Rupert, the ferry heads south along the eastern flank of Digby Island, then northwest through Brown Passage, and out into the wide open Hecate Strait. The first section can present a number of "inshore" seabirds that are less numerous farther out. These include all three scoter species, Harlequin Duck, Bald Eagle, Marbled Murrelet, Rhinoceros Auklet, Common Murre, Mew Gull, and Bonaparte's Gull. Obviously, many of the bird varieties you see on this trip will depend

Cassin's Auklet

on the time of year. Late summer to early fall is the best time for high diversity, but there should be lots to see throughout the year.

Once you're out into Hecate Strait itself, check for shearwaters, fulmars, and other "tubenoses" that might fly past close enough for a good look. Sooty Shearwaters and Northern Fulmars are usually the most abundant of this group, but in late fall (October to November), large numbers of Short-tailed Shearwaters are often seen. August to early October is a good time for Buller's and the scarce Flesh-footed Shearwater, whereas Pink-footed Shearwaters are relatively common between April and early October. Between spring and fall, you might be lucky enough to see either a Fork-tailed or Leach's Storm-Petrel, and there is always a chance of seeing one of the "big guys"—Black-footed Albatross—but they are few and far between on this side of the islands. Also look out for the rare but increasing Manx Shearwater, which is now being seen frequently off Alaska and has been recorded several times in the Hecate Strait. Moving onto other seabirds, Tufted Puffin is rare but regular between spring and fall, whereas both Cassin's and Rhinoceros Auklets can be numerous, especially in late summer and early fall.

Brandt's Cormorants are uncommon this far north but can be seen sometimes, along with the abundant Pelagic and Double-crested Cormorants, the latter usually closer to land.

Perhaps the most interesting feature about this ferry crossing, (in comparison with other pelagic opportunities farther south), is the nearly year-round possibility of seeing Yellow-billed Loon. In most of southern Canada and across the lower forty-eight U.S. states, Yellow-billed Loons turn up only occasionally and are usually young birds. This is because most of North America's nesting Yellow-billed Loons winter in eastern Siberia and Japan, with the rest remaining along the southern Alaska coastline. Over the last few years, increased birder coverage in the Hecate Strait and adjacent areas has shown the region to be an extension of this enigmatic species' non-breeding range—highlighted by winter high counts of more than forty individuals seen from the ferry in one day! Although October to May is the peak season for this species in the strait, both adults and immatures have been recorded in every month of the year—so keep your eyes peeled. Common and Pacific Loons are usually fairly common outside the breeding season, and Red-throated is also frequently seen, though usually closer to shore.

There are lots of possibilities in the gull department as well. Glaucous-winged Gull and Black-legged Kittiwake are the only two species that nest along the coast here, but late summer can see large numbers of dispersing California, Herring, and Mew Gulls. A little later on, in September, Thayer's Gulls begin to appear in the strait and by mid-October are often the most numerous species away from land. Western Gulls show up fairly frequently in small numbers throughout the year, but be aware that many hybrids occur (both Western x Glaucous-winged and Herring x Glaucous-winged). In fall and winter, Black-legged Kittiwakes can be seen in Prince Rupert, but in summer, they are scarce and usually only seen sitting on the small rocky islets north of the ferry route (just as it enters the open strait) or out in the middle of the strait itself. Bonaparte's Gulls are surprisingly infrequent on Haida Gwaii itself, so your best chance to see these little guys is along the Prince Rupert waterfront or during the first leg of the ferry crossing. Sabine's Gulls, however, prefer to stay offshore so are most often seen in the middle of the strait (spring and fall). It's possible to find all three jaeger species in spring and fall, with Long-tailed passing through in smaller time windows—August is best for this species.

> ## Queen Charlotte City

Queen Charlotte City is the main town close to the ferry terminal and a central location to begin your Haida Gwaii experience. There are many options for accommodation, from backpackers' hostels to frilly B&Bs. All major services are available here and in nearby Skidegate Landing, including gas stations and grocery stores. The Haida Heritage Centre is well worth a visit. Here you can learn all about Haida culture, as well as the human history of Haida Gwaii/Queen Charlotte Islands. This facility is located just northeast of the ferry terminal in Skidegate (off the main/only highway).

If you would rather go birding, why not start in town? Check the tidal flats along Oceanview Drive for shorebirds, particularly Black Turnstone (August to April) and Black Oystercatcher. Check the turnstone flocks for Ruddy Turnstones, Surfbirds, and Rock Sandpipers (October to April). Gulls are often present in sizable numbers, so put your gull identification skills to the test and see if you can pick out something spicy, such as a Black-tailed or Lesser Black-backed. This is Haida Gwaii after all—anything is possible!

Most of Haida Gwaii's forest birds can be found locally around the outskirts of town, including the endemic subspecies of Northern Goshawk, Hairy Woodpecker, Steller's Jay, and

Pine Grosbeak (sporadic). One of the better spots for these species is around the cemetery, which is reached by following the main road west out of the town, then turning left on Cemetery Road. There are also a few campsites available here. In spring and fall, it's a good idea to check the rows of salmonberry shrubs that line the streets and alleys around the edge of town. Among the common migrants, such as Townsend's and Orange-crowned Warblers, Dark-eyed Juncos, and Fox Sparrows, you might just find the next big rarity for the islands.

> ## Sandspit (Moresby Island)

Simply by looking at a map, you can tell that **Sandspit** is a natural magnet for birds. The main peninsula that the village is built on juts out into Hecate Strait, providing wayward migrants with an attractive mixture of tidal flats, grassy areas, and shrubs that is extremely scarce elsewhere on Haida Gwaii. These features, along with the more typical coastal forests and marine habitats, have translated into an impressive and diverse list of recorded bird species in the area.

To get to Sandspit and the rest of Moresby Island (that which is accessible by road), you need to take the small ferry from Skidegate to Alliford Bay. This short crossing of Skidegate Inlet can provide closer looks at some of the seabirds you scoped from land, such as all three scoter species, Black-legged Kittiwake, Common Murre, and Rhinoceros Auklet.

Once on the other side, follow the main road (the only one that's paved) west along the coast. It's around 10 kilometres to Sandspit, but you may want to stop along the way to look for forest birds and scan Skidegate Inlet. The alders near **Sacks Creek** (the first bridge after leaving Alliford Bay) can be hospitable to migrant flocks in spring and fall, and the creek mouth can be a good spot for loafing gulls and turnstone flocks. The next stop is **Onward Point** (6 kilometres from Alliford Bay), where you can park and walk along the short fern-clad Onward Point Trail to an overlook of Skidegate Inlet. Many of the typical forest breeding species can be seen here, including Chestnut-backed Chickadee, Red-breasted Nuthatch, Golden-crowned Kinglet, Pacific Wren, and Townsend's Warbler. Another 1.6 kilometres east along the road is the **Grassy Island rest area**. Equipped with tables and toilets, this makes for a delightful picnic spot and provides peek-a-boo views of the ocean and of Grassy Island itself, where Double-crested and Pelagic Cormorants and a variety of gulls can usually be seen.

The first worthwhile stop once you reach the village of Sandspit is **Sandspit Harbour/Coast Guard station**. This is immediately on your left after crossing Haans Creek, when the Sandspit peninsula comes into view. The creek mouth here is a particularly good draw for gulls and rock-piper flocks (turnstones, Surfbirds, and Rock Sandpipers). This is a prime spot to scope the western end of Shingle Bay, and the nearby creek can sometimes produce American Dipper.

Continue along the main drag for almost 3 kilometres until you get to School Road (see Map 26). You are now in Sandspit proper. Depending on tides and what kinds of birds you're after, there are several different ways to bird the area. The entire loop is 6 kilometres (flat terrain), so if you're up for that kind of walk then we suggest parking near the elementary school at the junction of School Road and Beach Road, then walking up along the west side, around the airport, then back west along School Road. Otherwise, you could just walk partway from either end then double-back to your car.

From the junction of School Road and Beach Road (the main road you came in on), continue northeast along Beach Road, taking the time to scan **Shingle Bay**. This shallow bay supports large numbers of sea ducks and grebes for most of the year (mainly between fall and spring), with Harlequin Ducks,

Barrow's Goldeneye, Bufflehead, and Black Scoter being some of the more conspicuous characters. Groups of shorebirds and gulls will often congregate on the flats. Look around for the resident pair of Bald Eagles that keeps watch over the bay. Major rarities such as Steller's Eider and Red-legged Kittiwake have been found in the area, so check those flocks carefully. Between fall and spring, four loon species regularly occur, and a mix of alcids and grebes can be scoped offshore. After passing the local post office and SuperValu, you will notice a large wooden pier. This is the favoured high-tide roost for flocks of migrating or wintering Black Turnstones (sometimes numbering more than three hundred!). Ruddy Turnstones, Surfbirds, and Rock Sandpipers are often mixed in with this flock (depending on the time of year), and a Ruff was seen here in September 2010.

Not too much farther beyond the pier, you will come to the end of the road at the southwest corner of the **Sandspit Airport**. From here, you must walk or bike around the perimeter of the airport—or return from whence you came. "Why should I walk around the airport?" you ask. Answer: Despite receiving relatively low birder coverage throughout the year, this patch has turned up an incredible number of vagrants (particularly shorebirds). Here's a list of some of the more notable finds: Baikal Teal, Least Tern, Eurasian Dotterel, Black-tailed Godwit, Common Greenshank, Red-necked Stint, Long-toed Stint, Little Stint, Sky Lark, Eastern Yellow Wagtail, Red-throated Pipit, and Smith's Longspur.

But it's not *all* about the rarities; because of the airport's geography, it's a fantastic place for birding in general, from the large flocks of sea ducks and alcids offshore to the geese, raptors, and ground-foraging passerines that prefer the grassy areas around the runway. When big winds blow in off the Hecate Strait, shearwaters and fulmars can often be seen flying close to shore. Although many of these birds are around the airport at any time, if you are hoping to maximize your shorebirding experience, it is best to start the loop at least 1.5 to 2 hours before high tide. Shorebird flocks tend to concentrate around the Little Spit (northeast corner), so that is where you should aim to be at least thirty minutes before high tide. You may still run into feeding flocks along the western side of the peninsula or near the Big Spit at the northwest end. If the tide is low, the best area to search is probably out on the shingle flats just west of Little Spit or on the spit itself. Do not walk out on Big Spit, as the tide can rise quickly and trap you. Once the tide rises all the way, some shorebirds may continue to feed in the kelp racks along the shore, particularly near the base of Little Spit or along the beach to the south. Otherwise, some of the flocks will sometimes fly onto the grassy fields along the runway, so be sure to scan carefully. In recent years, a male Ruff has turned up fairly reliably each May, usually around the grassy hollow along the southeast side of the airport.

In addition to the shorebirds and seabirds, check the rose thickets and other shrubs for migrating sparrows and warblers. It is always worthwhile to scan migrating flocks of pipits or long-spurs, as you never know what vagrant might be tagging along. In spring and fall, Short-eared Owls are often seen hunting around the perimeter of the airport, and Peregrine Falcons are usually one of the most prevalent raptors in the area.

When you reach the southeast corner of the airport, your progress might be blocked by a creek (depending on the time of year). If this is the case, there should be a small trail that skirts the water on the right (west) side; this will take you out to the east end of School Road. If you end up walking back along School Road, you can expect to run into a few of the common forest species in the mixed spruce forest. Pacific Wren, Golden-crowned

Kinglet, and Song Sparrow are usually the most abundant species, but Pine Siskins, Red Crossbills, and Pine Grosbeaks are sometimes present in sizable numbers, along with Northern Flicker, Hairy Woodpecker, Varied Thrush, and Brown Creeper. As with Queen Charlotte City, you should also check each salmonberry patch and alder stand for migrants, as many exciting birds have turned up in this neighbourhood, including Cape May and Black-throated Blue Warblers.

Another fruitful area to check out in Sandspit is **Copper Bay Road**. This road heads south from the eastern terminus of School Road and leads to Copper Bay. The first place to check is right at the start of the road—the conspicuous **Willows Golf Course**. This is a popular spot for migrating geese to forage—five species have been recorded here, as well as the Aleutian subspecies of Cackling Goose (identified by its white ring around the base of its neck and its disconnected white cheeks surrounded by black). There is scarce open fresh water near Sandspit, so if there is any water in the creek running through the golf course, this can be a great spot to check for dabbling ducks and has even yielded a lost White-faced Ibis on one occasion. The willows and crabapple trees along the course can be fantastic for passerines in migration season (if someone is around, be sure to obtain permission before crossing the fence).

As you continue south along Copper Bay Road, it may be worth checking the small alder patches on the ocean side of the road for migrant warblers. Near where the houses end, there are some picnic tables just back from the beach. This is where Haida Gwaii's first ever record of Grasshopper Sparrow was found, and there is plenty of potential for other exciting birds to turn up here. After the road passes the last house, it becomes surrounded by large alder trees on both sides—this is also one of the best local spots for mixed warbler flocks in spring and fall, and in November 2010, both a Chestnut-sided Warbler and a Black-throated Blue Warbler were photographed here.

At Croustcheff Point, the road turns from pavement to dirt. From here, a level but potholed road continues to **Copper Bay** (6.5 kilometres to the south). Most birders won't bother to drive down there, but it's a favourite spot of the locals for fishing, relaxing, and getting away from the Sandspit "city life." Summer to fall is probably the best time to visit, as many gulls and other water birds gather to take advantage of the large salmon runs in the area. Many of the native Haida Gwaii forest birds can be seen along this road as well, including Northern Goshawk, Northern Saw-Whet Owl (at night), Hairy Woodpecker, Red-breasted Sapsucker, Hermit Thrush, and Pacific-slope Flycatcher.

For those really wanting to get away from it all, **Gray Bay** might be just the place. This scenic bay of hard-packed grey sand is an awesome area to explore both the shoreline and the forest. There are twenty campsites available on a first-come, first-served basis, along with picnic tables, day-use shelters, and pit toilets. To get to Gray Bay, continue south from Copper Bay, following signs for Gray Bay (another 13 kilometres). In this area, there are several hiking trails that provide access to even more of the Moresby backcountry (Secret Cove Trail)—but now we're starting to get beyond the scope of this book. Happy exploring!

> Hwy. 16 North: Skidegate to Masset

From the ferry terminal at Skidegate Landing, it's a little more than 100 kilometres to Masset along Hwy. 16, and there are plenty of places to pull off and look for birds. The waterfront of **Skidegate Village** (2.5 kilometres from the ferry) can offer a similar variety of birds to Queen Charlotte City, and the next 37 kilometres of highway to **Tlell** parallel some beautiful beaches, where you can scan for seabirds offshore and comb the shoreline for shorebirds and other washed-up treasures. There is not much to the village of Tlell; for birding, the main draw is the series of open pastures and meadows that parallel the Tlell River. Like the Sandspit Airport, these open areas are oases for some birds, surrounded by forests, clear-cuts, and rocky beaches. In these fields, scan for flocks of geese, cranes, waterfowl, and shorebirds (especially if there is a bit of flooding), and explore the surrounding forests to find the usual forest species.

After passing Tlell, look for the Tlell River Provincial Park and Misty Meadows Park sign on your right, which marks the southern boundary of **Naikoon Provincial Park**. Turn into Tlell River Provincial Park for the Pesuta Shipwreck Hiking Trail and East Beach Trail, or continue on Hwy. 16 to Pure Lake and Mayer Lake Park. There are plenty of hiking, camping, and picnicking opportunities in the park, which encompasses 69,166 hectares (179,500 acres) of "sandy beaches, rolling sand dunes, forested old growth hiking trails, wetlands, bogs, rock cliffs, marine tidal pools, viewing look-outs, and historical shipwrecks," as described by the park's website. For more information about Naikoon Provincial Park, visit env.gov.bc.ca/bcparks/explore/parkpgs/naikoon.

Forty kilometres south of Masset is the logging community of **Port Clements**, former home of the famous Golden Spruce (Kiidk'yaas)—a mutant Sitka Spruce that was illegally cut down by Grant Hadwin in 1997 as a misguided protest to Haida Gwaii's logging industry. There isn't a lot of birding to do here, other than scanning the massive Masset Inlet. This part of the inlet can be hit or miss, with almost no birds on some days, though other times (particularly during migration), sizable numbers of loons, grebes, and other water birds are present. There is a small tidal flat on the northeast side of town that is usually the best place to look for waterfowl and shorebirds in season.

> Masset (Delkatla Wildlife Sanctuary)

Welcome to **Masset**, the largest community of Haida Gwaii, with around 940 residents. When you first glimpse the town as you approach from the south, find a safe place to pull over near the confluence of the Delkatla Inlet outflow and the main entrance channel of Masset Inlet. Outside of high tide, there is usually some exposed mud, which attracts a mix of dabbling ducks from late summer into spring and is usually the best place to find Eurasian Wigeon (October to April). Continue up the highway a few hundred metres more and turn left onto the bridge that takes you into downtown Masset. Instead of continuing into the main town, make an immediate right (northeast) on Delkatla Road/ Trumpeter Drive and sally along for 300 metres before turning right into the parking lot of the **Delkatla Wildlife Sanctuary Nature Interpretive Centre**. If the centre is open, be sure to have a look inside to learn more about the local birds and the conservation history of the area. Otherwise, there is a viewing tower close by, where you can get a good look at the **Delkatla Slough**.

Different seasons bring different birds, but there is usually a mix of water birds and raptors on offer. Like Sandspit, this has produced some impressive Asian vagrants, including TWO Rustic Buntings, Canada's first Wood Sandpiper, and Common Crane! By continuing north along Trumpeter Lane, you can reach more access trails to the sanctuary, where there is another viewing tower on the southeast side. To reach this one, drive back across the bridge, then instead of turning right (Hwy. 16 to Port Clements), turn left following signs to Tow Hill. You should see the tower and a pull-off on the left side around 850 metres from the bridge.

The bird mix along the Masset waterfront is fairly similar to that of Queen Charlotte City and Skidegate, with Pelagic Cormorants, Bald Eagles, Glaucous-winged Gulls, and Black

Oystercatchers being some of the typical year-round species. Like the other Haida Gwaii communities covered in this chapter, it is always worth walking around town and birding local gardens and hedges, as you never know what rare songbird might pop up.

> Tow Hill and South Beach

To reach Tow Hill and the north end of Naikoon Provincial Park, head northeast out of Masset (same directions as for the Delkatla Wildlife Sanctuary's second viewing tower) on Tow Hill Road. Soon you will pass the Masset Airport, then after another 2.9 kilometres, you will see the entrance road for the **Dixon Entrance Golf and Country Club.** Like the golf course in Sandspit, this spot offers a mix of shrub and grassland habitats attractive to migrants, as well as a few freshwater ditches. In general, birders are tolerated on the course, but be sure to gain permission (if possible) before walking on the grounds. You will also notice that the fairways surround a massive antenna array. Also known as the Elephant Cage, this is one of the world's two remaining FRD-10 circularly disposed antenna arrays—installed by the Canadian government in 1971 to triangulate radio signals for radio navigation, intelligence gathering, and search and rescue. The only other remaining operational FRD-10 in the world is in Gander, Newfoundland.

Back to the birds. Another impressive feature of the Dixon Entrance Golf Course is the large system of sand dunes and dune grass known as **South Beach.** From on top of the dunes, the panhandle of Alaska is visible on clear days, and this is also a prime spot for sea watching. Few people associate sand dunes and vast beaches with Haida Gwaii, but that is exactly what you will find here.

To see more of South Beach, which stretches for more than 20 kilometres from Entry Point near Old Masset to Yakan Point (just before Tow Hill), return to the main road and continue northeast. Soon you will leave the salmonberry scrub and enter into more mature coniferous forest. The beach houses along this stretch form the heart of Haida Gwaii's vibrant surfing community, and there are several charming B&Bs right on the beach. If you can find a public place to access the beach, you can then scan the expansive McIntyre Bay for loons, grebes, and sea ducks.

Just before crossing the Saangan River, the main road enters the north end of Naikoon Provincial Park. This 15-kilometre stretch of road is one of the most beautiful drives on Haida Gwaii. From the dunes of South Beach to the mystical rainforests of Naikoon, you can really get a taste of what the rest of Graham Island used to look like. There are campsites and picnic areas at **Agate Beach** (1.5 kilometres west of Tow Hill), which can be a great base for your explorations. The prominent landmark of this area, of course, at 109 metres high, is **Tow Hill**—a huge outcrop of basalt columns formed when volcanic rock solidified into faceted basalt pillars about 2 million years ago. It rises from the flat bogs of the Argonaut Plain at the mouth of the Hiellen River and provides fantastic views of the surrounding area. There are several hiking trails that take you through the forest and out to the shoreline. Common breeders here include Sooty Grouse, Hairy Woodpecker, Pacific Wren, Golden-crowned Kinglet, Varied Thrush, Townsend's Warbler, Red Crossbill, and Pine Siskin.

> Rose Spit

East of Tow Hill, on the other side of the Hiellen River, is **North Beach** and the massive sandy peninsula known as **Rose Spit**. North Beach, according to Haida legend, is the place where Raven first brought people into the world by coaxing them out of a clamshell, making this area the site of creation. You are allowed to drive your vehicle along the beach out to Rose Spit, but this should only be done around low tide and with four-wheel drive and good clearance. If your car gets stuck, your only hope is getting help from another passing vehicle, but they can be few and far between on this part of the island. Be smart and drive at your own risk.

Most people who head to Rose Spit bring supplies and camp, as it's a 30-kilometre round trip. This is doable as a day hike, but it won't give you much time for birding. Because of its position—jutting out into the sea, splitting the Hecate Strait from Dixon Entrance—many birders have drooled over maps of Rose Spit, dreaming of its huge potential for migration watching and, of course, rarity finding. However, because of its remoteness, very few birders have ever spent much time out there. Suitable weather for hiking and camping is in summer, but the birding is best toward the end of summer and throughout fall, when thousands of shearwaters, loons, grebes, scoters, and many other seabirds pass through on migration. Lost passerines probably turn up all the time in the windswept shrubs near the tip and among the driftwood lining the beaches—your job is to find them!

NORTHEAST
AND
FAR NORTH

Like the Okanagan Valley, the **Peace River** and **Fort Nelson Lowlands** of northeastern British Columbia provide birders with a completely different set of birds to play with. Thanks to their position on the eastern side of the Rocky Mountains, many "eastern" species that are rare elsewhere in the province can be added to your provincial list. Some of the locally common specialties in the region include Broad-winged Hawk, Franklin's Gull, Yellow-bellied Sapsucker, Eastern Phoebe, Yellow-bellied Flycatcher, Blue Jay, Blue-headed Vireo, Ovenbird, Black-and-White Warbler, Mourning Warbler, Palm Warbler, Canada Warbler, Black-throated Green Warbler, Rose-breasted Grosbeak, Swamp Sparrow, Le Conte's Sparrow, Baltimore Oriole, and Common Grackle. Even birders from eastern Canada and the United States will find the birding here rewarding, since several of the breeding specialties are very difficult to see while migrating through the eastern half of North America. Simply witnessing these species in their nesting habitat, as opposed to passing through the migrant traps of Texas, Ohio, and Ontario, is a unique treat.

We hope this guide will help you find all of your target birds in this corner of the province, including tougher ones such as Yellow Rail, Upland Sandpiper, Ruby-throated Hummingbird, Philadelphia Vireo, (eastern) Winter Wren, Cape May Warbler, Bay-breasted Warbler, Connecticut Warbler, and Nelson's Sparrow. Because many of these species are at the western limits of their breeding ranges, numbers will fluctuate from year to year. Baltimore Oriole, for instance, can be widespread and common in some years and nearly absent in others.

In this transition area, western birds meet eastern birds, and both of these meet northern birds. Where else can you see Western Wood-Pewees foraging alongside Boreal Chickadees and Philadelphia Vireos? Late May to early June is the best time to bird here, when breeding passerines are in peak song and migrant shorebirds are still passing through. August and September can also be interesting, when mixed flocks of warblers can turn up all sorts of goodies. July can be quiet, as many songbirds are silently feeding their young. Wind and rain can also make birding frustrating at times, but that's just how birding can be sometimes. We hope that the accounts below will give you a good idea of what is possible—use them to design an itinerary that suits your "wants." Also, remember what they say about the "early bird"!

CHETWYND

This quiet mill town stands at a birding crossroads. But before you continue, make sure to check your fuel because the next service station might be a ways away, depending on where you want to go. While filling up, it might be worthwhile to scan the skies for a Broad-winged Hawk (another eastern specialty) that is sometimes seen soaring high above town. Review the birding

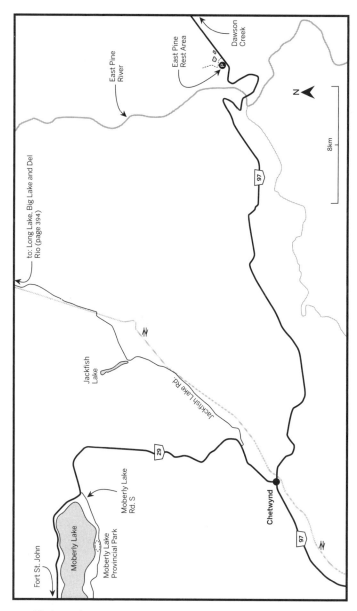

East Pine River

Dawson Creek

East Pine
Rest Area

N

8km

97

to: Long Lake, Big Lake and Del
Rio (page 394)

Jackfish
Lake

N

Jackfish Lake Rd.

29

Moberly Lake
Rd. S

Moberly Lake

Chetwynd

Moberly Lake
Provincial Park

Fort St. John

97

N

27 Chetwynd

options below to determine your route out of Chetwynd (see Map 27). If you're planning on driving to Fort St. John, there are rewarding birding spots along both Hwy. 29 (via Hudson's Hope) and Hwy. 97 (via Dawson Creek). If this is a return trip, we recommend picking one highway outbound then switching on the way back.

› Hwy. 29: Chetwynd to Fort St. John

Turn north at the main intersection in downtown Chetwynd (same as with Del Rio, see page 393), and continue up Hwy. 29 for nearly 20 kilometres until you reach Moberly Lake. Here Moberly Lake Road South turns off to the left and runs along the south end of Moberly Lake. It's a good road for about 30 kilometres, with patches of mixed forest filled with a variety of songbirds, including Least Flycatcher, Red-eyed and Blue-headed Vireo, American Redstart, Northern Waterthrush, and Black-throated Green Warbler. Broad-winged Hawks are often seen patrolling the sky, and the lake itself can be a great spot for migrating grebes, loons, and ducks in spring and fall.

Moberly Lake Provincial Park is the most convenient place from which to bird the lake and surrounding woodland (well-signed off Moberly Lake Road South). In addition to the camping facilities, day-use picnic sites, a boat launch, and several short walking trails make this an ideal pit stop. Black-throated Green Warblers are fairly common in the mixed spruce stands in the park, but be aware that you are in an overlap zone where Townsend's Warblers from the mountains occur in small numbers and hybridize with the Black-throated Greens. Another interesting overlap here is Mourning and MacGillivray's Warblers—both breed annually in the park in mixed forests with thick, scrubby understorey. Identifying these two sets of warblers by song can sometimes be problematic in this area, so be sure to get a good look.

Return to the highway and proceed toward Fort St. John. When you reach Hudson's Hope, look for signs for the **W.A.C. Bennett Dam**. Rock Wrens are sometimes heard singing from the dam itself, but otherwise, the good birding doesn't start until you reach the other side. Several forest service roads head off into the surrounding hills, where any number of Peace region specialties can be found. In recent years, this area has turned up some rarities, such as Hooded Warbler on the Table Creek Forest Service Road and Black-throated Blue Warbler on the Johnson Creek Forest Service Road. The Utah Forest Service Road can also be productive. *Note: Remember to always watch vigilantly for loaded trucks when navigating these narrow forestry roads. If you have a cb radio in your vehicle, tune in to the posted frequency and call your kilometres.*

Between Hudson's Hope and Watson Slough, there are many interesting areas to pull off and bird—we simply can't cover everything in this book! The large aspen grove just outside of Hudson's Hope can sometimes yield Connecticut Warbler, and any patch of roadside sedge can sometimes produce the sneaky Le Conte's Sparrow. **Watson Slough** is a refurbished tract of marshland (51 kilometres from Hudson's Hope) that has become a popular birding spot in recent years, thanks to both the high number of breeding species and its convenient location right next to Hwy. 29. If you park at the main pull-off (signed near the southwest end), there is a trail that leads down to the edge of the marsh. Blue-winged and Green-winged Teal, Mallard, Ring-necked Duck, Bufflehead, and Ruddy Duck are some of the resident waterfowl; Sora are common and American Bittern has also been recorded here. The wet sedge areas, especially at the southwest/Hudson's Hope end of the slough, can produce Solitary Sandpiper, Le Conte's Sparrow, Nelson's Sparrow, and even Yellow Rail (at least five heard calling in June 2011). The best time to look for these toughies is dawn or dusk, from late May to the end of June (they can also be heard at night). The boreal forest surrounding the slough can be productive as well, with Tennessee Warbler, Dark-eyed (Slate-colored) Junco, and Olive-sided Flycatcher being some of the more conspicuous singers. After birding Watson Slough, it's another 22 kilometres to link up with the Alaska Highway at Charlie Lake—just north of Fort St. John (see page 413 for birding directions to the Charlie Lake area from Fort St. John). *Note: B.C. Hydro has proposed a new hydroelectric dam project in the area (Site C). If this goes ahead, Watson Slough and the Bear Flats area will be under several metres of water.*

➤ Hwy. 97: Chetwynd to Dawson Creek

The other main option for birders heading to the Peace region is to continue along Hwy. 97 from Chetwynd to Dawson Creek. From Chetwynd, head straight through town and follow the highway east. After crossing the Pine River, the road climbs up onto a plateau of pastureland and aspen copses. The **East Pine rest area** is 38.2 kilometres from Chetwynd and up the hill from the Pine River Bridge. This is a reliable site for Upland Sandpiper, Le Conte's Sparrow, and, in some years, Yellow Rail. Park at the main pull-off (on the north side of the highway) and walk east down the highway until you see an old track heading to the north. You can either walk in there or continue along the highway, scanning the fields, fence posts, and power lines for the Upland Sandpipers. Be sure to keep your ears open too, as the sandpipers are very vocal, especially when in flight. Later in June, as the grass grows up, it becomes increasingly difficult to spot them along the ground. On the north side of the highway, fairly close to the rest stop, you will notice a flooded sedge wetland. This is where Yellow Rails have been heard on occasion, and Soras and Wilson's Phalaropes breed here every year. Western Meadowlarks, Black-billed Magpies, Red-winged Blackbirds, and Blue-winged Teal are some of the other breeders, and if you're lucky, you might see Le Conte's Sparrows singing from low perches toward the west end of the marsh. The aspen woodlands nearby can also produce a few exciting birds, including Rose-breasted Grosbeak, Clay-colored Sparrow, Black-and-White Warbler, and American Redstart.

Once you're satisfied with the birds (or frustrated with all the traffic!) continue down the highway for another 41.8 kilometres (80 kilometres from Chetwynd). Just before the highway crosses the Kiskatinaw River, the **Heritage Highway** (Hwy. 52) (an alternate route to and from Tumbler Ridge) heads off to the south. Even if you are not intending to go all the way to Tumbler Ridge, you may want to explore the first stretch of this road as it can be quite birdy at times. For about 14 kilometres the highway heads straight south through a mixture of farmland and aspen copses. You may notice small wetlands and Black Spruce bogs along the way, which can produce some thrilling stuff, such as Olive-sided Flycatcher, Blackpoll Warbler, Tennessee Warbler, and a diversity of sparrows (Chipping, Clay-colored, LeConte's, Lincoln's, Song, Fox, and Swamp). Members of the blackbird family can be in evidence as well—you'll see mainly Red-winged and Brewer's Blackbirds, but watch out also for fly-by Rusty Blackbirds. Baltimore Orioles can be heard whistling from the aspen and poplar groves, whereas Common Grackles work the fields with the Brewer's Blackbirds.

One of the most diverse birding roads in the region is a bit farther down Hwy. 52. In fewer than 15 kilometres of gravel road, the **Brassey Creek Road** boasts seventeen species of breeding wood-warblers, four nesting vireos, and nine flycatchers. Occasionally "western" species such as Steller's Jay and Northern Pygmy-Owl turn up, and when you factor in all the northern breeders (Boreal Chickadee, American Three-toed Woodpecker, and Pine Grosbeak), it's an interesting place to visit indeed.

The turnoff from Hwy. 52 is 25.6 kilometres from the junction with Hwy. 97 (labelled Chunter Brassey Road on Google Maps). *Note: There is a Brassey Road located 19.6 kilometres from Hwy. 97. Take the next right after that where signs advertise Brassey Plant.*

Truck traffic can be a problem on this road, so use extreme caution when going around turns and remember that early morning is best—both for birds and traffic. Around the kilometre 1 marker you will see a wide grassy buffer on the right (north) side of the road that meets with a large stand of open aspen woodland. You will notice that the understorey is very sparse—this is prime Connecticut Warbler habitat. If you visit in the spring or early summer, you have a chance of finding one of these loud but hard-to-see warblers. Remember that the similar-sounding Ovenbird and Northern Waterthrush are also common in the area, so be sure to listen to recordings beforehand. Connecticut Warblers spend a lot of time low down on logs and along the ground, but they usually sing from branches in the middle of the canopy. That means you need to walk into the forest to score a look. Other birds found in the big aspens and scrub along this first stretch include Red-eyed, Warbling, and Philadelphia Vireos; American Redstart; Black-and-White Warbler; Least Flycatcher; Rose-breasted Grosbeak; and Yellow-bellied Sapsucker.

At kilometre 5.8, park at the corner and take some time to explore a large spruce stand that is often one of the most reliable spots in the Lower Peace region for Cape May Warbler (the closer to dawn the better). Other spruce lovers such as Varied Thrush, Golden-crowned Kinglet, Boreal Chickadee, and Black-throated Green Warbler can be expected here. Continue up the hill to the right, where large aspens mix with thick scrub below. Unlike their cousin, the Connecticut Warbler (who likes old-growth aspen with little to no understorey), Mourning Warblers love this brushy mess, because it allows them to pursue their favourite activity—skulking. Another nice-looking but often hard-to-see bird found here is the Canada Warbler. These gems especially like the thick alder patches along moist slopes. Near kilometre 12, there is a T-junction. The second-growth mixed Lodgepole Pine forest in this area hosts Yellow-bellied Flycatcher in some years.

> Del Rio

Note: Be sure to have a full tank of gas before heading to Del Rio. Also, it's easy to get disoriented while exploring this area because new roads are put in every year by natural gas companies. Therefore, it is advisable to bring a copy of the Northern B.C. Backroad Mapbook and pay close attention to the directions in this chapter.

The rural area known as Del Rio by British Columbia birders boasts a variety of habitats and birds and is especially well known for its rich marshlands. To get to Del Rio, turn north at the main intersection, following signs for Hudson's Hope (Hwy. 29). After 3.5 kilometres, turn onto Jackfish Lake Road and continue along this road for 14.8 kilometres until you cross a set of railway tracks, then make an immediate left and continue north of Jackfish Lake Road. You will pass Jackfish Lake around kilometre 10, but the first good birding stop isn't until kilometre 22, where part of the old Jackfish Lake Road turns off to the left and crosses the railway tracks again. Just after you cross the tracks, continue straight and you will find the Long Lake Community Hall.

Park here and bird the forest behind the buildings, where trails lead to the south end of **Long Lake**. Listen for the explosive song of a Connecticut Warbler that haunts the aspen groves on both sides of the road. Although this species is considered one of the hardest warblers to see in North America, as many as three males have been recorded here at one time! Their song is loud and distinctive; however, it can be very difficult to catch a glimpse—patience is the key. On Long Lake, Trumpeter Swans,

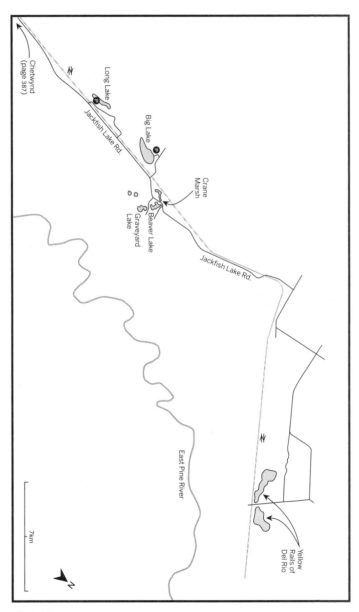

Chetwynd
(page 387)

Long Lake

Jackfish Lake Rd.

Big Lake

Crane
Marsh

Beaver Lake

Graveyard
Lake

Jackfish Lake Rd.

East Pine River

Yellow
Rails of
Del Rio

7km

Black Terns, Common Loons, Horned Grebes, and many other waterfowl species are annual breeders. Swamp Sparrows sing from prominent perches along the shoreline, and occasionally an American Bittern (rare in the Peace region) can be heard "pumping" from the cattails at the south end.

The **Big Lake recreation site** is a great place to stop for lunch or set up camp. Located at the north end of Big Lake (turn off Jackfish Lake Road at kilometre 28.4, or about 6.2 kilometres past the Long Lake turnoff), this site offers a mix of forest and water birds. White-throated Sparrow, Least Flycatcher, and Tennessee Warbler are three of the most abundant species here, but with a bit of effort, many more "eastern" birds such as Baltimore Oriole, Black-and-White Warbler, and Ovenbird can be found. Barrow's Goldeneye and White-winged Scoters are two of the more obvious waterfowl residents, and noisy Common Loons and both Red-necked and Horned Grebes compete for attention.

After Big Lake, the Jackfish Lake Road turns from asphalt to gravel and dirt and takes you deeper into the heart of **Del Rio**. There are many side roads to explore, where you will find wide open farmlands patrolled by the pale "Richardson's" Merlin; rich cattail marshes packed with Black Terns, Marsh Wrens, and Common Yellowthroats; and mixed woodlands where you can encounter almost any of the eastern specialties of the region. Listen for the soft, insect-like whispers of the secretive Le Conte's Sparrow in patches of sedge grass, and remember to keep scanning the sky for circling Broad-winged Hawks. Three of the more convenient wetlands to check out are **Graveyard Lake** (accessible from Pruckel Road, which runs to the east 1.3 kilometres past the Big Lake turnoff); **Crane Marsh** (west side of the road, 1.8 kilometres past the Big Lake turnoff); and **Beaver Lake** (turn down Willis Road, just a few hundred metres past Crane Marsh).

Yellow Rail

In most cases, the main reason keen birders venture into the back roads of Del Rio is for a chance encounter with one of British Columbia's most elusive breeders: the Yellow Rail. These fist-sized creatures spend their whole lives skulking around thick patches of sedge marsh and are usually only detected by the mechanical ticking calls they give from dusk until dawn. Yellow Rails arrive in British Columbia from mid-May to early June but *where* they arrive is always hard to predict, since water levels at any particular sedge marsh must be just right. Too dry means low food resources and exposure to predators, but too wet means they can't walk around on their stubby little legs. Del Rio has proven to be one of the most reliable areas to hear and sometimes see the rail.

To get to one of the larger patches of sedge wetlands, follow these directions: Continue north from the Big Lake turnoff for 12.8 kilometres, turn right at the T-junction, and then veer left at the next fork. After a straight stretch, you will come to a four-way junction (5.9 kilometres from the T-junction). Turn right (east) and keep straight (more or less) on this road for 10 kilometres, until you get to another T-junction. Turn right (southeast), and soon you will be getting into "the zone." Along this road, you can bird the mature aspen forest for deciduous-loving species such as Red-eyed and Philadelphia Vireos, Rose-breasted Grosbeak, Yellow-bellied Sapsucker, and Swainson's Thrush. Soon you will start to see sedge marshes on both sides of the road. The largest one, located on the right (southwest) side of the road, is the best spot for Yellow Rail (if you cross the railway tracks you've gone too far). The best time to listen is from an hour after dusk until dawn. Most people are happy to listen from the road, but if you're really gung-ho, you can put on rubber boots and walk into the back end of the marsh. Le Conte's Sparrows are thick in this area, and a few Nelson's Sparrows can be found here, too (the best spot for this species is right beside the gas well farther down the road, just before the railroad tracks). Solitary Sandpipers, both Lesser and Great Yellowlegs, and Wilson's Snipe are all common breeders in the wetlands, and Soras are often heard and sometimes seen. *Note: Although you can follow these gas roads to within a few kilometres of Fort St. John and Taylor, there is no way to cross the Pine and Peace Rivers. Once you finish birding the area, you must return to Chetwynd.*

TUMBLER RIDGE

Around the turn of the millennium, Tumbler Ridge was a struggling community known principally as a coal-producing mine town. Although coal is still the major component of the economy, there are now two other things the town is famous for.

Since 2000, more than seven hundred dinosaur bones have been discovered in the area (accounting for 99 percent of the provincial total). The Dinosaur Discovery Centre and Peace Region Palaeontology Research Centre have both been set up to accommodate these valuable treasures, and now visitors can get a look at some of the oldest birds in British Columbia. Included in the display are some shorebird tracks that are more than 100 million years old!

Continuing on the evolutionary theme, **Tumbler Ridge** is a birding convergence area, where east meets west. This is where Darren Irwin and David Toews conducted most of their research on the Winter Wren complex, which eventually led to an official split that created a new species—Pacific Wren. Both wrens can be found in the forests around Tumbler Ridge, as well as other east-west partners such as Mourning Warbler–MacGillivray's Warbler and Townsend's Warbler–Black-throated Green Warbler.

> Gwillim Lake Provincial Park

Located 46.4 kilometres south of Chetwynd on Hwy. 29, **Gwillim Lake** is a fantastic place to camp or experience some forest birding on your way to or from Tumbler Ridge. Expected species between May and September include Common Loon, Red-necked Grebe, Belted Kingfisher, Boreal Chickadee, Red-breasted Nuthatch, Golden-crowned Kinglet, Ruby-crowned Kinglet, Hermit Thrush, Varied Thrush, Townsend's Warbler, Song Sparrow, Lincoln's Sparrow, White-throated Sparrow, White-winged Crossbill, and Pine Siskin.

> Bullmoose Marsh

Bullmoose Marsh is a favourite spot for local birders because of the mix of habitat in a small area. Complete with boardwalks and viewing platforms, the marsh is easily accessed off Hwy. 29 (46.4 kilometres south of Gwillim Lake; 24.1 kilometres north of Tumbler Ridge). Look for the turnoff on the east side of the highway. Breeding species along the various trails include Bufflehead, Barrow's Goldeneye, Green-winged Teal, Northern Harrier, Northern Goshawk, American Bittern, Sora, Solitary Sandpiper,

White-tailed Ptarmigan

Great Horned Owl, Pileated Woodpecker, Blue-headed Vireo, Mountain Bluebird, and Bohemian Waxwing.

> ### Mount Spieker

This is one of the most reliable (and accessible) sites in British Columbia for White-tailed Ptarmigan—and it's also good for other birds. From Tumbler Ridge, drive north toward Chetwynd on Hwy. 29 to the Wolverine Forest Service Road (8.8 kilometres from Tumbler Ridge; about 15.5 kilometres south of Bullmoose Marsh). This is a radio-controlled road (frequency 153.020 MHZ), and there can be industrial traffic from Western Coal's Wolverine mine, so be careful and use a radio if you have one. The mine development has affected access to the trailhead. To gain access, go to the mine gate at kilometre 17 and ask at the security building for an escort through the mine. This will take you through the mine and onto the Perry Creek Road. It is advisable to call the mine at 250-242-6000 the day of your hike to arrange an escort. Follow the Perry Creek Road as it heads up the valley. There are junctions at the 10.2-kilometre and 12-kilometre marks—take the right fork at the first one and the left fork at the second one. The final junction is at 13.7 kilometres. Take the right fork at this one, and follow the road to its end at a large clearing with a gas well. From this parking area, you will proceed on foot up some switchbacks leading to a saddle.

Chipping Sparrows, Golden-crowned Sparrows, Fox Sparrows, and Yellow-rumped Warblers are common in this subalpine habitat. Once up on the saddle, you have three choices for alpine hiking: southwest (left), north, and east (both right). White-tailed Ptarmigan are possible anywhere above treeline on all three ridges but are most often seen on the ridge to the left (southwest). This could be because this is the shorter route and is more often birded. Regardless, the three main ridges of **Mount Spieker** are all fantastic for alpine birds, including both White-tailed and Willow Ptarmigan (Rock has been recorded but is very rare), Dusky Grouse, Golden Eagle, Horned Lark, Townsend's Solitaire, American Pipit, Savannah Sparrow, and Gray-crowned Rosy-Finch. Caribou, pika, and Hoary Marmot are some of the mammals that are often encountered.

If you're still missing Willow Ptarmigan after a long hike around the mountain, try hiking through the willow thickets just west from where you parked the car. Wilson's Warblers are common here, and higher up on the slopes, where the willows are more clumped and spread apart, you may find Brewer's (Timber-line) Sparrow.

› Quality Falls

From the east side of downtown Tumbler Ridge, head north on Mackenzie Way to reach Hwy. 52. At this junction, turn left (northbound), and in 6.1 kilometres, the parking lot for the **Quality Falls** walking trail will be on the left side. This is one of the best places to observe both the western Pacific and (eastern)

Winter Wren in the same spot. Listen for the slight differences in song, and look for the visual difference. Pacific Wrens are warmer brown with less white speckling, whereas Winter Wrens are a greyish brown with paler patterning on the upper parts. The song of the Pacific Wren is a bit buzzier and jumbled, whereas the Winter Wren's is fluid with quite distinct notes (compare with Tennessee Warbler). The call notes are also different—Pacific sounds similar to a Wilson's Warbler, and Winter recalls a Song Sparrow–like note.

Continue up Hwy. 52 to reach Hwy. 97. Along the way, you may want to check out **Brassey Creek Road** for a mix of boreal specialties and eastern birds such as Connecticut Warbler and Philadelphia Vireo (see page 391).

DAWSON CREEK

Dawson Creek is situated at Mile "0" of the Alaska Highway and thus is a popular spot for many birders to begin their journey northward. Whether you're spending a day or a whole week birding the area, there are many options. It is also known as the Capital of the Peace and is steeped in a long agricultural tradition, though in recent years, the natural gas industry has become a major player in the local economy. This increased activity in the backcountry has put a strain on some important natural areas, but there are still some wonderful birding sites to visit, and several of the notable ones are described below:

> McQueen's Slough

McQueen's Slough is close to town and is an easy-access way to see local birds. From the main traffic circle in downtown Dawson Creek, head east on the Spirit River Highway (Hwy. 49) for about 5 kilometres, then turn north (left) onto Rolla Road. After around 4.8 kilometres, you should see a wildlife viewing sign

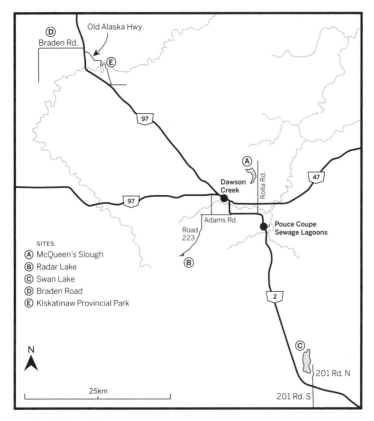

Old Alaska Hwy.

Ⓓ Braden Rd.

Ⓔ

97

Ⓐ

Dawson Creek

Rolla Rd.

47

Adams Rd.

Road 223

Pouce Coupe Sewage Lagoons

SITES
Ⓐ McQueen's Slough
Ⓑ Radar Lake
Ⓒ Swan Lake
Ⓓ Braden Road
Ⓔ Kiskatinaw Provincial Park

Ⓑ

2

N

Ⓒ

201 Rd. N

25km

201 Rd. S

29 South Peace Overview

and a gravel road on the west side (left); turn down this road and park where indicated. There is a nice set-up of trails and board-walks where you can easily view the large numbers of water birds on the main pond, including Eared Grebes, Mallards, American Wigeon, Northern Pintail, Green-winged and Blue-winged Teal, Lesser Scaup, Ring-necked Duck, Ruddy Duck, Canvasback, and Black Terns. Clay-colored Sparrows and Yellow Warblers are common in the surrounding willows, and both Le Conte's and Nelson's Sparrow can be heard and sometimes seen in the sedge grasses (especially in the area north of the main pond—keep right on the trail—near a small drop structure). Sandhill Cranes sometimes occur here but are often hidden from view, and Trumpeter Swans are usually present. Scan the sky for Broad-winged Hawk and "Richardson's" Merlin.

> Radar Lake

Only 15 kilometres out of Dawson Creek, **Radar Lake** is a convenient place to find a diversity of forest birds, including both eastern and northern specialties. Head south on 8th Street/the Pouce Coupe Highway (Hwy. 2) from the Mile "0" traffic circle. After 2.2 kilometres, keep right on 8th Street where the highway bends to the east, and take a right (west) on Adams Road. Continue straight on Adams Road for 4.8 kilometres, then turn left (south) on 223 Road; this will turn into Radar Lake Road, and after about 7.7 kilometres, the small Radar Lake will come up on the left side, where there is a short interpretive trail and boat launch. Hermit Thrush, Swainson's Thrush, American Redstart, and White-throated Sparrow are some of the common species. Many of the "eastern" warblers can be found in this area, including a few Black-throated Green Warblers (look for them in stands of White Spruce). Le Conte's Sparrows are fairly common around some of the roadside wetlands and fields, and of course, keep your eyes open for soaring Broad-winged Hawks.

> Swan Lake

If you have more time, we recommend a half-day or full-day trip down Hwy. 2 to the Alberta border. You can start by checking the **Pouce Coupe Sewage Lagoons** (accessed by turning east onto 52nd Avenue in Pouce Coupe and driving to the end, where you will see the signed gate for the lagoons). Least Flycatcher, Clay-colored Sparrow, Brown-headed Cowbird, and Yellow-bellied

Sapsucker are all common in the aspen copses, and Baltimore Oriole also breeds here. The ponds themselves can host a variety of waterfowl, and various shorebirds can be found, depending on the water levels and time of year. The next stop down the highway is **Swan Lake Provincial Park**. Slightly more than 30 kilometres from Dawson Creek (20 kilometres from Pouce Coupe), turn off to the east, following signs for Swan Lake Provincial Park. A great spot to camp or picnic, Swan Lake is just as good for birding. Several pairs of Eastern Phoebes can be found in the area (especially by the bridge over Tupper Creek), and Spotted Sandpiper, Northern Waterthrush, Least and Alder Flycatchers, Rose-breasted Grosbeak, Black-and-White Warbler, Western Tanager, and Baltimore Oriole are also common in and around the park. Swamp Sparrow and Common Grackle often hang out along the edges of the lake, and out on the water itself, scan for Franklin's and Bonaparte's Gulls, scoters, loons, and grebes. If you were hoping to camp here but find that it's full, check the privately run (and often quieter) Sudeten Campground directly across the highway from the Swan Lake turnoff.

Continuing south down Hwy. 2, turn north onto **Minnal 201 T** (formerly 201 Road North) (about 400 metres west of the Alberta border); a bit more than 1 kilometre up this road, park where it starts to curve to the right and an old track leads straight down to Swan Lake. Like elsewhere in the Peace region, Red-eyed Vireos, Least Flycatchers, Yellow Warblers, Baltimore Orioles, and others can be found in the aspen woodland, so the main reason to stop here is for the lake and marsh birds. Several male Swamp Sparrows hold territory along the shoreline, singing from prominent willow branches. Common Grackles are often skulking nearby, and Soras are common in the nearby cattail and sedge marshes. If you feel like getting wet (or have some sturdy boots), take a stroll through the wet grass along the shoreline to the

Baltimore Orioles

west and explore the vast wetland system at the south end of the lake. Both Le Conte's and Nelson's Sparrow can be found here, and Yellow Rails have been heard on many occasions. This site is also one of the better places in the Peace region to see Great Blue Heron (local rarity) and possibly American Bittern. Out on the lake itself, Red-necked Grebes and Common Loons can be seen and heard, and many species of ducks duck in and out of view as they feed along the perimeter of the lake.

For one of the greatest mixes of warblers in the area, cross the highway and continue up the hill on **Cornack 201 G** (formerly 201 Road South). After the road bends to the right (near the radio tower) and continues toward the top of the hill, you will notice a walking track on the left (south) side heading into the woods. Park where convenient and take some time to explore this area. Breeding warblers here include American Redstart, Yellow Warbler, Blackpoll Warbler, Black-throated Green Warbler, Ovenbird, Northern Waterthrush, Mourning Warbler, and Canada Warbler. Both the Mourning and Canada Warblers are most often seen along the main road in the thick brush. If you visit early in the day, listen for the loud and rich *churee churee churee* of the Mourning Warbler coming from high up in an aspen—otherwise, you'll have to spot him as he skulks through the thick underbrush. This is also a reliable area for Philadelphia, Blue-headed, Warbling, and Red-eyed Vireos—have fun telling them apart by voice. Broad-winged Hawks nest in the area, and of course, the large aspen groves attract large numbers of woodpeckers (mainly Flicker, Hairy, Downy, and Yellow-bellied Sapsucker). Ruffed Grouse are abundant, and Sharp-tailed Grouse are seen occasionally in the nearby farm fields and ditches.

> ## Kiskatinaw Provincial Park

About 27.5 kilometres northwest from Dawson Creek (Hwy. 97 to Fort St. John), turn right onto the Old Alaska Highway, following signs for **Kiskatinaw Provincial Park** and the historic Kiskatinaw curved bridge. Situated against the shaded riverbank of the meandering Kiskatinaw River, the park is an excellent place to camp or have a picnic and escape a hot afternoon. Birding around the campsite can be productive in spring and summer, with Canada Warbler (along slopes with thick vegetation), Black-throated Green Warbler, and Boreal Chickadee being some of the notable breeders.

> ## Braden Road

To visit a reliable Upland Sandpiper breeding site, turn west off Hwy. 97 onto Braden Road (18.3 kilometres south of the Peace River; 3 kilometres north of the Kiskatinaw River). After 2.1 kilometres, rolling pastureland will come up on the right (north) side. Scan carefully for these odd-looking shorebirds and listen for the loud whistling calls (May to July is best).

TAYLOR

The small town of Taylor is a fifteen-minute drive south of Fort St. John, positioned right above the north bank of the Peace

River along the Alaska Highway (Hwy. 97). During migration, the narrow Peace River Valley acts as a natural corridor for songbirds, so after periods of heavy rain, impressive fall-outs of warblers, vireos, and thrushes can sometimes occur. The two main birding roads near Taylor are right along the river (on the south side). The first is **Big Bam Road** (west side of the highway, close to the bridge), which eventually leads to the small Big Bam ski hill (only a couple of kilometres to the west). **Peace Island Park** is signed off the first stretch of road and can be a likely spot throughout the breeding season (June is best) for a variety of eastern specialties, including Eastern Phoebe, Black-and-White Warbler, Canada Warbler, Mourning Warbler, Ovenbird, Blue-headed Vireo, and Rose-breasted Grosbeak. Check the spruce stands along Big Bam Road and in parts of Peace Island Park for Black-throated Green Warbler, Cape May Warbler (dawn is best), and in spruce budworm irruption years, Bay-breasted Warbler. Least Flycatcher, Alder Flycatcher, Yellow-bellied Sapsucker, Red-eyed Vireo, Tennessee Warbler, American Redstart, Yellow Warbler, and Chipping Sparrow are some of the most abundant species, but many more species can be found with a little bit of effort (calm mornings are, of course, ideal).

Another 750 metres south on the highway (up the hill toward Dawson Creek), turn east onto **Johnson Road**. The first 5 kilometres pass through private farms but can be a wonderful stretch for open-country and "edge" specialists such as Eastern Phoebe, Black-billed Magpie, House Wren, Clay-colored Sparrow, Baltimore Oriole, Common Grackle, and Purple Finch. Several of the houses along this road (and on Taylor Sub Road, closer to the highway bridge) have hummingbird feeders. These days, Calliope Hummingbird is the most abundant hummer, followed by Rufous, then the much sought-after (by British Columbia birders anyway) Ruby-throated. Some of the feeders are visible from the road, but it's always best to ask the landowner's permission so as to avoid awkwardness. After passing the last house, the road dips down into the river flood plain and follows a sheltered oxbow. Here the road gets fairly rough, so you may want to proceed on foot. The birding in this zone is fantastic, with several pairs of Barred Owls in the area, as well as many of the eastern birds mentioned along Big Bam Road (above). The recently split (eastern) Winter Wren can also be found here, mostly along small creeks through conifer stands. As always, look out for raptors, especially Broad-winged Hawk, Cooper's Hawk (locally rare), and "Richardson's" Merlin.

FORT ST. JOHN

With around sixteen thousand residents, **Fort St. John** is the largest city in the British Columbia Peace region. It is a major hub for oil and gas work, as well as forestry, farming, and freight movement along the Alaska Highway. From town, the surrounding countryside might not look promising for birds, but there are many hidden gems. When you're figuring out directions, keep in mind that the two main roads in Fort St. John are 100th Avenue (runs east-west) and 100th Street (runs north-south). (See Map 30)

> ➤ North Sewage Lagoons

Fort St. John is blessed with not one but two sewage lagoons. The first is the **North Sewage Lagoons**, which are reached by travelling east on 100th Avenue, 4.8 kilometres from the junction with 100th Street. Stay left at the traffic circle, then proceed north on Airport Road for 750 metres before turning left (north) on 259 Road (the first left after the traffic circle). At 1.5 kilometres, the raised dykes of the sewage lagoons will be obvious. Park near the red gate and walk up onto the dyke on foot. Although birders are

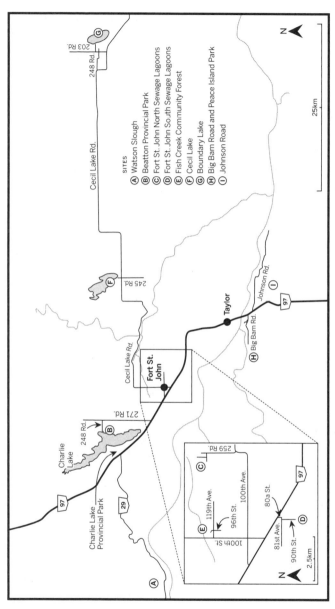

SITES
A Watson Slough
B Beatton Provincial Park
C Fort St. John North Sewage Lagoons
D Fort St. John South Sewage Lagoons
E Fish Creek Community Forest
F Cecil Lake
G Boundary Lake
H Big Bam Road and Peace Island Park
I Johnson Road

25km

203 Rd.
248 Rd.
Cecil Lake Rd.
245 Rd.
Johnson Rd.
97
Taylor
Big Bam Rd.
Cecil Lake Rd.
Fort St. John
271 Rd.
248 Rd.
Charlie Lake
97
Charlie Lake Provincial Park
29

259 Rd.
119th Ave.
96th St.
100th Ave.
100th St.
81st Ave.
90th St.
80a St.
97
2.5km

30 North Peace Overview

410 BIRDFINDING IN BRITISH COLUMBIA

generally tolerated by the facility's workers, it is probably best to visit this site (and the South Sewage Lagoons) outside of regular business hours, since the sewage trucks often flush many of the birds. *Note: Since our last visit to this location, a new chain-link fence has been erected near the gate of this facility, which may mean that public access will be difficult without direct permission from city employees. Use your discretion.*

The north lagoons feature five large ponds with four smaller cells in the southwest corner. From spring thaw through late fall, most of the large ponds are packed with a variety of waterfowl. Eared Grebes and Sora are present throughout summer, and shorebird numbers can be impressive if enough mud is exposed. Available habitat, time of year, and weather patterns are all important factors when looking for shorebirds. Early May to early June is the peak spring movement for most shorebirds here, then mid-July to early September. In addition to the regular Interior mix of shorebirds, Stilt Sandpipers pass through in above-average numbers; White-rumped Sandpipers are scarce but regular in spring (late May to early June), and Hudsonian Godwits are fairly regular (late April to mid-May in spring, then the adults return in mid-July, followed by a few juveniles in September). There is always a chance to see Buff-breasted Sandpipers either at the sewage ponds or in nearby fields. If it has rained recently and you are visiting the area in a migration window, it may be worthwhile to scan the nearby fields and around the nearby airport for golden-plovers, Buff-breasted Sandpiper, and Upland Sandpiper.

> South Sewage Lagoons

From the 100th Street and 100th Avenue intersection, head south on 100th Street, then turn left onto the highway; proceed southeast for 1.4 kilometres, then turn right on 89A Street, then right on 81 Avenue, then left on 90th Street and park at the end.

The bird situation at the **South Sewage Lagoons** is similar to that of the North Sewage Lagoons, but since they're equally productive, it's best to check them both just in case. In recent years, Hudsonian Godwits have been fairly regular in late summer, and other local rarities such as Double-crested Cormorant and Great Blue Heron have been seen. In addition to the large ponds, be sure to check the four small cells in the west portion of the lagoons for shorebirds.

> Fish Creek Community Forest

Travel north on 100th Street for 2 kilometres past 100th Avenue. Turn right on 119th Avenue/West Bypass Road, then left on 96th Street; park behind the college in the designated area. **Fish Creek Community Forest** is mostly composed of older White Spruce trees, making it a great spot for those tough high-pitched warblers: Cape May, Bay-breasted, and Blackburnian. None of these species can be guaranteed in any given year, as their populations fluctuate with spruce budworm outbreaks. Cape May is the most likely, followed by Bay-breasted, then the very rare Blackburnian. The best time is daybreak in early June. Tennessee and Black-throated Green Warblers are common throughout the park—accessible via a well-maintained trail system. American Three-toed Woodpecker, Gray Jay, Boreal Chickadee, and White-wined Crossbill are present year round, whereas Blue-headed Vireo, Ovenbird, and Pacific-slope Flycatcher are some of the summer breeders. The recently split (eastern) Winter Wren is also an annual breeder but can be tough to track down along the shaded gullies of the park.

> Cecil Lake and Boundary Lake

For those hoping to see breeding Palm Warblers in British Columbia, and who aren't travelling up to Fort Nelson, a trip toward the Alberta border will give you the best chance. The muskeg bogs around Cecil Lake and Boundary Lake have fairly poor species diversity but contain a few interesting specialties—namely, Yellow-bellied Flycatcher and Palm Warbler. From Fort St. John, head north on 100th Street past the turnoff for the Fish Creek Community Forest (100th Street will turn into Rose Prairie Road), then make a right on Cecil Lake Road. Zero your odometer and proceed roughly east (the road makes several turns along the way) for 20.4 kilometres. Here 245 Road heads off to the left (north), providing access to the south end of **Cecil Lake**. Don't keep driving in if the track is muddy (after recent rain), as it is very easy to get stuck. It is only about 1 kilometre to the lake, so you should be able to walk it. Palm Warblers are not expected here, but there should be a lot to look at in breeding season—similar species to those found at Swan Lake near Dawson Creek.

Continue along Cecil Lake Road for another 17.2 kilometres. There is a decent patch of muskeg on the north side of the road that has breeding Palm Warbler. Other species in this habitat include Ruby-crowned Kinglet, Hermit Thrush, Swainson's Thrush, Yellow-rumped Warbler, and Lincoln's Sparrow. If you don't find Palm Warblers here, continue along Cecil Lake Road for 21.5 kilometres, then turn left on **203 Road**. This road runs north just west of **Boundary Lake**, which straddles the British Columbia–Alberta border. Gas-extraction work is constant in this area, so be careful and keep in mind that road names can change constantly and new roads are created every year. There are some patches of muskeg with Palm Warbler potential along 203 Road; you may want to also check either way along 248 Road (the first crossroad from the turnoff). Just north of 248 Road is a gas well access road that runs east along a small channel to Boundary Lake itself. If the road is driveable, the lake is well worth a check. Eared Grebes and White-winged Scoters are two of the notable breeders on the lake, along with a range of other possibilities between spring and fall. Look for Rusty Blackbirds

Cape May Warbler

nesting in the area, and listen for the insect-like songs of both Le Conte's and Nelson's Sparrows coming from areas of wet sedge along the roadside. If you continue along the main road (Cecil Lake Road) to the Alberta border, you will reach a pond/slough that is a good spot for breeding Green-winged Teal, Sora, Northern Waterthrush, and a few other wetland species.

➤ Charlie Lake

From the 100th Street and 100th Avenue intersection in downtown Fort St. John, head due west on 100th Avenue and turn right (northwest) onto the highway. After 3.9 kilometres, turn right on 271 Road and follow this straight for 7.7 kilometres, then make a left on 248 Road, following signs to **Beatton Provincial Park**. This 330-hectare park (with camping facilities) is situated on the eastern shores of **Charlie Lake** and offers more than 12 kilometres of trails (groomed for cross-country skiing in the winter) through a mixture of aspen, birch, and spruce forest. In spring and fall, large flocks of diving ducks, including scoters, goldeneye, and scaup, can be seen from the waterfront picnic area. It's possible to find four species of loons (especially in fall), and Franklin's Gull numbers can reach into the thousands in early summer. This species does not breed in British Columbia but seems to enjoy hanging out in this area from May until July. The forest trails can produce a variety of Peace region specialties, the most notable being Cape May Warbler, which favours the large stand of White Spruce near the playing fields. Getting up at dawn is usually a must if you're searching for this species, but on occasion, they will sing at any time of day. Other birding highlights include Blue Jay, Baltimore Oriole, (eastern) Winter Wren, Boreal Chickadee, and, in some years, Bay-breasted Warbler (in the same area as the Cape May).

Return to the highway, turn right (northwest), then proceed for another 2 kilometres or so to another campsite on the right side. Here at the south end of Charlie Lake you can take another opportunity to scope the lake. A variety of shorebirds can sometimes be found here along the beach or where Fish Creek flows out of the lake.

Another 4.5 kilometres up the highway is **Charlie Lake Provincial Park**. It's similar in size to Beatton Provincial Park and also has a number of campsites, but reaching the lake requires a short hike. Many of the same species common at Beatton are present here, such as Least Flycatcher, Black-and-White Warbler, Ovenbird, Yellow Warbler, and Rose-breasted Grosbeak.

ALASKA HIGHWAY: FORT ST. JOHN TO FORT NELSON

The drive north from Fort St. John to Fort Nelson can seem monotonous and uneventful. But look out for both Great Gray Owl and Northern Hawk-Owl, as both species breed in this area and are regularly spotted from the highway at any time of year. Other wildlife such as moose, Black Bear, and caribou are often seen along the roadsides, and there are several short side trips you can make to break up the four-hour trip to Fort Nelson.

The first is **Beatton Airport Road**, which heads off to the east about 40 kilometres north of Fort St. John. This route is only advisable when road conditions are suitable. Out here there are miles and miles of backcountry to explore that could yield some northern specialties, such as Great Gray Owl, Northern Hawk-Owl, Boreal Owl, Sharp-tailed Grouse, Spruce Grouse, Boreal Chickadee, and Bohemian Waxwing. Many of the eastern Peace specialties can be found in appropriate habitat—this area is the northern edge of Black-throated Green Warbler's range in British Columbia.

Farther north up the Alaska Highway is the **Inga Lake recreation site** (around 70 kilometres north of Fort St. John), where you might want to stop for a birdy pit stop.

> Pink Mountain

Another 88 kilometres north is the settlement of Pink Mountain, which is almost halfway between Fort St. John and Fort Nelson. You may want to pay a visit to the little café in the hotel (across the street from the general store) for homemade cookies and sandwiches. From June to September (depending on weather conditions), a trip up to the top of **Pink Mountain** can be worthwhile (main attraction: Rock Ptarmigan). A vehicle with decent clearance and four-wheel drive is highly recommended, but it is possible for any vehicle to make it up, as long as there aren't too many snowdrifts (we did it in a loaded minivan!). From the highway, turn left onto Pink Mountain Road at the north end of town (opposite the old Husky gas station and the now closed Mae's Kitchen). For the next 16 kilometres, the road passes through a mixture of Black Spruce bog (good for breeding Rusty Blackbird), aspen woodland, and Lodgepole Pine stands. At kilometre 16.1, turn right onto an unsigned road (the only marker is a small metal sign for a Husky gas well). Keep right at the next fork and

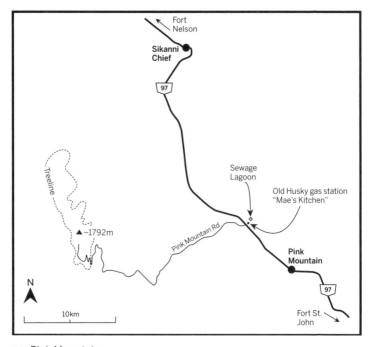

31 Pink Mountain

proceed up the switchbacks to the main ridge of Pink Mountain. You may want to stop here and there along the ascent, as the road passes through a variety of habitats.

Just as you start getting close to the subalpine, listen for singing Gray-cheeked Thrushes (irregular) in patches of thick willow and spruce. Once you're into the subalpine scrub, look out for Dusky Grouse along the roadside; there is a chance to find Willow Ptarmigan as well. Sometimes snowdrifts block the road, but if the entire stretch is passable, we suggest that you drive all the way to either the first summit or the second (at the weather station) and start your hike from there. All three ptarmigan species have been recorded on Pink Mountain; however, Rock and

Willow (albeit rare) are the only regular breeders—in fact, this is probably the most reliable spot in British Columbia for Rock Ptarmigan (around 75 percent success rate with proper effort). The ptarmigan are most often seen among the boulders on the eastern slope of the mountain (20 to 60 metres below the ridge) but are a possibility on top as well. In early June, the males are still mostly white, so they are easy to spot against the reddish and black rocks. Rock Wrens have been heard singing from the rocky bluffs on the west side of the main saddle in past years, making this the northernmost outpost in the world for this species. Indeed, as an isolated outlier of the Rocky Mountains, Pink Mountain is an interesting case study in mountain ecology. The views of the surrounding boreal plains are incredible, and other breeding birds to be found up top include Horned Lark, Townsend's Solitaire, American Pipit, Savannah Sparrow, and Golden-crowned Sparrow.

After returning to the highway, you may want to visit one of Pink Mountain's best-kept birding secrets: the Pink Mountain Sewage Lagoons. Hidden behind Mae's Kitchen (opposite the start of Pink Mountain Road), these minuscule retention ponds are not the most impressive bodies of water to look at, but you just never know what might pop up in the wader or waterfowl department.

FORT NELSON

The drive between Fort St. John and **Fort Nelson** is dominated by miles and miles of Black Spruce. As you approach the Fort Nelson Lowlands, the forests become more diverse and the trees (mainly aspen and White Spruce) are noticeably larger. Because of the abundance of old-growth habitat, many of the eastern forest bird species associated with the Lower Peace region (with the

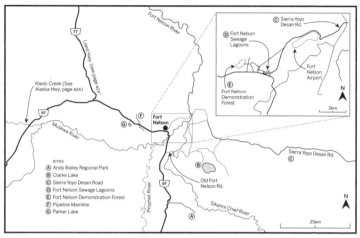

32 Fort Nelson

exception of Black-throated Green Warbler) are more abundant here. On the other hand, open-country specialties such as Baltimore Oriole and Common Grackle are markedly harder to find and in some years are not present at all. A booming natural gas industry has led to the construction of hundreds of roads around Fort Nelson, which has opened up the backcountry to avid birders hungry for exploration. At the same time, however, we must recognize the potential hazards that can come from this rampant escalation in development. Few people travel these forestry and gas roads other than the workers themselves; therefore, it is extremely important to carefully document the important natural features. This will help to show policy-makers what we have to lose. When birding the back roads of Fort Nelson, it is a very good idea to stick to the paved and gravelled roads. The dirt roads can turn into a slick gumbo with the slightest bit of moisture—even large four-wheel-drive vehicles can easily get stuck. Always be aware of other traffic on the roads, and carry a radio if possible.

> Andy Bailey Regional Park

Although this site is no longer a provincial park and thus is not regularly maintained, it is still a lovely place to camp (five sites available—no firewood, no camping fees) or picnic, and the mixed forest and wetland habitat is fantastic for nesting birds in May to July. Look for the signs off the highway (on the east side) 28 kilometres south of Fort Nelson. Stay right at the fork 2.7 kilometres down the road from Hwy. 97 (look for a small white sign indicating the road for the park). The rich mixed forest along the second half of the drive in, along with **Andy Bailey Regional Park** itself, can be great for both northern- and eastern-type birds, including Blue-headed Vireo, (eastern) Winter Wren, Boreal Chickadee, Ovenbird, Bay-breasted Warbler, Cape May Warbler, and Rose-breasted Grosbeak. There are also some wetlands just west of **Andy Bailey Lake** that have nesting waterfowl, Wilson's Snipe, Common Yellowthroat, Northern Waterthrush, Lincoln's Sparrow, Swamp Sparrow, and Rusty Blackbird, among others.

> Clarke Lake

It's impossible to reach the lake itself during the summer months, but the birding in this area can be very productive for forest birds. Just south of Fort Nelson, the Alaska Highway crosses the Muskwa River. Drive 5.5 kilometres south of this bridge (along the highway), and turn east onto Old Fort Nelson Road; this will take you down to the Fort Nelson River and across to the other side. From here, take a left at the first major fork, and the rest is up to you. The main road passes close to **Clarke Lake**, but you won't know it because it's blocked by thick forest. Be sure to carry a back roads map with you. Solitary Sandpiper, Swainson's Thrush, Yellow-breasted Sapsucker, American Three-toed Woodpecker, Least Flycatcher, Red-eyed

Vireo, Winter Wren, Ruby-crowned Kinglet, American Red-start, Chipping Sparrow, and White-throated Sparrow are some of the common species here.

> ## Sierra Yoyo Desan Road

Boasting one of the coolest-sounding names in British Columbia, this road is also the main service road into the extreme northeast corner of the province. It is a wide, gravelled road that is drivable by most vehicles in the summer months (if it has rained recently, avoid pulling off onto the slick muddy shoulders). This road is reached by following signs to the airport northeast of town, then continuing straight across the bridge. The **Fort Nelson Airport** might be worth a quick check, particularly in spring and fall, when longspurs, Upland Sandpipers, and other shorebirds touch down in the grassy flats (especially after periods of rain). Sand-hill Cranes are a possibility throughout summer, and a singing Sprague's Pipit was recorded in early June 2001. After crossing the bridge, the Sierra Yoyo Desan (s y d) is the main road for the next several hundred miles. We don't expect you to get out that far, but if you do plan an extended trip, be sure to have a full tank of gas and watch your mileage.

There are many good roads that branch off from the **Sierra Yoyo Desan Road**, so it's up to you to judge where you want to go. Two species that might lead you out this way include Bay-breasted Warbler—look and listen in patches of old-growth aspen stands mixed with White Spruce—and Palm Warbler, which sticks to the extensive mixed pine and muskeg bogs far-ther along the road, which is also habitat for Yellow-bellied Flycatchers. In addition to the variety of forest types, there are a few marshes along this road where Marsh Wrens, Le Conte's Sparrows, and Black Terns can be found (this is the northern edge of their respective breeding ranges).

Be aware that there has been a huge increase in natural gas work in this area, and traffic can be heavy along this road. Be sure to find safe pull-offs to park, and remember that traffic will be lighter on the side roads. Early morning is best for light traffic; plus it is by far the best time for birding. Finally, be prepared to encounter millions of mosquitoes!

> Fort Nelson Sewage Lagoons

There are two main sets of ponds—the first group is fairly obvious along the main street in town opposite the Woodlands Inn. The other group can be accessed via a dirt track leading northeast from the main ponds, but this road is often gated. You can either walk in or try accessing them from Airport Road (eastern branch—see Map 32). Both sets of ponds tend to be low on shorebirds because of high water levels, but sometimes you get lucky. Waterfowl numbers can be high, particularly in spring and fall, and a variety of gulls will use the ponds from time to time. The forest around the smaller ponds can be home to songbirds, including Blue-headed and Philadelphia Vireos (all four vireo species are common, making for an interesting challenge in birdsong identification). A pair of Eastern Phoebes nests on the service building beside the smaller set of ponds, whereas Clay-colored and Savannah Sparrows both nest in the grass clumps and shrubs right along the highway in front of the large ponds.

> Fort Nelson Demonstration Forest

If you're just passing through Fort Nelson and looking for one or two quick places to bird, this is an ideal place to stop. Near the west end of town, turn right (north) on 55th Street/Simpson Trail, then turn left (west) on Mountainview Drive after 750 metres. The **Fort Nelson Demonstration Forest** parking area is at the end of the short road and is a fabulous spot for a walk or ski. Because of the mix in timber and understorey, many eastern specialties can be found here during the breeding season, including Yellow-bellied Sapsucker, Blue Jay, Philadelphia Vireo, (eastern) Winter Wren, Tennessee Warbler, Cape May Warbler, Bay-breasted Warbler, Canada Warbler, Magnolia Warbler, Black-and-White Warbler, and Rose-breasted Grosbeak. We hope the bugs aren't too bad, but you may want to apply some spray. Spruce Grouse (Taiga subspecies), Ruffed Grouse, American Three-toed Woodpecker, Gray Jay, Boreal Chickadee, and White-winged Crossbills are also regular year round.

> Pipeline Mainline

About 8.5 kilometres west of Fort Nelson (along the Alaska Highway), look for the signed **Pipeline Mainline** at a yellow gate on the south side of the road. The gate is usually closed and locked, but sometimes it is open. Proceed by vehicle only if the road is dry. Otherwise, you can walk or bike in.

This is a nice birding road since there is virtually no traffic (as of 2011), and several of the tough eastern specialties can be found here, including Cape May Warbler (in the spruce trees along the first 2 kilometres of the road) and Connecticut Warbler (in the aspen copses just before you reach the Muskwa River (about 8.7 kilometres down the road). Palm Warbler and Yellow-bellied Flycatcher are numerous among the boggy patches of tamarack and Black Spruce between kilometres 3 and 5, and Le Conte's Sparrows, Solitary Sandpipers, and Green-winged Teal all nest or forage in the wet sedge marshes along the roadside and sometimes along the ditch beside the highway at the yellow gate. Both Canada and Mourning Warblers can sometimes be heard singing from the thick brush near the beginning of the road, and Broad-winged Hawks can sometimes be seen soaring above treeline.

> Parker Lake

Another 3.5 kilometres west along the highway from Pipeline
Road is the unmarked turnoff to **Parker Lake**. It's the first left
after Pipeline Road (south side, opposite a branch of the Old
Alaska Highway). The road is only 1 kilometre long but can sometimes be muddy and filled with deep ruts—most of the time it
should be drivable for any vehicle, though large campers and RVs
will have trouble turning around. At the end of the road, there is
a small wharf for fishing and launching small watercraft. Marsh
Wrens and Common Yellowthroats nest in the cattails along the
edge of the lake, and a male Yellow-bellied Flycatcher is often
heard giving its *chebenk* song from atop one of the spruce trees
near the end of the road. Bonaparte's Gulls nest nearby and can
often be seen on the lake and in the trees on the opposite side.
Common Loons, Red-necked Grebes, and Barrow's Goldeneyes
are some of the breeding water birds, but there are plenty of other
species that pass through before and after breeding, from swans
and scoters to terns, gulls, and jaegers.

> Liard Highway (Hwy. 77 North)

Around 27 kilometres west of Fort Nelson, the Alaska Highway
passes the turnoff for the **Liard Highway** (Hwy. 77) north to Fort
Liard in the Northwest Territories. In 2008 and 2009, paving
was completed along the British Columbia section, providing
yet another easy way to explore the north. There are many side
roads that branch off from Hwy. 77, but only a few are suitable
for casual birders. If Bay-breasted Warbler is one of your big targets, this area is probably the best in British Columbia (though
breeding populations will fluctuate year to year).

The first stop of interest is 10 kilometres up the road; look for
the **Beaver Lake recreation site** sign on the right (east) side. This
small camping area is a well-known spot for Cape May Warbler.

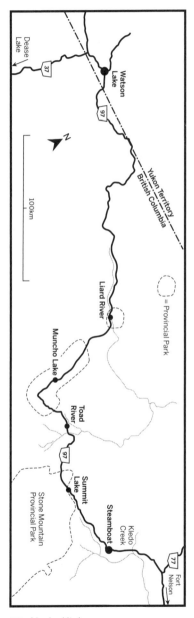

33 Alaska Highway

Both species of goldeneye, as well as Bufflehead, breed around the lake, and Spotted Sandpipers can usually be seen teetering along the shoreline in summer. Also in summer, listen for the noisy family of Yellow-breasted Sapsuckers that inhabits the aspens around the campsite. Other campsite nesters include Great Horned Owl, Merlin, (eastern) Winter Wren, Northern Waterthrush, and White-winged Crossbills.

Moving north up the highway, you may want to stop wherever looks safe and promising for birding, as many birds found deep in the forest can also be seen along the roadside. Another 34 kilometres north of Beaver Lake (just after you cross the Fort Nelson River), turn left onto an obvious forestry road. Although these side roads sometimes change names depending on which oil company is leasing them, this particular road is known by locals as the **Patry Mainline** and should be signed as such. Be wary of loaded logging trucks. Because it is gravelled, it can generally be driven in most weather conditions but gets quite dusty when dry. You wind down a small hill at the beginning, and then the road straightens out as it heads due west past a workers' camp. It should be noted that along this straight stretch you are driving past one of the few stands of Jack Pine in British Columbia (a tick for your tree list!). Stop if you want along this first stretch, but it's generally not worth it since traffic is usually busy and few birds use the pine trees other than Yellow-rumped Warblers, Chipping Sparrows, and Dark-eyed Juncos.

Between kilometres 9 and 10, you will come to an obvious fork (after passing a work camp on the right). Occasionally, the right-hand road at the fork is gated. If this is the case, park well off to the side and walk up the road. Although you won't be able to cover the same amount of ground, there is plenty of productive habitat along the first stretch of road. Both of these roads stretch for many kilometres and have been newly resurfaced (as of 2010), so they should be easy to drive on. (Once again: Be wary of logging and gas-work traffic, and use a radio if you have one.) Both roads are great for birds—particularly the much sought-after Bay-breasted Warbler and Philadelphia Vireo. The Bay-breasted Warblers favour stands of large mixed aspen and spruce; their slurred song is extremely high-pitched and can sound like a Cape May Warbler from a distance. Also be aware that both Black-and-White Warblers and American Redstarts can produce similar sounding songs.

In addition to the abundant birding (late May to mid-June is best—it can get eerily quiet for birdsong in July and August), this area is well known for larger wildlife as well. Small groups of Wood Bison are often seen along the Patry Mainline as well as the highway, and the Black Bears here are notoriously unafraid of humans, so be sure to act responsibly and safely when birding out in the bush.

A little more than 66 kilometres north of the Patry Mainline turnoff along Hwy. 77 (and only 26 kilometres from the Northwest Territories border) is the turnoff to **Maxhamish Lake Provincial Park**. This small park, about 15 kilometres west of the highway, lies on the southeast shore of the large Maxhamish Lake. In recent years, the quality of this road has deteriorated and is probably only drivable by a four-wheel-drive vehicle under dry conditions. The birding is similar to the rest of Hwy. 77, but since you're so far north, there is always room for some birding discoveries because few birders come by this way. Pacific Loon and Northern Shrike are two examples of species whose breeding ranges barely creep into British Columbia in this area; Arctic Tern and American Tree Sparrow might also be possibilities. If you're desperate for gas, Fort Liard is another 64 kilometres to the north; otherwise, turn around and head back to the Alaska Highway (Hwy. 97).

ALASKA HIGHWAY:
HWY. 77 JUNCTION TO WATSON LAKE, YUKON

> Kledo Creek

Around 25.5 kilometres west of the Liard Highway turnoff, the Alaska Highway passes over **Kledo Creek**. Here there is a pull-off on the north side of the highway. The cottonwoods along the creek provide habitat for a mix of songbirds, and both Barn and Cliff Swallows nest underneath the highway bridge. Just west of the bridge, there is a road heading south marked by a yellow gate. You may notice some No Trespassing signs, but birders are generally allowed to go in as long as you stick to the roads. The main stands of spruce can be promising spots for Cape May and Bay-breasted Warblers in some years, whereas the surrounding mixed scrub and riparian habitat is loaded with Least and Hammond's Flycatchers, Ovenbird, Mourning Warbler, American Redstart, Yellow Warbler, White-throated Sparrow, and more. If you're looking for more, the **Kledo Forest Service Road** branches off from the Alaska Highway northward just east of the bridge—it is not well maintained so may not be suitable to drive if conditions are poor; however, hiking along the first stretch can be very productive in the mornings.

> Stone Mountain Provincial Park

As you continue westward, the Northern Rockies will become more apparent and there are several rest stops where you can marvel at the changing scenery. As you approach the mountains, you are also entering an overlap zone in avifauna (much like Pine Pass and the Tumbler Ridge area to the south), where western birds such as Townsend's Warbler, MacGillivray's Warbler, and Pacific Wren mingle with their eastern counterparts—so be cautious when identifying birds by sound only.

The beautiful **Stone Mountain Provincial Park** is 82 kilometres west of Kledo Creek. Vehicle accessible campsites are available on a first-come, first-served basis at the east end of the park, near Summit Lake. There are numerous picnic sites and lots of awesome hiking opportunities. Not surprisingly, most of the park is covered in upper-elevation habitat, so the birdlife will reflect this—Gray Jays, Boreal Chickadee, Townsend's Solitaire, Yellow-rumped (Myrtle) Warbler, and Golden-crowned Sparrow are some of the common species, and all three ptarmigan species can be found in the alpine: Willow in willow, Rock in tundra, and White-tailed up on the rocky ridgelines. Also look out for American Tree Sparrow and Brewer's (Timberline) Sparrow in the alpine willow scrub. The **Summit Peak Trail** (north of the highway just east of Summit Lake) is probably the most reliable hiking trail for ptarmigan, whereas the road to the microwave tower and the **Flower Springs Lake Trail** are also recommended. Anecdotal reports of American Golden-Plover, Lapland Longspur, and Snow Bunting in summer suggest that this park could yield some surprises with more birding coverage. **Summit Lake**, as well as the other small lakes in the park, can be a good spot for summering waterfowl, including both Surf and White-winged Scoters.

> Toad River

Just west of Stone Mountain Provincial Park is the small, quirky settlement of **Toad River**. The aspen copses around this area, particularly on the opposite side of the airfield, can sometimes produce Connecticut Warbler, as well as other more common "eastern" birds, such as Blue-headed Vireo, Philadelphia Vireo, and Ovenbird. Eight kilometres west of the Toad River Lodge, take the first right turn (north) off the highway, marked by a sign for Stone Mountain Safaris. Cross the Toad River then continue on the main road (keep left at the turnoff for Stone Mountain Safaris on the right). This road is known as the **Nonda Creek Corridor** and is an easy way to get up into the alpine. Four-wheel drive and good clearance are recommended but not essential if the road is dry; it's around an 18-kilometre drive from the highway to the Northwestel repeater towers at the top.

Along the first stretch of Nonda Creek, listen for Townsend's Warbler, as well as Tennessee Warbler (abundant), Northern Waterthrush, Lincoln's Sparrow, and Ruffed Grouse. Both Spotted and Solitary Sandpipers can be found in the roadside ditches. As you climb into the subalpine, look and listen for Gray-cheeked Thrush, Wilson's Warbler, and Chipping Sparrow in the mixed spruce and willow. Three species of *Zonotrichia* sparrows can be found along the road: White-throated lower down, White-crowned in the subalpine, and Golden-crowned near the top in the stunted firs and willow scrub. In addition to the Gray-cheeked Thrushes, the other main draw of this road is, of course, the possibility of seeing ptarmigan. All three species are possible, though it seems that Willow Ptarmigan is the most regular. Once up at the top, American Pipit and Savannah Sparrows are common, and there is a possibility of finding Brewer's (Timberline) Sparrow. This ridge provides panoramic views of the Sentinel Range, including Mount McLearn directly to the north. If you plan to hike through the alpine away from the road, remember that you are now in Grizzly country, so bear spray and noisemakers are recommended.

> › Muncho Lake

Another 40 kilometres farther along the highway is **Muncho Lake Provincial Park**, boasting a gorgeous array of azure lakes, snow-capped mountains, alluvial fans, and alpine meadows. There are fewer hiking trails than in Stone Mountain Provincial Park, but there are still plenty of roadside wildlife-viewing areas, and the lake itself can host sizable numbers of scaup, scoters, loons, and gulls (mainly Mew and Herring) throughout summer. Although there are fuel and other supplies available at the Muncho Lake Lodge, be advised that they can be two or even three times the normal price.

> Liard River Hot Springs

Originally called Tropical Valley because of the warm swamps and diverse flora surrounding the hot pools, **Liard River Hot Springs Provincial Park** is a must-see location for Alaska Highway travellers. Take a break from the long drive by bathing in either of the natural pools, and look out for a few birds while you're at it. Nothing like combining birding and bathing! The only drawback is that the park can get a bit busy in summer (the pools are open year round). This area is well-signed off the highway about 60 kilometres north of Muncho Lake.

The boardwalk from the parking lot to the hot springs passes first through a large warm-water swamp where Mew Gull nest and moose are regularly seen. Once you're into the diverse forest in and around the pools, the birding can be fantastic, as this is the western limit for many of the Peace and Fort Nelson specialties, including Baltimore Oriole, Philadelphia Vireo, and Blue-headed Vireo. MacGillivray's and Mourning Warblers can be seen here singing side by side, as well as a variety of other northern species.

> Watson Lake to Whitehorse, Yukon

From the hot springs, it's another 135 kilometres to the Yukon border, then 72 kilometres more to Watson Lake, Yukon. The highway passes through a mix of habitats dominated by subalpine fir, spruce, and aspen—stop wherever you want, as there is no one spot that is better than any other. You may want to check the small lake on the right (south) side of the highway, just before you reach the Yukon border the first time (the highway dips back into British Columbia several times before reaching Whitehorse), as Pacific Loon is an annual breeder and Arctic Terns can often be seen in summer. In between here and Watson Lake, listen for Cape May and Bay-breasted Warblers in mature stands of White Spruce, particularly at Contact Creek and Irons Creek (signed from the highway). Boreal Chickadee, Yellow-bellied Flycatcher, Blackpoll Warbler, and White-winged Crossbills are usually present in large numbers, and Gray-checked Thrushes can be found in and around thick willow wetlands. Note that this is the northwest edge of White-throated Sparrow and Swamp Sparrow range, and be sure to keep an eye on the roadsides, as both Spruce Grouse and Ruffed Grouse are commonly seen.

ATLIN

Contributed in part by Syd Cannings

Atlin Road (Yukon Hwy. 7) is a stunning route that leaves Tagish Road 1.7 kilometres southwest of Jake's Corner on the Alaska Highway and winds through dry boreal forest to the small town of Atlin, 100 kilometres to the south. It is one of the most scenic roads in British Columbia, with sweeping views of expansive lakes and distant, snow-capped mountains. As the road reaches Little Atlin Lake, it passes the eastern slopes of the towering marble cliffs of White Mountain before traversing the open, sandy woodlands of Agay Mene Territorial Park. Just south of the Yukon border, you leave the sandy hills behind, and for the remainder of the journey, the road parallels the eastern shore of Atlin Lake (though the lake is almost always out of sight). At first, you are crossing the lower slopes of the mountains to the east, but as you approach Atlin, you travel through a broad forested plain of glacial debris, with many kettle lakes and wetlands.

As you travel south, the first notable roadside lake you will encounter is **Grayling Lake** (25.4 kilometres south of Yukon; 25 kilometres north of Atlin on the east side). Visit this lake, along with a few other smaller ones nearby, for waterfowl, as well as nesting Arctic Terns and Bonaparte's Gulls. Next up is **Davie Hall Lake** (38 kilometres south of Yukon; 12.4 kilometres north of Atlin)—another great lake for waterfowl migration (including scoters), as well as Bonaparte's Gulls and the occasional breeding pair of Pacific Loons.

Look for **Fourth of July Creek Road** on the left (east) side, 2.5 kilometres south of Davie Hall Lake. This road will take you up into the subalpine to the **MacDonald Lakes**, where Red-breasted Mergansers breed. There are numerous ponds and marshes in the area that harbour a plethora of water birds, both in spring and fall and during the breeding season. The lakes are 7.4 kilometres up the road, and farther along there is a side road that heads up the mountain to an old mine site. This will give a motorized head start for those wishing to explore the alpine here, where Willow Ptarmigan and other tundra-loving species can be found.

From the bottom of Fourth of July Creek Road it is fewer than 10 kilometres to the town of **Atlin**. You will pass a couple more small lakes along the way that might be worth scanning. From the town, you have a brilliant view of British Columbia's largest natural lake; perhaps you will appreciate why the locals call it "the most beautiful place on Earth; in any season, in any weather." Herring Gulls nest on the islets offshore, and a variety of water birds can be seen out on the big lake or in the marshes and ponds around town. For more information about Atlin and a few of the attractions to the south, visit discoveratlin.com.

HAINES ROAD

From Haines Junction, Yukon, it's a 238-kilometre drive to Haines, Alaska. Make sure to gas up in Haines Junction beforehand. If you are planning on spending several days birding **Haines Road**, it is essential that you stock up on camping and food supplies and bring an extra 20-litre jerry can of gasoline, since there are no services until you reach Haines, Alaska (and remember your passport if you want to enter the USA).

The attraction of this road for British Columbia birders is that it provides easy access to alpine habitats more typical of Alaska and Yukon. Northwestern specialties such as Willow Ptarmigan, Gyrfalcon, Arctic Tern, Gray-cheeked Thrush, American Tree-Sparrow, and Common Redpoll are common, and this is the only area south of the 60th parallel where Wandering Tattlers are known to breed in Canada. This used to be a reliable road for Smith's Longspur, but because of climate change, the willows have grown up around their former breeding sites near Kelsall Lake. They favour grassy meadows with small, stunted willows only 1 metre tall. It is still possible to find this habitat on the upper slopes of the surrounding hills, so perhaps an adventurous birder will be able to reconfirm the presence of this attractive denizen of mountain tundra. Since the area is so under-birded, it is certainly possible to make some neat discoveries.

It is almost exactly 100 kilometres to the British Columbia border from Haines Junction (Yukon Hwy. 3). On the drive south, you will pass two large lakes: Kathleen Lake to the west and Dezadeash Lake to the east. Once across into British Columbia, you have made it to the fabled Haines Triangle. From the British Columbia–Yukon border, the now-paved Haines Road slowly climbs up the Tatshenshini River Valley, across Datlasaka and

Mosquito Flats, covered in boggy fens and willow scrub, then up over the Chilkat Pass and down the Klehini River to the border with Alaska. Summer is generally the best time to visit, as weather is optimal and the birds are abundant. Birdsong peaks in June, but many of the summer breeders can still be seen in July and August.

We encourage you to stop wherever you please, but the **Twin Lakes** (signed) are certainly worth checking (14 kilometres south of the Yukon border). Arctic Terns can usually be observed in high numbers during summer, with a few Bonaparte's, Mew, and Herring Gulls mixed in. American Wigeon, Greater Scaup (uncommon), Lesser Yellowlegs, Short-billed Dowitcher, Wilson's Snipe, and Common Yellowthroat all breed here.

Check out **Kelsall Lake**. The access road is sometimes a little tricky to see, but you should be able to find it on the east side, about 12 kilometres south of the Twin Lakes. It is usually impossible to drive all the way to the lake because of washouts, but it is only a 3.5-kilometre hike from the road in flat but sometimes wet terrain. The willows here are loaded with Willow Ptarmigan, Wilson's Warbler, American Tree Sparrow, Golden-crowned Sparrow, Fox Sparrow, and Common Redpoll, whereas the wetlands can yield Wilson's Snipe, Lesser Yellowlegs, and Least Sandpiper. The lake itself can be quiet in summer, but you never know what you might find—May and September are best. *Note: Be extremely wary of Grizzly Bears, especially if you're hiking away from the main road. This area supports a healthy population, and they can easily be out of sight in the dense willows. If you plan to venture away from the road, we advise you not to go alone and inform others of your intentions. Carry bear spray and make lots of noise when passing through thick patches of willows.*

Along Haines Road, you will pass several hiking trailheads on the west side of the road—some are short and some are longer, but all follow creeks uphill into **Tatshenshini-Alsek Provincial**

Willow Ptarmigan

Park. Once you clear the willow scrub, it is easy to hike around the tundra at the base of the St. Elias Mountains. It is a good idea to bring a map and a GPS along, since once you lose sight of the main road it is easy to get confused by the abundance of small lakes and rivers. Once out of the willows, look for Semipalmated Plover, American Pipit, and Horned Lark in the mossy tundra. Wandering Tattlers are fairly common around the small lakes and shingle rivers—hiking up Stonehouse Creek (signed off Haines Road) is one of the quickest ways into their preferred habitat. Arctic Tern, Herring Gull, and Mew Gull all breed around these lakes, as well as Least Sandpiper and Savannah Sparrow. Snow Buntings have been recorded in the rocky slopes above, and perhaps an intrepid birder will one day confirm Northern Wheatear from those high rocky ridges. Both Rock and White-tailed Ptarmigan are possible in the high country, and Gyrfalcon and Golden Eagle nest on the cliffs.

After passing the impressive **Three Guardsmen** peaks, the road starts to descend swiftly toward Haines, Alaska. Just before the border, habitat along the roadside will take on the distinctly "coastal" feel of Western Hemlock and Sitka Spruce forest. Sooty Grouse, Red-breasted Sapsucker, and Chestnut-backed Chickadee are some of the coastal birds to be expected here.

ANNOTATED CHECKLIST

The following list provides information about some of the species that are harder to find in British Columbia, particularly those of interest to visiting birders.

Eurasian Wigeon: Fairly rare in the Interior (best time is spring and fall), and rare to uncommon on the coast (but increasing); often associated with flocks of American Wigeon. *Best Places:* Blackie Spit, Boundary Bay, Brunswick Point (all near Vancouver)—all three of these areas can sometimes produce more than twenty in winter if you're lucky.

Chukar: This introduced species from Eurasia is found in the dry grasslands and rocky slopes of the Thompson-Okanagan region and is more often heard than seen. *Best Places:* Vaseux Cliffs (Okanagan), Sun Rivers subdivision (Kamloops), and along the slopes of the Fraser Canyon between Spences Bridge and Ashcroft. In winter, a reliable spot is the hay stacks or cattle-feeding stations just west of Richter Pass (Hwy. 3 between Osoyoos and Keremeos).

Gray Partridge: Another Eurasian introduction, this secretive species is found in the grasslands and sagebrush lands of the Okanagan and Similkameen Valleys. *Best Places:* White Lake, Haynes' Lease Ecological Reserve, and Chopaka Customs (all in the South Okanagan region).

Spruce Grouse: Common throughout the boreal forests of British Columbia. Easiest time to see them is in spring, when the males are displaying, and in summer, when family groups are roaming around. *Best Places:* E.C. Manning Provincial Park alpine trails, kilometres 22 to 28 on the Shuttleworth Road (Okanagan Falls), and the subalpine hiking trails of the Rocky Mountains.

Willow Ptarmigan: Present in low numbers in the Northern Rockies and coastal mountains but most common (and easily accessed) in the Haines Triangle, where hundreds can be seen displaying in spring and early summer. *Best Places:* British Columbia section of Haines Road between Haines Junction, Yukon, and Haines, Alaska. Hudson Bay Mountain (in Smithers) and Mount Spieker (in Tumbler Ridge) are also fairly reliable sites.

Rock Ptarmigan: Similar to Willow in that they are found occasionally in the Rockies and Coast Mountains but are most numerous toward the Yukon border. *Best Place:* Pink Mountain (Peace region).

White-tailed Ptarmigan: Our most widespread ptarmigan species. Found in most mountain ranges above treeline. *Best Places:* Mount Quinesco (Cathedral Provincial Park), Mount Cheam (Chilliwack), Whistler, and many others. In spring and early summer, call playback can be an effective way to bring in territorial males.

Sooty Grouse: Common throughout coastal British Columbia (away from urban Vancouver) but difficult to locate outside of spring, when males are hooting. *Best Places:* Mount Wells (Victoria), Cypress Provincial Park (north of Vancouver), and E.C. Manning Provincial Park.

Dusky Grouse: Found throughout the open forests and grasslands of the southern Interior and farther north in alpine environments. *Best Places:* Kilpoola Lake and Anarchist Mountain areas (both near Osoyoos) and any alpine hiking area away from the Coast and Cascade Mountains. Some can be seen at Manning Park side by side with Sooties. Beware of intergrades in that area and in the Fraser Canyon.

Yellow-billed Loon: A rare migrant/winter visitor to most of the province but can be found in a few key areas. *Best Places:* The coastline between Comox and Oyster River (Vancouver Island) and the Hecate Strait ferry crossing (where more than twenty are regularly seen each winter).

Clark's Grebe: Rare and local; one to two pairs breed regularly at Salmon Arm Bay (mixed in with Westerns), and the same might be true for the less-frequented Western Grebe colony on Duck Lake (Creston).

Black-footed Albatross and other "tubenoses": The only reliable way to look for albatrosses, fulmars, and shearwaters is to get on a pelagic boat trip off the outer coast. *Best Places:* West coast of Vancouver Island and Hecate Strait ferry crossing.

Brandt's Cormorant: Breeds mostly along the outer coast of the southern half of British Columbia; more widespread in winter, when it can be commonly seen around Vancouver, Victoria, and the main ferry crossings. *Best Places:* Tsawwassen ferry jetty, Victoria waterfront, and Pacific Rim National Park.

Swainson's Hawk: A local breeder of open grasslands in the Thompson-Okanagan region. *Best Places*: Anarchist Mountain (east of Osoyoos), Vernon Commonage, and the grasslands surrounding Merritt, Kamloops, and Savona. Only present in British Columbia between April and early September.

Gyrfalcon: Breeds in the mountains of extreme northern British Columbia and winters in small numbers in the Interior and along the coast. *Best Places:* Haines Triangle (summer) and Boundary Bay (winter).

Yellow Rail: This secretive species is widespread but extremely local in the Peace River and Fort Nelson Lowlands, as well as the Chilcotin Plateau. *Best Places*: Watson Slough (Fort St. John), East Pine rest area (east of Chetwynd), and the Del Rio marshes (north of Chetwynd).

Wandering Tattler: Scarce but regular migrant along the British Columbia coast and breeds locally in the Haines Triangle. *Best Places:* For May and August migration, check the Ogden Point jetty (Victoria), Botanical Beach (Port Renfrew), the Iona south jetty (Richmond), and rocky shorelines in Pacific Rim National Park. If you're travelling along Haines Road in summer, look for tattlers along streams and lakes near the Chilkat Pass.

Upland Sandpiper: Local breeder in the grasslands and farm country of the Peace River Lowlands. *Best Places:* East Pine rest area (Chetwynd) and along Braden Road (south of Fort St. John).

Sharp-tailed Sandpiper: A rare but regular fall migrant along the British Columbia coast (September to October). *Best Places:* Reifel Refuge, Boundary Bay, Sandspit Airport, and anywhere else where large numbers of Pectoral Sandpipers congregate.

Heermann's Gull: Large numbers of this attractive gull show up around south Vancouver Island each summer and continue into early fall. *Best Places:* Victoria waterfront, Jordan River, and Pacific Rim National Park.

Ancient Murrelet: The best time to see this species is in late fall and early winter (October to February), when large numbers pass through the Georgia Strait on their southward dispersal routes. In summer, most head up to Haida Gwaii to breed, but a few can still be seen occasionally off the west coast of Vancouver Island. *Best Places*: Roberts Creek jetty (Sunshine Coast), the ferry between Little River and Powell River, Cape Lazo (Comox), Lighthouse Marine Park (Point Roberts, Washington), and any good headland between Victoria and Port Renfrew where you can scope the Strait of Juan de Fuca.

Tufted Puffin/Cassin's Auklet: Both are rare in the Georgia Strait, so if you want a shot at these two Pacific specialties, you'll either have to take a pelagic trip out of Ucluelet or Tofino or hope for some luck on the Hecate Strait ferry to Haida Gwaii. With luck you may see both species on the Port Angeles Ferry out of Victoria (late summer).

Flammulated Owl: Despite being locally common throughout the southern Interior during the breeding season (they migrate south in fall and return in early May), few people have actually seen one. The best strategy is to visit an area where they are known to occur between mid-May and early June, then at night listen for their soft hoots. *Best Places:* Lindley Creek Road (Merritt), Max Lake (Penticton), Lac du Bois (Kamloops), and Kilpoola Lake road (Osoyoos).

Spotted Owl: This species has declined to the point where extirpation will be inevitable without intensive re-introduction effort, habitat conservation, and Barred Owl control. There are probably only about ten individuals left in the wild and perhaps only one or two active pairs—all of which are in remote areas. *Best Places:* Your chances are extremely slim, but for the best shot, search in old-growth forests around the western end of E.C. Manning Provincial Park and in the Stein Valley (west of Lytton).

Boreal Owl: Boreal Owls are numerous in the Interior of British Columbia and are present all year. However, because their habitat tends to be cold, snowy, and far away from major urban centres, most people consider it a tough or even "mythical" bird. The best strategy is to visit potential breeding territories (mature stands of subalpine fir, spruce, and aspen, with nearby boggy meadows for hunting opportunities) between February and early May. If you're lucky, the owls will be giving their territorial song. *Best Places:* Upper sections of the Carmi/Shuttleworth/201 Roads (South Okanagan), Whitewater ski hill (Nelson), and practically every logging road in central and northern British Columbia. In the south, any high mountain pass or ski village with subalpine fir could be worth a check.

Burrowing Owl: Sadly, British Columbia's last truly "wild" Burrowing Owls were extirpated in the 1970s, but in the last two decades a significant captive breeding and re-introduction program has created a number of new colonies in the southern Interior grasslands. Most of the birds are on private land but with luck and persistence some can be seen from public roads. *Best Places:* Lac du Bois grasslands and Separation Lake (both near Kamloops) and Beaver Ranch/Guichon Flats (Nicola Valley).For more information on the recovery effort, visit burrowingowlbc.org.

Williamson's Sapsucker: Locally common in large stands of Western Larch and Trembling Aspen in the southern Interior of British Columbia. The best time is April, when the birds are setting up territories. Listen for their distinctive double-noted drum and grating calls. *Best Places:* Venner Meadows (east of Okanagan Falls), Wagon Wheel Road (Anarchist Mountain, east of Osoyoos), and Lindley Creek Road (Merritt).

White-headed Woodpecker: Like the Spotted Owl, White-headed Woodpecker numbers have declined drastically at the northern end of their range, mainly because of habitat loss. Unless one has been recently reported, your best shot is to search carefully in mature stands of Ponderosa Pine in the Similkameen, Okanagan, and Kettle Valleys. *Best Places:* McKinney Road between kilometres 9 and 12, as well as nearby side roads (east of Oliver); the forest around Mahoney Lake on the Green Lake Road (southwest of Okanagan Falls); and around the Regal Ridge development on the western and southern slopes of Anarchist Mountain (east of Osoyoos).

Gray Flycatcher: First discovered in Canada in 1984, these tail-wagging *Empids* are now regular but local breeders in the Okanagan Valley. *Best Place:* McKinney Road (Between kilometres 9 to 10.5). There are several other places but most are harder to get to and the birds are not present every year. The McKinney spot has been reliable for more than twenty years. Be aware that both Dusky and Hammond's Flycatchers breed in the same area, so make sure to study those call notes and fieldmarks beforehand.

Sky Lark: See page 25 for details. *Best Places:* Bulb fields along Middle Saanich Road and in the farm fields of Martindale Flats (Victoria area).

Sage Thrasher: Like many other grassland species, this one has declined significantly in Canada, and although the numbers are low (and sometimes nearly non-existent), the Okanagan Valley is probably the best place in the country to see them. Although some thrashers show up in mid-May, the majority of records come from pairs that show up in late June or July and remain into August—probably to raise second broods or to re-nest after a failed attempt farther south in the USA. In most years, there are only a few birds seen, but every once in a while, as many as ten or more pairs will nest in the South Okanagan and Similkameen Valleys. *Best Places*: White Lake (southwest of Penticton), Kilpoola Lake, and Chopaka Customs (both west of Osoyoos).

Cape May Warbler: This spruce-loving warbler is widespread in the Northern Rockies, Peace River and Fort Nelson Lowlands, and northern British Columbia but can often prove elusive because of its preference for remote spruce stands, early mornings, and an extremely high-pitched song that many have difficulty hearing over the chatter of every other bird in the neighbourhood. Numbers will fluctuate depending on spruce budworm outbreaks (the Cape May's favourite food), but there are several fairly reliable spots for them each year. *Best Places:* Brassey Creek Road (southwest of Dawson Creek), Beatton Provincial Park (Charlie Lake), and the Beaver Lake recreation site (Hwy. 77 west of Fort Nelson).

444 | BIRDFINDING IN BRITISH COLUMBIA

Connecticut Warbler: This warbler is notoriously hard to see anywhere, whether it be on the wintering grounds, during migration, or on the breeding grounds. It is a scarce but widespread breeder found east of the Rockies in mature stands of aspen with little or no understorey. Occasionally, they will also nest in Black Spruce bogs. Their explosive song is unmistakable (compare with Northern Waterthrush and Ovenbird). Although they spend most of their time foraging on the ground, males will usually give their song from mid-height or even near the top of a tree. *Best Places:* Brassey Creek Road (southwest of Dawson Creek), aspen stands along Jackfish Lake Road (northeast of Chetwynd), and along Hwy. 29 northeast of Hudson's Hope.

Canada Warbler: Many birders unfamiliar with eastern warblers find it hard to distinguish Canada Warbler song from Yellow or Magnolia Warbler and American Redstart songs. The key to finding this species in British Columbia is to recognize the habitat and listen for the sharp *tip* note that precedes the rest of the song (study those recordings!). Canadas love thick, shady deciduous thickets, particularly on slopes, so if you run into this habitat and you're on the east side of the Rockies, have a look. *Best Places:* Kiskatinaw Provincial Park, Johnson Road (Taylor), and the Fort Nelson Demonstration Forest.

Yellow-breasted Chat: If there's a chat around, you'll probably be able to hear it. However, because of their skulky habits and preference for thick habitat (the more rose, poison ivy, and stinging nettle the better), it can be quite hard to see them. Patience is the key. *Best Places:* Road 22 (north of Osoyoos) and River Road (north of Oliver).

Grasshopper Sparrow: This inconspicuous little tyke is another species that is barely holding on to its British Columbian range.

In 2006, there was a major invasion, with more than forty singing males detected in the Okanagan and Similkameen Valleys. Since then, however, only one to three pairs have been detected annually. *Best Places:* Same as Sage Thrasher, as well as Vernon Commonage.

Nelson's Sparrow: This species is a scarce but widespread breeder in the Peace River Lowlands, preferring slightly wetter sedge marshes than the similar but much more common Le Conte's Sparrow. Usually one of the last migrants to arrive on the breeding grounds, listen for its soft *hush* song—most often given at dusk and dawn and usually all night in the early stages of the breeding season. *Best Places:* Del Rio Marshes (northeast of Chetwynd), Watson Slough (southwest of Fort St. John), and McQueen's Slough (Dawson Creek).

Smith's Longspur: Although there are probably hundreds of breeding pairs in the province, this is an extremely hard species to see in British Columbia, unless you have ready access to a float plane or helicopter that can take you to the remote mountain plateaus near the Yukon border. They were once reliable songsters along Haines Road (near Kelsall Lake), but because of habitat changes, it seems they have left the area (but perhaps are still present higher up on the adjacent mountain slopes).

Bobolink: The males are conspicuous, but since there are so few breeding colonies left, you'll need to know where to look. *Best Places:* Road 22 (north of Osoyoos), Similkameen Valley pastureland around and south of Cawston, Kootenay Flats (southwest of Creston), and pastureland in the Columbia/Kootenay Valleys from Cranbrook north to Golden.

Gray-crowned Rosy-Finch: This species breeds wherever there are permanent snow fields above treeline, so the easiest places to find it in summer are high mountains with road or ski-lift access to high elevations. Some hiking is almost always necessary. *Best Places:* Cathedral Provincial Park is a reliable site, as are ski hills in the Rockies where gondolas run in the summer for hikers. In winter and spring, they are sporadically found at lower elevations in the Interior, usually on gravelly road banks in open habitats (for example, Mount Kobau, west of Osoyoos).

BIRDING
RESOURCES

EBIRD

The growing popularity of eBird (ebird.ca), a worldwide public database for bird sightings, has given birders a powerful resource with which to create checklists or access the latest bird sightings from any given area. You can explore the eBird database through easy data visualization tools such as range maps, bar graph checklists, and frequency graphs. If you create your own free account at eBird, you can enter your sightings as well, joining the thousands of birders who contribute to this amazing site. At the time of writing, there are more than 1.5 million bird records from British Columbia in eBird, and more than 20,000 more records are added every month. On the eBird website you can create bar graph checklists for any province or state, county or regional district, or even any public site (public birding sites are called hot spots in eBird). You can check online tools to see what interesting birds have been seen lately or subscribe to alerts that will email you the details of these sightings. There are even smartphone apps that use eBird data to help you explore local birding spots with up-to-date information.

ONLINE BIRDING FORUMS

There are many online birding forums in British Columbia. If you are planning a trip to a certain part of the province, it is a very good idea to monitor the appropriate forum and ask any questions you might have about your planned itinerary. Birders are generally very helpful and open with information, and you'll likely make some new birding friends through these forums. Here are some of the more active websites:

Birdrepbc: tech.groups.yahoo.com/group/birdrepbc
A province-wide forum for birding in British Columbia with an emphasis on the Lower Mainland

B.C. Interior Bird List: pets.groups.yahoo.com/group/bcintbird
A forum for birders in the Interior of the province, especially the Thompson-Okanagan region

BCVIbirds: groups.yahoo.com/group/BCVIBIRDS
A forum for birding on Vancouver Island

Fraser Valley Birding: fraservalleybirding.com
A website and forum about birding in the Fraser Valley (Abbotsford to Hope)

Sunshine Coast Birding: groups.yahoo.com/group/sunshinecoastbirding
A forum restricted to the Sunshine Coast (Sechelt and Powell River areas)

West Kootenay Birds: groups.yahoo.com/group/wkbirds
A forum for West Kootenay birding

NATURALISTS CLUBS

There are naturalists clubs in most communities across the province, and their members represent an amazing resource of local knowledge. Many have websites outlining field trip information and meeting times. If you are new to birding, this is the best way to expand your knowledge. Get out in the field with some of the local experts; they'll be glad to have you along! For a list of these groups, go to the B.C. Nature website (bcnature.ca).

REPORTING RARE BIRDS

If you have a rare bird to report or are looking for information about recent rarities seen around British Columbia, leave a comment on the B.C. Bird Alert website (bcbirdalert.blogspot.com).

INDEX

451